THE CRESS█████

GENERAL EDITOR: S0-BRO-565

THE VOYAGES OF CAPTAIN COOK

THE
VOYAGES
OF
CAPTAIN JAMES COOK
ROUND THE WORLD

*Selected from his Journals
and Edited by*
CHRISTOPHER LLOYD

NEW YORK
CHANTICLEER PRESS
MCMXLIX

PUBLISHED BY CHANTICLEER PRESS NEW YORK
41 EAST 50TH STREET, NEW YORK 22, NEW YORK
PRINTED IN GREAT BRITAIN BY
LATIMER, TREND AND CO. LTD., PLYMOUTH

Contents

THE FIRST VOYAGE
1768–1771

THE SECOND VOYAGE
1772–1775

THE THIRD VOYAGE
1776–1780

The Maps

Cook's Sketch of the Track of the Endeavour and the Coasts discovered on his First Voyage   Endpapers

The origin of this sketch is explained in the Memoirs of Dr. Burney, edited by his daughter Fanny: 'In February [1772] I had the honour of receiving the illustrious Captain Cooke to dine with me in Queen-square, previously to his second voyage round the world. Observing upon a table Bougainville's *Voyage autour du Monde*, he turned it over, and made some curious remarks on the illiberal conduct of that circumnavigator towards himself, when they met, and crossed each other; which made me desirous to know, in examining the chart of M. de Bougainville, the several tracks of the two navigators; and exactly where they had crossed or approached each other. Captain Cooke instantly took a pencil from his pocket book, and said he would trace the route; which he did in so clear and scientific a manner, that I would not take fifty pounds for the book. The pencil marks having been fixed by skim milk, will always be visible.'

Apart from the spelling of Cook's name, there is another error in this passage: Cook and Bougainville never met each other. Burney's copy of the book is now in the British Museum. The present editor is grateful to the Trustees for permission to reproduce this chart for the first time.

Introduction

The father of Captain Cook was an agricultural labourer living in the North Riding of Yorkshire, who, we are told, learned to read when he was nearly eighty years old "that he might gratify a parent's pride by perusing his son's first voyage round the world". James, the second of nine children, was born in a mud cottage in the remote village of Marton-in-Cleveland on 27 October 1728. That he received only the rudiments of a formal education is apparent from the style of the original text of the Journal of his first voyage as printed in this volume. Yet how infinitely preferable is his own natural turn of phrase to the inflated periods of the eighteenth-century editor responsible for the version usually reprinted as Cook's authentic journal!

Young Cook seems to have been a dour and obstinate boy. At an early age he helped his father on the farm and at seventeen he became the shop assistant of a country storekeeper. A disagreement soon arose between them, in consequence of which Cook was bound apprentice to the shipping firm of Walker at Whitby. The Walkers were a Quaker firm engaged in the coastal coal trade, and it was on board their vessel, the *Freelove*, that Cook learned the arts of navigation and seamanship. So well did the fine sailing qualities of the Whitby-built colliers impress him that when he was called upon to command a voyage round the world he insisted on the Admiralty buying a vessel of this type.

In the spring of 1755, when he was twenty-seven years old, his vessel was lying in the Thames when hostilities, which proved to be the preliminaries of the Seven Years' War, broke out. As mate of a collier, Cook enjoyed nominal immunity from the "hot press", but he volunteered to join the Navy, "having a mind to try his fortune that way". He was therefore entered as an Able Seaman on board the sixty-gun ship *Eagle*, under the command of Captain (later Admiral) Sir Hugh Palliser. To the latter's patronage he owed everything in later life. In this ship and in others he spent the war years on the North American station, chiefly engaged in charting the St. Lawrence. He was in charge of some of the boats on the night of Wolfe's landing at Quebec, where, by a curious coincidence, his rival in Pacific exploration, M. de Bougainville, played an important part in the defence of the city. In the years succeeding the war Cook continued his work with a series of remarkably accurate charts of Newfoundland at the time when Palliser was Governor of the island. His work as a Master (the equivalent of the modern Lieutenant [N]) made it clear to his superiors that he was, in fact, a natural genius. Outside the service, however, he was still quite unknown.

II

Earlier in the century the astronomer Halley had suggested that it would be possible to determine the distance of the earth from the sun by the observation of the transit of the planet Venus in 1769. At the instance of the Royal Society the Admiralty agreed to send a ship to Tahiti for this, and, as will be seen, other purposes. Who was to command the vessel? According to the Royal Society the obvious choice was Alexander Dalrymple, a Fellow of the Society, and a notable geographer, who later became the first Hydrographer of the Navy. No one knew as much about the Pacific as he did. His privately printed *Discoveries in the South Pacific* had just been written, and in it was what the author claimed to be the most accurate chart of that ocean in existence.

On the other hand, when Halley had been placed in command of one of H.M. ships for the purpose of making magnetic observations in the South Atlantic the appointment had not been a success. Their Lordships were unwilling to risk another expedition into distant parts of the world to the command of such an opinionated civilian as Dalrymple. On the advice of Palliser, the First Lord (Sir Edward Hawke) turned down his application in favour of James Cook, who was to be raised to the rank of Lieutenant for the purpose. He was promoted Commander after the First Voyage, and Captain after the Second.

The next question was the type of ship to be sent. On the two previous expeditions to the Pacific the copper-bottomed frigate *Dolphin* had been used. She made remarkably fast voyages, but it was clear that she was too heavily armed for this sort of service, and Cook was of the opinion that repairs to the copper sheathing might prove difficult on remote islands. He accordingly advised the purchase of a bluff-bowed, Whitby-built collier originally called the *Earl of Pembroke*, which was to be registered on the lists of the Royal Navy by the name of the *Endeavour*, bark, in order to distinguish her from another vessel of the same name. Her dimensions were 366 tons, deck length 97' 8", breadth 29' 2", depth 11' 4". Though a small vessel, she was of roomy build, square in the stern, sheathed with wood, and square rigged on all three masts.

In addition to a naval complement of eighty-four, she carried eleven civilians, of whom the most notable was Sir Joseph Banks, a wealthy young amateur of science who, when advised to go on the usual Grand Tour of Europe, replied: "Every blockhead does that. My grand tour should be round the world." In the public mind, and certainly in that of the Royal Society, the voyage of the *Endeavour* was in fact associated with the name of Banks, not with that of Cook. Apart from Banks there was his botanist, Dr. Solander; Parkinson, his painter of natural history; Buchan, his landscape artist; a number of personal servants, and Charles Green, sent by the Astronomer Royal to make the necessary observations. Thus with the patronage of the King and of the Royal Society, with Banks's money, and the personal favour of some of the Lords of the Admiralty, Cook embarked on what was certainly the best-equipped expedition which had ever left England.

III

The pretext of the voyage was the observation of the transit of Venus; but the secret, and far more important, problem was the search for a great southern continent. That some vast land mass called *Terra Incognita* or, more optimistically, *Nondum Cognita*, existed in the South Pacific and the South Atlantic was a belief of great antiquity. It had never been held so firmly as at the date when Cook sailed. This was partly owing to the fact that it was Dalrymple's *idée fixe*, and partly because the French, having lost Canada in the late war, showed a keen interest in the prospect of discovering another empire in as yet unexplored parts of the world. The consequence was a series of voyages by the ships of both nations, of which Cook's was the triumphant climax. Ship after ship chased each other across the ocean, coming across nothing more than palm-fringed islands, on which a musket, a broken sword, a handful of coins, or a leaden plate nailed to a tree betokened that a rival had been there before. The *Dolphin* (in which many of Cook's shipmates sailed) went twice round the world, the first time under Captain John Byron in 1764–6, the second time under Captain Samuel Wallis in 1766–8. Wallis returned on May 20th, two months before Cook sailed, and it was his discovery of Tahiti which was responsible for the decision to make that island one of the sites of observation. The other ship that sailed with Wallis, the *Swallow* (Captain Carteret), parted company and did not return till after the *Endeavour* had sailed. Nor did Cook know anything of the expedition of Bougainville until towards the end of his voyage. Bougainville's aim was, like Cook's, scientific as well as political, and he made an important contribution to the myth of the Noble Savage, which played such a part in the ideas of philosophers like Rousseau and Diderot; but few discoveries of importance were made, chiefly because Bougainville sailed too late, arriving at Tahiti eight months after Wallis had left.

All circumnavigators from the time of Magellan were at the mercy of geographical factors. No sailing vessel which entered the Pacific by way of Cape Horn or the Straits of Magellan could sail due west on account of the Westerlies. All such vessels were accordingly swept north by the Chile or Humboldt current until they were in the latitude of the South-East Trades, where they were carried across the ocean in a diagonal direction, usually fetching up in the Marianas or the Philippines. Consequently little had been discovered in the South Pacific beyond scattered islands like Tahiti, Easter or Pitcairn. That left an enormous area in which it might reasonably be supposed that a southern continent lay. The two voyages which were largely responsible for delimiting the shape of this supposed continent, which haunted the minds of geographers like Dalrymple in Britain and de Brosses in France, were those of Quiros and Tasman. In 1605 Quiros, with Torres in command of his second ship, sailed west from the port of Lima to discover what the former called Austrialia del Espiritu Santo. This was actually the northernmost of the New Hebrides, but Quiros (and his disciple, Dalrymple) was convinced it was the northern tip of *Terra Australis*. Thereafter the two ships parted company, Quiros returning to America and Torres continuing west through the Straits which bear his name, a notable discovery which was concealed by the Spaniards until Dalrymple's researches revived it. In 1642 Tasman, the only navigator to attack the problem from the west, discovered the southern part of Tasmania and part of the western coast of New Zealand, which was thenceforward regarded as the coast of *Terra Australis*. Thus, according to the best charts available to Cook, an imaginary land mass lay between the west coast of New Zealand and Staten Land (east of Tierra del Fuego), rising again somewhere in the Atlantic. Of what we call Australia, only the north and west coasts, together with the southern tip of Tasmania, had been discovered hitherto. The name itself was not even in use, the known parts being referred to as New Holland and Van Diemen's Land.

By his First Voyage Cook demonstrated that New Zealand consisted of two islands and that New Holland was bounded on the east by a coast he called New South Wales. By his Second he entirely exploded the ancient myth of *Terra Australis*, the confines of which had beautified so many old maps and deluded for so long so many geographers.

Cook himself sailed with an open mind on these matters. He had, as a letter on a later voyage shows, the instinct of the explorer: "I, who had ambition not only to go farther than any man had ever been before, but as far as it was possible for a man to go. . . ." But on his First Voyage the Secret Instructions issued to him (which, incidentally, were not printed till 1928)[1]

[1] See Navy Records Society, *Miscellany*, Vol. III.

showed him the way. The relevant passage is as follows:

"Whereas there is reason to imagine that a continent or land of great extent, may be found to the southward of the tract lately made by Capt. Wallis in His Majesty's ship the *Dolphin* (of which you will herewith receive a copy) or of the tract of any former navigators in pursuits of the like kind; you are therefore in pursuance of His Majesty's pleasure hereby required and directed to put to sea with the bark you command, as soon as the observation of the transit of the planet Venus shall be finished, and observe the following instructions.

"You are to proceed to the southward in order to make discovery of the continent above-mentioned until you arrive in the latitude of 40°, unless you sooner fall in with it; but not having discovered it, or any evident signs of it, in that run, you are to proceed in search of it to the westward, between the latitude before mentioned and the latitude of 35° until you discover it or fall in with the Eastern side of the land discovered by Tasman and now called New Zealand."

The other problem which Cook is usually said to have solved was the conquest of scurvy; but credit must be given to those to whom it is due. Up to the middle of the eighteenth century this disease, due to a deficiency of vitamin C, was the curse of long sea voyages. Anson's circumnavigation is the classical instance, and the appalling losses suffered led to the publication of Dr. James Lind's *Treatise on the Scurvy* in 1754. Benefiting from the long experience of the East Indiamen, which had not yet penetrated to the Navy, Lind advised the use of fresh vegetables, lemon and orange juice. These ideas were first put into practice by Wallis, who lost only one man during his voyage round the world. Cook himself stressed the importance of a dry, clean ship and plenty of fresh water. For the other remedies used—evaporated malt in the form of beer called "wort", and salted cabbage fermented with juniper berries, called "sauerkraut"—Pelham, the secretary to the Commissioners of Victualling, was actually responsible. Pelham's foresight was vital, since the stock provisions were swarming with maggots before the *Endeavour* reached the Pacific.

In both these instances Cook followed out, with the minutest attention, ideas suggested by others. But in the planning of his Second Voyage he seems to have virtually formulated his own instructions. Needless to say, Dalrymple was furious at the way in which his own ideas had been falsified: he insisted that the continent must lie in the South-Eastern Pacific, as well as in the South Atlantic. Cook planned his route to lay this ghost once and for all time by (in the words of his Instructions) "keeping in as high a latitude as you can, and prosecuting your discoveries as near to the South Pole as possible", both in the Atlantic and in the Pacific. By doing this he reduced *Terra Australis* to the limits of Antarctica. He sailed south from the Cape of Good Hope, then east to New Zealand; he skirted the ice floes of Antarctic seas; he twice circled the South Pacific in order to give his men some respite from the gripping cold of high latitudes, so that on his return he was able to say: "I have now done with the Southern Pacific Ocean and flatter myself that no one will think that I have left it unexplored." And again, in one of his official letters: "If I have failed in discovering a continent, it is because it does not exist in a navigable sea, and not for want of looking after."

The other achievement of the Second Voyage was the successful determination of longitude by the use of the first chronometer. While it had long been possible for seamen to determine a position north and south by the use of the cross staff, the quadrant or the sextant, enormous errors were still made when it came to determining a position east or west. For this purpose the log line had been used from time immemorial, a clumsy method by which only a rough estimate of the distance travelled by a ship could be made. Maskelyne, the Astronomer Royal, had recently perfected a method of lunar observation which, used in conjunction with his new Nautical Almanac, gave pretty accurate results on Cook's First Voyage. But John Harrison (another self-educated Yorkshireman) had already gone far to win the reward offered by Parliament for a clock which would maintain accurate time at sea, and thus determine how far east or west a ship was from the prime meridian. The watchmaker, Larcum Kendall, duplicated Harrison's fourth model, and it was this miraculously constructed watch which Cook found to be "our never-failing guide" on his Second and Third Voyages. The extraordinary accuracy of his charts and positions is due to the use of this watch, and his own supremely scientific temperament.

In the brief interval between his voyages Cook received some part of the credit due to him for his achievements. He was honoured by the Royal Society for his paper on scurvy; the narrative of his voyage brought him popular fame; he was presented to the King; and appointed fourth captain of Greenwich Hospital. There, at the age of forty-seven, he might have retired honourably. As he told his old master at Whitby: "A few months ago the whole Southern Hemisphere was hardly enough for me, and now I am going to be confined within the narrow limits of Greenwich Hospital, which are far too small for an active mind like mine. I must confess it is a fine retreat, and a pretty income, but whether I can bring myself to like ease and retirement, time will show."

In fact he was not allowed time enough to take up his residence there. Since he had solved the problem of the South Pacific so successfully, it was decided, in 1776, to send him to the North Pacific on an even older quest: that of the North-West Passage, thought to lie between Hudson Bay and somewhere north of California. After a long interval this search of the Elizabethans had recently been revived, and a handsome reward was offered by Parliament to the first captain to make the voyage. A number of voyages into polar seas were being undertaken from the Atlantic side, on one of which Midshipman Nelson sailed. More important was the work of Samuel Hearne, of the Hudson Bay Company, who in 1771 first travelled over the part of Canada lying north-west of Hudson Bay. Although Hearne's report made the existence of such a passage unlikely, it was decided to send Cook in command of the *Resolution* and *Discovery* to search for the Pacific entrance, which Drake had failed to find two centuries previously. At the same time he was to explore what lay between Drake's New Albion (California) and the Russian discoveries of Vitus Bering in 1728 and 1741, which had determined the existence of the Bering Strait, the Aleutian Islands and part of Alaska; but whether these constituted an archipelago or a continuation of the North American coast remained to be decided. No fresh discoveries had been made in the North Pacific ocean after the circular Manila route from Mexico to the Philippines, out with the North-East Trades and home with the Westerlies, had been adopted by the Spaniards. Because Cook followed a new diagonal route from Tahiti to America he discovered the Hawaiian group, or, as he called them, the Sandwich Islands. Having made his landfall on the North American coast, he followed it up until he passed through the Bering Strait and reached the latitude of 70° 44', where he was "stopped by an impenetrable body of ice". He intended to renew the search the following year; but having returned to winter at Hawaii, on 14 February 1779 he was killed, like Magellan, in covering the retreat of his men.

IV

Few of Cook's personal letters have survived; indeed, it is doubtful if he wrote many. What we know of the man himself has to be deduced from his journals and the impressions he made on other people. The predominating impression is, I think, that of tenacity of purpose, call it obstinacy or firmness of will. Of course he was lucky in the patronage he enjoyed; but it argued a long career of unswerving devotion to duty for a man of his humble upbringing to deserve the favour which gave him his big opportunity. Once given it, that same unruffled firmness enabled him to carry out his task in the face of enormous difficulties. Two other characteristics helped him to do this: the high degree of moral courage necessary to every great explorer, and a sense of modesty which made it difficult for anyone to quarrel with him. The best illustration of his modesty is the letter he wrote to the Admiralty recounting the discoveries made on his First Voyage (see below, p. 94). Only a man who had the humility of the really great could have written that letter. Moreover it is this impression of calm self-confidence which assured the loyalty of his crews. There were a few attempted desertions; but it is only necessary to compare what happened to Bligh a few years later with Cook's series of longer voyages in those same seas to appreciate the assurance and the humanity with which he treated his subordinates.

To these qualities which make Cook such an outstanding leader of men we must add those which make him the ideal explorer: an open mind, an immense capacity for taking pains, a meticulous accuracy of statement, which is equally apparent in the geographical details of his voyages as in the anthropological observations occupying so many of his pages, observations which later researchers have saluted for their fidelity. One can understand the delight with which the sophisticated eighteenth-century reader enjoyed Cook's description of the romantic and idyllic societies of Tahiti or the Friendly Isles at a date when the Noble Savage was a literary convention in Europe. To-day the value of Cook's accounts is enhanced by a realization of the scientific value of the unprejudiced attitude with which he observed the strange manners of the islanders—their sexual licence, their propensity to theft, their funeral customs and formal dances, besides the darker mysteries of human sacrifice and cannibalism. The key concepts of modern anthropology—totem and taboo—find their first expression in his pages. Fifty years after his death, Ellis, the first serious ethnologist to study Polynesian societies, declared that although the inferences drawn by Cook, and the reasons he assigned to the customs he observed, might be incorrect, "in the description of what he saw and heard there is throughout a degree of accuracy, seldom if ever exceeded in accounts equally minute and extended". A modern anthropologist would agree with that judgment. In Cook's journals will be found an account of the primitive life of the Maoris, the Fuegians, the natives of Tonga, Tahiti or Hawaii which is of unique value because those peoples were as yet untouched by Western civilization. Perhaps it was because of the assurance and benevolence of his presence, combined with the unpatronizing attitude with which he invariably treated natives, that this dour northerner succeeded in winning the confidence of the chiefs of the islands more easily than he did that of his own countrymen. Hence the tragedy of the manner of his death at the hands of those who really venerated him is all the more ironic.

It was part of his duty to write full accounts of the places he visited. He learned how to do it from scientists like Banks and Solander, who taught him the habit of observing and describing native life with the same accuracy he was professionally trained to adopt in navigational matters. In consequence of what he saw at first hand he failed to share the rosy illusions of Rousseau and his fellow philosophers about the Noble Savage. He insists, for example, that the Maoris "are certainly in some state of civilization", but that "an intercourse with foreigners would reform their manners, and polish their savage minds". At the same time he only too clearly foresaw the fate which inevitably befell the innocent islanders as soon as his task of opening up the Pacific was completed. He himself did his utmost to restrain his own men: "It was ever a maxim with me to punish the least crime any of my people committed against these uncivilized nations. Their robbing us with impunity is by no means a sufficient reason why we should treat them in the same manner." Would that the black-birders and beachcombers who came after him had thought likewise!

The most unprejudiced and illuminating view of Cook's personality is that of Zimmermann, a Swiss seaman who signed on for the Third Voyage. Cook impressed this ordinary seaman as a 'tall, handsome, strong, but somewhat spare man. His hair was dark brown, his expression somewhat stern, and so hasty tempered that the least contradiction on the part of an officer or sailor made him very angry. He was inexorable regarding the ship's regulations and the punishments connected with them." He was ordinarily very reserved in speech, but on ocaasion could be "exceedingly affable to the crew". He made the right sort of speech at the right time. He never swore. He was scrupulously clean in habits as in person. He ate sparingly, though "on Saturdays he was usually very affable, and on that day he frequently drank an extra glass of punch, pledging a toast to all beautiful women". Fearlessness, says Zimmermann, was an outstanding characteristic, combined with an uncanny instinct for any danger that might threaten the safety of the ship. When the news of his death was received on board, "everyone on the ships was silent and depressed; we all felt that we had lost a father."

If we wish for an epitaph on this great man we may find it in a letter written earlier in his lifetime by David Wray, a Fellow of the Royal Society: "He is a right-headed and unaffected man; and I have great authority for calling him our best navigator." His monument is the map of the Pacific Ocean.

v

In view of Cook's international reputation, and the fact that his voyages added more to the British Empire than almost any war in history, it is curious that no critical edition of the whole of his journals has yet been published. It is therefore satisfactory to note that the Hakluyt Society announced in the spring of 1949 that, with the generous assistance of the New Zealand Government, it proposes to undertake the very considerable and costly task of preparing a complete *variorum* edition in four volumes. The literature on Cook's life and achievements already in existence is, however, enormous. Biographies of him abound, and his Voyages have always been one of the most popular books on exploration (though most of the one-volume editions are merely shortened paraphrases). The present volume of selections is addressed to those who wish to know something of his achievements, of the lands he discovered, and the peoples he encountered, at a date when there were still new worlds to find, and the Pacific had not yet become an atomic bombing range.

The method adopted by the editor has been to select those passages which illustrate the course of the voyages and the customs of the natives, without immersing the reader in the mass of detail contained in the million words of the original journals. Each passage is, if not as Cook actually wrote it, in the words of his earliest or his best editor. Between the dates marking the beginning of each passage much has been excluded; otherwise, unless omissions are marked, no cuts or alterations have been made. The spelling of the original has been modernized.

The text followed for the First Voyage is that of Cook's own journal printed by Admiral W. J. L. Wharton in 1893. This journal was officially "edited" by Dr. J. Hawkesworth in 1773, because Cook's own seamanlike style was thought unsuitable for publication in the age of Dr. Johnson. It is often reprinted as an authoritative version; but what Hawkesworth actually did was to amalgamate Cook's journal with that of Banks, and to intersperse both with moralizings of his own in such a way that the reader never knows if he is reading Cook or Banks or Hawkesworth. The book sold well at the time, but it was severely criticized by the pious for its scepticism, and by the scientific-minded for its inaccuracies.

The accounts of the Second and Third Voyages are taken from Volumes III–VI of the seven-volume edition printed in 1821, which is a reprint of the official quartos of 1777 and 1784. Cook's journals for these voyages were edited by Canon John Douglas, who generally "faithfully adhered" to the original, as is shown by a collation with certain passages in the MS. journal of the Second Voyage now at the National Maritime Museum. Cook was perfectly satisfied with this version: "I can only say that it is my own narrative, and as it was written during the voyage." Though his name appears on none of the title pages, Douglas adopted the same treatment towards the journal of the last voyage, the conclusion of which from a month before Cook's death to the return of the ships is by Captain King, whose narrative occupies the last volume of the original set.

CHRISTOPHER LLOYD

The First Voyage

1768—1771

BOOK I

The Voyage from England to Tahiti
1768–1769

VOYAGE TO THE PACIFIC BY WAY OF CAPE HORN—THE FUEGIANS—
ARRIVAL AT TAHITI—THE TRANSIT OF VENUS—DEPARTURE FROM
TAHITI—MANNERS AND CUSTOMS OF THE ISLANDERS

May 27 to July 29   River Thames. Moderate and fair weather;
at 11 a.m. hoisted the pendant, and took charge of the ship,
agreeable to my commission of the 25th inst., she lying in the
basin in Deptford Yard. From this day to July 21st we
were constantly employed in fitting the ship, taking on board
stores and provisions, etc. The same day we sailed from Deptford
and anchored in Gallions Reach, where we remained until the
30th. The transactions of each day, both while we lay here and
at Deptford, are inserted in the Log Book, and as they contain
nothing but common occurrences, it was thought not necessary
to insert them here.

July 30 to August 7   Saturday, July 30th, weighed from Gallions,
and made sail down the river, the same day anchored at Graves-
end, and the next morning weighed from thence, and at noon
anchored at the buoy of the fairway. On Wednesday, August
3rd, anchored in the Downs in nine fathoms of water, Deal
Castle NW. by W. On Sunday 7th, I joined the ship, discharged
the pilot, and the next day sailed for Plymouth.

October 26   First part light airs and cloudy weather, the remainder a moderate breeze and cloudy. After we had got an observa-

tion, and it was no longer doubted that we were to the southward of the Line, the ceremony on this occasion practised by all nations was not omitted. Every one that could not prove upon the sea chart that he had before Crossed the Line was either to pay a bottle of rum or be ducked in the sea, which former case was the fate of by far the greatest part on board; and as several of the men chose to be ducked, and the weather was favourable for that purpose, this ceremony was performed on about twenty or thirty, to the no small diversion of the rest.[1]

January 16 A fresh breeze of wind at S. and S.W., with frequent showers of rain and snow. At 2 p.m. anchored in the Bay of Success[2] in nine fathoms, the bottom ooze and sand. The south point of the Bay bore S.E. and the north point E.N.E. This bay I shall describe when I come to speak of the rest of the coast. Hoisted out the boats and moored with the stream anchor. While this was doing I went ashore accompanied by Mr. Banks and Dr. Solander to look for a watering place and to speak with the natives, who were assembled on the beach at the head of the bay

[1] Though Cook himself had never previously crossed the Line he escaped the ceremony of initiation by reason of his position on board. Banks's account is as follows : "About dinner time a list was brought into the cabin containing the names of every boy and thing aboard the ship (in which the dogs and cats were not forgotten); to this was affixed a signed petition from the ship's company desiring leave to examine everybody in the list that it might be known whether or no they had crossed the Line before. This was immediately granted, everybody being called upon the quarter-deck and examined by one of the lieutenants who had crossed the Line: he marked every name either to be ducked or to be let off as their qualifications directed. Captain Cook and Dr. Solander were on the black list, as were I myself, and my servants, and dogs, for all of whom I was obliged to compound by giving the duckers a certain quantity of brandy, for which they willingly excused us the ceremony. Many of the men, however, chose to be ducked rather than give up four days' allowance of wine, which was the price fixed upon, and as for the boys they were always ducked of course, so that about twenty-one underwent the ceremony."

[2] After a visit to Rio, Cook, in accordance with his orders, made his way to the Pacific by the Straits of Le Maire (between Staten Island and Tierra del Fuego) and Cape Horn. His first encounter with the natives was at the Bay of Success in the Straits, where he paused to strike the guns into the hold and make other preparations for the passage before him. Bougainville had passed through the Magellan Straits the previous year, and found the Fuegians "troublesome and disgusting", and complained of "the insupportable stench of the hideous women". Darwin later echoed Cook's view: "I believe that in this extreme part of the world man exists in a lower state of improvement than in any other." On the other hand there were no signs of the giants reported by Captain John Byron and other explorers.

to the number of thirty or forty. They were so far from being afraid or surprised at our coming amongst them that three of them came on board without the least hesitation. They are something above the middle size, of a dark copper colour with long black hair; they paint their bodies in streaks, mostly red and black. Their clothing consists wholly in a guanaco skin or that of a seal, in the same form as it came from the animal's back.

The women wear a piece of skin over their privy parts, but the men observe no such decency. Their huts are made like a beehive, and open on one side where they have their fires; they are made of small sticks and covered with branches of trees, long grass, etc., in such a manner that they are neither proof against wind, hail, rain or snow, a sufficient proof that these people must be a very hardy race. They live chiefly on shell fish, such as mussels, which they gather from off the rocks along the seashore, and this seems to be the work of the women. Their arms are bows and arrows neatly made; their arrows are bearded, some with glass and others with fine flint; several pieces of the former we saw amongst them with other European things, such as rings, buttons, cloth, canvas, etc., which I think proves that they must sometimes travel to the northward, as we know of no ship that hath been in these parts for many years; besides, they were not at all surprised at our firearms; on the contrary, they seemed to know the use of them, by making signs to us to fire at seals or birds that might come in the way. They have no boats that we saw or anything to go upon the water with; their number doth not exceed fifty or sixty young and old, and there are fewer women than men. They are extremely fond of any red thing, and seemed to set more value on beads than anything we could give them; in this consists their whole pride, few, either men or women, are without a necklace or string of beads made of small shells or bones about their necks. They would not taste any strong liquor, neither did they seem fond of our provisions. We could not discover that they had any head or chief or form of government, neither have they any useful or necessary utensil except it be a bag or basket to gather their mussels into. In a word they are perhaps as miserable a set of people as are this day upon earth.

Having found a convenient place on the south side of the bay to wood and water at, we set about that work in the morning, and Mr. Banks with a party went into the country to gather plants, etc.[3]

January 25   This point[4] is pretty high and consists of peaked craggy rocks, and not far from it lay several others high above water. It lies in the latitude of 55° 53' S. and S.W., twenty-six leagues from Straits Le Maire, and by some on board thought to be Cape Horn; but I was of another opinion, and with good reason, because we saw land to the southward of it about three or four leagues. It appeared not unlike an island with a very high round hummock upon it; this I believe to be Cape Horn, for after we had stood about three leagues the weather cleared up for about a quarter of an hour, which gave us a sight of the land bearing W.S.W., but we could see no land to the southward or westward of it, and therefore conclude that it must be the Cape, but whether it be an island of itself, a part of the southernmost of Hermits Islands, or a part of Terra del Fuego, I am not able to determine. However, this is of very little consequence to navigation: I only wished to be certain whether or no it was the southernmost land on or near to Terra del Fuego; but the thick foggy weather and the westerly winds which carried us from the land prevented me from satisfying my curiosity in this point, but from its latitude and the reasons before given I think it must, and if so it must be Cape Horn, and lies in the latitude of 55° 53' S. and longitude 68° 13' W. from the meridian of Greenwich, being the mean result of several observations of the sun and moon made the day after we left the land, and which agreed with those made at Straits Le Maire, allowing for the distance between one

[3] This party, which included Banks and Solander and their servants, climbed a mountain nearby and nearly perished from the cold. Two of the black servants, indeed, succumbed.

[4] Near Cape Horn. Early navigators found great difficulty in determining the longitude of the Cape, because of the strong current. The actual position is 55° 58' S., 67° 16' W. Twenty-nine years earlier Commodore Anson, having underestimated his longitude by 350 miles, turned north too soon and narrowly escaped shipwreck. Cook spent thirty-three days rounding Tierra del Fuego, as compared with the three months it would have taken him by way of the Magellan Straits.

place and the other, which I found means very accurately to determine.

April 4   A steady fresh Trade and clear weather. At half past ten a.m. saw land bearing south, distance three or four leagues. Hauled up for it, and soon found it to be an island of about two leagues in circuit and of an oval form, with a lagoon in the middle, for which I named it Lagoon Island.[5] The border of land circumscribing this lagoon is in many places very low and narrow, particularly on the south side, where it is mostly a beach or reef of rocks; it is the same on the N. side in three places, and these disjoin the firm land and make it appear like so many islands covered with wood. On the W. end of the island is a large tree which looks like a large tower, and about the middle of the island are two coconut trees that appear above all the other wood, which as we approached the island looked very much like a flag. We approached the north side of this island within a mile, and found no bottom with 130 fathoms of line, nor did there appear to be anchorage about it. We saw several of the inhabitants, the most of them men, and these marched along the shore abreast of the ships with long clubs in their hands as though they meant to oppose our landing. They were all naked except their privy parts, and were of a dark copper colour with long black hair, but upon our leaving the island some of them were seen to put on a covering, and one or two we saw in the skirts of the wood was clothed in white; these we supposed to be women.

April 13   The first part cloudy and squally, with showers of rain; remainder, gentle breezes and clear weather. At 4 p.m. the N.E. point of Royal Bay W. ½ N.; run under an easy sail all night, and had soundings from twenty-two to twelve fathoms two or three miles from the shore. At 5 a.m. made sail for the bay, and at 7 anchored in thirteen fathoms.[6] At this time we had

[5] Vahitahi, one of the Low or Tuamotu archipelago; this was the first land sighted after leaving Cape Horn.

[6] The *Endeavour* anchored in Matavai Bay on the north side of Tahiti; Fort Venus was established a little to the east of it. Wallis in the *Dolphin* (in which the First Lieutenant, Gore, and the Master, Molyneux, and others had

but very few men upon the sick list, and these had but slight complaints. The ship's company had in general been very healthy, owing in a great measure to the sauerkraut, portable soup and malt; the two first were served to the people, the one on beef days and the other on banyan days.[7] Wort was made of the malt, and at the discretion of the surgeon given to every man that had the least symptoms of scurvy upon him. By this means, and the care and vigilance of Mr. Monkhouse, the surgeon, this disease was prevented from getting a footing in the ship. The sauerkraut, the men at first would not eat it, until I put it in practice—a method I never once knew to fail with seamen—and this was to have some of it dressed every day for the cabin table, and permitted all the officers, without exception, to make use of it, and left it to the option of the men either to take as much as they pleased or none at all; but this practice was not continued above a week before I found it necessary to put every one on board to an allowance; for such are the tempers and disposition of seamen in general that whatever you give them out of the common way —although it be ever so much for their good—it will not go down, and you will hear nothing but murmurings against the man that first invented it; but the moment they see their superiors set a value upon it, it becomes the finest stuff in the world and the inventor an honest fellow. Wind easterly.

We had no sooner come to an anchor in Royal Bay, as before-mentioned, than a great number of the natives in their canoes came off to the ship and brought with them coconuts, etc.; these they seemed to set a great value upon. Amongst those that came off to the ship was an elderly man whose name was Owhaa, him the gentleman that had been here before in the *Dolphin* knew and had often spoke of as one that had been of service to them. This man (together with some others) I took on board and made

served) had anchored in another bay when the island was discovered on 19 June 1767 and given the name of George's Island, though it was usually called Otaheite. On 4 April 1768, Bougainville (with thirty-four men sick of scurvy) took possession of it under the name of La Nouvelle Cythère. Though the *Endeavour* had been at sea 127 days, very few cases of scurvy had developed. One of the few to be affected was Banks, who cured himself from his private supply of lemon juice.

[7] *i.e.* meatless days.

much of, thinking that he might on some occasions be of use to us. As our stay at this place was not likely to be very short, I thought it very necessary that some order should be observed in trafficking with the natives, that such merchandise as we had on board for that purpose might continue to bear a proper value, and not leave it to everyone's own particular fancy, which could not fail to bring on confusion and quarrels between us and the natives, and would infallibly lessen the value of such articles as we had to traffick with. In order to prevent this, the following rules were ordered to be observed; viz.:

Rules to be observed by every person in or belonging to His Majesty's Bark the *Endeavour* for the better establishing a regular and uniform trade for provisions, etc., with the inhabitants of George's Island:

1. To endeavour by every fair means to cultivate a friendship with the natives, and to treat them with all imaginable humanity.

2. A proper person or persons will be appointed to trade with the natives for all manner of provisions, fruits, and other Productions of the earth; and no officer or seaman or other person belonging to the ship, excepting such as are so appointed, shall trade or offer to trade for any sort of provisions, fruit or other productions of the earth, unless they have my leave so to do.

3. Every person employed on shore on any duty whatsoever is strictly to attend to the same, and if by neglect he loses any of his arms or working tools, or suffers them to be stole the full value thereof will be charged against his pay, according to the custom of the Navy in such cases, and he shall receive such further punishment as the nature of the offence may deserve.

4. The same penalty will be inflicted upon every person who is found to embezzle, trade or offer to trade, with any of the ship's stores of what nature so ever.

5. No sort of iron or anything that is made of iron, or any sort of cloth or other useful or necessary articles, are to be given in exchange for anything but provisions.

J.C.

As soon as the ship was properly secured I went on shore,

accompanied by Mr. Banks and the other gentlemen, with a party of men under arms; we took along with us Owhaa—who took us to the place where the *Dolphin* watered, and made signs to us as well as we could understand that we might occupy that ground, but it happened not to be fit for our purpose. No one of the natives made the least opposition at our landing, but came to us with all imaginable marks of friendship and submission. We afterwards made a circuit through the woods, and then came on board. We did not find the inhabitants to be numerous, and we imagined that several of them had fled from their habitations upon our arrival in the bay.

April 14 This morning we had a great many canoes about the ship; the most of them came from the westward, and brought nothing with them but a few coconuts, etc. Two that appeared to be chiefs we had on board, together with several others, for it was a hard matter to keep them out of the ship, as they climb like monkeys; but it was still harder to keep them from stealing but everything that came within their reach; in this they are prodigious expert. I made each of these two chiefs a present of a hatchet, things that they seemed mostly to value. As soon as we had partly got clear of these people I took two boats and went to the westward, all the gentlemen being along with me. My design was to see if there was not a more commodious harbour, and to try the disposition of the natives, having along with us the two chiefs above mentioned; the first place we landed at was in great Canoe Harbour (so called by Captain Wallis); here the natives flocked about us in great numbers, and in as friendly a manner as we could wish, only that they showed a great inclination to pick our pockets. We were conducted to a chief, who for distinction sake we called Hercules. After staying a short time with him, and distributing a few presents about us, we proceeded farther, and came to a chief who I shall call Lycurgus; this man entertained us with broiled fish, coconuts, etc., with great hospitality, and all the time took great care to tell us to take care of our pockets, as a great number of people had crowded about us. Notwithstanding the care we took, Dr. Solander and Dr. Monkhouse had each of them their pockets picked: the one of his spy glass and the other of his snuff box. As soon as Lycurgus was made acquainted with the theft he dispersed the people in a moment, and the method he made use of was to lay hold on the first thing that came in his way and throw it at them, and happy was he or she that could get first out of his way. He seemed very much concerned for what had happened, and by way of recompense offered us but everything that was in his house; but we refused to accept of anything, and made signs to him that we only wanted the things again. He had already sent people out after them, and it was not long before they were returned. We found the natives very numerous wherever we came, and from what we could judge seemed very peaceably inclined. About six o'clock in the evening we returned on board, very well satisfied with our little excursion.

April 15   Winds at east during the day, in the night a light breeze off the land; and as I apprehend it be usual here for the Trade wind to blow during a great part of the day from the eastern board, and to have it calm or light breezes from the land that is southerly during the night with fair weather, I shall only mention the wind and weather when they deviate from this rule. This morning several of the chiefs we had seen yesterday came on board, and brought with them hogs, bread fruit, etc., and for these we gave them hatchets, linen, and such things as they valued. Having not met with yesterday a more convenient situation for every purpose we wanted than the place we now are, I therefore, without delay, resolved to pitch upon some spot upon the N.E. point of the bay, properly situated for observing the transit of Venus, and at the same time under the command of the ship's guns, and there to throw up a small fort for our defence. Accordingly I went ashore with a party of men, accompanied by Mr. Banks, Dr. Solander, and Mr. Green. We took along with us one of Mr. Banks's tents, and after we had fixed upon a place fit for our purpose we set up the tent and marked out the ground we intended to occupy. By this time a number of the natives had got collected together about us, seemingly only to look on, as not one of them had any weapon, either offensive or defensive. I would suffer none to come within the lines I had marked out, excepting one who appeared to be a chief and old Owhaa—to these two men we endeavoured to explain, as well as we could, that we wanted that ground to sleep upon such a number of nights and then we should go away. Whether they understood us or no is uncertain, but no one appeared the least displeased at what we was about; indeed the ground we had fixed upon was of no use to them, being part of the sandy beach upon the shore of the bay, and not near to any of their habitations. It being too late in the day to do anything more, a party with a petty officer was left to guard the tent, while we with another party took a walk into the woods, and with us most of the natives. We had but just crossed the river when Mr. Banks shot three ducks at one shot, which surprised them so much that most of them fell down as though they had been shot likewise. I was in hopes this would have had some good effect, but the event did not prove it, for we had not been long from the tent before the natives again began to gather about, and one of them more daring than the rest pushed one of the sentinels down, snatched the musket out of his hand and made a push at him, and then made off, and with him all the rest. Immediately upon this the officer ordered the party to fire, and the man who took the musket was shot dead before he had got far from the tent, but the musket was carried quite off when this happened. I and Mr. Banks with the other party was about half a mile off, returning out of the woods, upon hearing the firing of muskets, and the natives leaving us at the same time, we suspected that something was the matter and hastened our march, but before we arrived the whole was over, and every one of the natives fled except old Owhaa, who stuck by us the whole time, and I believe from the first he either knew or had some suspicion that the people would attempt something at the tent, as he was very much against our going into the woods out of sight of the tent.

April 17   At 2 o'clock this morning, departed this life, Mr. Alex Buchan, Landskip Draftsman to Mr. Banks, a gentleman well skill'd in his profession and one that will be greatly missed in the course of this voyage.[8] He had long been subject to a disorder in his bowels, which had more than once brought him to the very point of death, and was at one time subject to fits, of one of which he was taken on Saturday morning; this brought on his former disorder, which put a period to his life. Mr. Banks thought it not so advisable to inter the body ashore in a place where we were utter strangers to the custom of the natives on such occasions; it was therefore sent out to sea and committed to that element with all the decency the circumstance of the place would admit of. This morning several of the chiefs from the westward made us a visit: they brought with them emblems of peace, which are young plantain trees. These they put on board the ship before they would venture themselves. They brought us a present of two hogs (an article we find here very scarce) and some bread fruit;[9] for these they had hatchets and other things. In the afternoon we set up one of the ship's tents ashore, and Mr. Green and myself stayed there the night to observe an eclipse of Jupiter's first satellite, which we was hindered from seeing by clouds.

April 20   Mr. Banks and Dr. Solander lay ashore to-night for the first time, their marquees being set up within the walls of the fort and fit for their reception.

April 21   Got the copper oven ashore and fixed it in the bank of the breastwork. Yesterday, as Mr. Green and Dr. Monkhouse were taking a walk, they happened to meet with the body of the man we had shot, as the natives made them fully understand; the manner in which the body was interred being a little extra-ordinary. I went to-day, with some others, to see it. Close by the house wherein he resided when living was built a small shed, but whether for the purpose or no I cannot say, for it was in all re-

---

[8] This was the fourth death to be recorded. In addition to the two negroes who died of cold, a marine had committed suicide.

[9] The transplantation of the bread fruit tree from Tahiti to the West Indies was the occasion of Bligh's voyage in the *Bounty* in 1789, undertaken on the advice of Banks.

spects like some of the sheds or houses they live in.[10] This shed
was about fourteen or sixteen feet long, ten or twelve broad, and
of a proportionable height. One end was wholly open, the other
end and two sides were partly inclosed with a kind of wickered
work. In this shed lay the corpse, upon a bier or frame of wood,
with a matted bottom, like a cot frame used at sea, and supported
by four posts about five feet from the ground. The body was
covered with a mat, and over that a white cloth; alongside of the
body lay a wooden club, one of their weapons of war. The head
of the corpse lay next the close end of the shed, and at this end lay
two coconut shells, such as they sometimes use to carry water in;
at the other end of the shed was a bunch of green leaves, with
some dried twigs tied all together and stuck in the ground, and
a stone lying by them as big as a coconut. Near to these lay a
young plantain tree, such as they use as emblems of peace, and
by it lay a stone axe. At the open end of the shed was stuck upright in the ground the stem of a plantain tree about five feet
high, on the top of which stood a coconut shell full of fresh
water, and on the side of the post hung a small bag, wherein was
a few pieces of bread fruit roasted ready for eating. Some of the
pieces were fresh and others stale. The natives did not seem to
like that we should go near the body, and stood at a little distance themselves while we examined these matters, and appeared
to be pleased when we came away. It certainly was no very
agreeable place, for it stank intolerably, and yet it was not above
ten yards from the huts wherein several of the living resided. The
first day we landed we saw the skeleton of a human being lying
in this manner under a shade that was just big enough to cover it,
and some days after that, when some of the gentlemen went with
a design to examine it more narrowly, it was gone. It was at this
time thought that this manner of interring their dead was not
common to all ranks of people, as this was the first we had seen
except the skeleton just mentioned; but various were the opinions
concerning the provisions, etc., laid about the dead. Upon the
whole, it should seem that these people not only believe in a

[10] These sheds, called "marai", were family burial places, where tribal relics
were preserved.

supreme being, but in a future state also, and this must be meant either as an offering to some deity or for the use of the dead in the other world; but this latter is not very probable, as there appeared to be no priest craft in the thing, for whatever provisions were put there it appeared very plain to us that there it remained until it consumed away of itself. It is most likely that we shall see more of this before we leave the island, but if it is a religious ceremony we may not be able to understand it, for the mysteries of most religions are very dark and not easily understood, even by those who profess them.

April 28   This morning a great number of the natives came to us in their canoes from different parts of the island, several of whom we had not seen before. One of these was the woman called by the *Dolphins* the Queen of this island;[11] she first went to Mr. Banks's tent at the fort, where she was not known, till the Master, happening to go ashore, who knew her, and brought her on board with two men and several women, who seemed to be all of her family. I made them all some presents or other, but to *Oberiea* (for that is this woman's name) I gave several things, in return for which, as soon as I went on shore with her, she gave me a hog and several bunches of plantains. These she caused to be carried from her canoes up to the fort in a kind of procession, she and I bringing up the rear. This woman is about forty years of age, and, like most of the other women, very masculine. She is head or chief of her own family or tribe, but to all appearance hath no authority over the rest of the inhabitants, whatever she might have when the *Dolphin* was here. Hercules, whose real name is *Tootaha*, is, to all appearance, the chief man of the island, and hath generally visited us twice a week since we have been here, and came always attended by a number of canoes and people; and at those times we were sure to have a supply, more or less, of everything the island afforded, both from himself and from those that came with him, and it is a chance thing that we

[11] O Berea ("the stoutest woman I ever saw", as a midshipman in the *Dolphin* described her) had lost much of the power she possessed when she entertained Captain Wallis and his men in 1767. The Master's name was Molyneux.

get a hog at any other time. He was with us at this time, and did not appear very well pleased at the notice we took of Oberiea.

May 2   This morning, about nine o'clock, when Mr. Green and I went to set up the quadrant, it was not to be found.[12] It had never been taken out of the packing case (which was about eighteen inches square) since it came from Mr. Bird, the maker; and the whole was pretty heavy, so that it was a matter of astonishment to us all how it could be taken away, as a sentinel stood the whole night within five yards of the door of the tent, where it was put, together with several other instruments; but none of them was missing but this. However, it was not long before we got information that one of the natives had taken it away and carried it to the eastward. Immediately a resolution was taken to detain all the large canoes that were in the bay, and to seize upon Tootaha and some others of the principal people, and keep them in custody until the quadrant was produced; but this last we did not think proper immediately to put in execution, as we had only Oberiea in our power, and the detaining of her by force would have alarmed all the rest. In the meantime, Mr. Banks (who is always very alert upon all occasions wherein the natives are concerned) and Mr. Green went into the woods to enquire of Toobouratomita which way and where the quadrant was gone. I very soon was informed that these three was gone to the eastward in quest of it; and some time after I followed myself with a small party of men; but before I went away I gave orders that if Tootaha came either to the ship or the fort he was not to be detained, for I found he had no hand in taking away the quadrant, and that there was almost a certainty of getting it again. I met Mr. Banks and Mr. Green about four miles from the fort, returning with the quadrant. This was about sunset, and we all got back to the fort about eight o'clock, where I found Tootaha in custody, and a number of the natives crowding about the gate of the fort. My going into the woods with a party of armed men so alarmed

---

[12] Without his quadrant (the predecessor of the sextant) Mr. Green the astronomer would be unable to take the lunar observations by which longitude was ascertained on this voyage.

the natives that in the evening they began to move off with their effects, and a double canoe putting off from the bottom of the bay was observed by the ship, and a boat sent after her. In this canoe happened to be Tootaha, and as soon as our boat came up with her, he and all the people that were in the canoe jumped overboard, and he only was taken up and brought on board the ship, together with the canoe; the rest were permitted to swim to the shore. From the ship Tootaha was sent to the fort, where Mr. Hicks thought proper to detain him until I returned. The scene between Toobouratomita and Tootaha, when the former came into the fort and found the latter in custody, was really moving. They wept over each other for some time. As for Tootaha, he was so far prepossessed with the thought that he was to be killed that he could not be made sensible to the contrary till he was carried out of the fort to the people, many of whom expressed their joy by embracing him; and, after all, he would not go away until he had given us two hogs, notwithstanding we did all in our power to hinder him, for it is very certain that the treatment he had met with from us did not merit such a reward. However, we had it in our power to make him a present of equal value whenever we pleased.

May 12   Cloudy weather with showers of rain. This morning a man and two young women, with some others, came to the fort, whom we had not seen before, and as their manner of introducing themselves was a little uncommon, I shall insert it. Mr. Banks was as usual at the gate of the fort trading with the people, when he was told that some strangers were coming, and therefore stood to receive them. The company had with them about a dozen young plantain trees, and some other small plants, these they laid down about twenty feet from Mr. Banks; the people then made a lane between him and them. When this was done the man (who appeared to be only a servant to the two women) brought the young plantains singly, together with some of the other plants, and gave them to Mr. Banks, and at the delivery of each pronounced a short sentence which we understood not. After he had thus disposed of all his plantain trees, he took several pieces

17

of cloth and spread them on the ground. One of the young women then stepped upon the cloth, and with as much innocency as one could possibly conceive, exposed herself, entirely naked, from the waist downwards; in this manner she turned herself once or twice round, I am not certain which, then stepped off the cloth, and dropped down her clothes. More cloth was then spread upon the former, and she again performed the same ceremony. The cloth was then rolled up and given to Mr. Banks, and the two young women went and embraced him, which ended the ceremony.

June 3   This day proved as favourable to our purpose as we could wish. Not a cloud was to be seen the whole day, and the air was perfectly clear, so that we had every advantage we could desire in observing the whole of the passage of the planet Venus over the sun's disk.[13] We very distinctly saw an atmosphere or dusky shade round the body of the planet, which very much disturbed the times of the contact, particularly the two internal ones. Dr. Solander observed as well as Mr. Green and myself, and we differed from one another in observing the times of the contact much more than could be expected. Mr. Green's telescope and mine were of the same magnifying power, but that of the doctor was greater than ours. It was nearly calm the whole day, and the thermometer exposed to the sun about the middle of the day rose to a degree of heat we have not before met with.

June 4   Punished Archd. Wolf with two dozen lashes for theft, having broken into one of the storerooms and stolen from thence a large quantity of spike nails; some few of them were found upon him. This evening the gentlemen that were sent to observe the transit of Venus, returned with success; those that were sent to York Island were well received by the natives. That island appeared to them not to be very fruitful.

June 5   Got some of the bread ashore out of the bread room to

[13] Although the Tahiti observations were successful, those taken in other parts of the world failed, so no calculation of the sun's distance could be made.

18

dry and clean. Yesterday being His Majesty's birthday, we kept it to-day and had several of the chiefs to dine with us.

June 6   This day and for some days past we have been informed by several of the natives that about ten or fifteen months ago two ships touched at this island and stayed ten days in a harbour to the eastward, called *Ohidea*, the Commander's name was Toot-teraso[14]—so at least the natives call him—and that one of the natives, brother to the chief of Ohidea, went away with him. They likewise say these ships brought the venereal distemper to this island, where it is now as common as in any part of the world, and which the people bear with as little concern as if they have been accustomed to it for ages past. We had not been here many days before some of our people got this disease, and as no such thing happened to any of the *Dolphin's* people while she was here, that I ever heard of, I had reason (notwithstanding the improbability of the thing) to think that we had brought it along with us, which gave me no small uneasiness, and did all in my power to prevent its progress, but all I could do was to little purpose, as I was obliged to have the most part of the ship's company ashore every day to work upon the fort, and a strong guard every night; and the women were so very liberal with their favours—or else nails, shirts, etc., were temptations that they could not withstand, that this distemper very soon spread itself over the greatest part of the ship's company, but now I have the satisfaction to find that the natives all agree that we did not bring it here.

We have several times seen iron tools and other articles with these people that we suspected came not from the *Dolphin*, and these they now say they had from these two ships.

June 7 to June 9   These three days we have been employed in careening both sides of the ship, and paying them with pitch and brimstone. We found her bottom in good order, and that the worm had not got into it.

[14] *i.e.* Bougainville. In his journal he accused Wallis (his predecessor here by eight months) of introducing venereal disease into the island. The latter returned the charge on the evidence of his surgeon's log, which proved that his men were free of it for six months preceding and six months succeeding his visit.

June 20   Got all the powder ashore to air, all of which we found in a bad condition, and the gunner informs me that it was very little better when it came first on board. Last night Oberiea made us a visit, whom we have not seen for some time. We were told of her coming, and that she would bring with her some of the stolen things, which we gave credit to because we knew several of them were in her possession; but we were surprised to find this woman put herself wholly in our power, and not bring with her one article of what we had lost. The excuse she made was that her gallant, a man that used to be along with her, did steal them, and she had beat him and turned him away, but she was so sensible of her own guilt that she was ready to drop down through fear, and yet she had resolution enough to insist upon sleeping in Mr. Banks's tent all night, and was with difficulty prevailed upon to go to her canoe, although no one took the least notice of her. In the morning she brought her canoe, with everything she had, to the gate of the fort, after which we could not help admiring her for her courage and the confidence she seemed to place in us, and thought that we could do no less than to receive her into favour, and accept the present she had brought us, which consisted of a hog, a dog, some bread fruit and plantains.

We refused to accept of the dog, as being an animal we had no use for; at which she seemed a little surprised, and told us it was very good eating, and we very soon had an opportunity to find that it was so, for Mr. Banks, having bought a basket of fruit in which was the thigh of a dog ready dressed, of this several of us tasted, and found that it was meat not to be despised, and therefore took Oberiea's dog and had him immediately dressed by some of the natives in the following manner: they first made a hole in the ground about a foot deep, in which they made a fire and heated some small stones. While this was doing the dog was strangled and the hair got off by laying him frequently on the fire, and as clean as if it had been scalded off with hot water. His entrails were taken out, and the whole washed clean, and as soon as the stones and hole was sufficiently heated the fire was put out and part of the stones were left in the bottom of the hole. Upon these stones were laid green leaves, and upon them the dog, together with the entrails, these were likewise covered with leaves, and over them hot stones; and then the hole was close covered with mould. After he had laid here about four hours, the oven (for so I must call it) was opened, and the dog taken out, whole and well done, and it was the opinion of every one who tasted it that they never eat sweeter meat, therefore we resolved for the future never to despise dog's flesh. It is in this manner that the natives dress and bake all their victuals that require it—flesh, fish, and fruit.

July 9   When, sometime in the middle watch, Clement Webb and Samuel Gibson, both marines and young men, found means to get away from the fort (which was now no hard matter to do) and in the morning were not to be found.[15] As it was known to everybody that all hands were to go on board on the Monday morning, and that the ship would sail in a day or two, there was reason to think that these two men intended to stay behind. However I was willing to stay one day to see if they would return before I took any step to find them.

July 10   The two marines not returning this morning, I began to enquire after them, and was informed by some of the natives that they were gone to the mountains, and that they had got each of them a wife and would not return; but at the same time no one would give us any certain intelligence where they were, upon which a resolution was taken to seize upon as many of the chiefs as we could. This was thought to be the readiest method to induce the other natives to produce the two men. We had in our custody Oberiea, Toobouratomita, and two other chiefs, but that I knew Tootaha would have more weight with the natives than all these put together, I dispatched Lieutenant Hicks away in the pinnace to the place where Tootaha was, to endeavour to decoy him into the boat and bring him on board, which Mr. Hicks per-

---

[15] These deserters anticipated the mutineers of the *Bounty*. When Cook examined them on their return they declared "that an acquaintance they had contracted with two girls, and to whom they had strongly attached themselves, was the sole reason of their attempting to stay behind." They received two dozen lashes each. For a similar attempt on the Second Voyage, see below p. 188.

formed without the least disturbance. We had no sooner taken the other chiefs into custody in Mr. Banks's tent than they became as desirous of having the men brought back as they were before of keeping them, and only desired that one of our people might be sent with some of theirs for them. Accordingly I sent a petty officer and the corporal of marines with three or four of their people, not doubting but they would return with the two men in the evening; but they not coming as soon as I expected, I took all the chiefs on board the ship for greater safety. About nine o'clock in the evening Webb, the marine, was brought in by some of the natives and sent on board. He informed me that the petty officer and corporal that had been sent in quest of them were disarmed and seized upon by the natives, and that Gibson was with them. Immediately upon getting this information I dispatched Mr. Hicks away in the long boat with a strong party of men to rescue them; but before he went Tootaha and the other chiefs was made to understand that they must send some of their people with Mr. Hicks to show him the place where our men were, and at the same time to send orders for their immediate release, for if any harm came to the men they (the chiefs) would suffer for it; and I believe at this time they wished as much to see the men return in safety as I did, for the guides conducted Mr. Hicks to the place before daylight, and he recovered the men without the least opposition, and returned with them about seven o'clock in the morning of

July 11   I then told the chiefs that there remained nothing more to be done to regain their liberty but to deliver up the arms the people had taken from the petty officer and corporal, and these were brought on board in less than half an hour, and then I sent them all on shore.

July 13   Between eleven and twelve o'clock we got under sail, and took our final leave of these people, after a stay of just three months, the most part of which time we have been upon good terms with them. Some few differences have now and then happened owing partly to the want of rightly understanding each other, and partly to their natural thievish disposition, which we could not at all times bear with or guard against; but these have been attended with no ill consequence to either side except the first, in which one of them was killed, and this I was very sorry for, because from what had happened to them by the *Dolphin* I thought it would have been no hard matter to have got and kept a footing with them without bloodshed. For some time before we left this island several of the natives were daily offering themselves to go away with us; and as it was thought they must be of use to us in our future discoveries we resolved to bring away one whose name is *Tupia*, a chief and a priest.[16] This man had been with us most part of the time we had been upon the island, which gave us an opportunity to know something of him. We found him to be a very intelligent person, and to know more of the geography of the islands situated in these seas, their produce, and the religion, laws, and customs of the inhabitants, than any one we had met with, and was the likeliest person to answer our purpose. For these reasons, and at the request of Mr. Banks, I received him on board, together with a young boy, his servant.

DESCRIPTION OF TAHITI

The produce of this island is bread fruit, coconuts, bananas, plantains, a fruit like an apple, sweet potatoes, yams, a fruit known by the name of *Eag Melloa*, and reckoned most delicious; sugar cane which the inhabitants eat raw; a root of the salop kind, called by the inhabitants *pea*; the root also of a plant called *ether*; and a fruit in a pod like a kidney bean, which when roasted eats like a chestnut, and is called *ahee*; the fruit of a tree which they call *wharra*, something like a pineapple; the fruit of a tree called by them *nano*; the roots of a fern and the roots of a plant called *thive*. All these articles the earth almost spontaneously produces,

---

[16] Tupia was O Berea's chief priest and rejected lover. As a recent conspirator against the new ruler of the island, he probably welcomed this opportunity to escape. His son, who had sailed with Bougainville, scored a notable success in the part of the Noble Savage in the *salons* of Paris, but died before he returned home.

or, at least, they are raised with very little labour. In the article of food these people may almost be said to be exempt from the curse of our forefathers, scarcely can it be said that they earn their bread with the sweat of their brow; benevolent nature hath not only supplied them with necessaries, but with abundance of superfluities. The sea coast supplies them with vast variety of most excellent fish, but these they get not without some trouble and perseverance. Fish seems to be one of their greatest luxuries, and they eat it either raw or dressed and seem to relish it one way as well as the other. Not only fish but almost everything that comes out of the sea is ate and esteemed by these people; shell fish, lobsters, crabs, and even sea insects, and what is commonly called blubbers of many kinds, conduce to their support.

For tame animals they have hogs, fowls, and dogs, the latter of which we learned to eat from them, and few were there of us but what allowed that a South Sea dog was next to an English lamb. One thing in their favour is that they live entirely upon vegetables; probably our dogs would not eat half so well. Little can be said in favour of their fowls, but their pork is most excellent, they have no beasts of prey of any sort, and wild fowls are scarce and confined to a few species. When any of the chiefs kill a hog it seems to be almost equally divided among all his dependants, and as these are generally very numerous, it is but a little that comes to each person's share, so that their chief food is vegetables, and of these they eat a large quantity. . . .

It is not common for any two to eat together, the better sort hardly ever; and the women never upon any account eat with the men, but always by themselves. What can be the reason of so unusual a custom it is hard to say, especially as they are a people, in every other instance, fond of society and much so of their women. They were often asked the reason, but they never gave no other answer, but that they did it because it was right, and expressed much dislike at the custom of men and women eating together of the same victuals. We have often used all the entreaties we were masters of to invite the women to partake of our victuals at our tables, but there never was an instance of one of them doing it public, but they would often go five or six together into the servants' apartments, and there eat very heartily of whatever they could find, nor were they the least disturbed if any of us came in while they were dining; and it hath sometimes happened that when a woman was alone in our company she would eat with us, but always took care that her own people should not know what she had done, so that whatever may be the reasons for this custom, it certainly affects their outward manners more than their principle.

PERSON OF THE NATIVES

With respect to their persons the men in general are tall, strong-limbed, and well-shaped. One of the tallest we saw measured six feet three inches and a half. The superior women are in every respect as large as Europeans, but the inferior sort are in general small, owing possibly to their early amours, which they are more addicted to than their superiors. They are of various colours: those of the inferior sort, who are obliged to be much exposed to the sun and air, are of a very dark brown; the superiors again, who spend most of their time in their houses under shelter, are not browner than people who are born or reside longer in the West Indies; nay, some of the women are almost as fair as Europeans. Their hair is almost universally black, thick, and strong; this the women wear short cropped round their ears. The men, on the other hand, wear it different ways: the better sort let it grow long, and sometimes tying it up on the top of their heads, or letting it hang loose over their shoulders; but many of the inferiors, and such who, in the exercise of their professions, fishing, etc., are obliged to be much upon or in the water, wear it cropped short like the women. They always pluck out a part of their beards, and keep what remains neat and clean. Both sexes eradicate every hair from under their armpits, and look upon it as a mark of uncleanliness in us that we do not do the same.

They have all fine white teeth, and for the most part short, flat noses and thick lips; yet their features are agreeable, and their gait graceful, and their behaviour to strangers and to each other is open, affable, and courteous, and, from all I could see, free from treachery, only that they are thieves to a man, and would steal but everything that came in their way, and that with such dexterity as would shame the most noted pickpocket in Europe. They are very cleanly people, both in their persons and diet, always washing their hands and mouth immediately before and after their meals, and wash or bathe themselves in fresh water three times a day, morning, noon, and night.

The only disagreeable thing about them is the oil with which they annoint their heads, *monoe*, as they call it; this is made of coconut oil, in which some sweet herbs or flowers are infused. The oil is generally very rancid, which makes the wearer of it smell not very agreeable. Another custom they have that is disagreeable to Europeans, which is eating lice, a pretty good stock of which they generally carry about them. However, this custom is not universal; for I seldom saw it done but among children and common people, and I am persuaded that had they the means they would keep themselves as free from lice as we do; but the want of combs in a hot climate makes this hardly possible. There are some very fine men upon this island whose skins are whiter than any European's, but of a dead colour, like that of the nose of a white horse; their eyes, eyebrows, hair and beards are also white. Their bodies were covered, more or less, with a kind of white down. Their skins are spotted, some parts being much whiter than others. They are short-sighted, with their eyes ofttimes full of rheum, and always looked unwholesome, and have neither the spirit nor the activity of the other natives. I did not see above three or four upon the whole island, and these were old men; so that I concluded that this difference of colour, etc., was accidental, and did not run in families, for if it did they must have been more numerous. The inhabitants of this island are troubled with a sort of leprosy, or scab all over their bodies. I have seen men, women, and children, but not many, who have had this distemper to that degree as not to be able to walk. This distemper, I believe, runs in families, because I have seen both mother and child have it.

Both sexes paint their bodies, *tattow*, as it is called in their language. This is done by inlaying the colour of black under their skins, in such a manner as to be indelible. Some have ill-designed figures of men, birds, or dogs; the women generally have this figure Z simply on every joint of their fingers and toes; the men have it likewise, and both have other different figures, such as circles, crescents, etc., which they have on their arms and legs; in short, they are so various in the application of these figures that both the quantity and situation of them seem to depend entirely upon the humour of each individual, yet all agree in having their buttocks covered with a deep black. Over this most have arches drawn one over another as high as their short ribs, which are near a quarter of an inch broad. These arches seem to be their great pride, as both men and women show them with great pleasure.

Their method of tattowing I shall now describe. The colour they use is lamp black, prepared from the smoke of a kind of oily nut, used by them instead of candles. The instrument for pricking it under the skin is made of very thin flat pieces of bone or shell, from a quarter of an inch to an inch and a half broad, according to the purpose it is to be used for, and about an inch and a half long. One end is cut into sharp teeth, and the other fastened to a handle. The teeth are dipped into black liquor, and then drove, by quick, sharp blows struck upon the handle with a stick for that purpose, into the skin so deep that every stroke is followed with a small quantity of blood. The part so marked remains sore for some days before it heals. As this is a painful operation, especially the tattowing their buttocks, it is performed but once in their lifetimes; it is never done until they are twelve or fourteen years of age.

Their clothing is either of cloth or matting of several different sorts; the dress of both men and women are much the same, which is a piece of cloth or matting wrapped two or three times round their waist, and hangs down below their knees, both behind and before, like a petticoat; another piece, or sometimes two or three, about two yards or two and a half yards long, with a hole in the middle, through which they put their heads. This hangs over their shoulders down behind and before, and is tied round their waist with a long piece of thin cloth, and being open at the sides gives free liberty to their arms. This is the common dress of all ranks of people, and there are few without such a one except the children, who go quite naked, the boys until they are six or seven years of age, and the girls until three or four. At these ages they begin to cover what nature teaches them to hide. Besides the dress I have mentioned some of the better sort, such as can afford it, but more especially the women, will one way or other wrap round them several pieces of cloth, each eight or ten yards long and two or three broad, so much that I have often wondered how they could bear it in so hot a climate. Again, on the other hand, many of the inferior sort during the heat of the day, go almost naked, the women wearing nothing but the petticoat afore-mentioned, and sometimes hardly that. The men wear a piece of cloth like a sack, which goes between their thighs, and brought up before and behind, and then wrapped round their waist. This every man wears always without exception, and it is no uncommon thing to see many of the better sort have nothing else on, as it is reckoned no shame for any part of the body to be exposed to view, except those which all mankind hide.

Both sexes sometimes shade their faces from the sun with little bonnets made of coconut leaves. Some have them of fine matting, but this is less common. They sometimes wear turbans, but their chief headdress is what they call *tomou*, which is human hair plaited scarce thicker than common thread. Of this I can safely affirm that I have seen pieces near a mile in length worked upon one end without a knot. These are made and worn only by the women, five or six such pieces of which they will sometimes wind round their heads, the effect of which, if done with taste, is very becoming. They have earrings by way of ornament, but wear them only at one ear. These are made of shells, stones, berries, red pease, and some small pearls which they wear three tied together; but our beads, buttons, etc., very soon supplied their places.

MANNERS AND CUSTOMS

After their meals in the heat of the day they often sleep, middle-aged people especially, the better sort of whom seem to spend most of their time in eating and sleeping. Diversions they have but few, shooting with the bow and wrestling are the chief; the first of which is confined almost wholly to the chiefs; they shoot for distance only, kneeling upon one knee and dropping the bow the instant of the arrow's parting from it. I have seen one of them shoot an arrow 274 yards, yet he looked upon it as no great shot.

Music is little known to them, yet they are very fond of it; they have only two instruments—the flute and the drum. The former is made of hollow bamboo about fifteen inches long, in which are three holes; into one of them they blow with one nostril, stopping the other with the thumb of the left hand, the other two holes they stop and unstop with their fingers, and by this means produce four notes, of which they have made one tune, which serves them upon all occasions, to which they sing a number of songs generally consisting of two lines and generally in rhyme. At any time of the day when they are lazy they amuse themselves by singing these couplets, but especially after dark when their candles are lighted, which are made of the kernels of a nut abounding much in oil; these are stuck upon a skewer of wood one upon another, and give a very tolerable light, which they often keep burning an hour after dark, and if they have strangers in the house much longer. Their drums are made of a hollow block of wood covered with shark's skin, and instead of drumsticks they use their hands. Of these they make out five or six tunes and accompany the flutes.

The drums are chiefly used at their *heivas*, which are a set of musicians, two or three drums for instance, as many flutes and singers, which go about from house to house and play, and are always received and rewarded by the master of the family, who gives them a piece of cloth or whatever he can spare, for which they will stay three or four hours, during which time his house will be crowded full, for the people are extravagantly fond of this diversion. The young girls whenever they can collect eight or ten together dance a very indecent dance, which they call *Timorodee*, singing most indecent songs and using most indecent actions, in the practice of which they are brought up from their earliest childhood; in doing this they keep time to a great nicety. This exercise is generally left off as soon as they arrive at years of maturity, for as soon as they have formed a connection with man they are expected to leave off dancing *Timorodee*.

One amusement or custom more I must mention, though I confess I do not expect to be believed, it is founded upon a custom so inhuman and contrary to the principles of human nature. It is this: that more than one half of the better sort of the inhabitants have entered into a resolution of enjoying free liberty in love, without being troubled or disturbed by its consequences. These mix and cohabit together with the utmost freedom, and the children who are so unfortunate as to be thus begot are smothered at the moment of their birth; many of these people contract intimacies and live together as man and wife for years, in the course of which the children that are born are destroyed. They are so far from concealing it that they look upon it as a branch of freedom upon which they value themselves. They are called *Arreoys*, and have meetings among themselves, where the men amuse themselves with wrestling, etc., and the women in dancing the indecent dance before-mentioned, in the course of which they give full liberty to their desires, but I believe keep up to the appearance of decency. I never saw one of these meetings; Dr. Monkhouse saw part of one, enough to make him give credit to what we had been told.

Both sexes express the most indecent ideas in conversation without the least emotion, and they delight in such conversation beyond any other. Chastity, indeed, is but little valued, especially among the middle people,—if a wife is found guilty of a breach of it her only punishment is a beating from her husband. The men will very readily offer the young women to strangers, even their own daughters, and think it very strange if you refuse them; but this is done merely for the sake of gain. . . .

30

Their canoes or proes are built all of them very narrow, and some of the largest are sixty or seventy feet long. These consist of several pieces; the bottom is round and made of large logs hollowed out to the thickness of about three inches, and may consist of three or four pieces; the sides are of plank of nearly the same thickness, and are built nearly perpendicular, rounding in a little towards the gunwale. The pieces on which they are built are well fitted, and fastened or sewed together with strong platting something in the same manner as old china, wooden bowls, etc., are mended. The greatest breadth is at the after part, which is generally about eighteen or twenty inches, and the fore part about one-third narrower; the height from the bottom to the gunwale seldom exceeds two and a half or three feet. They build them with high curved sterns which are generally ornamented with carved work; the head or fore part curves little or nothing. The smaller canoes are built after the same plan, some out of one, two, or more trees according to their size or the use they are for. In order to prevent them from oversetting when in the water, all those that go single, both great and small, have what is called outriggers, which are pieces of wood fastened to the gunwale and project out on one side about six, eight or ten feet, according to the size of the boat. At the end is fastened in a parallel direction to the canoe a long log of wood simply; or some have it shaped in the form of a small boat, but this is not common; this lays in the water and balances the boat. Those that are for sailing have outriggers only on the other side abreast of the mast; these serve to fasten the shrouds to, and are of use in trimming the boat when it blows fresh; the sailing proes have some one and some two masts; the sails are of matting and are made narrow at the head and square at the foot, something like a shoulder of mutton sail, such as are generally used in man-of-war barges, etc. . . .

Having given the best account I can of the manners and customs of these people, it will be expected that I should give some account of their religion, which is a thing I have learned so little of that I hardly dare to touch upon it, and should have passed it over in silence, were it not my duty as well as inclination to insert in this journal every and the least knowledge I may obtain of a people, who for many centuries have been shut up from almost every other part of the world.

They believe that there is one supreme god whom they call *Tane*; from him sprung a number of inferior deities, *Eatuas* as they call them—these they think preside over them and intermeddle in their affairs. To these they offer oblations such as hogs, dogs, fish, fruit, etc., and invoke them on some particular occasions, as in time of real or apparent danger, the setting out of a long voyage, sicknesses, etc.; but the ceremony made use of on these occasions I know not. The *mories*, which we at first thought were burying places, are wholly built for places of worship, and for the performing of religious ceremonies in.[17] The viands are laid upon altars erected eight, ten, or twelve feet high, by stout posts, and the table of the altar on which the viands lay, is generally made of palm leaves; they are not always in the *mories*, but very often at some distance from them. Their *mories*, as well as the tombs of the dead, they seem to hold sacred, and the women never enter the former, whatever they may do the latter. The viands laid near the tombs of the dead are, from what I can learn, not for the deceased, but as an offering to the *Eatua* made upon that occasion who, if not, would destroy the body and not accept of the soul—for they believe of a future state of rewards and punishments; but what their ideas are of it I know not. We have seen in some few places small houses set apart on purpose for the oblations offered to the *Eatua*, which consists of small strips of cloth, viands, etc. I am of opinion they offer to the *Eatua* a strip or small piece of every piece of cloth they make before they use it themselves, and it is not unlikely but what they observe the same thing with respect to their victuals, but as there are but few of these houses this cannot be a common custom; it may only be observed by the priests and such families as are more religious than others.

Now I have mentioned priests, there are men that exercise that function, of which numbers Tupia is one. They seem to be in no

---

[17] It was only on his Second Voyage that Cook discovered that human sacrifices were offered. Cannibalism was never a practice. A full knowledge of the island was not obtained until the landing of missionaries from the *Duff* in 1797. French missionaries appeared in 1836 and France annexed the island in 1843.

great repute, neither can they live wholly by their profession, and this leads me to think that these people are no bigots to their religion. The priests on some occasions do the office of physicians, and their prescriptions consist in performing some religious ceremony before the sick person. They likewise crown the *Eare dehi*, or King, in the performing of which we are told much form and ceremony is used, after which everyone is at liberty to treat and play as many tricks with the new King as he pleaseth during the remainder of the day.

There is a ceremony which they perform at or after the funerals of the dead which I had forgot to mention at the time; we happened to see it some time before we left the island. An old woman, a relation of Toobouratomita's, happened to die and was interred in the usual manner. For several successive evenings after, one of her relations dressed himself in a very odd dress, which I cannot tell how to describe or to convey a better idea of it than to suppose a man dressed with plumes of feathers, something in the same manner as those worn by coaches, hearses, horses, etc., at the funerals in London. It was very neatly made up of black or brown and white cloth, black and white feathers, and pearl oyster shells. It covered the head, face, and body, as low as the calf of the legs or lower, and not only looked grand but awful likewise. The man thus equipped, and attended by two or three more men and women with their faces and bodies besmeared with soot, and a club in their hands, would about sunset take a compass of near a mile running here and there, and wherever they came the people would fly from them as though they had been so many hobgoblins, not one daring to come in their way. I know not the reason for their performing this ceremony, which they call *heiva*, a name they give to most of their divertisements.

BOOK II

From Leaving Tahiti to the Completion of the Survey of New Zealand
1769–1770

IN SEARCH OF THE SOUTHERN CONTINENT—DISCOVERY OF NEW
ZEALAND—CIRCUMNAVIGATION OF THE NORTH ISLAND—QUEEN
CHARLOTTE'S SOUND—CUSTOMS OF THE MAORIS—CIRCUMNAVIGA-
TION OF THE SOUTH ISLAND—ACCOUNT OF NEW ZEALAND

August 28   Fresh gales and cloudy, with rain in the latter part.[1]
At 10 a.m. departed this life John Reading, boatswain's mate;
his death was occasioned by the boatswain out of mere good
nature giving him part of a bottle of rum last night, which it is
supposed he drank all at once. He was found to be very much in
liquor last night, but as this was no more than what was common
with him when he could get any, no farther notice was taken of
him than to put him to bed, where this morning about eight
o'clock he was found speechless and past recovery.

September 2   Very strong gales, with heavy squalls of wind,
hail, and rain. At 4 p.m., being in the latitude of 40° 22′ S., and
having not the least visible signs of land, we wore, and brought
to under the foresail, and reefed the mainsail, and handed it. I did

---

[1] The *Endeavour* was now on her way south from Tahiti. Before leaving the
neighbouring islands, which he called the Society Islands, Cook spent a month
charting them and planting the seeds provided by Banks. He then began the more
secret part of his voyage—the search for *Terra Australis*—by sailing south as far
as latitude 40° and then turning west.

intend to have stood to the southward if the winds had been moderate, so long as they continued westerly, notwithstanding we had no prospect of meeting with land, rather than stand back to the northward, on the same track as we came, but as the weather was so very tempestuous I laid aside this design, and thought it more advisable to stand to the northward into better weather, lest we should receive such damage in our sails and rigging as might hinder the further prosecutions of the voyage. Some albatrosses, pintado birds, and doves about the ship, and a bird larger than a duck, his plumage of a dark brown, with a yellow beak. We saw of these birds in our passage to the northward, after doubling Cape Horn.

October 7   Gentle breezes and settled weather. At 2 p.m. saw land[2] from the masthead bearing W. by N., which we stood directly for, and could but just see it of the deck at sunset. Variation per azimuth and amplitude 15° 4½′ E.; by observation of the sun and moon made this afternoon the longitude of the ship is 180° 55′ W., by the mean of these and subsequent observations the error of the ship's account in longitude from George's Island is 3° 16′; that is, so much to the westward of the longitude resulting from the Log, which is what is inserted in the columns. At midnight brought to and sounded, but had no ground with 170 fathoms. At daylight made sail in for the land, at noon it bore from S.W. to N.W. by N., distant eight leagues. Latitude observed 38° 57′ S.; wind N.E., S.E., variable; course S. 70° W.; distance 41 m.; latitude 38° 47′ observation S.; longitude 177° 54′ W.

October 8   Gentle breezes and clear weather. At 5 p.m., seeing the opening of a bay that appeared to run pretty far inland, hauled our wind and stood in for it; but as soon as night came on

---

[2] *i.e.* New Zealand. Cook named his landfall on the eastern side of the North Island Young Nick's Head, after the boy, Nick Young, who sighted it; the town of Gisborne is situated near it. The last European to encounter the warlike Maoris was Tasman in 1642: from his experience he named the bay where he anchored near Nelson on the South Island "Massacre Bay". According to one Maori tradition the natives thought that the *Endeavour* was a large bird; according to another she was a floating island, which they attempted to capture by force of arms.

we kept plying on and off until daylight, when we found ourselves to leeward of the bay, the wind being at N. By noon we fetched in with the S.W. point, but not being able to weather it we tacked and stood off. We saw in the bay several canoes, people upon the shore, and some houses in the country. The land on the sea coast is high, with steep cliffs; and back inland are very high mountains. The face of the country is of a hilly surface, and appears to be clothed with wood and verdure. Wind between the E.N.E. and N.

October 9   Gentle breezes and clear weather. Afternoon stood into the bay and anchored on the north-east side before the entrance of a small river, in ten fathoms, a fine sandy bottom. The north-east point of the bay bore E. by S. $\frac{1}{2}$ S., and the south-west point S., distance from the shore half a league. After this I went ashore with a party of men in the pinnace and yawl accompanied by Mr. Banks and Dr. Solander. We landed abreast of the ship and on the east side of the river just mentioned; but seeing some of the natives on the other side of the river of whom I was desirous of speaking with, and finding that we could not ford the river, I ordered the yawl in to carry us over, and the pinnace to lay at the entrance. In the meantime the Indians made off. However we went as far as their huts which lay about two or three hundred yards from the waterside, leaving four boys to take care of the yawl, which we had no sooner left than four men came out of the woods on the other side of the river, and would certainly have cut her off had not the people in the pinnace discovered them and called to her to drop down the stream, which they did, being closely pursued by the Indians. The coxswain of the pinnace, who had the charge of the boats, seeing this, fired two muskets over their heads; the first made them stop and look round them, but the second they took no notice of; upon which a third was fired and killed one of them upon the spot just as he was going to dart his spear at the boat. At this the other three stood motionless for a minute or two, seemingly quite surprised; wondering, no doubt, what it was that had thus killed their comrade; but as soon as they recovered themselves they made off, dragging the dead body a little way and then left it. Upon our hearing the report of the muskets we immediately repaired to the boats, and after viewing the dead body we returned on board. In the morning, seeing a number of the natives at the same place where we saw them last night, I went on shore with the boats, manned and armed, and landed on the opposite side of the river. Mr. Banks, Dr. Solander, and myself only landed at first, and went to the side of the river, the natives being got together on the opposite side. We called to them in the George's Island language, but they answered us by flourishing their weapons over their heads and dancing, as we supposed, the war dance; upon this we retired until the marines were landed, which I ordered to be drawn up about two hundred yards behind us. We went again to the riverside, having Tupia, Mr. Green, and Dr. Monkhouse along with us. Tupia spoke to them in his own language, and it was an agreeable surprise to us to find that they perfectly understood him. After some little conversation had passed one of them swam over to us, and after him twenty or thirty more; these last brought their arms, which the first man did not. We made them every one presents, but this did not satisfy them; they wanted everything we had about us, particularly our arms, and made several attempts to snatch them out of our hands. Tupia told us several times, as soon as they came over, to take care of ourselves for they were not our friends; and this we very soon found, for one of them snatched Mr. Green's hanger from him and would not give it up; this encouraged the rest to be more insolent, and seeing others coming over to join them, I ordered the man who had taken the hanger to be fired at, which was accordingly done, and wounded in such a manner that he died soon after. Upon the first fire, which was only two muskets, the others retired to a rock which lay nearly in the middle of the river; but on seeing the man fall they returned, probably to carry him off or his arms, the last of which they accomplished, and this we could not prevent unless we had run our bayonets into them, for upon their returning from off the rock, we had discharged off our pieces, which were loaded with small shot, and wounded three more; but these got over the river and were carried off by the others, who now thought proper to retire. Finding nothing was to be done with the people on this side, and the water in the river being salt, I embarked with an intent to row round the head of the bay in search of fresh water, and if possible to surprise some of the natives and to take them on board, and by good treatment and presents endeavour to gain their friendship with this view.

October 10 Afternoon, I rowed round the head of the bay, but could find no place to land on account of the great surf which beat everywhere upon the shore. Seeing two boats or canoes coming in from sea I rowed to one of them, in order to seize upon the people; and came so near before they took notice of us that Tupia called to them to come alongside and we would not hurt them; but instead of doing this they endeavoured to get away, upon which I ordered a musket to be fired over their heads, thinking this would either make them surrender, or jump overboard; but here I was mistaken, for they immediately took to their arms or whatever they had in the boat, and began to attack us. This obliged us to fire upon them, and unfortunately either two or three were killed and one wounded, and three jumped overboard. These last we took up and brought on board, where they were clothed and treated with all imaginable kindness; and to the surprise of everybody became at once as cheerful and as merry as if they had been with their own friends. They were all three young, the eldest not above twenty years of age, and the youngest about ten or twelve. I am aware that most humane men who have not experienced things of this nature will censure my conduct in firing upon the people in their boat, nor do I myself think that the reason I had for seizing upon her will at all justify me; and had I thought that they would have made the least resistance I would not have come near them; but as they did, I was not to stand still and suffer either myself or those that were with me to be knocked on the head.

October 12 Gentle breezes at N.W. and N., with frequent calms. In the afternoon, while we lay becalmed, several canoes came off to the ship, but kept at a distance until one, who appeared to come from a different part, came off and put alongside at once, and after her all the rest. The people in this boat had heard of the treatment those had met with we had had on board before, and therefore came on board without hesitation; they were all kindly treated, and very soon entered into a traffic with our people for George's Island cloth, etc.; giving in exchange their paddles, having little else to dispose of, and hardly left themselves a sufficient number to paddle ashore; nay, the people in one canoe, after disposing of their paddles, offered to sell the canoe. After a stay of about two hours they went away, but by some means or other three were left on board, and not one boat would put back to take them in, and, what was more surprising, those aboard did not seem at all uneasy with their situation. In the evening a light breeze springing up at N.W., we steered along shore under an easy sail, until midnight, then brought to. Soon after it fell calm, and continued so until 8 a.m., when a breeze sprang up at N., with which we stood along shore S.S.W. At and after sunrise found the variation to be 14° 46′ E. About this time two canoes came off to the ship, one of which was prevailed upon to come alongside to take in the three people we had had on board all night, who now seemed glad of the opportunity to get ashore. As the people in the canoe were a little shy at first, it was observed that one argument those on board made use on to entice the others alongside, was in telling them that we did not eat men; from which it should seem that these people have such a custom among them.

October 15   At 8 a.m., being abreast of the south-west point of the bay,[3] some fishing boats came off to us and sold us some stinking fish; however it was such as they had, and we were glad to enter into traffic with them upon any terms. These people behaved at first very well, until a large armed boat, wherein were twenty-two men, came alongside. We soon saw that this boat had nothing for traffic, yet as they came boldly alongside we gave

[3] *i.e.* Hawke's Bay, to the south of which lies the town of Napier. After making his landfall, Cook sailed south along the east coast; then, "seeing no likelihood of meeting with a harbour, and the face of the country visibly altering for the worse", he turned north to circumnavigate the North Island.

them two or three pieces of cloth, articles they seemed the most fond of. One man in this boat had on him a black skin, something like a bear skin, which I was desirous of having that I might be a better judge what sort of an animal the first owner was. I offered him for it a piece of red cloth, which he seemed to jump at by immediately putting off the skin and holding it up to us, but would not part with it until he had the cloth in his possession and after that not at all, but put off the boat and went away, and with them all the rest. But in a very short time they returned again, and one of the fishing boats came alongside and offered us some more fish. The Indian boy Tiata, Tupia's servant, being over the side, they seized hold of him, pulled him into the boat and endeavoured to carry him off; this obliged us to fire upon them, which gave the boy an opportunity to jump overboard. We brought the ship to, lowered a boat into the water, and took him up unhurt. Two or three paid for this daring attempt with the loss of their lives, and many more would have suffered had it not been for fear of killing the boy. This affair occasioned my giving this point of land the name of *Cape Kidnapper*. It is remarkable on account of two white rocks in form of haystacks standing very near it. On each side of the cape are tolerable high white steep cliffs, latitude 39° 43′ S.; longitude 182° 24′ W.; it lies S.W. by W., distant thirteen leagues from the Island of Portland. Between them is a large bay wherein we have been for these three days past; this bay I have named *Hawke's Bay* in honour of Sir Edward First Lord of the Admiralty; we found in it from twenty-four to eight and seven fathoms, everywhere good anchoring.

October 28   Gentle breezes southerly and fine weather. Employed wooding, cutting, and making of brooms, there being a shrub here very fit for that purpose; and as I intended to sail in the morning some hands were employed picking of celery to take to sea with us. This is found here in great plenty, and I have caused it to be boiled with portable soup and oatmeal every morning for the people's breakfast; and this I design to continue as long as it will last, or any is to be got, and I look upon it to be very wholesome and a great antiscorbutic.

November 4 At 1 p.m. three canoes came off from the main to the ship, and after parading about a little while they darted two pikes at us. The first was at one of our men as he was going to give them a rope, thinking they were coming on board; but the second they throwed into the ship; the firing of one musket sent them away. Each of these canoes were made out of one large tree, and were without any sort of ornament, and the people in them were mostly quite naked. At 2 p.m. saw a large opening or inlet in the land, which we bore up for with an intent to come to an anchor. At this time had forty-one fathoms, which gradually decreased to nine fathoms, at which time we were one and a half miles from a high towered rock lying near the south point of the inlet; the rock and the northernmost of the Court of Aldermen being in one bearing S. 61° E. At half-past seven anchored in seven fathoms a little within the south entrance of the bay or inlet.[4] We were accompanied in here by several canoes, who stayed about the ship until dark; and before they went away they were so generous as to tell us that they would come and attack us in the morning; but some of them paid us a visit in the night, thinking, no doubt, but what they should find all hands asleep, but as soon as they found their mistake they went off. My reasons for putting in here were the hopes of discovering a good harbour, and the desire I had of being in some convenient place to observe the transit of Mercury, which happens on the 9th instant, and will be wholly visible here if the day is clear. If we be so fortunate as to obtain this observation, the longitude of this place and country will thereby be very accurately determined. Between five and six o'clock in the morning several canoes came off to us from all parts of the bay; in them were about 130 or 140 people. To all appearances their first design was to attack us, being all completely armed in their way; however, this they never attempted, but after parading about the ship near three hours, sometimes trading with us, and at other times tricking of us, they dispersed; but not before we had fired a few muskets and one great gun, not with any design to hurt any of them, but to show them what sort of weapons we had, and that we could revenge any insult they

[4] *i.e.* Mercury Bay, on the North Island.

offered to us. It was observable that they paid but little regard to the muskets that were fired, notwithstanding one ball was fired through one of their canoes, but what effect the great gun had I know not, for this was not fired until they were going away.

November 12   I went with the pinnace and yawl, accompanied by Mr. Banks and Dr. Solander, over to the north side of the bay in order to take a view of the country and the fortified village[5] which stands there. We landed about a mile from it, and were met by the inhabitants in our way thither, who, with a great deal of good nature and friendship, conducted us into the place and showed us everything that was there.

This village is built upon a high promontory or point on the north side and near the head of the bay. It is in some places quite inaccessible to man, and in others very difficult, except on that side which faced the narrow ridge of the hill on which it stands. Here it is defended by a double ditch, a bank and two rows of picketing, the inner row upon the bank; but not so near the crown but what there was good room for men to walk and handle their arms between the picketing and the inner ditch. The outer picketing was between the two ditches, and laid sloping with their upper ends hanging over the inner ditch. The depth of this ditch from the bottom to the crown of the bank was twenty-four feet. Close within the inner picketing was erected by strong posts a stage thirty feet high and forty in length and six feet broad. The use of this stage was to stand upon to throw darts at the assailants, and a number of darts lay upon it for that purpose. At right angles to this stage and a few paces from it was another of the same construction and bigness; this stood likewise within the picketing, and was intended for the same use as the other—viz., to stand upon to throw stones and darts upon the enemy as they advanced up the side of the hill where lay the main way into the place. It likewise might be intended to defend some little outworks and huts that lay at the skirts and on this side of the hill. These outworks were not intended as advanced posts, but

[5] Called a "pa"; Cook adds the definite article in his spelling "hippa".

for such of the inhabitants to live in as had not room in the main works, but had taken shelter under it. Besides the works on the land side, above described, the whole village was pallisaded round with a line of pretty strong picketing run round the edge of the hill. The ground within having not been level at first, but laid sloping, they had divided it into little squares and levelled each of these. These squares lay in the form of an amphitheatre, and were each of them pallisaded round, and had communication one with another by narrow lanes and little gateways, which could easily be stopped up, so that if an enemy had forced the outer picketing he had several others to encounter before the place could be easily reduced, supposing them to defend every one of the places one after another. The main way leading into this fortification was up a very steep part of the hill and through a narrow passage about twelve feet long and under one of the stages. I saw no door nor gate, but it might very soon have been barricaded up. Upon the whole I looked upon it to be a very strong and well-chosen post, and where a small number of resolute men might defend themselves a long time against a vast superior force, armed in the manner as these people are. These seemed to be prepared against a siege, having laid up in store an immense quantity of fern roots and a good many dried fish; but we did not see that they had any fresh water nearer than a brook which runs close under the foot of a hill, from which I suppose they can at times get water, though besieged, and keep it in gourds until they use it.

January 16   Variable light airs and clear settled weather. At 1 p.m. hauled close round the south-west end of the island, on which stands the village before mentioned, the inhabitants of which were all in arms. At two o'clock we anchored in a very snug cove,[6] which is on the north-west side of the bay facing the

6 Named Ship Cove in Queen Charlotte's Sound, some seventy miles south-east of "Murtherer's Bay", *i.e.* Tasman's Massacre Bay on the South Island. Cook frequently returned to this anchorage on later voyages. He had now almost completed the circumnavigation of the North Island. When off North Cape on 14 December, he was actually within thirty miles of a French ship, Surville's *St. Jean Baptiste*, which was approaching New Zealand from the opposite direction. Surville, who had sailed from India for Tahiti to follow up Bougainville's visit,

south-west end of the island in eleven fathoms; soft ground, and moored with the stream anchor. By this time several of the natives had come off to the ship in their canoes, and after heaving a few stones at us and having some conversation with Tupia, some of them ventured on board, where they made but a very short stay before they went into their canoes again, and soon after left us altogether. I then went ashore in the bottom of the cove, accompanied by most of the gentlemen on board. We found a fine stream of excellent water, and as to wood the land is here one entire forest. Having the seine with us we made a few hauls and caught 300 lb. weight of different sorts of fish, which were equally distributed to the ship's company. Morning, careened the ship, scrubbed and payed [tarred] the larboard side. Several of the natives visited us this morning, and brought with them some stinking fish, which, however, I ordered to be bought up to encourage them in this kind of traffic, but trade at this time seemed not to be their object, but were more inclinable to quarrel, and as the ship was upon the careen I thought they might give us some trouble, and perhaps hurt some of our people that were in the boats alongside. For this reason I fired some small shot at one of the first offenders; this made them keep at a proper distance while they stayed, which was not long before they all went away. These people declared to us this morning, that they never either saw or heard of a ship like ours being upon this coast before. From this it appears that they have no tradition among them of Tasman being here, for I believe Murtherer's Bay, the place where he anchored, not to be far from this place; but this cannot be it from the latitude, for I find by an observation made this day at noon that we are at an anchor in 41° 5′ 32″ S., which is fifteen miles to the southward of Murtherer's Bay.

January 17   Light airs, calm and pleasant weather. Afternoon, righted ship and got the other side ready for heeling out, and in the evening hauled the seine and caught a few fish. While this was doing

sighted the North Island on 12 December and continued by sailing down the east coast at the same time as Cook was sailing down the west; he had already lost a third of his men from scurvy, so decided to continue direct to Peru, but he was drowned before he reached his destination.

some of us went in the pinnace into another cove, not far from where the ship lays; in going thither we met with a woman floating upon the water, who to all appearance had not been dead many days. Soon after we landed we met with two or three of the natives who not long before must have been regaling themselves upon human flesh, for I got from one of them the bone of the forearm of a man or woman which was quite fresh, and the flesh had been but lately picked off, which they told us they had eat; they gave us to understand that but a few days before they had taken, killed, and eat a boat's crew of their enemies or strangers, for I believe they look upon all strangers as enemies. From what we could learn the woman we had seen floating upon the water was in this boat and had been drowned in the fray. There was not one of us that had the least doubt but what these people were cannibals; but the finding this bone with part of the sinews fresh upon it was a stronger proof than any we had yet met with, and, in order to be fully satisfied of the truth of what they had told us, we told one of them that it was not the bone of a man, but that of a dog; but he, with great fervency, took hold of his forearm, and told us again that it was that bone: and to convince us that they had eat the flesh he took hold of the flesh of his own arm with his teeth and made signs of eating. Morning, careened, scrubbed, and payed the starboard side of the ship; while this was doing some of the natives came alongside seemingly only to look at us. There was a woman among them who had her arms, thighs, and legs cut in several places; this was done by way of mourning for her husband who had very lately been killed and eat by some of their enemies as they told us and pointed towards the place where it was done, which lay somewhere to the eastward. Mr. Banks got from one of them a bone of the forearm, much in the same state as the one before mentioned; and to show us that they eat the flesh, they bit and gnawed the bone and drawed it through their mouths, and this in such a manner as plainly showed that the flesh to them was a dainty bit.

January 23   Afternoon, winds southerly, a fresh breeze. I took one hand with me and climbed up to the top of one of the hills, but when I came there I was hindered from seeing up the inlet by higher hills, which I could not come at for impenetrable woods, but I was abundantly recompensed for the trouble I had in ascending the hill, for from it I saw what I took to be the Eastern Sea, and a strait or passage from it into the Western Sea;[7] a little to the eastward of the entrance of the inlet in which we now lay with the ship. The mainland which lies on the south-east side of this inlet appeared to me to be a narrow ridge of very high hills, and to form a part of the south-west side of the strait; the land on the opposite side seemed to tend away east, as far as the eye could see. To the south-east appeared an open sea, and this I took to be the eastern. I likewise saw some islands lying on the east side of the inlet, which before I had taken to be a part of the mainland. As soon as I had descended the hill and we had refreshed ourselves, we set out in order to return to the ship, and on our way passed through and examined the harbours, coves, etc., that lay behind the islands above mentioned. In this route we met with an old village in which were a good many houses, but nobody had lived in them lately; we likewise saw another that was inhabited, but the day being so far spent, that we had not time to go to it, but made the best of our way to the ship, which we reached between eight and nine o'clock.

January 31   Little wind and variable. In the afternoon the carpenters having prepared the two posts with inscriptions upon them, setting forth the ship's name, month, and year, one of them was set up at the watering place, on which we hoisted the Union flag;[8] and in the morning I took the other over to the island which is known by the name of *Motuouru*, and is the one that lies nearest to the sea; but before I attempted to set up the post I went first

[7] Tasman supposed that this strait between the North and South Islands was a bay. Banks gave it its present name. He writes: "While Dr. Solander and I were botanising, the Captain went to the top of a hill and in about an hour returned in high spirits, having seen the Eastern Sea and satisfied himself of the existence of a strait communicating with it, the idea of which has occurred to us all from Tasman's as well as our own observations."

[8] The scene is near Cape Jackson in Queen Charlotte's Sound. The *Endeavour* left the Sound to complete the circumnavigation of the North Island a week later. After that, Cook turned south to examine the eastern coast of the South Island.

to the *hippa*, having Dr. Monkhouse and Tupia along with me. We here met with the old man I have before spoken of. The first thing I did was to inquire after the man said to be killed by our people, and the one that was wounded at the same time, when it did not appear to me that any such accidents had happened. I next (by means of Tupia) explained to the old man and several others that we were come to set up a mark upon the island, in order to show to any ship that might put into this place that we had been here before. They not only gave their free consent to set it up, but promised never to pull it down. I then gave every one a present of one thing or another; to the old man I gave silver, three penny pieces dated 1763; and spike nails with the King's broad arrow cut deep in them; things that I thought were most likely to remain long among them. After I had thus prepared the way for setting up the post, we took it up to the highest part of the island, and after fixing it fast in the ground, hoisted thereon the Union flag, and I dignified this inlet with the name of Queen Charlotte's Sound, and took formal possession of it and the adjacent lands in the name and for the use of His Majesty. We then drank Her Majesty's health on a bottle of wine, and gave the empty bottle to the old man (who had attended us up the hill), with which he was highly pleased. Whilst the post was setting up we asked the old man about the strait or passage into the Eastern Sea, and he very plainly told us there was a passage, and as I had some conjectures that the lands to the south-west of this strait (which we are now at) was an island, and not a continent, we questioned the old man about it, who said it consisted of two *Wannuas*, that is two lands or islands that might be circumnavigated in a few days, even in four. This man spoke of three lands, the two above mentioned which he called *Tovy-poinammu*, which signifies green talk or stone, such as they make their tools or ornaments, etc.,[9] and for the third he pointed to the land on the east side of the strait; this, he said, was a large land, and that it would take up a great many moons to sail round it; this he called *Aeheino Mouwe*, a name many others before had called it by. That part which borders on the strait he called *Teiria Whitte*. After we

---

[9] New Zealand jade, of which axes and clubs were also made.

had done our business upon the island we returned on board, bringing the old man along with us, who after dinner went ashore in a canoe that came to attend upon him.

February 17   Yesterday Lieutenant Gore, having the morning watch at the time we first saw this island,[10] thought he saw land bearing S.S.E. and S.E. by E.; but I, who was upon deck at the same time, was very certain that it was only clouds, which dissipated as the sun rose. But neither this, nor the running fourteen leagues to the south, nor the seeing no land to the eastward of us in the evening, could satisfy Mr. Gore but what he saw in the morning was, or might be, land; although there was hardly a possibility of its being so, because we must have been more than double the distance from it at that time to what we were either last night or this morning, at both of which times the weather was exceeding clear, and yet we could see no land either to the eastward or southward of us. Notwithstanding all this, Mr. Gore was of the same opinion this morning; upon this I ordered the ship to be wore, and to be steered E.S.E. by compass on the other tack, the point on which he said the land bore at this time from us. At noon we were in the latitude of 44° 7′ S.; the S. point of Banks Island bore N., distant five leagues.

February 18   Gentle breezes at N. and fair weather. Afternoon stood E.S.E. in search of Mr. Gore's imaginary land until seven o'clock, at which time we had run twenty-eight miles since noon; but seeing no land but that we had left, or signs of any, we bore away S. by W., and continued upon that course until noon, when we found ourselves in the latitude of 45° 16′ S. Our course and distance sailed since yesterday is S. 8° E., seventy miles; the south-point of Banks Island N. 6° 30′ W., distant twenty-eight leagues; variation per amplitude this morning 15° 30′. Seeing no signs of

[10] One of the few errors which Cook made was to mistake the Banks peninsula (on which Lyttelton, the port of Christchurch, is situated) for an island. He appears to have named it after Banks in revenge for the latter's naming the Cook Strait. To leave nothing unexplored, he made a big detour out to sea before continuing south, to make sure that Gore's suggestion was not really *Terra Australis*.

land, I thought it to no purpose standing any farther to the south-ward, and therefore hauled to the westward, thinking we were far enough to the southward to weather all the land we had left; but this opinion was only founded on the information we had had from the natives of Queen Charlotte's Sound.

March 10   Afternoon. Moderate breezes at N.W. by N. and N. with which we stood close upon a wind to the westward. At sunset the southernmost point of land, which I afterwards named South Cape,[11] and which lies in the latitude of 47° 19′ S., longitude 192° 12′ W. from Greenwich, bore N. 38° E., distant four leagues, and the westernmost land in sight bore N. 2° E. This last was a small island, lying off the point of the main. I began now to think that this was the southernmost land, and that we should be able to get round it by the W., for we have had a large hollow swell from the south-west, ever since we had the last gale of wind from that quarter, which makes one think there is no land in that direction. In the night it began to blow, so that at or before day-light we were brought under our two courses; but at 8 a.m. it fell moderate, and we set the topsails close reefed, and the mizzen and mizzen staysail being split, we unbent them and bent others. At noon, the wind coming at W, we tacked and stood to the northward, having no land in sight; our latitude by observation was 47° 33′ S., longitude west from the South Cape 0° 59′.

March 23   Having now nearly run down the whole of this north-west coast of *Tovy Poenammu*, it is time I should describe the face of the country as it hath at different times appeared to us.[12] I have mentioned on the 11th instant, at which time we were off the southern part of the island, that the land seen then was

---

[11] The southern point of Stewart Island, which Cook thought was joined to New Zealand. The "small island" was Long Island, a little to the westward. Banks's journal has this entry: "Blew fresh all day; we were carried round the point, to the total destruction of our aerial fabric called continent." He and one of the midshipmen were the only persons on board who really believed in Dalrymple's southern continent.

[12] Cook is writing off Cape Farewell, the north point of the South Island. He covered the 400 miles of the west coast here described in twelve days. Foggy weather prevented him seeing Mount Cook.

rugged and mountainous; and there is great reason to believe that the same ridge of mountains extends nearly the whole length of the island from between the westernmost land seen that day and the easternmost seen on the 13th. There is a space of about six or eight leagues of the sea coast unexplored, but the mountains inland were visible enough. The land near the shore about Cape West is rather low, and rises with a gradual ascent up to the foot of the mountains, and appeared to be mostly covered with wood. From Point Five Fingers down to the latitude of 44° 20′ there is a narrow ridge of hills rising directly from the sea, which are clothed with wood; close behind these hills lies the ridge of mountains, which are of a prodigious height, and appear to consist of nothing but barren rocks, covered in many places with large patches of snow, which perhaps have lain there since the Creation. No country upon earth can appear with a more rugged and barren aspect than this doth; from the sea for as far inland as the eye can reach nothing is to be seen but the summits of these rocky mountains, which seem to lay so near one another as not to admit any valleys between them. From the latitude of 44° 20′ to the latitude 42° 8′ these mountains lay farther inland; the country between them and the sea consists of woody hills and valleys of various extent, both for height and depth, and hath much the appearance of fertility. Many of the valleys are large, low, and flat, and appeared to be wholly covered with wood; but it is very probable that great part of the land is taken up in lakes, ponds, etc., as is very common in such like places. From the last mentioned latitude to Cape Farewell, afterwards so called, the land is not distinguished by anything remarkable; it rises into hills directly from the sea, and is covered with wood. While we were upon this part of the coast the weather was foggy, in so much that we could see but a very little way inland; however, we sometimes saw the summits of the mountains above the fog and clouds, which plainly showed that the inland parts were high and mountainous, and gave me great reason to think that there is a continued chain of mountains from the one end of the island to the other.

March 31   Upon my return to the ship, in the evening, I found the water, etc., all on board, and the ship ready for sea;[13] and being now resolved to quit this country altogether, and to bend my thoughts towards returning home by such a route as might conduce most to the advantage of the service I am upon, I consulted with the officers upon the most eligible way of putting this in execution. To return by the way of Cape Horn was what I most wished, because by this route we should have been able to prove the existence or non-existence of a southern continent, which yet remains doubtful; but in order to ascertain this we must have kept in a higher latitude in the very depth of winter, but the condition of the ship, in every respect, was not thought sufficient for such an undertaking. For the same reason the thoughts of proceeding directly to the Cape of Good Hope was laid aside, especially as no discovery of any moment could be hoped for in that route. It was therefore resolved to return by way of the East Indies by the following route: upon leaving this coast to steer to the westward until we fall in with the east coast of New Holland, and then to follow the direction of that coast to the northward, or what other direction it might take us, until we arrive at its northern extremity; and if this should be found impracticable, then to endeavour to fall in with the land or islands discovered by Quiros.[14]

ACCOUNT OF NEW ZEALAND

Before I quit this land altogether I shall give a short general description of the country, its inhabitants, their manners, customs, etc., in which it is necessary to observe that many things are founded only on conjecture, for we were too short a time in

[13] The *Endeavour* now lay in Admiralty Bay, near Queen Charlotte's Sound, having completed the circumnavigation of both islands. Cook's instructions gave him a free choice of his route home. After summoning a council of officers, it was decided to continue west, in consequence of which he discovered the eastern coast of Australia.

[14] *i.e.* Espiritu Santo, the northern island of the New Hebrides, discovered by Quiros in 1606. The only land marked on Cook's charts was this supposed north western tip of *Terra Australis* and the southern part of Tasman's Van Diemen's land.

any one place to learn much of their interior policy, and therefore could only draw conclusions from what we saw at different times.

Part of the [west] coast of this country was first discovered by Abel Tasman in 1642, and by him called New Zealand; he, however, never landed upon it; probably he was discouraged from it by the natives killing three or four of his people at the first and only place he anchored at. This country, which before now was thought to be a part of the imaginary Southern Continent, consists of two large islands, divided from each other by a strait or passage of four or five leagues broad. They are situated between the latitude of 34° and 48° S., and between the longitude of 181° and 194° W. from the meridian of Greenwich. The situation of few parts of the world are better determined than these islands are, being settled by some hundreds of observations of the sun and moon, and one of the transit of Mercury made by Mr. Green, who was sent out by the Royal Society to observe the transit of Venus.

The northernmost of these islands, as I have before observed, is called by the natives *Aeheino Mouwe* and the southernmost *Tovy Poenammu*. The former name, we were well assured, comprehends the whole of the northern island; but we were not so well satisfied with the latter whether it comprehended the whole of the southern islands or only a part of it. This last, according to the natives of Queen Charlotte's Sound, ought to consist of two islands, one of which at least we were to have sailed round in a few days; but this was not verified by our own observations. I am inclinable to think that they knowed no more of this land than what came within the limits of their sight. The chart[15] which I have drawn will best point out the figure and extent of these islands, the situation of the bays and harbours they contain, and the lesser islands lay about them. . . .

So far as I have been able to judge of the genius of these people

[15] Crozet, a French naval officer who visited New Zealand in 1772, says of this chart; "I found it of an exactitude and of a thoroughness of detail which astonished me beyond all powers of expression; I doubt whether our own coasts of France have been delineated with more precision." Stewart Island, however, is marked as part of the South Island.

it does not appear to me to be at all difficult for strangers to form a settlement in this country; they seem to be too much divided among themselves to unite in opposing, by which means, and kind and gentle usage, the colonists would be able to form strong parties among them.

The natives of this country are a strong, raw-boned, well made, active people, rather above than under the common size, expecially the men; they are of a very dark brown colour, with black hair, thin black beards, and white teeth, and such as do not disfigure their faces by tattooing, etc., have in general very good features. The men generally wear their hair long, combed up, and tied upon the crown of their heads; some of the women wear it long and loose upon their shoulders, old women especially; others again wear it cropped short. Their combs are made some of bones, and others of wood; they sometimes wear them as an ornament stuck upright in their hair. They seem to enjoy a good state of health, and many of them live to a good old age. Many of the old and some of the middle-aged men have their faces marked or tattooed with black, and some few we have seen who have had their buttocks, thighs, and other parts of their bodies marked, but this is less common. The figures they mostly use are spirals, drawn and connected together with great nicety and judgment. They are so exact in the application of these figures that no difference can be found between the one side of the face and the other, if the whole is marked, for some have only one side, and some a little on both sides; hardly any but the old men have the whole tattooed. From this I conclude that it takes up some time, perhaps years, to finish the operation, which all who have begun may not have perseverance enough to go through, as the manner in which it must be done must certainly cause intolerable pain, and may be the reason why so few are marked at all —at least I know no other. The women inlay the colour of black under the skins of their lips, and both sexes paint their faces and bodies at times more or less with red ochre, mixed with fish oil.

Their common clothing are very much like square thrumbed mats, that are made of rope yarns, to lay at the doors or passages into houses to clean one's shoes upon. These they tie round their necks, the thrumbed side out, and are generally large enough to cover the body as low as the knee; they are made with very little preparation of the broad grass plant before mentioned. Besides the thrumbed mats, as I call them, they have other much finer clothing, made of the same plant after it is bleached and prepared in such a manner that it is as white and almost as soft as flax, but much stronger. Of this they make pieces of cloth about five feet long and four broad; these are wove some pieces close and others very open; the former are as stout as the strongest sail cloth, and not unlike it, and yet it is all worked or made by hand with no other instrument than a needle or bodkin. To one end of every piece is generally worked a very neat border of different colours of four or six inches broad, and they very often trim them with pieces of dog skin or birds' feathers. These pieces of cloth they wear as they do the other, tying one end round their necks with a piece of string, to one end of which is fixed a needle or bodkin made of bone, by means of which they can easily fasten, or put the string through any part of the cloth; they sometimes wear pieces of this kind of cloth round their middles, as well as over their shoulders. But this is not common, especially with the men, who hardly wear anything round their middles, observing no sort of decency in that respect; neither is it at all uncommon for them to go quite naked without any one thing about them besides a belt round their waists, to which is generally fastened a small string, which they tie round the prepuce; in this manner I have seen hundreds of them come off to and on board the ship, but they generally had their proper clothing in the boat along with them to put on if it rained, etc. The women, on the other hand, always wear something round their middle; generally a short, thrumbed mat, which reaches as low as their knees. Sometimes, indeed, I have seen them with only a bunch of grass or plants before, tied on with a piece of fine platting made of sweet-scented grass; they likewise wear a piece of cloth over their shoulders as the men do; this is generally of the thrum kind. I hardly ever saw a woman wear a piece of fine cloth. One day at Talago I saw a strong proof that the women never appear naked, at least before strangers. Some of us happened to land upon a small island where several of them were naked in the water, gathering of lobsters and shell fish; as soon as they saw us some of them hid themselves among the rocks and the rest remained in the sea until they had made themselves aprons of the seaweed; and even then, when they came out to us, they showed manifest signs of shame, and those who had no method of hiding their nakedness would by no means appear before us. . . .

Whenever we were visited by any number of them that had never heard or seen anything of us before they generally came off in the largest canoe they had, some of which will carry sixty, eighty, or one hundred people. They always brought their best clothes along with them, which they put on as soon as they came near the ship. In each canoe were generally an old man, in some two or three; these used always to direct the others, were better clothed, and generally carried a halberd or battle axe in their hands, or some such like thing that distinguished them from the others. As soon as they came within about a stone's throw of the ship they would there lay, and call out: "Haromoi harenta a patoo ago!" that is: "Come here, come ashore with us, and we will kill you with our patoo patoos!" and at the same time would shake them at us. At times they would dance the war dance, and other times they would trade with and talk to us, and answer such questions as were put to them with all the calmness imaginable, and then again begin the war dance, shaking their paddles, patoo patoos, etc., and make strange contortions at the same time. As soon as they had worked themselves up to a proper pitch they would begin to attack us with stones and darts, and oblige us, whether we would or no, to fire upon them. Musketry they never regarded unless they felt the effect; but great guns they did, because they threw stones farther than they could comprehend. After they found that our arms were so much superior to theirs, and that we took no advantage of that superiority, and a little time given them to reflect upon it, they ever after were our very good friends; and we never had an instance of their attempting to surprise or cut off any of our people when they were ashore; opportunity for so doing they must have had at one time or another.

It is hard to account for what we have everywhere been told, of their eating their enemies killed in battle, which they most certainly do; circumstances enough we have seen to convince us of the truth of this. Tupia, who holds this custom in great aversion, hath very often argued with them against it, but they have always as strenuously supported it, and never would own that it was wrong. It is reasonable to suppose that men with whom this custom is found, seldom, if ever, give quarter to those they overcome in battle; and if so, they must fight desperately to the very last. A strong proof of this supposition we had from the people of Queen Charlotte's Sound, who told us, but a few days before we arrived that they had killed and eat a whole boat's crew. Surely a single boat's crew, or at least a part of them, when they found themselves beset and overpowered by numbers would have surrendered themselves prisoners was such a thing practised among them. The heads of these unfortunate people they preserved as trophies; four or five of them they brought off to show to us, one of which Mr. Banks bought, or rather forced them to sell, for they parted with it with the utmost reluctancy, and afterwards would not so much as let us see one more for anything we could offer them.

In the article of food these people have no great variety; fern roots, dogs, fish, and wild fowl is their chief diet, for cocos, yams, and sweet potatoes is not cultivated everywhere. They dress their victuals in the same manner as the people in the South Sea Islands; that is, dogs and large fish they bake in a hole in the ground, and small fish, birds, and shell fish, etc., they broil on the fire. Fern roots they likewise heat over the fire, then beat them out flat upon a stone with a wooden mallet; after this they are fit for eating, in the doing of which they suck out the moist and glutinous part, and spit out the fibrous parts. These ferns are much like, if not the same as, the mountain ferns in England.

They catch fish with seines, hooks and line, but more commonly with hooped nets very ingeniously made; in the middle of these they tie the bait, such as sea ears, fish guts, etc., then sink the net to the bottom with a stone; after it has laid there a little time they haul it gently up, and hardly ever without fish, and very often a large quantity. All their nets are made of the broad grass plant before mentioned; generally with no other preparation than by splitting the blade of the plant into threads. Their fish hooks are made of crooked pieces of wood, bones, and shells.

The people show great ingenuity and good workmanship in the building and framing their boats or canoes. They are long and narrow, and shaped very much like a New England whale boat. Their large canoes are, I believe, built wholly for war, and will carry from forty to eighty or one hundred men with their arms, etc. I shall give the dimensions of one which I measured that lay ashore at Tolago. Length sixty-eight and a half feet, breadth five feet, and depth three and a half; the bottom sharp, inclining to a wedge, and was made of three pieces hollowed out to about two inches or an inch and a half thick, and well fastened together with strong platting. Each side consisted of one plank only, which was sixty-three feet long and ten or twelve inches broad, and about one and a quarter inch thick, and these were well fitted and lashed to the bottom part. There were a number of thwarts laid across and lashed to each gunwale as a strengthening to the boat. The head ornament projected five or six feet without the body of the boat, and was four feet high; the stern ornament was fourteen feet high, about two feet broad, and about one and a half inch thick; it was fixed upon the stern of the canoe like the stern post of a ship upon her keel. The ornaments of both head and stern and the two side boards were of carved work, and, in my opinion, neither ill designed nor executed. All their canoes are built after this plan, and few are less than twenty feet long. Some of the small ones we have seen with outriggers, but this is not common. In their war canoes they generally have a quantity of birds' feathers hung in strings, and tied about the head and stern as additional ornament. They are as various in the heads of their canoes as we are in those of our shipping; but what is most common is an odd-designed figure of a man, with as ugly a face as can be conceived, a very large tongue sticking out of his mouth, and large white eyes made of the shells of sea ears. Their paddles are small, light, and neatly made; they hardly ever make use of sails, at least that we saw, and those they have are but ill contrived, being generally a piece of netting spread between two poles, which serve for both masts and yards. . . .

With respect to religion, I believe these people trouble themselves very little about it; they, however, believe that there is one supreme god, whom they call *Tawney*, and likewise a number of other inferior deities; but whether or no they worship or pray to either one or the other we know not with any degree of certainty. It is reasonable to suppose that they do, and I believe it; yet I never saw the least action or thing among them that tended to prove it. They have the same notions of the creation of the world, mankind, etc., as the people of the South Sea Islands have; indeed, many of their notions and customs are the very same. But nothing is so great a proof of their all having had one source as their language, which differs but in a very few words the one from the other, as will appear from the following specimens, which I had from Mr. Banks, who understands their language as well, or better than, anyone on board.

English	New Zealand	South Sea Islands
A chief	Eareete	Eare
A man	Taata	Taata
A woman	Ivahina	Ivahine
The head	Eupo	Eupo [etc.]

What is meant by the South Sea Islands are those islands we ourselves touched at; but I gave it that title because we have always been told that the same language is universally spoke by all the islanders, and that this is a sufficient proof that both they and the New Zealanders have had one origin or source, but where this is even time perhaps may never discover.

It certainly is neither to the southward nor eastward, for I cannot persuade myself that ever they came from America; and as to a Southern Continent, I do not believe any such thing exists, unless in a high latitude. But as the contrary opinion hath for many years prevailed, and may yet prevail, it is necessary I should say something in support of mine more than what will be directly pointed out by the track of this ship in those seas; for from that alone it will evidently appear that there is a large space extending quite to the tropic in which we were not, or any other before us that we can ever learn for certain. In our route to the northward, after doubling Cape Horn, when in the latitude of 40°, we were in the longitude of 110°; and in our return to the southward, after leaving Ulietea, when in the same latitude, we were in the longitude of 145°; the difference in this latitude is 35° of longitude. In the latitude of 30° the difference of the two tracks is 21°, and that difference continues as low as 20°; but a view of the chart will best illustrate this.

Here is now room enough for the North Cape of the Southern Continent to extend to the northward, even to a pretty low latitude. But what foundation have we for such a supposition? None, that I know of, but this, that it must either be here or nowhere. Geographers have indeed laid down part of Quiros's discoveries in this longitude, and have told us that he had these signs of a continent, a part of which they have actually laid down in the maps; but by what authority I know not. Quiros, in the latitude of 25° or 26° S., discovered two islands, which, I suppose, may lay between the longitude of 130° and 140° W. Dalrymple lays them down in 146° W., and says that Quiros saw to the southward very large hanging clouds and a very thick horizon, with other known signs of a continent. Other accounts of their voyage says not a word about this; but supposing this to be true, hanging clouds and a thick horizon are certainly no signs of a continent— I have had many proofs to the contrary in the course of this voyage; neither do I believe that Quiros looked upon such things as known signs of land, for if he had he certainly would have stood to the southward, in order to have satisfied himself before he had gone to the northward, for no man seems to have had discoveries more at heart than he had. Besides this, this was the ultimate object of his voyage. If Quiros was in the latitude of 26° and longitude 146° W., then I am certain that no part of the Southern Continent can nowhere extend so far to the northward as the above mentioned latitude. But the voyage which seems to thrust it farthest back in the longitude I am speaking of, viz., between 130° and 150° W., is that of Admiral Roggeween, a Dutchman, made in 1722, who, after leaving Juan Fernandes, went in search of Davis's Island; but not finding it, he ran 12° more to the west, and in the latitude of 28½° discovered Easter Island. Dalrymple and some others have laid it down in 27° S. and 106° 30′ W., and supposes it to be the same as Davis's Isle, which I think cannot be from the circumstance of the voyage; on the other hand Mr. Pingre, in his treatise concerning the transit of Venus, gives an extract of Roggeween's voyage and a map of the South Seas, wherein he places Easter Island in the latitude of 28½° S., and in the longitude of 123° W.; his reason for so doing may be seen at large in the said treatise. He likewise lays down Roggeween's route through those South Seas very different from any other author I have seen; for after leaving Easter Island he makes him steer S.W. to the height of 34° S., and afterwards W.N.W. If Roggeween really took this route, then it is not probable that there is any mainland to the northward of 35° S. However, Mr. Dalrymple and some geographers have laid down Roggeween's track very different from Mr. Pingre. From Easter Isle they have laid down his track to the north-west, and afterwards very little different from that of Le Maire; and this I think is not probable, that a man who, at his own request, was sent to discover the Southern Continent should take the same route through these seas as others had done before who had the same thing in view; by so doing he must be morally certain of not finding what he was in search of, and of course must fail as they had done. Be this as it may, it is a point that cannot be cleared up from the published accounts of the voyage, which, so far from taking proper notice of their longitude, have not even mentioned the latitude of several of the islands they discovered, so that I find it impossible to lay down Roggeween's route with the least degree of accuracy.[16]

But to return to our own voyage, which must be allowed to have set aside the most, if not all, the arguments and proofs that have been advanced by different authors to prove that there must be a Southern Continent; I mean to the northward of 40° S., for what may lie to the southward of that latitude I know not. Certain it is

[16] Roggevein's track is still unknown. Davis Land was mythical and became identified with Easter Island, see below, p. 173.

that we saw no visible signs of land, according to my opinion, neither in our route to the northward, southward, or westward, until a few days before we made the coast of New Zealand. . . .

Thus I have given my opinion freely and without prejudice, not with any view to discourage any future attempts being made towards discovering the Southern Continent; on the contrary, as I think this voyage will evidently make it appear that there is left but a small space to the northward of 40° where the grand object can lay. I think it would be a great pity that this thing, which at times has been the object of many ages and nations, should not now be wholly cleared up; which might very easily be done in one voyage without either much trouble or danger or fear of miscarrying, as the navigator would know where to go to look for it; but if, after all, no continent was to be found, then he might turn his thoughts towards the discovery of those multitude of islands which, we are told, lay within the tropical regions to the south of the Line, and this we have from very good authority, as I have before hinted. This he will always have in his power; for, unless he be directed to search for the southern lands in a high latitude, he will not, as we were, be obliged to go farther to the westward in the latitude of 40° than 140° or 145° W., and therefore will always have it in his power to go to George's Island, where he will be sure of meeting with refreshments to recruit his people before he sets out upon the discovery of the islands. But should it be thought proper to send a ship out upon this service while Tupia lives, and he to come out in her, in that case she would have a prodigious advantage over every ship that hath been upon discoveries in those seas before; for by means of Tupia, supposing he did not accompany you himself, you would always get people to direct you from island to island, and would be sure of meeting with a friendly reception and refreshment at every island you came to. This would enable the navigator to make his discoveries the more perfect and complete; at least it would give him time so to do, for he would not be obliged to hurry through those seas through any apprehensions of wanting provisions.[17]

[17] The programme outlined in this passage was carried out on the Second Voyage, but Tupia died before that.

BOOK III

The Discovery of New South Wales and the Voyage up the East Coast of Australia

1770

────────────

April 19   In the afternoon had fresh gales at S.S.W. and cloudy squally weather, with a large southerly sea; at 6 took in the top-sails, and at 1 a.m. brought to and sounded, but had no ground with 130 fathoms of line. At 5, set the topsails close reefed, and 6, saw land extending from N.E. to W., distance five or six leagues, having eighty fathoms, fine sandy bottom. We continued standing to the westward with the wind at S.S.W. until 8, at which time we got topgallant yards across, made all sail, and bore away along shore north-east for the easternmost land we had in sight, being at this time in the latitude of 37° 58′ S., and longitude of 210° 39′ W. The southernmost point of land we had in sight, which bore from us W. ¼ S., I judged to lay in the latitude of 38° 0′ S. and in the longitude of 211° 7′ W. from the meridian of Greenwich. I have named it Point Hicks, because Lieutenant Hicks was the first who discovered this land.[1] To the southward of this point we could see no land, and yet

───

[1] Point Hicks is just south of Cape Howe, the south-eastern point of Australia. Tasmania (Van Diemen's Land) lies about 300 miles to the south-west. As Cook steered north after striking the coast, he could not realise that the latter was an island. The strait was discovered by Bass in 1798.

it was clear in that quarter, and by our longitude compared with that of Tasman's, the body of Van Diemen's Land ought to have bore due south from us, and from the soon falling of the sea after the wind abated I had reason to think it did; but as we did not see it, and finding the coast to trend N.E. and S.W., or rather more to the westward, makes me doubtful whether they are one land or no. However, everyone who compares this journal with that of Tasman's will be as good a judge as I am; but it is necessary to observe that I do not take the situation of Van Diemen's from the printed charts, but from the extract of Tasman's Journal, published by Dirk Rembrantse. At noon we were in the latitude of 37° 50′ and longitude of 210° 29′ W. The extremes of the land extending from N.W. to E.N.E., a remarkable point, bore N. 20° E., distant four leagues. This point rises to a round hillock very much like the Ramhead going into Plymouth Sound, on which account I called it by the same name. What we have as yet seen of this land appears rather low, and not very hilly, the face of the country green and woody, but the seashore is all a white sand.

April 28   In the afternoon hoisted out the pinnace and yawl in order to attempt a landing, but the pinnace took in the water so fast that she was obliged to be hoisted in again to stop her leaks. At this time we saw several people ashore, four of whom were carrying a small boat or canoe, which we imagined they were going to put into the water in order to come off to us; but in this we were mistaken. Being now not above two miles from the shore Mr. Banks, Dr. Solander, Tupia, and myself put off in the yawl, and pulled in for the land to a place where we saw four or five of the natives, who took to the woods as we approached the shore; which disappointed us in the expectation we had of getting a near view of them, if not to speak to them. But our disappointment was heightened when we found that we nowhere could effect a landing by reason of the great surf which beat everywhere upon the shore. We saw hauled up upon the beach three or four small canoes, which to us appeared not much unlike the small ones of New Zealand. In the wood were several trees of the palm

63

kind, and no underwood; and this was all we were able to observe from the boat, after which we returned to the ship about
5 in the evening. At this time it fell calm, and we were not above
a mile and a half from the shore, in eleven fathoms, and within
some breakers that lay to the southward of us; but luckily a light
breeze came off from the land, which carried us out of danger,
and with which we stood to the northward. At daylight in the
morning we discovered a bay,[2] which appeared to be tolerably
well sheltered from all winds, into which I resolved to go with
the ship, and with this view sent [the] Master in the pinnace to
sound the entrance, while we kept turning up with the ship,
having the wind right out. At noon the entrance bore N.N.W.,
distance one mile.

April 29   In the afternoon wind southerly and clear weather, with
which we stood into the bay and anchored under the south shore
about two miles within the entrance in five fathoms, the south
point bearing S.E. and the north point E. Saw, as we came in,
on both points of the bay, several of the natives and a few huts;
men, women, and children on the south shore abreast of the ship,
to which place I went in the boats in hopes of speaking with them,
accompanied by Mr. Banks, Dr. Solander, and Tupia. As we
approached the shore they all made off, except two men, who
seemed resolved to oppose our landing. As soon as I saw this I
ordered the boats to lay upon their oars, in order to speak to them;
but this was to little purpose, for neither us nor Tupia could
understand one word they said. We then threw them some nails,
beads, etc., ashore, which they took up, and seemed not ill
pleased with, in so much that I thought that they beckoned to us
to come ashore; but in this we were mistaken, for as soon as we

[2] Botany Bay lies a few miles south of Sydney. The Cook family tradition was
that Isaac Smith, Mrs. Cook's nineteen year old nephew, was the first to land.
This was the spot intended for the first convict settlement, but Captain Phillip
preferred Port Jackson, Sydney. In Hawkesworth's account of the landing on
29 April, a curious detail is added: "We saw four small canoes, each with one man
on board, who were busily engaged in striking fish with a long pike or spear.
They were so intent on what they were doing, that although the ship passed
within a quarter of a mile of them, they scarcely turned their eyes toward
her."

put the boat in they again came to oppose us, upon which I fired a musket between the two, which had no other effect than to make them retire back, where bundles of their darts lay, and one of them took up a stone and threw at us, which caused my firing a second musket, loaded with small shot; and although some of the shot struck the man, yet it had no other effect than making him lay hold on a target. Immediately after this we landed, which we had no sooner done than they throwed two darts at us; this obliged me to fire a third shot, soon after which they both made off, but not in such haste but what we might have taken one; but Mr. Banks being of the opinion that the darts were poisoned, made me cautious how I advanced into the woods. We found here a few small huts made of the bark of trees, in one of which were four or five small children, with whom we left some strings of beads, etc. A quantity of darts lay about the huts; these we took away with us. Three canoes lay upon the beach, the worst I think I ever saw; they were about twelve or fourteen feet long, made of one piece of the bark of a tree, drawn or tied up at each end, and the middle kept open by means of pieces of stick by way of thwarts. After searching for fresh water without success, except a little in a small hole dug in the sand, we embarked, and went over to the northern point of the bay, where in coming in we saw several people; but when we landed now there were nobody to be seen. We found here some fresh water, which came trickling down and stood in pools among the rocks; but as this was troublesome to come at I sent a party of men ashore in the morning to the place where we first landed to dig holes in the sand, by which means and a small stream they found fresh water sufficient to water the ship. The string of beads, etc., we had left with the children last night were found lying in the huts this morning; probably the natives were afraid to take them away. After breakfast we sent some empty casks ashore and a party of men to cut wood, and I went myself in the pinnace to sound and explore the bay, in the doing of which I saw some of the natives; but they all fled at my approach. I landed in two places, one of which the people had but just left, as there were small fires and fresh mussels broiling upon them; here likewise lay vast heaps of the largest oyster shells I ever saw.

May 1   Gentle breezes, northerly. In the afternoon ten of the natives again visited the watering place. I, being on board at this time, went immediately ashore, but before I got there they were going away. I followed them alone and unarmed some distance along the shore, but they would not stop until they got farther off than I chose to trust myself. These were armed in the same manner as those that came yesterday. In the evening I sent some hands to haul the seine, but they caught but a very few fish. A little after sunrise I found the variation to be 11° 3′ E. Last night Forby Sutherland, Seaman, departed this life, and in the morning his body was buried ashore at the watering place, which occasioned my calling the south point of this bay after his name. This morning a party of us went ashore to some huts, not far from the watering place, where some of the natives are daily seen; here we left several articles, such as cloth, looking-glasses, combs, beads, nails, etc.; after this we made an excursion into the country, which we found diversified with woods, lawns, and marshes. The woods are free from underwood of every kind, and the trees are at such a distance from one another that the whole country, or at least great part of it, might be cultivated without being obliged to cut down a single tree. We found the soil everywhere, except in the marshes, to be a light white sand, and produceth a quantity of good grass, which grows in little tufts about as big as one can hold in one's hand, and pretty close to one another; in this manner the surface of the ground is coated. In the woods between the trees Dr. Solander had a bare sight of a small animal something like a rabbit, and we found the dung of an animal[3] which must feed upon grass, and which, we judge, could not be less than a deer; we also saw the track of a dog, or some such like animal. We met with some huts and places where the natives had been, and at our first setting out one of them was seen; the others, I

---

[3] *i.e.* the kangaroo, which was first seen further north on 24 June. In his description of the aborigines Cook agrees with Dampier, the only Englishman to have seen them previously, when he visited northern Australia in 1686: "The inhabitants of this country are the miserablest people in the world."

suppose, had fled upon our approach. I saw some trees that had been cut down by the natives with some sort of a blunt instrument, and several trees that were barked, the bark of which had been cut by the same instrument.

May 6   In the evening the yawl returned from fishing, having caught two sting rays weighing near 600 lb. The great quantity of plants Mr. Banks and Dr. Solander found in this place occasioned my giving it the name of Botany Bay.[4] It is situated in the latitude of 34° 0' S., longitude 208° 37' W. It is capacious, safe, and commodious; it may be known by the land on the sea coast, which is of a pretty even and moderate height, rather higher than it is inland, with steep rocky cliffs next the sea, and looks like a long island lying close under the shore. The entrance of the bay lies about the middle of this land. In coming from the southward it is discovered before you are abreast of it, which you cannot do in coming from the northward; the entrance is little more than a quarter of a mile broad, and lies in W.N.W. . . . . The natives do not appear to be numerous, neither do they seem to live in large bodies, but dispersed in small parties along by the waterside. Those I saw were about as tall as Europeans, of a very dark brown colour, but not black, nor had the woolly, frizzled hair, but black and lank like ours. No sort of clothing or ornaments were ever seen by any of us upon any one of them, or in or about any of their huts; from which I conclude that they never wear any. Some that we saw had their faces and bodies painted with a sort of white paint or pigment. Although I have said that shell fish is their chief support, yet they catch other sorts of fish, some of which we found roasting on the fire the first time we landed; some of these they strike with gigs,[5] and others they catch with

[4] In Cook's personal journal the original name is "Stingray Harbour", nor do any of the logs use the name "Botany Bay"; but in the fair copy sent to the Admiralty the name is altered for the reason given here. Many years later Banks bought some old French maps of about 1540, usually called the Dieppe maps, in one of which this area is marked "Coste des Herbaiges". Dalrymple accused Cook of knowing of these maps and concealing his knowledge to claim a fresh discovery. Nobody has solved the mystery of these maps and no voyage to Australia at that date has been recorded.

[5] *i.e.* tridents.

hook and line; we have seen them strike fish with gigs, and hooks and lines are found in their huts. Sting rays, I believe, they do not eat, because I never saw the least remains of one near any of their huts or fireplaces. However, we could know but very little of their customs, as we never were able to form any connections with them; they had not so much as touched the things we had left in their huts on purpose for them to take away. During our stay in this harbour I caused the English colours to be displayed ashore every day, and an inscription to be cut out upon one of the trees near the watering place, setting forth the ship's name, date, etc. Having seen everything this place afforded, we, at daylight in the morning, weighed with a light breeze at N.W., and put to sea, and the wind soon after coming to the southward we steered along shore N.N.E., and at noon we were by observation in the latitude of 33° 50′ S., about two or three miles from the land, and abreast of a bay, wherein there appeared to be safe anchorage, which I called Port Jackson. It lies three leagues to the northward of Botany Bay.[6]

May 23   Last night, some time in the middle watch, a very extraordinary affair happened to Mr. Orton, my clerk. He having been drinking in the evening, some malicious person or persons in the ship took advantage of his being drunk, and cut off all the clothes from off his back; not being satisfied with this, they some time after went into his cabin and cut off a part of both his ears as he lay asleep in his bed. The person whom he suspected to have done this was Mr. Magra, one of the midshipmen; but this did not appear to me. Upon inquiry, however, as I had been told that Magra had once or twice before this in their drunken frolics cut off his clothes, and had been heard to say (as I was told) that if it were not for the Law he would murder him, these things considered, induced me to think that Magra was not altogether innocent. I therefore for the present dismissed him the quarter deck, and suspended him from doing any duty in the ship, he being

[6] On the shores of the great inlet which Cook called Port Jackson lies the city of Sydney; he could not see the magnificent harbour because he did not examine the bay.

one of those gentlemen frequently found on board King's ships that can very well be spared; besides, it was necessary in me to show my immediate resentment against the person on whom the suspicion fell, lest they should not have stopped here. With respect to Mr. Orton, he is a man not without faults; yet from all the inquiry I could make, it evidently appeared to me that so far from deserving such treatment, he had not designed injuring any person in the ship; so that I do—and shall always—look upon him as an injured man. Some reasons, however, might be given why this misfortune came upon him, in which he himself was in some measure to blame; but as this is only conjecture, and would tend to fix it upon some people in the ship, whom I would fain believe would hardly be guilty of such an action, I shall say nothing about it, unless I shall hereafter discover the offenders, which I shall take every method in my power to do, for I look upon such proceedings as highly dangerous in such voyages as this, and the greatest insult that could be offered to my authority in this ship, as I have always been ready to hear and redress every complaint that has been made against any person in the ship.[7]

June 11   My intention was to stretch off all night as well to avoid the danger we saw ahead as to see if any islands lay in the offing, especially as we now began to draw near the latitude of those discovered by Quiros, which some geographers, for what reason I know not, have thought proper to tack to this land. Having the advantage of a fine breeze of wind, and a clear moonlight night in standing off from six until near nine o'clock, we deepened our water from fourteen to twenty-one fathoms, when all at once we fell into twelve, ten and eight fathoms. At this time I had everybody at their stations to put about and come to an anchor; but in this I was not so fortunate, for meeting again with

[7] The brutal style of this practical joke, and the fact that Cook takes the drunkenness of his clerk as a matter of course, illustrate the spirit of the times.   Magra was not restored to duty for three weeks.   He was an American by birth, changed his name to Matra, and made the first written proposal in 1783 for the foundation of a settlement in New South Wales. An additional phrase used by Cook to describe him is erased in the MS.—'to speak more plainly, good for nothing.' He had previously thought of deserting at Tahiti. (See Brit. Museum, Add. MSS. 33,979/29). James Matra died as consul of Tangier in 1806.

deep water, I thought there could be no danger in standing on. Before ten o'clock we had twenty and twenty-one fathoms, and continued in that depth until a few minutes before eleven, when we had seventeen, and before the man at the lead could heave another cast, the ship struck and stuck fast.[8] Immediately upon this we took in all our sails, hoisted out the boats and sounded round the ship, and found that we had got upon the south-east edge of a reef of coral rocks, having in some places round the ship three and four fathoms of water, and in other places not quite as many feet, and about a ship's length from us on the starboard side (the ship laying with her head to the north-east) were eight, ten and twelve fathoms. As soon as the longboat was out we struck yards and topmast, and carried out the stream anchor on our starboard bow, got the coasting anchor and cable into the boat, and were going to carry it out in the same way; but upon my sounding the second time round the ship I found the most water astern, and therefore had this anchor carried out upon the starboard quarter, and hove upon it a very great strain; which was to no purpose, the ship being quite fast, upon which we went to work to lighten her as fast as possible, which seemed to be the only means we had left to get her off. As we went ashore about the top of high water we not only started water, but threw overboard our guns, iron and stone ballast, casks, hoop staves, oil jars, decayed stores, etc.; many of these last articles lay in the way at coming at heavier. All this time the ship made little or no water. At 11 a.m., being high water as we thought, we tried to heave her off without success, she not being afloat by a foot or more, notwithstanding by this time we had thrown overboard

[8] As he made his way up the Queensland coast, Cook was unaware that he was sailing inside the Great Barrier Reef, which converges towards the shore in the neighbourhood of Cooktown. By far the most dangerous crisis of the voyage occurred when the *Endeavour* struck the inner side of the coral formation, on the part now called Endeavour Reef. Two years earlier Bougainville, approaching from the east in search of Torres Strait, had struck the outer edge about 150 miles away. In consequence he was prevented from discovering the east coast of Australia, since he made his way to Java round the north of New Guinea. Had Cook known of the Dieppe maps he would have seen that this part is marked "Coste Dangereuse". He seems to have had an uncanny instinct that he was entering dangerous waters because he was taking soundings frequently. What made the situation desperate was that the ship struck "at the top of high water" and the nearest harbour for repairs was Batavia, 1,500 miles away.

forty or fifty tons weight. As this was not found sufficient we continued to lighten her by every method we could think of; as the tide fell the ship began to make water as much as two pumps could free: at noon she lay with three or four streaks heel to starboard; latitude observed 15° 45' S.

June 12   Fortunately we had little wind, fine weather, and a smooth sea, all this twenty-four hours, which in the afternoon gave us an opportunity to carry out the two bower anchors, one on the starboard quarter, and the other right astern, got blocks and tackles upon the cables, brought the falls in abaft and hove taut. By this time it was 5 p.m.; the tide we observed now began to rise, and the leak increased upon us, which obliged us to set the third pump to work, as we should have done the fourth also, but could not make it work. At nine the ship righted, and the leak gained upon the pumps considerably. This was an alarming and, I may say, terrible circumstance, and threatened immediate destruction to us. However, I resolved to risk all, and heave her off in case it was practical, and accordingly turned as many hands to the capstan and windlass as could be spared from the pumps; and about twenty minutes past ten o'clock the ship floated, and we hove her into deep water, having at this time three feet nine inches of water in the hold. This done I sent the longboat to take up the stream anchor, got the anchor, but lost the cable among the rocks; after this turned all hands to the pumps, the leak increasing upon us.

A mistake soon after happened, which for the first time caused fear to approach upon every man in the ship. The man that attended the well took the depth of water above the ceiling; he, being relieved by another who did not know in what manner the former had sounded, took the depth of water from the outside plank, the difference being sixteen or eighteen inches, and made it appear that the leak had gained this upon the pumps in a short time. This mistake was no sooner cleared up than it acted upon every man like a charm; they redoubled their vigour, insomuch that before eight o'clock in the morning they gained considerably upon the leak. We now hove up the best bower, but found it impossible to save the small bower, so cut it away at a whole cable; got up the fore topmast and foreyard, warped the ship to the south-east, and at eleven got under sail, and stood in for the land, with a light breeze at E.S.E. Some hands employed sewing oakum, wool, etc., into a lower steering sail to fother the ship; others employed at the pumps, which still gained upon the leak.

June 13   In the afternoon had light airs at E.S.E., with which we kept edging in for the land. Got up the maintopmast and mainyard, and having got the sail ready for fothering of the ship, we put it over under the starboard fore chains, where we suspected the ship had suffered most, and soon after the leak decreased, so as to be kept clear with one pump with ease; this fortunate circumstance gave new life to everyone on board.

It is much easier to conceive than to describe the satisfaction felt by everybody on this occasion. But a few minutes before our utmost wishes were to get hold of some place upon the main, or an island, to run the ship ashore, where out of her materials we might build a vessel to carry us to the East Indies; no sooner were we made sensible that the outward application to the ship's bottom had taken effect, than the field of every man's hopes enlarged, so that we thought of nothing but ranging along shore in search of a harbour, when we could repair the damages we had sustained. In justice to the ship's company, I must say that no men ever behaved better than they have done on this occasion; animated by the behaviour of every gentleman on board, every man seemed to have a just sense of the danger we were in, and exerted himself to the very utmost.[9] . . . The leak now decreaseth, but for fear it should break out again we got the sail ready filled

---

[9] Banks was much impressed by Cook's handling of the crisis and the behaviour of the ship's company: "No grumbling or growling was to be heard throughout the ship, not even an oath—though the ship was in general as well furnished with them as most in His Majesty's service. . . . During the whole time of this distress, I must say for the credit of our people that I believe every man exerted his utmost for the preservation of the ship, contrary to what I have universally heard to be the behaviour of seamen, who, commonly, as soon as a ship is in a desperate situation, begin to plunder and refuse all command. This was no doubt owing to the cool and steady conduct of the officers, who, during the whole time, never gave an order which did not show them to be perfectly composed and unmoved by the circumstances, however dreadful they might appear."

for fothering; the manner this is done is thus: we mix oakum and wool together (but oakum alone would do), and chop it up small, and then stick it loosely by handfuls all over the sail, and throw over it sheep dung or other filth. Horse dung for this purpose is the best. The sail thus prepared is hauled under the ship's bottom by ropes, and if the place of the leak is uncertain, it must be hauled from one part of her bottom to another until one finds the place where it takes effect. While the sail is under the ship the oakum, etc., is washed off, and part of it carried along with the water into the leak, and in part stops up the hole. Mr. Monkhouse, one of my midshipmen, was once in a merchant ship which sprung a leak, and made forty-eight inches of water per hour; but by this means was brought home from Virginia to London with only her proper crew; to him I gave the direction of this, who executed it very much to my satisfaction.

June 22   Winds at S.E., fair weather. At 4 p.m., having got out most of the coals, cast loose the ship's moorings, and warped her a little higher up the harbour to a place I had pitched upon to lay her ashore to stop the leak;[10] draught of water forward 7 feet 9 inches and abaft 13 feet 6 inches. At eight, being high water, hauled her bow close ashore, but kept her stern afloat, because I was afraid of neaping her, and yet it was necessary to lay the whole of her as near the ground as possible. At 2 a.m. the tide left her, which gave us an opportunity to examine the leak, which we found to be at her floor heads, a little before the starboard fore chains; here the rocks had made their way through four planks, quite to, and even into the timbers, and wounded three more. The manner these planks were damaged—or cut out, as I may say—is hardly credible; scarce a splinter was to be seen, but the whole was cut away as if it had been done by the hands of man with a blunt-edged tool. Fortunately for us the timbers in this place were very close; otherwise it would have been impossible to have saved the ship, and even as it was it appeared very

[10] As soon as the *Endeavour* could be got off Cook made his way to the nearest point on the coast, where he beached her in Endeavour River, the site of the modern Cooktown. 'Neaping', in the next sentence, means failing to heave off at neap tide.

extraordinary that she made no more water than what she did. A large piece of coral rock was sticking in one hole, and several pieces of the fothering, small stones, etc., had made its way in, and lodged between the timbers, which had stopped the water from forcing its way in in great quantities. Part of the sheathing was gone from under the larboard bow, part of the false keel was gone, and the remainder in such a shattered condition that we should be much better off if it was gone also; her forefoot and some part of her main keel was also damaged, but not materially. What damage she may have received abaft we could not see, but believe not much, as the ship makes but little water, while the tide keeps below the leak forward. At nine the carpenters went to work upon the ship, while the armourers were busy making bolts, nails, etc.

August 4   The refreshments we got here[11] were chiefly turtle, but as we had to go five leagues out to sea for them, and had much blowing weather, we were not over-stocked with this article; however, what with these and the fish we caught with the seine we had not much reason to complain, considering the country we were in. Whatever refreshment we got that would bear a division I caused to be equally divided among the whole company, generally by weight; the meanest person in the ship had an equal share with myself or anyone on board, and this method every commander of a ship on such a voyage as this ought ever to observe. We found in several places on the sandy beaches and sandhills near the sea, purslain and beans, which grows on a creeping kind of a vine. The first we found very good when boiled, and the latter not to be despised, and were at first very serviceable to the sick; but the best greens we found here was the tarra, or coco tops, called in the West Indies Indian Kale, which grows in most boggy places; these eat as well as, or better, than spinach. The roots, for want of being transplanted and properly cultivated, were not good, yet we could have dispensed with

[11] Over a month was spent in Endeavour River repairing the leak as best they could. Since this was the longest of the four occasions on which Cook landed in Australia, his account of the country becomes more detailed.

them could we have got them in any tolerable plenty; but having a good way to go for them, it took up too much time and too many hands to gather both root and branch. The few cabbage palms we found here were in general small, and yielded so little cabbage that they were not worth the looking after, and this was the case with most of the fruit, etc., we found in the woods.

Besides the animals which I have before mentioned, called by the natives kangooroo, or kanguru, here are wolves,[12] possums, an animal like a rat, and snakes, both of the venomous and other sorts. Tame animals here are none except dogs, and of these we never saw but one, who frequently came about our tents to pick up bones, etc. The kanguru are in the greatest number, for we seldom went into the country without seeing some. The land fowls we met here, which far from being numerous, were crows, kites, hawks, cockadores[13] of two sorts, the one white, and the other brown, very beautiful loryquets of two or three sorts, pigeons, doves, and a few other sorts of small birds. The sea or water fowl are herns, whistling ducks, which perch and, I believe, roost on trees; curlews, etc., and not many of these neither. Some of our gentlemen who were in the country heard and saw wild geese in the night.

The country, as far as I could see, is diversified with hills and plains, and these with woods and lawns; the soil of the hills is hard, dry, and very stony; yet it produces a thin coarse grass, and some wood. The soil of the plains and valleys are sandy, and in some places clay, and in many parts very rocky and stony, as well as the hills, but in general the land is pretty well clothed with long grass, wood, shrubs, etc. The whole country abounds with an immense number of ant hills, some of which are six or eight feet high, and more than twice that in circuit. Here are but few sorts of trees besides the gum tree, which is the most numerous, and is the same that we found on the southern part of the coast,

[12] Dingos. A sailor encountering one of the strange animals (probably a flying fox) thought it was the devil and wisely refrained from challenging it. Cook's previous description of the kangaroo is: "One of the men saw an animal something less than a greyhound; it was a mouse colour, very slender made, and swift of foot."
[13] Cockatoos.

only here they do not grow near so large. On each side of the river, all the way up it, are mangroves, which extended in some places a mile from its banks; the country in general is not badly watered, there being several fine rivulets at no very great distance from one another, but none near to the place where we lay; at least not in the dry season, which is at this time. However we were very well supplied with water by springs which were not far off.

August 7   After having well viewed our situation from the mast head,[14] I saw that we were surrounded on every side with dangers, in so much that I was quite at a loss which way to steer when the weather will permit us to get under sail, for to beat back to the south-east the way we came, as the Master would have had me done, would be an endless piece of work, as the winds blow constantly from that quarter, and very strong, without hardly any intermission; on the other hand, if we do not find a passage to the northward we shall have to come back at last. At eleven the ship drove, and obliged us to bear away to a cable and one third, which brought us up again; but in the morning the gale increasing, she drove again. This made us let go the small bower anchor, and bear away a whole cable on it and two on the other; and even after this she still kept driving slowly, until we had got down top gallant masts, struck yards and top masts close down, and made all snug; then she rode fast, Capt. Bedford bearing W.S.W., distant three and a half leagues. In this situation we had shoals to the eastward of us extending from the S.E. by S. to the N.N.W., distant from the nearest part of them about two miles.

August 14   Winds at S.E., a steady gale. By 2 p.m. we got out to the outermost reefs, and just fetched to windward of one of the openings I had discovered from the island; we tacked and made a short trip to the south-west, while the Master went in the pinnace to examine the channel, who soon made the signal for the ship to follow, which we accordingly did, and in a short time

14 The *Endeavour* had sailed on 4 August. By sending the pinnace ahead, Cook was able to work the ship through to the outer edge of the Barrier Reef, where the S.E. Trades blow strongly at this time of year. A ship 'driving' means drifting off her course.

got safely out.[15] This channel lies N.E. $\frac{1}{2}$ N., three leagues from Lizard Island; it is about one-third of a mile broad, and twenty-five or thirty fathoms deep or more. The moment we were without the breakers we had no ground with 100 fathoms of line, and found a large sea rolling in from the south-east. By this I was well assured we were got without all the shoals, which gave us no small joy, after having been entangled among islands and shoals, more or less, ever since the 26th of May, in which time we have sailed above 360 leagues by the lead without ever having a leadsman out of the chains, when the ship was under sail; a circumstance that perhaps never happened to any ship before, and yet it was here absolutely necessary. I should have been very happy to have had it in my power to have kept in with the land, in order to have explored the coast to the northern extremity of the country, which I think we were not far off, for I firmly believe this land doth not join to New Guinea. But this I hope soon either to prove or disprove, and the reasons I have before assigned will, I presume, be thought sufficient for my leaving the coast at this time; not but what I intend to get in with it again as soon as I can do it with safety.

August 16   We had not stood above two miles to the S.S.E. before it fell quite calm. We both sounded now and several times before, but had not bottom with 140 fathoms of line. A little after four o'clock the roaring of the surf was plainly heard, and at daybreak the vast foaming breakers were too plainly to be seen not a mile from us, towards which we found the ship was carried by the waves surprisingly fast. We had at this time not an air of wind, and the depth of water was unfathomable, so that there was not a possibility of anchoring. In this distressed situation we had nothing but Providence and the small assistance the boats could give us to trust to; the pinnace was under repair, and could not immediately be hoisted out. The yawl was put in the water, and the longboat hoisted out, and both sent ahead to tow, which, together with the help of our sweeps abaft, got the ship's head round to the northward, which seemed to be the best way

---

[15] Their new situation outside the reef was no better than it had been inside it.

to keep her off the reef, or at least to delay time. Before this was effected it was six o'clock, and we were not above eighty or one hundred yards from the breakers. The same sea that washed the side of the ship rose in a breaker prodigiously high the very next time it did rise, so that between us and destruction was only a dismal valley, the breadth of one wave, and even now no ground could be felt with 120 fathom. The pinnace was by this time patched up, and hoisted out and sent ahead to tow. Still we had hardly any hopes of saving the ship, and full as little our lives, as we were full ten leagues from the nearest land, and the boats not sufficient to carry the whole of us; yet in this truly terrible situation not one man ceased to do his utmost, and that with as much calmness as if no danger had been near.[16] All the dangers we had escaped were little in comparison of being thrown upon this reef, where the ship must be dashed to pieces in a moment. A reef such as one speaks of here is scarcely known in Europe. It is a wall of coral rock rising almost perpendicular out of the unfathomable ocean, always overflown at high water generally seven or eight feet, and dry in places at low water. The large waves of the vast ocean meeting with so sudden a resistance makes a most terrible surf, breaking mountains high, especially as in our case, when the general Trade wind blows directly upon it. At this critical juncture, when all our endeavours seemed too little, a small air of wind sprung up, but so small that at any other time in a calm we should not have observed it. With this, and the assistance of our boats, we could observe the ship to move off from the reef in a slanting direction; but in less than ten minutes we had as flat a calm as ever, when our fears were again renewed, for as yet we were not above two hundred yards from the breakers. Soon after our friendly breeze visited us again, and lasted about as long as before. A small opening was now seen in the reef about a quarter of a mile from us, which I sent one of the mates to examine. Its

[16] A fine example of British phlegm is provided by the entry in Mr. Green's log made during this dangerous attempt to repass inside the Reef through a narrow channel. Green was engaged in taking sights to obtain the longitude while "we were about 100 yards from the reef, where we expected the ship to strike every minute, it being calm, no soundings, and the swell heaving us right on." Cook was so impressed by this danger that he determined that in future two vessels should always be sent on voyages of exploration.

breadth was not more than the length of the ship, but within was smooth water. Into this place it was resolved to push her if possible, having no other probable views to save her, for we were still in the very jaws of destruction, and it was a doubt whether or no we could reach this opening. However, we soon got off it, when to our surprise we found the tide of ebb gushing out like a mill stream, so that it was impossible to get in. We however took all the advantage possible of it, and it carried us out about a quarter of a mile from the breakers; but it was too narrow for us to keep in long. However, what with the help of this ebb, and our boats, we by noon had got an offing of one and a half or two miles, yet we could hardly flatter ourselves with hopes of getting clear, even if a breeze should spring up, as we were by this time embayed by the reef, and the ship, in spite of our endeavours, driving before the sea into the bight. The ebb had been in our favour, and we had reason to suppose the flood which was now made would be against us. The only hopes we had was another opening we saw about a mile to the westward of us, which I sent Lieutenant Hicks in the small boat to examine. Latitude observed 12° 37′ S., the mainland in sight distant about ten leagues.

August 17   While Mr. Hicks was examining the opening we struggled hard with the flood, sometimes gaining a little and at other times losing. At two o'clock Mr. Hicks returned with a favourable account of the opening. It was immediately resolved to try to secure the ship in it. Narrow and dangerous as it was, it seemed to be the only means we had of saving her, as well as ourselves. A light breeze soon after sprang up at E.N.E., with which, the help of our boats, and a flood tide, we soon entered the opening, and was hurried through in a short time by a rapid tide like a mill race, which kept us from driving against either side, though the channel was not more than a quarter of a mile broad, having two boats ahead of us sounding. Our depth of water was from thirty to seven fathoms; very irregular soundings and foul ground until we had got quite within the reef, where we anchored in nineteen fathoms, a coral and shelly bottom. The channel we came in by, which I have named Providential Channel, bore E.N.E., distant ten or twelve miles, being about eight or nine leagues from the mainland, which extended from N. 66° W. to S.W. by S.

It is but a few days ago that I rejoiced at having got without the reef; but that joy was nothing when compared to what I now felt at being safe at an anchor within it. Such are the vicissitudes attending this kind of service, and must always attend an unknown navigation where one steers wholly in the dark without any manner of guide whatever. Was it not from the pleasure which naturally results to a man from his being the first discoverer, even was it nothing more than land or shoals, this kind of service would be insupportable, especially in far distant parts like this, short of provisions and almost every other necessary. People will hardly admit of an excuse for a man leaving a coast unexplored he has once discovered. If dangers are his excuse, he is then charged with timorousness and want of perseverance, and at once pronounced to be the most unfit man in the world to be employed as a discoverer; if, on the other hand, he boldly encounters all the dangers and obstacles he meets with, and is unfortunate enough not to succeed, he is then charged with temerity, and, perhaps, want of conduct. The former of these aspersions, I am confident, can never be laid to my charge, and if I am fortunate to surmount all the dangers we meet with, the latter will never be brought in question; although I must own that I have engaged more among the islands and shoals upon this coast than perhaps in prudence I ought to have done with a single ship and every other thing considered. But if I had not I should not have been able to give any better account of the one half of it than if I had never seen it; at best, I should not have been able to say whether it was mainland or islands; and as to its produce, that we should have been totally ignorant of as being inseparable with the other; and in this case it would have been far more satisfaction to me never to have discovered it. But it is time I should have done with this subject, which at best is but disagreeable, and which I was led into on reflecting on our late dangers.

August 22   Having satisfied myself of the great probability of a passage,[17] through which I intend going with the ship, and therefore may land no more upon this eastern coast of New Holland, and on the western side I can make no new discovery, the honour of which belongs to the Dutch navigators, but the eastern coast from the latitude of 38° S. down to this place, I am confident, was never seen or visited by any European before us; and notwithstanding I had in the name of His Majesty taken possession of several places upon this coast, I now once more hoisted English colours, and in the name of His Majesty King George III took possession of the whole eastern coast from the above latitude down to this place by the name of New Wales, together with all the bays, harbours, rivers, and islands, situated upon the said coast; after which we fired three volleys of small arms, which were answered by the like number from the ship.

August 23   The most northernmost land we had in sight (being part of the same chain of islands we have had to the northward of us since we entered the passage) bore N. 71° E.; latitude in, by observation, 10° 33′ S., longitude 219° 22′ W.[18] In this situation we had no part of the mainland in sight. Being now near the island, and having but little wind, Mr. Banks and I landed upon it, and found it to be mostly a barren rock frequented by birds, such as boobies, a few of which we shot, and occasioned my giving it the name of Booby Island. I made but very short stay at this island before I returned to the ship; in the meantime the wind had got to the south-west, and although it blowed but very faint, yet it was accompanied with a swell from the same quarter. This, together with other concurring circumstances, left me no

---

[17] *i.e.* round Cape Yorke. Having returned inside the reef, Cook was able to work up the coast to the northernmost point of Australia. Here he went ashore to take possession of the eastern coastline, which he originally named New Wales (possibly on the analogy of Dampier's New Britain). The name "New South Wales" occurs in another copy of the journal. Hitherto Australia had been known as New Holland, the modern name coming into use in 1803 after the first circum-navigation by Matthew Flinders.

[18] The ship was now passing through Endeavour Strait, separated from Torres Strait by Prince of Wales Island and the chain mentioned here. The only other European to have passed between New Guinea and Australia was Torres in 1606. Dalrymple revived the knowledge of his discovery and marked the strait in the book which he gave Banks to take with him on this voyage. Cook proved that, for once, Dalrymple was right.

room to doubt but we had got to the westward of Carpentaria, or the northern extremity of New Holland, and had now an open sea to the westward; which gave me no small satisfaction, not only because the danger and fatigues of the voyage was drawing near to an end, but by being able to prove that New Holland and New Guinea are two separate lands or islands, which until this day has been a doubtful point with geographers.

The north-east entrance of this passage or strait lies in the latitude of 10° 27' S., and in the longitude of 218° 36' W. from the meridian of Greenwich. It is formed by the main, or the northern extremity of New Holland, on the south-east, and by a congeries of islands to the north-west, which I named Prince of Wales's Islands. It is very probable that the islands extend quite to New Guinea; they are of various extent both for height and circuit, and many of them seemed to be indifferently well clothed with wood, etc., and, from the smokes we saw, some, if not all of them, must be inhabited. It is also very probable that among these islands are as good, if not better, passages than the one we have come through, although one need hardly wish for a better, was the access to it from the eastward less dangerous; but this difficulty will remain until some better way is found out than the one we came, which no doubt may be done was it ever to become an object to be looked for. The northern extent of the main or outer reef, which limit or bounds the shoals to the eastward, seems to be the only thing wanting to clear up this point; and this was a thing I had neither time nor inclination to go about, having been already sufficiently harassed with dangers without going to look for more.

SOME ACCOUNT OF NEW [SOUTH] WALES

In the course of this journal I have at different times made mention of the appearance or aspect of the face of the country, the nature of the soil, its produce, etc. By the first it will appear that to the southward of 33° or 34° the land in general is low and level, with very few hills or mountains; further to the northward it may in some places be called a hilly, but hardly anywhere can be called a mountainous, country, for the hills and mountains put together take up but a small part of the surface in comparison to what the plains and valleys do which intersect or divide these hills and mountains. It is indifferently well watered, even in the dry seasons, with small brooks and springs, but no great rivers, unless it be in the wet season, when the lowlands and valleys near the sea, I do suppose, are mostly laid under water. The small brooks may then become large rivers; but this can only happen with the tropic. It was only in Thirsty Sound that we could find no fresh water, and that no doubt was owing to the country being there very much intersected with salt creeks and mangrove land.

The lowland by the sea, and even as far inland as we were, is for the most friable, loose, sandy soil yet indifferently fertile, and clothed with woods, long grass, shrubs, plants, etc. The mountains or hills are chequered with woods and lawns; some of the hills are wholly covered with flourishing trees; others but thinly and the few that are upon them are small, and the spot of lawns or savannas are rocky and barren, especially to the northward, where the country did not afford or produce near the vegetation that it does to the southward, nor were the trees in the woods half so tall and stout. The woods do not produce any great variety of trees; there are only two or three sorts that can be called timber. The largest is the gum tree, which grows all over the country; the wood of this tree is too hard and ponderous for most common uses. The tree which resembles our pines I saw nowhere in perfection but in Botany Bay; this wood, as I have before observed, is something of the same nature as American live oak; in short, most of the large trees in this country are of a hard and ponderous nature, and could not be applied to many purposes. Here are several sorts of the palm kind, mangrove, and several other sorts of small trees and shrubs quite unknown to me, besides a very great number of plants hitherto unknown; but these things are wholly out of my way to describe, nor will this be of any loss, since not only plants, but everything that can be of use to the learned world will be very accurately described by Mr. Banks and Dr. Solander. The land naturally produces hardly anything fit for man to eat, and the natives know nothing of cultivation. There are, indeed, growing wild in the wood a few sorts of fruit (the most of them unknown to us), which when ripe do not eat amiss, one sort especially, which we called apples, being about the size of a crab apple; it is black and pulpy when ripe, and tastes like a damson; it has a large hard stone or kernel, and grows on trees or shrubs. . . .

The natives of this country are of a middle stature, straight bodied and slender limbed; their skins the colour of wood soot, their hair mostly black, some lank and others curled; they all wear it cropped short; their beards, which are generally black, they likewise crop short, or singe off. Their features are far from being disagreeable, and their voices are soft and tunable. They go quite naked, both men and women, without any manner of clothing whatever; even the women do not so much as cover their privities, although none of us was ever very near any of their women, one gentleman excepted, yet we are all of us as well satisfied of this as if we had lived among them. Notwithstanding we had several interviews with the men while we lay in Endeavour River, yet, whether through jealousy or disregard, they never brought any of their women along with them to the ship, but always left them on the opposite side of the river, where we had frequent opportunities [of] viewing them through our glasses. They wear as ornaments, necklaces made of shells, bracelets, or hoops, about their arms, made mostly of hair twisted and made like a cord hoop; these they wear tight about the upper parts of their arms, and some have girdles made in the same manner. The men wear a bone, about three or four inches long and a finger's thick, run through the bridge of their nose; they likewise have holes in their ears for earrings, but we never saw them wear any; neither are all the other ornaments worn in common, for we have seen as many without as with them. Some of these we saw on Possession Island wore breast plates, which we supposed were made of mother of pearl shells. Many of them paint their bodies and faces with a sort of white paste or pigment; this they apply different ways, each according to his fancy.

Their offensive weapons are darts; some are only pointed at

one end, others are barbed, some with wood, others with stings of rays, and some with sharks' teeth, etc.; these last are stuck fast on with gum. They throw the darts with only one hand, in the doing of which they make use of a piece of wood about three feet long, made thin like the blade of a cutlass, with a little hook at one end to take hold of the end of the dart, and at the other end is fixed a thin piece of bone about three or four inches long; the use of this is, I believe, to keep the dart steady, and to make it quit the hand in a proper direction. By the help of these throwing sticks, as we call them, they will hit a mark at the distance of forty or fifty yards, with almost, if not as much, certainty as we can do with a musket, and much more so than with a ball. These throwing sticks we at first took for wooden swords, and perhaps on some occasions they may use them as such; that is, when all their darts are expended. Be this as it may, they never travel without both them and their darts, not for fear of enemies, but for killing of game, etc., as I shall show hereafter. Their defensive weapons are targets, made of wood; but these we never saw used but once in Botany Bay.

I do not look upon them to be a warlike people; on the contrary, I think them a timorous and inoffensive race, no ways inclined to cruelty, as appeared from their behaviour to one of our people in Endeavour River, which I have before mentioned, neither are they very numerous. They live in small parties along by the sea coast, the banks of lakes, rivers, creeks, etc. They seem to have no fixed habitation, but move about from place to place like wild beasts in search of food, and, I believe, depend wholly upon the success of the present day for their subsistence. They have wooden fish gigs, with two, three, or four prongs, each very ingeniously made, with which they strike fish. We have also seen them strike both fish and birds with their darts. With these they likewise kill other animals; they have also wooden harpoons for striking turtle, but of these I believe they get but few, except at the seasons they come ashore to lay. In short, these people live wholly by fishing and hunting, but mostly by the former, for we never saw one inch of cultivated land in the whole country. They know, however, the use of *taara*, and sometimes eat them;

we do not know that they eat anything raw, but roast or broil all they eat on slow small fires. Their houses are mean, small hovels, not much bigger than an oven, made of pieces of sticks, bark, grass, etc., and even these are seldom used but in the wet seasons, for in the daytimes we know they as often sleep in the open air as anywhere else. We have seen many of their sleeping places, where there has been only some branches or pieces of bark, grass, etc., about a foot high on the windward side.

Their canoes are as mean as can be conceived, especially to the southward, where all we saw were made of one piece of the bark of trees about twelve or fourteen feet long, drawn or tied together at one end. As I have before made mention, these canoes will not carry above two people, in general there is never more than one in them; but, bad as they are, they do very well for the purpose they apply them to, better than if they were larger, for as they draw but little water they go in them upon the mud-banks, and pick up shell fish, etc., without going out of the canoe. The few canoes we saw to the northward were made out of a log of wood hollowed out, about fourteen feet long and very narrow, with outriggers; these will carry four people. During our whole stay in Endeavour River we saw but one canoe, and had great reason to think that the few people that resided about that place had no more; this one served them to cross the river and to go a-fishing in, etc. They attend the shoals, and flats, one where or another, every day at low water to gather shell fish, or whatever they can find to eat, and have each a little bag to put what they get in; this bag is made of net work. They have not the least knowledge of iron or any other metal that we know of; their working tools must be made of stone, bone, and shells; those made of the former are very bad, if I may judge from one of their adzes I have seen.

Bad and mean as their canoes are, they at certain seasons of the year (so far as we know) go in them to the most distant islands which lay upon the coast, for we never landed upon one but what we saw signs of people having been there before. We were surprised to find houses, etc., upon Lizard Island, which lies five leagues from the nearest part of the main; a distance we before thought they could not have gone in their canoes.

The coast of this country, at least so much of it as lies to the northward of 25° of latitude, abounds with a great number of fine bays and harbours, which are sheltered from all winds; but the country itself, so far as we know, doth not produce any one thing that can become an article in trade to invite Europeans to fix a settlement upon it. However, this eastern side is not that barren and miserable country that Dampier and others have described the western side to be. We are to consider that we see this country in the pure state of nature; the industry of man has had nothing to do with any part of it, and yet we find all such things as nature hath bestowed upon it in a flourishing state. In this extensive country it can never be doubted but what most sorts of grain, fruit, roots, etc., of every kind would flourish here were they once brought hither, planted and cultivated by the hands of industry; and here are provender for more cattle, at all seasons of the year, than ever can be brought into the country. . . .

From what I have said of the natives of New Holland they may appear to some to be the most wretched people upon earth; but in reality they are far more happier than we Europeans, being wholly unacquainted not only with the superfluous, but with the necessary conveniences so much sought after in Europe; they are happy in not knowing the use of them. They live in a tranquillity which is not disturbed by the inequality of condition. The earth and sea of their own accord furnishes them with all things necessary for life. They covet not magnificent houses, household stuff, etc.; they live in a warm and fine climate, and enjoy every wholesome air, so that they have very little need of clothing; and this they seem to be fully sensible of, for many to whom we gave cloth, etc., left it carelessly upon the sea beach and in the woods, as a thing they had no manner of use for; in short, they seemed to set no value upon anything we gave them, nor would they ever part with anything of their own for any one article we could offer them. This, in my opinion, argues that they think themselves provided with all the necessaries of life, and that they have no superfluities.

BOOK IV

From Leaving Australia to the Return to
England by way of Java and the Cape of
Good Hope
1770—1771

NEW GUINEA—STRAITS OF SUNDA—BATAVIA—STATE OF THE SHIP
AND HER CREW—EPIDEMIC OF DYSENTERY—CAPE OF GOOD HOPE—
VOYAGE HOME— LAND'S END—POSTSCRIPT

September 3   It's true I might have gone farther along the coast[1]
to the northward and westward until we had found a place where
the ship could lay so near the shore as to cover the people with
her guns when landed; but it is very probable that before we had
found such a place we should have been carried so far to the
west as to have been obliged to have gone to Batavia by the way
of Moluccas, and on the north side of Java, where we were all
utter strangers. This I did not think was so safe a passage as to go
to the south of Java and through the Straits of Sunda, the way I
propose to myself to go. Besides, as the ship is leaky, we are not
yet sure whether or no we shall not be obliged to heave her down
at Batavia; in this case it becomes the more necessary that we
should make the best of our way to that place, especially as no

---

[1] Emerging from Endeavour Strait, Cook sailed north-west until he fell in with
the coast of New Guinea. The decision to make for Java was welcomed by all
on board, of whom the greater part, says Banks, "were now pretty far gone with
the longing for home which the physicians have gone so far as to esteem a disease
under the name of Nostalgia"—the earliest recorded use of the word.

new discovery can be expected to be made in these seas, which the Dutch have, I believe, long ago narrowly examined, as appears from three maps bound up with the French History of Voyages to the *Terra Australis*, published in 1756,[2] which maps, I do suppose, by some means have been got from the Dutch, as we found the names of many of the places are in that language.

It should likewise seem from the same maps that the Spaniards and Dutch have at one time or another circumnavigated the whole of the island of New Guinea, as the most of the names are in these two languages; and such part of the coast as we were upon I found the chart tolerable good, which obliges me to give some credit to all the rest, notwithstanding we neither know by whom or when they were taken, and I always understood, before I had a sight of these maps, that it was unknown whether or no New Holland and New Guinea was not one continued land, and so it is said in the very History of Voyages these maps are bound up in. However, we have now put this wholly out of dispute; but, as I believe, it was known before, though not publicly, I claim no other merit than the clearing up of a doubtful point. Another doubtful point I should have liked to have cleared up, although it is of very little, if of any consequence, which is, whether the natives of New Holland and those of New Guinea are, or were, originally, one people, which one might well suppose, as these two countries lie so near to each other, and the intermediate space filled up with islands. On the other hand, if these two people have or ever had any friendly communication with each other it seems strange, as I have before observed, that they should not have transplanted from New Guinea over to New Holland coconuts, bread fruit, plantains, etc., etc., all very useful articles for the support of man, that we never saw grow in the latter, and which we have now seen in the former. Le Maire has given us a vocabulary of words spoken by the people of New Britain (which before Dampier's time was taken to be a part of New Guinea), by which it appears that the people of New Britain speak a very different language from those of New Holland. Now should it be found that the natives of New Britain

[2] By the President de Brosses.

and those of New Guinea have had one origin, and speak the same language, it will follow, of course, that the New Hollanders are a different people from both.

September 7   Navigation formerly wanted many of these helps towards keeping an accurate journal which the present age is possessed of;[3] it is not they that are wholly to blame for the faultiness of the charts, but the compilers and publishers, who publish to the world the rude sketches of the navigator as accurate surveys, without telling what authority they have for so doing; for were they to do this we should then be as good or better judge than they, and know where to depend upon the charts, and where not. Neither can I clear seamen of this fault; among the few I have known who are capable of drawing a chart or sketch of a sea coast I have generally, nay, almost always, observed them run into this error. I have known them lay down the line of a coast they have never seen, and put down soundings where they never have sounded; and, after all, are so fond of their performances as to pass the whole off as sterling under the title of a Survey Plan, etc. These things must in time be attended with bad consequences, and cannot fail of bringing the whole of their works in disrepute. If he is so modest as to say, such and such parts, or the whole of his plan is defective, the publishers or vendors will have it left out, because they say it hurts the sale of the work; so that between the one and the other we can hardly tell when we are possessed of a good sea chart until we ourselves have proved it.

September 30   Fresh gales and fair weather. In the morning I took into my possession the Officers', Petty Officers' and Seamen's Log Books and Journals, at least all that I could find, and enjoined everyone not to divulge where they had been.[4] At noon our course and distance sailed since yesterday at noon, is N. 20° W., 126 miles, which brought us into the latitude of 7° 34′ S. and longitude 252° 23′ W.

[3] This passage illustrates the revolution in honest and accurate surveying which Cook may be said to have initiated.

[4] As the ship approached the Dutch port of Batavia, Cook took precautions to keep his discoveries secret by impounding the logs.

October 1   First and latter parts fresh breezes at S.E. and fair weather; the middle squally with lightning and rain. At 7 p.m., being then in the latitude of Java Head, and not seeing any land, assured us that we had got too far to the westward; upon which we hauled up E.N.E., having before steered N. by E. At twelve o'clock saw the land bearing E., tacked, and stood to the S.W. until four, then stood again to the eastward, having very unsettled squally weather which split the main topsail very much, and obliged us to bend the other; many of our sails are now so bad that they will hardly stand the least puff of wind. At six o'clock Java Head, on the west end of Java, bore S.E. by E., distant five leagues; soon after this saw Princes Island, bearing E. ½ S. At ten o'clock saw the Island of Cracatoa[5] bearing N.E., distant seven leagues; Princes Island extending from S. 53° E. to S. by W., distant three leagues. Course and distance sailed since yesterday at noon is N. 24° 30′ E., seventy miles. Latitude in per observation, 6° 29′ S., longitude 251° 54′; but either our longitude must be erroneous or the Straits of Sunda must be faultily laid down in all books and charts; but this no doubt we shall have an opportunity to settle.

October 10, according to our reckoning, but by the people here
October 11   At four o'clock in the afternoon anchored in Batavia Road, where we found the *Harcourt* Indiaman from England, two English country ships,[6] thirteen sail of large Dutch ships, and a number of small vessels. As soon as we anchored I sent Lieutenant Hicks ashore to acquaint the Governor of our arrival, and to make an excuse for not saluting; as we could only do it with three guns I thought it was better let alone.

---

[5] The volcanic eruption which destroyed the island of Krakatoa occurred in 1883. Cook's longitude was nearly three degrees in error, owing to the strength of the current running against them.

[6] The Journal gives little idea of the excitement which must have prevailed on reaching the first civilised port for two years. Banks tells how they now heard for the first time that the American colonists were refusing to pay taxes, and that the cry in England was "Down with King George, King Wilkes for ever!" What must have interested Cook was the news that Carteret's *Swallow* (given up for lost when they left home) and Bougainville's *Boudeuse* (of which he had not previously heard) had lately visited the port.

A "country ship" is a vessel belonging to an English port abroad.

The carpenter now delivered me in the defects of the ship, of which the following is a copy:

"The defects of His Majesty's Bark *Endeavour*, Lieutenant James Cook, Commander.

"The ship very leaky (as she makes from 12 to 6 Inches water per hour), occasioned by her Main Keel being wounded in many places and the Scarfe of her Stem being very open. The false Keel gone beyond the Midships (from Forward and perhaps further), as I had no opportunity of seeing for the water when hauld ashore for repair. Wounded on her Starboard side under the Main Chains, where I immagine is the greatest leakes (but could not come at it for the water). One pump on the Starboard side useless, the others decayed within 1½ inch of the bore, otherwise masts, yards, boats and hull in pretty good condition.

"Dated in Batavia Road,

"this 10th of October, 1770.   "J. SATTERLY."

Previous to the above, I had consulted with the carpenter and all the other officers concerning the leak, and they were all unanimously of opinion that it was not safe to proceed to Europe without first seeing her bottom; accordingly I resolved to apply for leave to heave her down at this place, and, as I understood that this was to be done in writing, I drew up the following request to be presented to the Governor, etc., etc.:

"Lieutenant James Cook, commander of His Brittanick Majesty's Bark *Endeavour*, requests of the Right Hon'ble Petrus Albertus Van der Parra, Governor-General, etc., etc., etc., the Indulgence of the following Articles, viz.:

"Firstly, that he may be allow'd a proper and convenient place to heave down and repair His Britannick Majesty's ship under his command.

"Secondly, that he may have leave to purchase such few Trifling Naval stores as he may be in want of.

"Thirdly, that he may be permitted daily to purchase such provisions as he may want; also such an Additional quantity as

may enable him to proceed on his passage home to England.
  "Dated on board His Britannick Majesty's
  "Bark *Endeavour*, in Batavia Road,
  "the 11th October, 1770   "JAMES COOK."

In the morning I went on shore myself and had the foregoing
request translated into Dutch by a Scotch Gentleman, a merchant
here.

October 12   At 5 o'clock p.m. I was introduced to the Governor-
General, who received me very politely and told me that I
should have everything I wanted, and that in the morning my
request should be laid before the council where I was desired to
attend.

October 15   Fresh sea and land breezes and fair weather. I had
forgot to mention, that upon our arrival here I had not one
man upon the sick list; Lieut. Hicks, Mr. Green, and Tupia were
the only people that had any complaints occasioned by a long
continuance at sea.[7]

October 24   Employed clearing the ship, having a storehouse
to put our stores, etc., in. In the afternoon I went up to town in
order to put on board the first Dutch ship that sails, a packet for
the Admiralty containing a copy of my journal, a chart of the
South Sea, another of New Zealand, and one of the east coast of
New Holland. In the morning the General, accompanied by the
Water Fiscall, some of the Council, and the Commodore, each in
their respective boats, went out into the Road on board the oldest
captain, in order to appoint him Commodore of the Fleet, ready
to sail for Holland. The ships were drawn up in two lines, between which the General passed to the new Commodore's ship,
which lay the farthest out. Each ship as he passed and repassed
gave him three cheers, and as soon as he was on board, and the
Dutch flag hoisted at the main topmast head, the other commo-

[7] This brief entry records one of the greatest triumphs of the voyage. There
had been outbreaks of scurvy on board, but no fatal cases. Up-to-date, eight
deaths had been recorded, all from other causes. After leaving Batavia a very
different situation prevailed.

dore saluted him with twenty-one guns, and immediately after struck his Broad Pendant, which was again hoisted as soon as the General left the other ship; he was then saluted with seventeen guns by the new-made Commodore, who now hoisted a Common Pendant. This ceremony of appointing a commodore over the Grand Fleet, as they call it, we were told is yearly performed. I went out in my boat on purpose to see it, accompanied by Mr. Banks and Dr. Solander, because we were told it was one of the grandest sights Batavia afforded; that may be too, and yet it did not recompense us for our trouble. I thought that the whole was but ill conducted, and the Fleet appeared to be very badly manned. This fleet consists of ten or twelve stout ships; not only these, but all or most of their other ships are pierced for fifty guns, but have only their upper tier mounted, and these are more by half than they have men to fight.

October 25   In the evening I sent the Admiralty packet on board the *Kronenburg*, Captain Fredrick Kelger, Commodore, who, together with another ship, sails immediately for the Cape, where she waits for the remainder of the Fleet.[8]

[8] The final paragraph of the letter sent to Phillip Stephens, the Secretary of the Admiralty, runs as follows :

"I send herewith a copy of my Journal, containing the Proceedings of the whole Voyage, together with such Charts as I have had time to Copy, which I judge will be sufficient for the present to illustrate said Journal. In this Journal I have with undisguised truth and without gloss inserted the whole Transactions of the Voyage, and made such remarks and have given such descriptions of things as I thought was necessary in the best manner I was Capable off. Altho' the discoverys made in this Voyage are not great, yet I flatter myself they are such as may Merit the Attention of their Lordships; and altho' I have failed in discovering the so much talked of Southern Continent (which perhaps do not exist), and which I myself had much at heart, yet I am confident that no part of the Failure of such discovery can be laid to my charge. Had we been so fortunate not to have run a shore much more would have been done in the latter part of the Voyage than what was; but as it is, I presume this Voyage will be found as compleat as any before made to the So. Seas on the same account. The plans I have drawn of the places I have been at were made with all the Care and accuracy that time and Circumstances would admit of. Thus far I am certain that the Latitude and Longitude of few parts of the World are better settled than these. In this I was very much assisted by Mr. Green, who let slip no one opportunity for making of Observations for settling the Longitude during the whole Course of the Voyage; and the many Valuable discoveries made by Mr. Banks and Dr. Solander in Natural History, and other things useful to the learned World, cannot fail of contributing very much to the Success of the Voyage. In justice to the Officers and the whole Crew, I must say they have gone through the fatigues and dangers of the whole

December 26   In the evening myself, Mr. Banks, and all the
gentlemen came on board, and at 6 a.m. weighed and came to
sail with a light breeze at S.W. The *Elgin* Indiaman saluted us
with three cheers and thirteen guns, and soon after the Garrison
with fourteen, both of which we returned. Soon after this the
sea breeze set in at N. by W., which obliged us to anchor just
without the ships in the Road. The number of sick on board at
this time amounts to forty or upwards, and the rest of the ship's
company are in a weakly condition, having been every one sick
except the sailmaker, an old man about seventy or eighty years
of age; and what is still more extraordinary in this man is his
being generally more or less drunk every day. But notwithstanding this general sickness, we lost but seven men in the whole:
the surgeon, three seamen, Mr. Green's servant, and Tupia and
his servant, both of which fell a sacrifice to this unwholesome
climate before they had reached the object of their wishes.[9]
Tupia's death, indeed, cannot be said to be owing wholly to the
unwholesome air of Batavia; the long want of a vegetable diet,
which he had all his life before been used to, had brought upon
him all the disorders attending a sea life. He was a shrewd, sensible, ingenious man, but proud and obstinate, which often made
his situation on board both disagreeable to himself and those
about him, and tended much to promote the diseases which put
a period to his life. . . .

    Batavia is certainly a place that Europeans need not covet to
go to; but if necessity obliges them, they will do well to make

Voyage with that cheerfulness and Allertness that will always do Honour to
British Seamen, and I have the satisfaction to say that I have not lost one Man by
sickness during the whole Voyage. I hope that the repairs wanting to the Ship
will not be so great as to detain us any length of time. You may be assured that I
shall make no unnecessary delay either here or at any other place, but shall make
the best of my way home. I have the Honour to be with the greatest respect,
                              Sir,
                              Your most Obedient and Humble Servant,
                              JAMES COOK.

Endeavour Bark,
at Onrust, near Batavia,
the 23rd of October, 1770."

   [9] Three months spent repairing the ship at Batavia during the rainy season
resulted in an epidemic of malaria and dysentery (the "flux"). Tupia and Monkhouse the surgeon died there; Banks and Solander fell seriously ill; and Cook
himself was affected.

their stay as short as possible, otherwise they will soon feel the effects of the unwholesome air of Batavia, which, I firmly believe, is the death of more Europeans than any other place upon the globe of the same extent. Such, at least, is my opinion of it, which is founded on facts. We came in here with as healthy a ship's company as need go to sea, and after a stay of not quite three months left it in the condition of an hospital ship, besides the loss of seven men; and yet all the Dutch captains I had an opportunity to converse with said that we had been very lucky, and wondered that we had not lost half our people in that time.

March 15[10]   After our leaving Java Head we were eleven days before we got the general S.E. Trade wind, in which time we did not advance above 5° to the south and 3° to the west, having all the time variable light airs of wind, interrupted by frequent calms, the weather all the time hot and sultry, and the air unwholesome, occasioned most probably by the vast vapours brought into these latitudes by the Easterly Trade wind and Westerly Monsoons, both of which blow at this time of the year in this sea. The easterly winds prevail as far as 12° or 10° S., and the westerly winds as far as 6° or 8°; between them the winds are variable, and I believe always more or less unwholesome, but to us it was remarkable from the fatal consequences that attended it, for whatever might be the cause of first bringing on the flux among our people, this unwholesome air had a great share in it, and increased it to that degree that a man was no sooner taken with it than he looked upon himself as dead. Such was the despondency that reigned among the sick at this time, nor could it be by any means prevented, when every man saw that medicine, however skilfully administered, had not the least effect. I shall mention what effect only the imaginary approach of this disorder had upon one man. He had long tended upon the sick, and enjoyed a tolerably good state of health; one morning, coming

[10] This entry was made the day before anchoring at Table Bay, Cape Town. At one stage during their two and a half months' voyage from Batavia there were only twelve men left fit for duty. Banks and Solander recovered, but Green and twenty-six others died. Of the ninety-four persons who sailed from England, fifty-six returned.

upon deck, he found himself a little griped, and immediately began to stamp with his feet, and exclaim: "I have got the gripes, I have got the gripes; I shall die, I shall die!" In this manner he continued until he threw himself into a fit, and was carried off the deck, in a manner, dead; however he soon recovered, and did very well.

We had no sooner got into the S.E. Trade wind than we felt its happy effect, though we lost several men after, but they were such as were brought so low and weak that there was hardly a possibility of their recovery; and yet some of them lingered out in a state of suspense a month after, who, in all probability, would not have lived twenty-four hours before this change happened. Those that were not so far gone remained in the same state for some time, and at last began to recover; some few, however, were seized with the disorder after we got into the Trade wind, but they had it but slightly, and soon got over it. It is worth remarking, that of all those who had it in its last stage only one man lived, who is now in a fair way of recovering; and I think Mr. Banks was the only one that was cured at the first attack that had it to a great degree, or indeed at all, before we got into the S.E. Trade, for it was before that time that his cure was happily effected.

It is to be wished, for the good of all seamen, and mankind in general, that some preventative was found out against this disease, and put in practice in climates where it is common, for it is impossible to victual and water a ship in those climates but what some one article or another, according to different people's opinions, must have been the means of bringing on the flux.

April 15   The Cape of Good Hope has been so often described by authors, and is so well known to Europeans, that any description I can give of it may appear unnecessary. However, I cannot help observing that most authors, particularly the author of Mr. Byron's voyage, have heightened the picture to a very great degree above what it will bear; so that a stranger is at once struck with surprise and disappointment, for no country we have seen this voyage affords so barren a prospect as this, and not only so in appearance, but in reality. . . .

Notwithstanding the many disadvantages this country labours under, such is the industry, economy, and good management of the Dutch that not only the necessary, but all the luxuries, of life are raised here in as great abundance, and are sold as cheap, if not cheaper, than in any part of Europe, some few articles excepted. Naval stores, however, do not want for price any more here than they do at Batavia; these are only sold by the company, who have a certain fixed exorbitant price, from which they never deviate.

The inhabitants of the Cape Town are in general well bred and extremely civil and polite to all strangers; indeed, it is their interest so to do, for the whole town may be considered as one great inn fitted up for the reception of all comers and goers. Upon the whole, there is perhaps not a place in the known world that can equal this in affording refreshments of all kinds to shipping. The bay is capacious, pretty safe, and commodious; it lies open to the north-west winds, which winds, we are told, very seldom blow very strong, but sometimes sends in a great sea, for which reason ships moor north-east and south-west, and in such a manner as to have an open hawse with north-west winds.[11] The south-east winds blow frequently with great violence; but as this is right out of the bay it is attended with no danger. Near the town is a wharf built of wood, run out a proper distance into the sea for the convenience of landing and shipping off goods. To this wharf water is conveyed in pipes and by means of cocks. Several boats may fill water at one and the same time. The company keeps several large boats or hoys to carry goods, provisions, water, etc., to and from shipping, as well strangers as their own. Fuel is one of the scarcest articles they have, and is brought a long way out of the country, and consists of roots of trees, shrubs, etc. Except a few English oaks which they have planted, this country

[11] Cook explains that the Dutch used False Bay, Simonstown, from May to August, when the winds made Table Bay unsafe. The Master, Molyneux, died here, and Hicks, the First Lieutenant, died soon after leaving. The former was replaced by Pickersgill, the latter by John Gore, while Charles Clerke (who had also been round the world with Wallis) was promoted junior lieutenant in his place. "Open hawse" *i.e.* "the cables are directed to their anchor, without lying athwart the stem." (Falconer, *Marine Dictionary*, 1815.)

is wholly destitute of wood, except at too great a distance to be brought to the Cape.

July 10   At noon we saw land from the mast head, bearing north, which we judged to be about the Land's End.[12]

July 11   Steady fresh breezes and clear weather. At two in the afternoon saw the Lizardland, and at six o'clock the lighthouse bore N.W., distant five leagues, we being at this time, by my reckoning, in the longitude of 5° 30′ W.; soon after two ships under their topsails between us and the land, which we took for men of war. At seven o'clock in the morning the Start Point bore N.W. by N., distant three leagues, and at noon we reckoned ourselves about five leagues short of Portland. This forenoon a small cutter built vessel came under our stern, and inquired after the India Fleet, which, they said, they were cruising for and had not seen.

July 12   Winds at S.W., a fresh gale, with which we ran briskly up Channel. At half past three p.m. passed the Bill of Portland, and at seven Peverell Point; at 6 a.m. passed Beachy Head at the distance of four or five miles; at ten Dungeness, at the distance of two miles, and at noon we were abreast of Dover.

July 13   At three o'clock in the afternoon anchored in the Downs, and soon after I landed in order to repair to London.

POSTSCRIPT

Now I am upon the subject of discoveries, I hope it will not be taken amiss if I give it as my opinion that the most feasible

---

[12] For the voyage home from the Cape Cook's Journal gives only the barest details. During this part of the voyage the *Endeavour* sailed in company with the India fleet, but she was too slow to keep up for long. The crew were paid off on 1 August. Mention should be made of the goat which went twice round the world with Wallis and Cook to provide milk for "the gentlemen's coffee"; Dr. Johnson wrote a Latin epigram in her honour.

method of making further discoveries in the South Sea is to enter it by the way of New Zealand, first touching and refreshing at the Cape of Good Hope; from thence proceed to the southward of New Holland for Queen Charlotte's Sound, where again refresh wood and water, taking care to be ready to leave that place by the latter end of September, or beginning of October at farthest, when you would have the whole summer before you, and after getting through the strait, might, with the prevailing westerly winds, run to the eastward in as high a latitude as you please, and if you meet with no lands would have time enough to get round Cape Horn before the summer was too far spent; but if after meeting with no continent, and you had other objects in view, then haul to the northward, and after visiting some of the islands already discovered, after which proceed with the Trade wind back to the westward in search of those before mentioned —thus the discoveries in the South Sea would be complete.[13]

[13] This programme was carried out on the Second Voyage. The passage occurs in the postcript which concludes Cook's first MS. Journal.

The Second Voyage

1772—1775

Introduction to the Second Voyage

Before I begin my narrative of the expedition entrusted to my care, it will be necessary to add here some account of its equipment, and of some other matters, equally interesting, connected with my subject.

Soon after my return home in the *Endeavour*, it was resolved to equip two ships, to complete the discovery of the Southern Hemisphere. The nature of this voyage required ships of a particular construction, and the *Endeavour* being gone to the Falkland Islands as a store ship, the Navy Board was directed to purchase two such ships as were most suitable for this service.

At this time various opinions were espoused by different people, touching the size and kind of vessels most proper for such a voyage. Some were for having large ships; and proposed those of forty guns, or East India Company's ships. Others preferred large, good sailing frigates, or three-decked ships, employed in the Jamaica trade, fitted with round-houses. But of all that was said and offered to the Admiralty's consideration on this subject, as far as has come to my knowledge, what, in my opinion, was most to the purpose, was suggested by the Navy Board.

As the kind of ships most proper to be employed on discoveries is a very interesting consideration to the adventurers in such undertakings, it may possibly be of use to those who, in future, may be so employed, to give here the purport of the sentiments of the Navy Board thereon, with whom, after the experience of two voyages of three years each, I perfectly agree.

The success of such undertakings as making discoveries in distant parts of the world will principally depend on the preparations being well adapted to what ought to be the first considerations, namely, the preservation of the adventurers and ships; and this will ever chiefly depend on the kind, the size, and the properties of the ships chosen for the service.

These primary considerations will not admit of any other that

may interfere with the necessary properties of the ships. Therefore, in choosing the ships, should any of the most advantageous
properties be wanting, and the necessary room in them be in any
degree diminished, for less important purposes, such a step would
be laying a foundation for rendering the undertaking abortive in
the first instance.

As the greatest danger to be apprehended and provided against
on a voyage of discovery, especially to the most distant parts of
the globe, is that of the ship's being liable to be run aground on
an unknown desert, or, perhaps, savage coast, so no consideration
should be set in competition with that of her being of a construction of the safest kind, in which the officers may, with the least
hazard, venture upon a strange coast. A ship of this kind must not
be of a great draught of water, yet of a sufficient burden and
capacity to carry a proper quantity of provisions and necessaries
for her complement of men, and for the time requisite to perform the voyage.

She must also be of a construction that will bear to take the
ground; and of a size which, in case of necessity, may be safely
and conveniently laid on shore, to repair any accidental damage
or defects. These properties are not to be found in ships of war of
forty guns, nor in frigates, nor in East India Company's ships,
nor in large three-decked West India ships, nor indeed in any
other but North-Country-built ships, or such as are built for the
coal trade, which are peculiarly adapted to this purpose.

In such a vessel an able sea-officer will be most venturesome,
and better enabled to fulfil his instructions, than he possibly can
(or indeed than would be prudent for him to attempt) in one of
any other sort or size.

Upon the whole, I am firmly of opinion, that no ships are so
proper for discoveries in distant unknown parts as those constructed as was the *Endeavour*, in which I performed my former
voyage. For no ships of any other kind can contain stores and
provisions sufficient (in proportion to the necessary number of
men), considering the length of time it will be necessary they
should last. And, even if another kind of ship could stow a sufficiency, yet, on arriving at the parts for discovery, they would

still, from the nature of their construction and size, be less fit for the purpose.

Hence, it may be concluded, so little progress had been hitherto made in discoveries in the southern hemisphere. For all ships which attempted it before the *Endeavour* were unfit for it, although the officers employed in them had done the utmost in their power.

It was upon these considerations that the *Endeavour* was chosen for that voyage. It was to these properties in her that those on board owed their preservation; and hence we were enabled to prosecute discoveries in those seas so much longer than any other ship ever did or could do. And, although discovery was not the first object of that voyage, I could venture to traverse a far greater space of sea, till then unnavigated, to discover greater tracts of country in high and low south latitudes, and to persevere longer in exploring and surveying more correctly the extensive coasts of those new-discovered countries, than any former navigator, perhaps, had done during one voyage.

In short, these properties in the ships, with perseverance and resolution in their commanders, will enable them to execute their orders; to go beyond former discoverers; and continue to Britain the reputation of taking the lead of all nations in exploring the globe.

These considerations concurring with Lord Sandwich's opinion on the same subject, the Admiralty determined to have two such ships as are here recommended. Accordingly, two were purchased of Captain William Hammond of Hull. They were both built at Whitby, by the same person who built the *Endeavour*, being about fourteen or sixteen months old at the time they were purchased, and were, in my opinion, as well adapted to the intended service as if they had been built for the purpose. The larger of the two was 462 tons burden. She was named *Resolution*, and was sent to Deptford to be equipped. The other was 336 tons burden. She was named *Adventure*, and sent to be equipped at Woolwich.[1]

---

[1] The original names of these colliers, *Drake* and *Raleigh*, were changed in deference to Spanish susceptibilities. They were built by Fishburn of Whitby. The

It was first proposed to sheath them with copper; but, on considering that copper corrodes the ironwork, especially about the rudder, this intention was laid aside, and the old method of sheathing and fitting pursued, as being the most secure; for, although it is usual to make the rudder-bands of the same composition, it is not, however, so durable as iron, nor would it, I am well assured, last out such a voyage as the *Resolution* performed.

Therefore, till a remedy is found to prevent the effect of copper upon the ironwork, it would not be advisable to use it on a voyage of this kind, as the principal fastenings of the ship being iron, they may be destroyed.

On November 28th, 1771, I was appointed to the command of the *Resolution*; and Tobias Furneaux (who had been second lieutenant with Captain Wallis) was promoted, on this occasion, to the command of the *Adventure*. . . .

In the equipping of these ships, they were not confined to ordinary establishments, but were fitted in the most complete manner, and supplied with every extra article that was suggested to be necessary.

Lord Sandwich paid an extraordinary attention to this equipment, by visiting the ships from time to time, to satisfy himself that the whole was completed to his wish, and to the satisfaction of those who were to embark in them.

---

alterations to the *Resolution* made to fulfil Banks's requirements made her so top-heavy that Clerke, her First Lieutenant, informed him: "She is so very bad that the pilot declares he will not run the risk of his character so far as to take charge of her farther than the Nore without a fair wind; that he cannot with safety to himself, attempt working her to the Downs. Hope you know me too well to impute my giving this intelligence to any ridiculous apprehension for myself. By God, I'll go to sea in a grog-tub, if required, or in the *Resolution* as soon as you please; but must say I think her by far the most unsafe ship I ever saw or heard of. However, if you think proper to embark to the South Pole in a ship which the pilot (who I think by no means a timorous man) will not undertake to carry down the river, all I can say is that you will be most cheerfully attended, so long as we can keep her above water."

Her upper works were therefore altered once more, whereupon Banks refused to sail in her. His place was taken by the German naturalists, John Reinhold Forster and his son George. The complement of the *Resolution* was 112 (excluding five civilians), that of the *Adventure* eighty-one. The *Endeavour*, having been sold by the Admiralty, became a French privateer and was ultimately sold to a Rhode Island firm, which allowed her to drop to pieces in Newport harbour.

Nor were the Navy and Victualling Boards wanting in providing them with the very best of stores and provisions, and whatever else was necessary for so long a voyage. Some alterations were adopted in the species of provisions usually made use of in the Navy. That is, we were supplied with wheat in lieu of so much oatmeal, and sugar in lieu of so much oil; and when completed, each ship had two years and a half provisions on board, of all species.

We had, besides, many extra articles, such as *malt, sauerkraut, salted cabbage, portable broth, saloup, mustard, marmalade of carrots,* and *inspissated juice of wort and beer.*[2] Some of these articles had before been found to be highly antiscorbutic; and others were now sent out on trial, or by way of experiment—the inspissated juice of beer and wort, and marmalade of carrots especially. As several of these antiscorbutic articles are not generally known, a more particular account of them may not be amiss.

Of *malt* is made *sweet wort*, which is given to such persons as have got the scurvy, or whose habits of body threatens them with it, from one to five or six pints a day, as the surgeon sees necessary.

Sauerkraut, is cabbage cut small, to which is put a little salt, juniper berries, and annis-seeds; it is then fermented, and afterwards close packed in casks: in which state it will keep good a long time. This is a wholesome vegetable food, and a great antiscorbutic. The allowance to each man is two pounds a week, but I increased or diminished their allowance as I thought proper.

Salted cabbage is cabbage cut to pieces, and salted down in casks, which will preserve it a long time.

Portable broth is so well known, that it needs no description. We were supplied with it both for the sick and well and it was exceedingly beneficial.

Saloup, and *rob of lemons* and *oranges*, were for the sick and scorbutic only, and wholly under the surgeon's care.

Marmalade of carrots is the juice of yellow carrots inspissated till it is of the thickness of fluid honey, or treacle, which last it re-

---

[2] *i.e.* condensed infusion of malt before it is fermented into beer. "*Rob*", mentioned later, means "syrup".

sembles both in taste and colour. It was recommended by Baron Storsch, of Berlin, as a very great antiscorbutic; but we did not find that it had much of this quality.

For the *inspissated juice of wort*, and *beer*, we were indebted to Mr. Pelham, secretary to the commissioners of the Victualling Office. This gentleman, some years ago, considered that if the juice of malt, either as beer or wort, was inspissated by evaporation, it was probable this inspissated juice would keep good at sea; and, if so, a supply of beer might be had at any time, by mixing it with water. Mr. Pelham made several experiments, which succeeded so well, that the commissioners caused thirty-one half-barrels of this juice to be prepared, and sent out with our ships for trial; nineteen on board the *Resolution*, and the remainder on board the *Adventure*. The success of the experiments will be mentioned in the narrative, in the order they were made.

The frame of a small vessel, twenty tons burden, was properly prepared, and put on board each of the ships, to be set up (if found necessary) to serve as tenders upon any emergency, or to transport the crew in case the ship was lost.

We were also well provided with fishing-nets, lines and hooks of every kind for catching fish. And, in order to enable us to procure refreshments in such inhabited parts of the world as we might touch at, where money was of no value, the Admiralty caused to be put on board both the ships, several articles of merchandise; as well to trade with the natives for provisions, as to make them presents to gain their friendship and esteem.

Their Lordships also caused a number of medals to be struck, the one side representing His Majesty, and the other the two ships. These medals were to be given to the natives of new-discovered countries, and left there, as testimonies of our being the first discoverers.

Some additional clothing, adapted to a cold climate, was put on board; to be given to the seamen whenever it was thought necessary. In short, nothing was wanting that could tend to promote the success of the undertaking, or contribute to the conveniences and health of those who embarked in it.

The Admiralty showed no less attention to science in general, by engaging Mr. William Hodges, a landscape painter, to embark in this voyage, on order to make drawings and paintings of such places, in the countries we should touch at, as might be proper to give a more perfect idea thereof than could be formed from written descriptions only.

And it being thought of public utility, that some person skilled in natural history should be engaged to accompany me on this voyage, the Parliament granted an ample sum for that purpose, and Mr. John Reinhold Forster, with his son, were pitched upon for this employment.

The Board of Longitude agreed with Mr. William Wales, and Mr. William Bayley, to make astronomical observations; the former on board the *Resolution*, the latter on board the *Adventure*. The great improvements which astronomy and navigation have met with from the many interesting observations they have made, would have done honour to any person whose reputation for mathematical knowledge was not so well known as theirs.

The same Board furnished them with the best of instruments, for making both astronomical and nautical observations and experiments; and likewise with four time-pieces, or watch machines; three made by Mr. Arnold, and one made by Mr. Kendall on Mr. Harrison's principles. A particular account of the going of these watches, as also the astronomical and nautical observations made by the astronomers, will be laid before the public by order of the Board of Longitude, under the inspection of Mr. Wales.[3]

Besides the obligations I was under to this gentleman for communicating to me the observations he made, from time to time, during the voyage, I have since been indebted to him for the perusal of his journal, with leave to take from it whatever I thought might contribute to the improvement of this work.

For the convenience of the generality of readers, I have reduced the time from the nautical to the civil computation, so

[3] For these chronometers see above p. xvii. The Kendall-Harrison watch is still going in the National Maritime Museum, Greenwich. Charles Lamb describes Wales when a master at Christ's Hospital: "a perpetual fund of humour, a constant glee about him, heightened by an inveterate provincialism of North country dialect, absolutely took away the sting from his severities."

that whenever the terms a.m. and p.m. are used, the former signifies the forenoon, and the latter the afternoon of the same day.

In all the courses, bearings, etc., the variation of the compass is allowed, unless the contrary is expressed.

And now it may be necessary to say, that, as I am on the point of sailing on a third expedition, I leave this account of my last voyage in the hands of some friends, who in my absence have kindly accepted the office of correcting the press for me; who are pleased to think, that what I have here to relate is better to be given in my own words, than in the words of another person, especially as it is a work designed for information, and not merely for amusement; in which it is their opinion, that candour and fidelity will counterbalance the want of ornament.[4]

I shall, therefore, conclude this introductory discourse with desiring the reader to excuse the inaccuracies of style, which doubtless he will frequently meet with in the following narrative; and that, when such occur, he will recollect that it is the production of a man, who has not had the advantage of much school education, but who has been constantly at sea from his youth; and though, with the assistance of a few good friends, he has passed through all the stations belonging to a seaman, from an apprentice boy in the coal trade, to a post captain in the Royal Navy, he has had no opportunity of cultivating letters. After this account of myself, the public must not expect from me the elegance of a fine writer, or the plausibility of a professed book-maker; but will, I hope, consider me as a plain man, zealously exerting himself in the service of his country, and determined to give the best account he is able of his proceedings.

Plymouth Sound,
July 7th, 1776.

[4] For Cook's dissatisfaction with Hawkesworth's treatment of the First Voyage see above p. xxiii. The friend who edited the Journal of the Second Voyage was Canon John Douglas. An arrangement whereby Forster should help broke down, whereupon he published his own somewhat scurrilous account separately.

BOOK I

From our Departure from England to Leaving the Society Isles the First Time
1772-1773

SAIL FROM DEPTFORD FOR CAPE OF GOOD HOPE—SEARCH FOR BOUVET ISLAND—ANTARCTIC CIRCLE—THE SHIPS SEPARATED—RE-UNION AT QUEEN CHARLOTTE'S SOUND, NEW ZEALAND—ARRIVAL AT TAHITI—OMAI TAKEN ON BOARD—DESCRIPTION OF SOCIETY ISLES

April 9   I sailed from Deptford, but got no farther than Woolwich; where I was detained by easterly winds till the 22nd, when the ship fell down to Long Reach, and the next day was joined by the *Adventure*. Here both ships received on board their powder, guns, gunners' stores, and marines.

On May 10th we left Long Reach with orders to touch at Plymouth; but in plying down the river, the *Resolution* was found to be very crank, which made it necessary to put into Sheerness, in order to remove this evil, by making some altera-tions in her upper works. These the officers of the yard were ordered to take in hand immediately; and Lord Sandwich and Sir Hugh Palliser came down to see them executed in such a manner as might effectually answer the purpose intended.

On June 22nd the ship was again completed for sea, when I sailed from Sheerness; and on July 3rd, joined the *Adventure* in Plymouth Sound. The evening before, we met, off the Sound, Lord Sandwich, in the *Augusta* yacht (who was on his return from visiting the several dockyards), with the *Glory* frigate and *Hazard* sloop. We saluted his Lordship with seventeen guns; and soon after he and Sir Hugh Palliser gave us the last mark of the very great attention they had paid to this equipment, by coming on board, to satisfy themselves that everything was done to my wish, and that the ship was found to answer to my satisfaction.

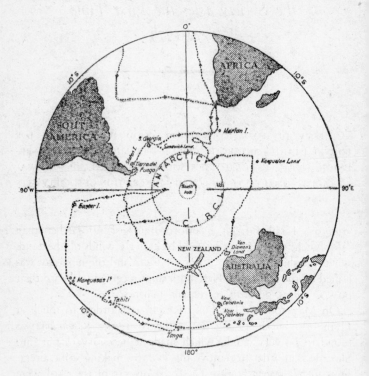

At Plymouth I received my instructions, dated June 25th, directing me to take under my command the *Adventure*; to make the best of my way to the island of Madeira, there to take in a supply of wine, and then proceed to the Cape of Good Hope, where I was to refresh the ships' companies, and take on board such provisions and necessaries as I might stand in need of. After leaving the Cape of Good Hope, I was to proceed to the southward and endeavour to fall in with Cape Circumcision, which was said by Monsieur Bouvet to lie in the latitude of 54° S., and in about 11° 20′ E. longitude from Greenwich.[1] If I discovered this cape, I was to satisfy myself whether it was a part of the continent, which had so much engaged the attention of geographers and former navigators, or a part of an island. If it proved to be the former, I was to employ myself diligently in exploring as great an extent of it as I could; and to make such notations thereon, and observations of every kind, as might be useful either to navigation or commerce, or tend to the promotion of natural knowledge. I was also directed to observe the genius, temper, disposition, and number, of the inhabitants, if there were any, and endeavour, by all proper means, to cultivate a friendship and alliance with them; making them presents of such things as they might value; inviting them to traffic, and showing them every kind of civility and regard. I was to continue to employ myself on this service, and making discoveries, either to the eastward or westward, as my situation might render most eligible; keeping in as high a latitude as I could, and prosecuting my discoveries as near to the South Pole as possible, so long as the condition of the ships, the health of their crews, and the state of their provisions, would admit of; taking care to reserve as much of the latter as would enable me to reach some known port, where I was to procure a sufficiency to bring me home to England. But if Cape Circumcision should prove to be part of an island only, or if I should not be able to find the said cape, I was, in the first case, to make the necessary survey of the island, and then to stand on to the southward, so long as I judged there was a likelihood of falling in with the continent; which I was also to do in the latter case; and then to proceed to the eastward, in further search of the said continent, as well as to make discoveries of such islands as might be situated in that unexplored part of the southern hemisphere; keeping in high latitudes, and prosecuting my discoveries as above-mentioned, as near the Pole as possible, until I had circumnavigated the globe; after which I was to proceed to the Cape of Good Hope, and from thence to Spithead.

[1] Sailing from Rio to the Cape of Good Hope in 1739, Captain Bouvet sighted the tiny island which bears his name which he imagined to be part of the Southern Continent. Actually it lies in the S. Atlantic 2,000 miles from the nearest land. Cook twice went in search of it, but never found it.

In the prosecution of these discoveries, whenever the season of the year rendered it unsafe for me to continue in high latitudes, I was to retire to some known place to the northward, to refresh my people, and refit the ships; and to return again to the southward, as soon as the season of the year would admit of it. In all unforeseen cases, I was authorized to proceed according to my own discretion; and in case the *Resolution* should be lost or disabled, I was to prosecute the voyage on board the *Adventure*.

November 23   Having got clear of the land,[2] I directed my course for Cape Circumcision. The wind continued at N.W. a moderate gale, until the 24th; when it veered round to the eastward. On the noon of this day, we were in the latitude of 35° 25′ S., and 29′ W. of the Cape; and had abundance of albatrosses about us, several of which were caught with hook and line; and were very well relished by many of the people, notwithstanding they were at this time served with fresh mutton. Judging that we should soon come into cold weather, I ordered slops to be served to such as were in want; and gave to each man the fearnought jacket and trousers allowed them by the Admiralty.[3]

The wind continued easterly for two days, and blew a moderate gale, which brought us into the latitude of 39° 4′, and 2° of longitude west of the Cape; thermometer 52½. The wind now came to W. and S.W., and on the 29th fixed at W.N.W. and increased to a storm, which continued, with some few intervals of moderate weather, till the 6th of December; when we were in the latitude of 48° 41′ S., and longitude 18° 24′ E. This gale, which was attended with rain and hail, blew at times with such violence that

---

[2] *i.e.* the Cape of Good Hope, where Cook heard that two French ships under Kerguelen had discovered the island which bears his name in lat. 49° S. on a voyage from Mauritius to Batavia. He was also told that Marion de Fresne had taken possession of New Zealand after the *Endeavour's* visit there on the previous voyage. Marion had been sent to return Bougainville's islander to Tahiti, but the unfortunate native died before they reached the Pacific, and Marion himself was killed by the Maoris.

[3] *Slops*—"a name given to all species of wearing apparel etc. which are supplied to H.M. ships". *Fearnought*—"a peculiar sort of thick woollen stuff, generally hung on a screen without the magazine door in time of action to prevent sparks from communicating to the powder; thence it derives its appellation." (Falconer).

we could carry no sails; by which means we were driven far to the eastward of our intended course, and no hopes were left me of reaching Cape Circumcision. But the greatest misfortune that attended us, was the loss of great part of our livestock; which we had brought from the Cape; and which consisted of sheep, hogs, and geese. Indeed this sudden transition from warm mild weather, to extreme cold and wet, made every man in the ship feel its effects. For by this time the mercury in the thermometer had fallen to 38; whereas at the Cape it was generally at 67 and upwards. I now made some addition to the people's allowance of spirit, by giving them a dram whenever I thought it necessary, and ordered Captain Furneaux to do the same. The night proved clear and serene, and the only one that was so since we left the Cape; and the next morning the rising sun gave us such flattering hopes of a fine day, that we were induced to let all the reefs out of the topsails, and to get top-gallant-yards across, in order to make the most of a fresh gale at N. Our hopes, however, soon vanished; for before eight o'clock, the serenity of the sky was changed into a thick haze, accompanied with rain. The gale increasing obliged us to hand the mainsail, close-reef our topsails, and to strike top-gallant-yards. The barometer at this time was unusually low, which foreboded an approaching storm; and this happened accordingly; for, by 1 p.m., the wind, which was at N.W., blew with such strength as obliged us to take in all our sails, to strike top-gallant-masts, and to get the sprit-sail-yard in. And I thought proper to wear, and lie to, under a mizzen staysail, with the ships' heads to the N.E., as they would bow the sea, which ran prodigiously high, better on this tack.

At eight o'clock next morning, being the 8th, we wore, and lay on the other tack; the gale was a little abated, but the sea ran too high to make sail, any more than the fore-top-mast stay-sail. In the evening, being in the latitude of 49° 40′ S., and 1½° east of the Cape, we saw two penguins, and some sea or rock weed, which occasioned us to sound, without finding ground at 100 fathoms. At 8 p.m. we wore, and lay with our heads to the northeast till three o'clock in the morning of the 9th, then wore again to the southward, the wind blowing in squalls, attended with

showers of snow. At eight, being something more moderate, I
made the *Adventure* signal to make sail, and soon after made sail
ourselves under the courses, and close-reefed top-sails. In the
evening, took in the top-sails and main-sail, and brought to,
under fore-sail and mizzen; thermometer at 36°. The wind, still
at N.W., blew a fresh gale, accompanied with a very high sea. In
the night, had a pretty smart frost with snow.

In the morning of the 10th, we made sail under courses and
top-sails close-reefed; and made the signal for the *Adventure* to
make sail and lead. At eight o'clock, saw an island of ice to the
westward of us, being then in the latitude of 50° 40′ S., and longitude 2° 0′ E. of the Cape of Good Hope. Soon after, the wind
moderated, and we let all the reefs out of the top-sails, got the
spritsail-yard out, and top-gallant-mast up. The weather coming
hazy, I called the *Adventure* by signal under my stern; which was
no sooner done, than the haze increased so much, with snow and
sleet, that we did not see an island of ice, which we were steering
directly for, till we were less than a mile from it. I judged it to
be about fifty feet high, and half a mile in circuit. It was flat at
top, and its sides rose in a perpendicular direction, against which
the sea broke exceedingly high. Captain Furneaux at first took
this ice for land, and hauled off from it, until called back by
signal. As the weather was foggy, it was necessary to proceed
with caution. We therefore reefed our top-sails, and at the same
time sounded, but found no ground with 150 fathoms. We kept
on to the southward with the wind at north till night, which we
spent in making short trips, first one way and then another, under
an easy sail; thermometer this twenty-four hours from 36½ to
31.

January 2   This longitude[4] is nearly the same that is assigned
to Cape Circumcision, and at the going down of the sun, we

[4] *i.e.* 9° 34′ E. The ship was now in lat. 58° S. After reaching 67° S. Cook
found progress to the southward blocked by ice, so he decided to haul away to the
northward in search of Kerguelen Island. He failed to find it on this voyage,
though he did so on his Third Voyage. On 7 February the ships became separated
and worked their way independently to the rendezvous at Queen Charlotte's
Sound, having sailed 3,600 leagues in 117 days, much of the time to the south of
the Antarctic Circle.

were about ninety-five leagues to the south of the latitude it is
said to lie in. At this time the weather was so clear, that
we might have seen land at fourteen or fifteen leagues distance.
It is therefore very probable that what Bouvet took for land
was nothing but mountains of ice, surrounded by loose or field
ice. We ourselves were undoubtedly deceived by the ice hills
the day we first fell in with the field ice. Nor was it an improbable conjecture, that that ice joined to land. The probability was
however now greatly lessened, if not entirely set aside. For the
space between the northern edge of the ice, along which we
sailed, and our route to the west, when south of it, nowhere
exceeded 100 leagues; and in some places not sixty. But a view of
the chart will best explain this. The clear weather continued no
longer than three o'clock the next morning, when it was succeeded by a thick fog, sleet, and snow. The wind also veered to
north-east and blew a fresh gale, with which we stood to south-
east. It increased in such a manner, that before noon we were
brought under close-reefed top-sails. The wind continued to veer
to the north, at last fixed at north-west, and was attended with
intervals of clear weather.

Our course was E. ¾ N., till noon the next day, when we were
in the latitude of 59° 2′ S., and nearly under the same meridian
as we were when we fell in with the last field of ice, five days
before; so that had it remained in the same situation, we must
now have been in the middle of it. Whereas we did not so much
as see any. We cannot suppose that so large a float of ice as this
was, could be destroyed in so short a time. It therefore must have
drifted to the northward, and this makes it probable that there is
land under this meridian, between the latitude of 55° and 59°,
where we had supposed some to lie, as mentioned above.

As we were now only sailing over a part of the sea where we
had been before, I directed the course E.S.E. in order to get more
to the south. We had the advantage of a fresh gale, and the dis-
advantage of a thick fog, much snow and sleet, which, as usual,
froze on our rigging as it fell, so that every rope was covered
·with the finest transparent ice I ever saw. This afforded an agreeable sight enough to the eye, but conveyed to the mind an idea

of coldness, much greater than it really was; for the weather was rather milder than it had been for some time past, and the sea less encumbered with ice. But the worst was, the ice so clogged the rigging, sails, and blocks, as to make them exceedingly bad to handle. Our people however surmounted those difficulties with a steady perseverance, and withstood this intense cold much better than I expected.

We continued to steer to the E.S.E. with a fresh gale at N.W. attended with snow and sleet, till the 8th, when we were in the latitude of 61° 12′ S., longitude 31° 47′ E. In the afternoon we passed more ice islands than we had seen for several days. Indeed they were now so familiar to us, that they were often passed unnoticed, but more generally unseen on account of the thick weather. At nine o'clock in the evening, we came to one which had a quantity of loose ice about it. As the wind was moderate, and the weather tolerably fair, we shortened sail, and stood on and off, with a view of taking some on board on the return of light; but at four o'clock in the morning, finding ourselves to leeward of this ice, we bore down to an island to leeward of us, there being about it some loose ice, part of which we saw break off. There we brought to, hoisted out three boats, and in about five or six hours, took up as much ice as yielded fifteen tons of good fresh water. The pieces we took up were hard, and solid as a rock, some of them were so large, that we were obliged to break them with pick-axes, before they could be taken into the boats.

The salt water which adhered to the ice, was so trifling as not to be tasted, and after it had lain on deck a short time, entirely drained off; and the water which the ice yielded was perfectly sweet and well-tasted. Part of the ice we broke in pieces, and put into casks, some we melted in the coppers, and filled up the casks with the water, and some we kept on deck for present use. The melting and stowing away the ice is a little tedious, and takes up some time, otherwise this is the most expeditious way of watering I ever met with.

Having got on board this supply of water, and the *Adventure* about two-thirds as much (of which we stood in great need), as we had once broke the ice, I did not doubt of getting more whenever we were in want. I therefore, without hesitation, directed our course more to the south, with a gentle gale at N.W. attended, as usual, with snow showers.

March 17   I continued to steer to the east, inclining to the south, with a fresh gale at S.W. till five o'clock the next morning, when, being in the latitude of 59° 7′ S., longitude 146° 53′ E. I bore away north-east and at noon north, having come to a resolution to quit the high southern latitudes, and to proceed to New Zealand, to look for the *Adventure*, and to refresh my people. I had also some thoughts, and even a desire, to visit the east coast of Van Diemen's Land, in order to satisfy myself if it joined the coast of New South Wales.[5]

In the night of the 17th, the wind shifted to north-west and blew in squalls, attended with thick hazy weather and rain. This continued all the 18th, in the evening of which day, being in the latitude of 56° 15′ S., longitude 150°, the sky cleared up, and we found the variation by several azimuths to be 13° 30′ E. Soon after, we hauled up with the log a piece of rock-weed, which was in a state of decay, and covered with barnacles. In the night the southern lights were very bright.

The next morning we saw a seal, and towards noon some penguins, and more rock-weed, being at this time in the latitude of 55° 1′, longitude 152° 1′ E. In the latitude of 54° 4′, we also saw a Port Egmont hen, and some weed. Navigators have generally looked upon all these to be certain signs of the vicinity of land; I cannot, however, support this opinion. At this time we knew of no land, nor is it even probable that there is any, nearer than New Holland, or Van Diemen's Land, from which we were distant 260 leagues. We had, at the same time, several porpoises playing about us; into one of which Mr. Cooper struck a harpoon; but, as the ship was running seven knots, it broke its hold, after towing it some minutes, and before we could deaden the ship's way.

As the wind, which continued between the north and the west,

---

[5] Furneaux, in the *Adventure*, made an unsatisfactory attempt to do this, see p. 138. The ships had separated on February 7.

would not permit me to touch at Van Diemen's Land, I shaped my course to New Zealand; and, being under no apprehensions of meeting with any danger, I was not backward in carrying sail, as well by night as day, having the advantage of a very strong gale, which was attended with hazy rainy weather, and a very large swell from the W. and W.S.W. We continued to meet with, now and then, a seal, Port Egmont hens, and sea-weed.

On the morning of the 22nd, the wind shifted to south, and brought with it fair weather. At noon we found ourselves in the latitude of 49° 55′, longitude 159° 28′, having a very large swell out of the south-west. For the three days past the mercury in the thermometer had risen to 46, and the weather was quite mild. Seven or eight degrees of latitude had made a surprising difference in the temperature of the air, which we felt with an agreeable satisfaction.

We continued to advance to the north-east at a good rate, having a brisk gale between the south and east; meeting with seals, Port Egmont hens, egg-birds, sea-weed, etc., and having constantly a very large swell from the south-west. At ten-o'clock in the morning of the 25th, the land of New Zealand was seen from the masthead; and, at noon, from the deck; extending from N.E. by E. to E., distant ten leagues. As I intended to put into Dusky Bay, or any other port I could find, on the southern part of *Tavai Poenammoo*, we steered in for the land, under all the sail we could carry, having the advantage of a fresh gale at west, and tolerably clear weather. This last was not of long duration; for, at half an hour after four o'clock, the land, which was not above four miles distant, was in a manner wholly obscured in a thick haze. At this time, we were before the entrance of a bay, which I had mistaken for Dusky Bay, being deceived by some islands that lay in the mouth of it.

Fearing to run, in thick weather, into a place to which we were all strangers, and seeing some breakers and broken ground ahead, I tacked in twenty-five fathom water, and stood out to sea with the wind at north-west. This bay lies on the south-east side of Cape West, and may be known by a white cliff on one of the isles which lies in the entrance of the bay. This part of the coast

I did not see but at a great distance, in my former voyage; and we now saw it under so many disadvantageous circumstances, that the less I say about it, the fewer mistakes I shall make. We stood out to sea, under close-reefed top-sails and courses, till eleven o'clock at night; when we wore and stood to the northward, having a very high and irregular sea. At five o'clock next morning, the gale abated, and we bore up for the land; at eight o'clock, the West Cape bore E. by N. ½ N. for which we steered, and entered Dusky Bay about noon. In the entrance of it, we found forty-four fathoms of water, a sandy bottom, the West Cape bearing S.S.E. and Five Fingers Point, or the north point of the bay, N. Here we had a great swell rolling in from the south-west. The depth of water decreased to forty fathoms; afterwards we had no ground with sixty. We were, however, too far advanced to return; and therefore stood on, not doubting but that we should find anchorage. For in this bay we were all strangers; in my former voyage, having done no more than discover, and name it.

After running about two leagues up the bay, and passing several of the isles which lay in it, I brought to, and hoisted out two boats; one of which I sent away with an officer round a point on the larboard hand, to look for anchorage. This he found, and signified the same by signal. We then followed with the ship, and anchored in fifty fathoms of water, so near the shore as to reach it with an hawser. This was on Friday, March 26th, at three in the afternoon, after having been 117 days at sea; in which time we had sailed 3,660 leagues, without having once sight of land.

After such a long continuance at sea, in a high southern latitude, it is but reasonable to think that many of my people must be ill of the scurvy. The contrary, however, happened. Mention has already been made of sweet wort being given to such as were scorbutic. This had so far the desired effect, that we had only one man on board that could be called very ill of this disease; occasioned, chiefly, by a bad habit of body, and a complication of other disorders. We did not attribute the general good state of health in the crew, wholly to the sweet wort, but to the frequent airing and sweetening the ship by fires, etc. We must also allow portable broth, and sauerkraut to have had some share in it. This last can never be enough recommended.

My first care, after the ship was moored, was to send a boat and people a-fishing; in the meantime, some of the gentlemen killed a seal (out of many that were upon a rock), which made us a fresh meal.

As I did not like the place we had anchored in, I sent Lieutenant Pickersgill over to the south-east side of the bay, to search for a better; and I went myself to the other side, for the same purpose, where I met with an exceedingly snug harbour, but nothing else worthy of notice. Mr. Pickersgill reported, upon his return, that he had found a good harbour, with every convenience. As I liked the situation of this, better than the other of my own finding, I determined to go there in the morning. The fishing-boat was very successful; returning with fish sufficient for all hands for supper, and, in a few hours in the morning, caught as many as served for dinner. This gave us certain hopes of being plentifully supplied with this article. Nor did the shores and woods appear less destitute of wild fowl; so that we hoped to enjoy with ease, what in our situation might be called the luxuries of life. This determined me to stay some time in this bay, in order to examine it thoroughly; as no one had ever landed before, on any of the southern parts of this country.

On the 27th, at nine o'clock in the morning, we got under sail with a light breeze at south-west and working over to Pickersgill Harbour, entered it by a channel scarcely twice the width of the ship; and, in a small creek, moored head and stern, so near the shore as to reach it with a brow or stage, which nature had in a manner prepared for us in a large tree, whose end or top reached our gunwale. Wood, for fuel and other purposes, was here so convenient, that our yards were locked in the branches of the trees; and, about 100 yards from our stern, was a fine stream of fresh water. Thus situated, we began to clear places in the woods, in order to set up the astronomer's observatory, the forge to repair our ironwork, tents for the sail-makers and coopers to repair the sails and casks in; to land our empty casks, to fill with water, and to cut down wood for fuel; all of which were absolutely necessary occupations. We also began to brew beer from the branches or leaves of a tree, which much resembles the American black spruce. From the knowledge I had of this tree, and the similarity it bore to the spruce, I judged that with the addition of inspissated juice of wort and molasses, it would make a very wholesome beer, and supply the want of vegetables, which this place did not afford; and the event proved that I was not mistaken.

Now I have mentioned the inspissated juice of wort, it will not be amiss, in this place, to inform the reader that I had made several trials of it since I left the Cape of Good Hope, and found it to answer in a cold climate, beyond all expectation. The juice, diluted in warm water, in the proportion of twelve parts water to one part juice, made a very good and well-tasted small beer. Some juice which I had of Mr. Pelham's own preparing, would bear sixteen parts water. By making use of warm water (which I think ought always to be done) and keeping it in a warm place if the weather be cold, no difficulty will be found in fermenting it. A little grounds of either small or strong beer will answer as well as yeast.

The few sheep and goats we had left, were not likely to fare quite so well as ourselves; there being no grass here, but what was coarse and harsh. It was, however, not so bad, but that we expected they would devour it with great greediness, and were the more surprised to find that they would not taste it; nor did they seem over-fond of the leaves of more tender plants. Upon examination, we found their teeth loose; and that many of them had every other symptom of an inveterate sea-scurvy. Out of four ewes and two rams which I brought from the Cape, with an intent to put ashore in this country, I had only been able to preserve one of each; and even these were in so bad a state, that it was doubtful if they could recover; notwithstanding all the care possible had been taken of them.

Some of the officers, on the 28th, went up the bay in a small boat on a shooting party; but discovering inhabitants, they returned before noon, to acquaint me therewith; for hitherto we had not seen the least vestige of any. They had but just got aboard, when a canoe appeared off a point about a mile from us, and soon after, returned behind the point out of sight, probably owing to a shower of rain which then fell: for it was no sooner over, than the canoe again appeared, and came within musket-shot of the ship. There were in it seven or eight people. They remained looking at us for some time, and then returned; all the signs of friendship we could make, did not prevail on them to come nearer. After dinner I took two boats and went in search of them, in the cove where they were first seen, accompanied by several of the officers and gentlemen. We found the canoe (at least a canoe) hauled upon the shore near to two small huts, where were several fireplaces, some fishing-nets, a few fish lying on the shore, and some in the canoe. But we saw no people; they, probably, had retired into the woods. After a short stay, and leaving in the canoes some medals, looking-glasses, beads, etc., we embarked and rowed to the head of the cove, where we found nothing remarkable. In returning back we put ashore at the same place as before; but still saw no people. However, they could not be far off, as we smelled the smoke of fire, though we did not see it. But I did not care to search further, or to force an interview which they seemed to avoid; well knowing that the way to obtain this, was to leave the time and place to themselves. It did not appear that anything I had left had been touched; however, I now added a hatchet, and with the night returned on board.

On the 29th, were showers till the afternoon; when a party of the officers made an excursion up the bay; and Mr. Forster and his party were out botanizing. Both parties returned in the evening without meeting with anything worthy of notice; and the two following days, everyone was confined to the ship on account of rainy stormy weather.

In the afternoon of April 1st, accompanied by several of the gentlemen, I went to see if any of the articles I had left for the Indians were taken away. We found everything remaining in the canoe; nor did it appear that anybody had been there since. After shooting some birds, one of which was a duck, with a blue-grey plumage and soft bill, we, in the evening, returned on board. The 2nd, being a pleasant morning, Lieutenants Clerke and

Edgcumbe, and the two Mr. Forsters, went in a boat up the bay to search for the productions of nature;[6] and myself, Lieutenant Pickersgill, and Mr. Hodges, went to take a view of the north-west side. In our way, we touched at the seal rock, and killed three seals, one of which afforded us much sport. After passing several isles, we at length came to the most northern and western arms of the bay; the same as is formed by the land of Five Fingers Point. In the bottom of this arm or cove we found many ducks, wood-hens, and other wild fowl, some of which we killed, and returned on board at ten o'clock in the evening; where the other party had arrived several hours before us, after having had but indifferent sport. They took with them a black dog we had got at the Cape, who, at the first musket they fired, ran into the woods, from whence he would not return. The three following days were rainy, so that no excursions were made.

Early in the morning on the 6th, a shooting party, made up of the officers, went to Goose Cove, the place where I was on the 2nd; and myself, accompanied by the two Mr. Forsters and Mr. Hodges, set out to continue the survey of the bay. My attention was directed to the north side, where I discovered a fine capacious cove, in the bottom of which is a fresh-water river; on the west side several beautiful small cascades; and the shores are so steep that a ship might lie near enough to convey the water into her by a hose. In this cove we shot fourteen ducks, beside other birds, which occasioned my calling it Duck Cove.

As we returned in the evening, we had a short interview with three of the natives, one man and two women. They were the first that discovered themselves on the north-east point of Indian Island, named so on this occasion. We should have passed without seeing them, had not the man hallooed to us. He stood with his club in his hand upon the point of a rock, and behind him, at the skirts of the wood, stood the two women, with each of them a

6 From Forster's Journal: "After supper we listened awhile to the original comic vein of our boat's crew, who huddled round the fire, made their meal, and recited a number of droll stories, intermixed with hearty curses, oaths and indecent expressions, but seldom without real humour. Then strewing our tent with heaps of fern leaves, and wrapping ourselves in our boat cloaks, with our guns and shooting bags for pillows, we composed ourselves to sleep." Dusky Bay, where the ship now lay, is on the S.W. coast of the southern island of New Zealand.

spear. The man could not help discovering great signs of fear when we approached the rock with our boat. He, however, stood firm; nor did he move to take up some things we threw him ashore. At length I landed, went up, and embraced him; and presented him with such articles as I had about me, which at once dissipated his fears. Presently after, we were joined by the two women, the gentlemen that were with me, and some of the seamen. After this, we spent about half an hour in chit-chat, little understood on either side, in which the youngest of the two women bore by far the greatest share. This occasioned one of the seamen to say, that women did not want tongue in any part of the world. We presented them with fish and fowl which we had in our boat; but these they threw into the boat again, giving us to understand that such things they wanted not. Night approaching, obliged us to take leave of them; when the youngest of the two women, whose volubility of tongue exceeded everything I ever met with, gave us a dance; but the man viewed us with great attention. Some hours after we got on board, the other party returned, having had but indifferent sport.

April 17   It rained all the 17th; but the 18th bringing fair and clear weather, in the evening, our friends the natives before mentioned paid us another visit; and the next morning, the chief and his daughter were induced to come on board, while the others went out in the canoe fishing. Before they came on board I showed them our goats and sheep that were on shore; which they viewed, for a moment, with a kind of stupid insensibility. After this, I conducted them to the brow; but before the chief set his foot upon it to come into the ship, he took a small green branch in his hand, with which he struck the ship's side several times, repeating a speech or prayer. When this was over, he threw the branch into the main chains, and came on board. This custom and manner of making peace, as it were, is practised by all the nations in the South Seas that I have seen.

I took them both down into the cabin, where we were to breakfast. They sat at table with us, but would not taste any of our victuals. The chief wanted to know where we slept, and in-

deed to pry into every corner of the cabin, every part of which
he viewed with some surprise. But it was not possible to fix his
attention to any one thing a single moment. The works of art
appeared to him in the same light as those of nature, and were as
far removed beyond his comprehension. What seemed to strike
them most was the number and strength of our decks, and other
parts of the ship. The chief, before he came aboard, presented me
with a piece of cloth and a green talk [jade] hatchet; to Mr. Forster
he also gave a piece of cloth; and the girl gave another to Mr.
Hodges. This custom of making presents, before they receive any,
is common with the natives of the South Sea Isles; but I never saw it
practised in New Zealand before. Of all the various articles I gave
my guests, hatchets and spike-nails were the most valuable in his
eyes. These he never would suffer to go out of his hands after he
had once laid hold of them; whereas many other articles he would
lay carelessly down anywhere, and at last leave them behind
him.

As soon as I could get quit of them, they were conducted into
the gun-room, where I left them, and set out with two boats to
examine the head of the bay; myself in one, accompanied by Mr.
Forster and Mr. Hodges; and Lieutenant Cooper in the other. We
proceeded up the south side; and, without meeting with anything remarkable, got to the head of the bay by sunset; where we
took up our lodging for the night at the first place we could land
upon; for the flats hindered us from getting quite to the head.

At daylight in the morning, I took two men in the small boat,
and, with Mr. Forster, went to take a view of the flat land at the
head of the bay, near to where we spent the night. We landed on
one side, and ordered the boat to meet us on the other side; but
had not been long on shore before we saw some ducks, which,
by their creeping through the bushes, we got a shot at, and killed
one. The moment we had fired, the natives, whom we had not
discovered before, set up a most hideous noise in two or three
places close by us. We hallooed in our turn; and, at the same time,
retired to our boat, which was full half a mile off. The natives
kept up their clamouring noise, but did not follow us. Indeed we
found, afterwards, that they could not, because of a branch of the

river between us and them; nor did we find their numbers answerable to the noise they made. As soon as we got to our boat, and found that there was a river that would admit us, I rowed in, and was soon after joined by Mr. Cooper, in the other boat. With this reinforcement I proceeded up the river, shooting wild ducks, of which there were great numbers; as we went along, now and then, hearing the natives in the woods. At length two appeared on the banks of the river, a man and a woman; and the latter kept waving something white in her hand, as a sign of friendship. Mr. Cooper being near them, I called to him to land, as I wanted to take the advantage of the tide to get as high up as possible, which did not much exceed half a mile, when I was stopped by the strength of the stream and great stones which lay in the bed of the river.

On my return, I found that, as Mr. Cooper did not land when the natives expected him, they had retired into the woods; but two others now appeared on the opposite bank. I endeavoured to have an interview with them; but this I could not effect. For, as I approached the shore, they always retired farther into the woods, which were so thick as to cover them from our sight. The falling tide obliged me to retire out of the river, to the place where we had spent the night. There we breakfasted, and afterwards embarked, in order to return on board; but, just as we were going, we saw two men, on the opposite shore, hallooing to us, which induced me to row over to them. I landed, with two others, unarmed; the two natives standing about 100 yards from the waterside, with each a spear in his hand. When we three advanced, they retired; but stood when I advanced alone.

It was some little time before I could prevail upon them to lay down their spears: this, at last, one of them did, and met me with a grass plant in his hand, one end of which he gave me to hold, while he held the other: standing in this manner, he began a speech, not one word of which I understood; and made some long pauses; waiting, as I thought, for me to answer; for when I spoke, he proceeded. As soon as this ceremony was over, which was not long, we saluted each other. He then took his *hahou*, or coat, from off his own back, and put it upon mine; after which, peace seemed firmly established. More people joining us did not in the least alarm them; on the contrary, they saluted every one as he came up.

I gave to each a hatchet and a knife, having nothing else with me: perhaps these were the most valuable things I could give them; at least they were the most useful. They wanted us to go to their habitation, telling us they would give us something to eat; and I was sorry that the tide, and other circumstances, would not permit me to accept of their invitation. More people were seen in the skirts of the wood, but none of them joined us, probably these were their wives and children. When we took leave they followed us to our boat, and seeing the muskets lying across the stern, they made signs for them to be taken away; which being done, they came alongside, and assisted us to launch her. At this time, it was necessary for us to look well after them, for they wanted to take away everything they could lay their hands upon, except the muskets; these they took care not to touch, being taught by the slaughter they had seen us make among the wild fowl, to look upon them as instruments of death.

We saw no canoes or other boats with them; two or three logs of wood tied together served the same purpose; and were indeed sufficient for the navigation of the river, on the banks of which they lived. There fish and fowl were in such plenty, that they had no occasion to go far for food; and they have but few neighbours to disturb them. The whole number at this place, I believe, does not exceed three families.

It was noon when we took leave of these two men, and proceeded down the north side of the bay; which I explored in my way, and the isles that lie in the middle; night, however, overtook us, and obliged me to leave one arm unlooked into, and hasten to the ship, which we reached by eight o'clock. I then learnt that the man and his daughter stayed on board the day before till noon; and that, having understood from our people what things were left in Cascade Cove, the place where they were first seen, he sent and took them away. He and his family remained near us till to-day, when they all went away, and we saw them no more; which was the more extraordinary, as he never left us empty-handed. From one or another he did not get less than nine or ten hatchets, three or four times that number of large spike nails, besides many other articles. So far as these things may be counted riches in New Zealand, he exceeds every man there; being at this time possessed of more hatchets and axes than are in the whole country besides.

May 11   As there are few places where I have been in New Zealand that afford the necessary refreshments in such plenty as Dusky Bay, a short description of it, and of the adjacent country, may prove of use to some future navigators, as well as acceptable to the curious reader. For although this country be far remote from the present trading part of the world, we can by no means tell what use future ages may make of the discoveries made in the present. . . .

The country is exceedingly mountainous; not only about Dusky Bay, but through all the southern part of this western coast of *Tavia Poenammoo*. A prospect more rude and craggy is rarely to be met with; for inland appears nothing but the summits of mountains of a stupendous height, and consisting of rocks that are totally barren and naked, except where they are covered with snow.[7] But the land bordering on the sea coast, and all the islands, are thickly clothed with wood, almost down to the water's edge. The trees are of various kinds, such as are common to other parts of this country, and are fit for the shipwright, house-carpenter, cabinet-maker, and many other uses. Except in the River Thames I have not seen finer timber in all New Zealand: both here and in that river, the most considerable for size is the spruce tree, as we called it, from the similarity of its foliage to the American spruce, though the wood is more ponderous and bears a greater resemblance to the pitch pine. Many of these trees are from six to eight, and ten feet in girt, and from sixty to eighty or one hundred feet in length; large enough to make a mainmast for a fifty-gun ship.

Here are, as well as in all other parts of New Zealand, a great

[7] Mount Cook, somewhat to the north of this point on the S.W. coast, is 12,349 feet high.

number of aromatic trees and shrubs, most of the myrtle kind; but amidst all this variety we met with none which bore fruit fit to eat.

In many parts the woods are so overrun with supple-jacks, that it is scarcely possible to force one's way amongst them. I have seen several which were fifty or sixty fathoms long.

The soil is a deep black mould, evidently composed of decayed vegetables, and so loose that it sinks under you at every step; and this may be the reason why we meet with so many large trees as we do, blown down by the wind, even in the thickest part of the woods. All the ground amongst the trees is covered with moss and fern, of both of which there is great variety; but except the flax or hemp plant, and a few other plants, there is very little herbage of any sort, and none that was eatable that we found, except about a handful of water-cresses, and about the same quantity of celery. What Dusky Bay most abounds with is fish: a boat with six or eight men with hooks and lines, caught daily sufficient to serve the whole ship's company: of this article the variety is almost equal to the plenty; and of such kinds as are common to the more northern coast; but some are superior; and in particular the cole fish, as we called it, which is both larger and finer flavoured than any I had seen before, and was, in the opinion of most on board, the highest luxury the sea afforded us. The shell fish are mussels, cockles, scallops, crayfish, and many other sorts; all such as are to be found in every other part of the coast. The only amphibious animals are seals; these are to be found in great numbers about this bay, on the small rocks and isles near the sea coast.

We found here five different kinds of duck, some of which I do not recollect to have anywhere seen before; the largest are as big as a Muscovy duck, with a very beautiful variegated plumage, on which account we called it the painted duck: both male and female have a large white spot on each wing; the head and neck of the latter is white, but all the other feathers, as well as those on the head and neck of the drake, are of a dark variegated colour. The second sort have a brown plumage, with bright green feathers in their wings, and are about the size of an English tame duck. The third sort is the blue-grey duck before mentioned, or the whistling duck, as some called them, from the whistling noise they made. What is most remarkable in these is, that the end of their beaks is soft, and of a skinny, or more properly, cartilaginous substance. The fourth sort is something bigger than teal, and all black except the drake, which has some white feathers in his wing. There are but few of this sort; and we saw them nowhere but in the river at the head of the bay. The last sort is a good deal like a teal, and very common I am told in England. The other fowls, whether belonging to the sea or land, are the same that are to be found in common in other parts of this country, except the blue petrel, before mentioned, and the water or wood hens: these last, although they are numerous enough here, are so scarce in other parts, that I never saw but one. The reason may be, that, as they cannot fly, they inhabit the skirts of the woods, and feed on the sea beach; and are so very tame or foolish, as to stand and stare at us till we knocked them down with a stick. The natives may have in a manner wholly destroyed them; they are a sort of rail, about the size, and a good deal like a common dunghill hen; most of them are of a dirty black or dark brown colour, and eat very well in a pie or fricassee. Amongst the small birds I must not omit to particularize the wattle-bird, poy-bird, and fan-tail, on account of their singularity, especially as I find they are not mentioned in the narrative of my former voyage.

The wattle-bird, so called because it has two wattles under its beak, as large as those of a small dunghill cock, is larger, particularly in length, than an English blackbird; its bill is short and thick, and its feathers of a dark lead colour; the colour of its wattles is a dull yellow, almost an orange colour.

The poy-bird is less than the wattle-bird; the feathers of a fine mazarine blue, except those of its neck, which are of a most beautiful silver-grey, and two or three short white ones, which are on the pinion-joint of the wing; under its throat hang two little tufts of curled snow-white feathers, called its *poies*, which being the Otaheitean word for earrings, occasioned our giving that name to the bird; which is not more remarkable for the beauty of its plumage than for the sweetness of its note; the flesh is also most delicious, and was the greatest luxury the woods afforded us.

Of the fan-tail, there are different sorts, but the body of the most remarkable one is scarcely larger than a good filbert, yet it spreads a tail of most beautiful plumage, full three-quarters of a semicircle, of at least four or five inches radius.

For three or four days after we arrived in Pickersgill Harbour, and as we were clearing the woods to set up our tents, etc., a four-footed animal was seen by three or four of our people; but as no two gave the same description of it, I cannot say of what kind it is; all, however, agreed, that it was about the size of a cat, with short legs, and of mouse colour: one of the seamen, and he who had the best view of it, said it had a bushy tail, and was the most like a jackal of any animal he knew. The most probable conjecture is, that it is of a new species; be this as it may, we are now certain, that this country is not so destitute of quadrupeds as was once thought.

The most mischievous animals here, are the small black sand flies, which are very numerous, and so troublesome, that they exceed everything of the kind I ever met with; wherever they bite they cause a swelling, and such an intolerable itching, that it is not possible to refrain from scratching, which at last brings on ulcers like the smallpox.

The almost continual rains may be reckoned another evil attending this bay; though, perhaps, this may only happen at this season of the year. Nevertheless, the situation of the country, the vast height, and nearness of the mountains, seem to subject it to much rain at all times. Our people, who were daily exposed to the rain, felt no ill effects from it; on the contrary, such as were sick and ailing when we came in, recovered daily, and the whole crew soon became strong and vigorous; which can only be attributed to the healthiness of the place, and the fresh provisions it afforded. The beer certainly contributed not a little: as I have already observed, we at first made it of a decoction of the spruce leaves; but finding that this alone made the beer too astringent, we afterwards mixed with it an equal quantity of the tea plant (a name it obtained in my former voyage, from our using it as tea then, as we also did now), which partly destroyed the astringency of the other, and made the beer exceedingly palatable, and esteemed by everyone on board. We brewed it in the same manner as spruce beer, and the process is as follows: first make a strong decoction of the small branches of the spruce and tea plants, by boiling them three or four hours, or until the bark will strip with ease from off the branches; then take them out of the copper, and put in the proper quantity of molasses; ten gallons of which is sufficient to make a ton or two hundred and forty gallons of beer; let this mixture just boil; then put it into the casks; and, to it, add an equal quantity of cold water, more or less according to the strength of the decoction, or your taste: when the whole is milk-warm, put in a little grounds of beer, or yeast, if you have it, or anything else that will cause fermentation, and in a few days the beer will be fit to drink. After the casks have been brewed in two or three times, the beer will generally ferment itself, especially if the weather is warm. As I had inspissated juice of wort on board, and could not apply it to a better purpose, we used it together with molasses or sugar, to make these two articles go further; for of the former I had but one cask, and of the latter little to spare for this brewing. Had I known how well this beer would have succeeded, and the great use it was of to the people, I should have come better provided; indeed I was partly discouraged by an experiment made during my former voyage; which did not succeed, then, owing, as I now believe, to some mismanagement.

Anyone who is in the least acquainted with spruce pines, will find the tree which I have distinguished by that name. There are three sorts of it; that which has the smallest leaves and deepest colours, is the sort we brewed with, but doubtless all three might safely serve that purpose. The tea plant is a small tree or shrub, with five white petals, or flower-leaves, shaped like those of a rose, having smaller ones of the same figure in the intermediate spaces, and twenty or more filaments or threads. The tree sometimes grows to a moderate height, and is generally bare on the lower part, with a number of small branches growing close together towards the top. The leaves are small and pointed, like those of the myrtle; it bears a dry roundish seed-case, and grows commonly in dry places near the shores. The leaves, as I have already observed, were used by many of us as tea, which has a very agreeable bitter flavour, when they are recent, but loses some of both when they are dried. When the infusion was made strong, it proved emetic to some, in the same manner as green tea.

The inhabitants of this bay are of the same race of people with those in the other parts of this country, speak the same language, and observe nearly the same customs. These, indeed, seem to have a custom of making presents before they receive any, in which they come nearer to the Otaheiteans than the rest of their countrymen. What could induce three or four families (for I believe there are not more) to separate themselves so far from the society of the rest of their fellow-creatures, is not easy to guess. By our meeting with inhabitants in this place, it seems probable, that there are people scattered over all this southern island. But the many vestiges of them in different parts of this bay, compared with the number that we actually saw, indicates that they live a wandering life; and, if one may judge from appearances and circumstances, few as they are, they live not in perfect amity one family with another. For, if they did, why do they not form themselves into some society? a thing not only natural to man, but observed even by the brute creation.

May 17   After leaving Dusky Bay, as has been already mentioned, I directed my course along shore for Queen Charlotte's Sound, where I expected to find the *Adventure*. In this passage we met with nothing remarkable or worthy of notice till the 17th, at four o'clock in the afternoon. Being then about three leagues to the westward of Cape Stephens, having a gentle gale at W. by S., and clear weather, the wind at once flattened to a calm, the sky became suddenly obscured by dark, dense clouds, and seemed to forebode much wind. This occasioned us to clew up all our sails, and presently after six waterspouts were seen. Four rose and spent themselves between us and the land; that is to the south-west of us; the fifth was without us; the sixth appeared in the south-west at the distance of two or three miles at least from us.

Its progressive motion was to the north-east, not in a straight, but in a crooked line, and passed within fifty yards of our stern, without our feeling any of its effects. The diameter of the base of this spout I judged to be about fifty or sixty feet; that is, the sea within this space was much agitated, and foamed up to a great height. From this a tube or round body was formed, by which the water or air, or both, was carried in a spiral stream up to the clouds. Some of our people said they saw a bird in the one near us; which was whirled round like the fly of a jack as it was carried upwards. During the time these spouts lasted, we had, now and then, light puffs of wind from all points of the compass; with some few slight showers of rain, which generally fell in large drops; and the weather continued thick and hazy, for some hours after, with variable light breezes of wind. At length the wind fixed in its old point, and the sky resumed its former serenity. Some of these spouts appeared, at times, to be stationary; and, at other times, to have a quick, but very unequal, progressive motion, and always in a crooked line, sometimes one way, and sometimes another; so that, once or twice, we observed them to cross one another. From the ascending motion of the bird, and several other circumstances, it was very plain to us that these spouts were caused by whirlwinds, and that the water in them was violently hurried upwards, and did not descend from the clouds, as I have heard some assert. . . .

At daylight the next morning (being the 18th) we appeared off Queen Charlotte's Sound, where we discovered our consort the *Adventure*, by the signals which she made to us; an event which everyone felt with an agreeable satisfaction. The fresh westerly wind now died away, and was succeeded by light airs from the south and south-west so that we had to work in, with our boats ahead towing. In the doing of this, we discovered a rock, which we did not see in my former voyage. It lies in the direction of S. by E. ½ E. distant four miles from the outermost of the Two Brothers, and in a line with the White Rocks, on with the middle of Long Island. It is just even with the surface of the sea, and has deep water all round it. At noon, Lieutenant Kempe of the *Adventure* came on board;

from whom I learnt that their ship had been here about six weeks. With the assistance of a light breeze, our boats, and the tides, we, at six o'clock in the evening, got to an anchor in Ship Cove near the *Adventure*; when Captain Furneaux came on board, and gave me the following account of his proceedings, from the time we parted, to my arrival here.

"On February 7th, 1773, in the morning, the *Resolution* being then about two miles ahead, the wind shifting then to the westward, brought on a very thick fog, so that we lost sight of her. We soon after heard a gun, the report of which we imagined to be on the larboard beam; we then hauled up S.E. and kept firing a four-pounder every half-hour; but had no answer, nor further sight of her; then we kept the course we steered on before the fog came on. In the evening it began to blow hard, and was, at intervals, more clear; but could see nothing of her, which gave us much uneasiness. We then tacked and stood to the westward, to cruise in the place where we last saw her, according to agreement in case of separation; but, next day, came on a very heavy gale of wind and thick weather, that obliged us to bring to, and thereby prevented us reaching the intended spot. However, the wind coming more moderate, and the fog in some measure clearing away, we cruised as near the place as we could get, for three days; when giving over all hopes of joining company again, we bore away for winter quarters, distant fourteen hundred leagues, through a sea entirely unknown, and reduced the allowance of water to one quart per day. . . .

"While we lay here,[8] we saw several smokes and large fires, about eight or ten miles inshore to the northward, but did not see any of the natives; though they frequently come into this bay, as there were several wigwams or huts, where we found some bags and nets made of grass, in which I imagine they carry their provisions and other necessaries. In one of them there was the stone they strike fire with, and tinder made of bark, but of what tree could not be distinguished. We found in one of their huts, one of their spears, which was made sharp at one end, I

[8] *i.e.* Tasmania. The natives of the island are now extinct.

suppose, with a shell or stone. Those things we brought away, leaving in the room of them, medals, gun-flints, a few nails, and an old empty barrel with the iron hoops on it. They seem to be quite ignorant of every sort of metal. The boughs, of which their huts are made, are either broken or split, and tied together with grass in a circular form, the largest end stuck in the ground, and the smaller parts meeting in a point at the top, and covered with fern and bark; so poorly done that they will hardly keep out a shower of rain. In the middle is the fireplace, surrounded with heaps of mussel, pearl scallop, and crayfish shells; which I believe to be their chief food, though we could not find any of them. They lie on the ground, on dried grass, round the fire; and, I believe, they have no settled place of habitation (as their houses seemed built only for a few days), but wander about in small parties from place to place in search of food, and are actuated by no other motive. We never found more than three or four huts in a place, capable of containing three or four persons each only; and what is remarkable, we never saw the least marks either of canoe or boat, and it is generally thought they have none; being altogether, from what we could judge, a very ignorant and wretched set of people, though natives of a country capable of producing every necessary of life, and a climate the finest in the world. We found not the least signs of any minerals or metals.

"Having completed our wood and water, we sailed from Adventure Bay, intending to coast it up along shore, till we should fall in with the land seen by Captain Cook, and discover whether Van Diemen's Land joins with New Holland. On the 16th we passed Maria's Islands, so named by Tasman; they appear to be the same as the mainland. On the 17th, having passed Schouten's Islands, we hauled in for the mainland, and stood along shore at the distance of two or three leagues off. The country here appears to be very thickly inhabited, as there was a continual fire along shore as we sailed. The land hereabouts is much pleasanter, low and even; but no signs of a harbour or bay, where a ship might anchor with safety. The weather being bad, and blowing hard at S.S.E., we could not send a boat on shore to have any intercourse with the inhabitants. In the latitude of 40°

50' S., the land trenches away to the westward, which I believe forms a deep bay, as we saw from the deck several smokes arising aback of the islands that lay before it, when we could not see the least signs of land from the mast head.

"From the latitude of 40° 50' S., to the latitude of 39° 50' S., is nothing but islands and shoals; the land high, rocky, and barren. On the 19th, in the latitude of 40° 30' S., observing breakers about half a mile within shore of us, we sounded, and finding but eight fathoms, immediately hauled off, deepened our water to fifteen fathoms, then bore away, and kept along shore again. From the latitude of 39° 50' to 39° S. we saw no land, but had regular soundings from fifteen to thirty fathoms. As we stood on to the northward, we made land again in about 39°; after which we discontinued our northerly course, as we found the ground very uneven, and shoal water some distance off. I think it a very dangerous shore to fall in with.

"The coast, from Adventure Bay to the place where we stood away for New Zealand, lies in the direction S. ½ W. and N. ½ E. about seventy-five leagues; and it is my opinion that there is no straits between New Holland and Van Diemen's Land, but a very deep bay.[9] I should have stood farther to the northward, but the wind blowing strong at S.S.E., and looking likely to haul round to the eastward, which would have blown right on the land, I therefore thought it more proper to leave the coast, and steer for New Zealand."

June 7   Both ships being now ready for sea, I gave Captain Furneaux an account in writing of the route I intended to take; which was to proceed to the east, between the latitudes of 41° and 46° S., until I arrived in the longitude of 140° or 135° W.; then, provided no land was discovered, to proceed to Otaheite; from thence back to this place by the shortest route; and after taking in wood and water, to proceed to the south, and explore all the unknown parts of the sea between the meridian of New Zealand and Cape Horn; therefore, in case of separation before

---

[9] George Bass discovered the strait in 1798 in an open boat voyage lasting eleven weeks.

we reached Otaheite, I appointed that island for the place of rendezvous, where he was to wait till August 20th: if not joined by me before that time, he was then to make the best of his way back to Queen Charlotte's Sound, where he was to wait until November 20th; after which (if not joined by me) he was to put to sea, and carry into execution their lordships' instructions.

Some may think it an extraordinary step in me to proceed on discoveries as far south as 46° of latitude, in the very depth of winter. But though it must be owned, that winter is by no means favourable for discoveries, it nevertheless appeared to me necessary that something should be done in it, in order to lessen the work I was upon, lest I should not be able to finish the discovery of the southern part of the South Pacific Ocean the ensuing summer. Besides, if I should discover any land in my route to the east, I should be ready to begin, with the summer, to explore it. Setting aside all these considerations, I had little to fear; having two good ships well provided, and healthy crews. Where then could I spend my time better? If I did nothing more, I was at least in hopes of being able to point out to posterity, that these seas may be navigated, and that it is practicable to go on discoveries, even in the very depth of winter.

During our stay in the sound, I had observed that this second visit made to this country, had not mended the morals of the natives of either sex. I had always looked upon the females of New Zealand to be more chaste than the generality of Indian women. Whatever favours a few of them might have granted to the people in the *Endeavour*, it was generally done in a private manner, and the men did not seem to interest themselves much in it; but now I was told they were the chief promoters of a shameful traffic, and that, for a spike nail, or any other thing they value, they would oblige the women to prostitute themselves, whether they would or no; and even without any regard to that privacy which decency required.

During our stay here Mr. Wales lost no opportunity to observe equal altitudes of the sun, for obtaining the rates of the watches. The result of his labours proved that Mr. Kendal's was gaining

9″, 5 per day, and Mr. Arnold's losing 94″, 158 per day, on mean time.

On June 7th, at four in the morning, the wind being more favourable, we unmoored, and at seven weighed and put to sea, with the *Adventure* in company.

July 29　On the 29th, I sent on board the *Adventure* to inquire into the state of her crew, having heard that they were sickly, and this I now found was but too true; her cook was dead, and about twenty of her best men were down in the scurvy and flux. At this time, *we* had only three men on the sick list, and only one of them attacked with the scurvy; several more, however, began to show symptoms of it, and were accordingly put upon the wort, marmalade of carrots, rob of lemons and oranges.

I know not how to account for the scurvy raging more in the one ship than the other, unless it was owing to the crew of the *Adventure* being more scorbutic when they arrived in New Zealand than we were, and to their eating few or no vegetables while they lay in Queen Charlotte's Sound, partly for want of knowing the right sorts, and partly because it was a new diet, which alone was sufficient for seamen to reject it. To introduce any new article of food among seamen, let it be ever so much for their good, requires both the example and authority of a commander; without both of which, it will be dropped before the people are sensible of the benefits resulting from it: were it necessary, I could name fifty instances in support of this remark. Many of my people, officers as well as seamen, at first disliked celery, scurvy-grass, etc., being boiled in the peas and wheat; and some refused to eat it; but as this had no effect on my conduct, this obstinate kind of prejudice, by little and little, wore off; they began to like it as well as the others and now, I believe, there was hardly a man in the ship that did not attribute our being so free from the scurvy, to the beer and vegetables we made use of at New Zealand; after this, I seldom found it necessary to order any of my people to gather vegetables, whenever we came where any were to be got, and if scarce, happy was he who could lay hold on them first. I appointed one of my seamen to be cook of the *Adventure*, and wrote to Captain Furneaux, desiring him to make use of every method in his power to stop the spreading of the disease amongst his people, and proposing such as I thought might tend towards it; but I afterwards found all this unnecessary, as every method had been used they could think of.

The wind continued in the north-west quarter, and blew fresh, at times, attended with rain; with which we stood to the N.E. On August 1st, at noon, we were in the latitude of 25° 1', longitude 134° 6' W., and had a great hollow swell from N.W. The situation we were now in, was nearly the same that Captain Cartaret assigns for Pitcairn's Island, discovered by him in 1767.[10] We therefore looked well out for it; but saw nothing. According to the longitude in which he has placed it, we must have passed about fifteen leagues to the west of it. But as this was uncertain, I did not think it prudent, considering the situation of the *Adventure's* people, to lose any time in looking for it. A sight of it would, however, have been of use in verifying or correcting, not only the longitude of this island, but of the others that Captain Cartaret discovered in this neighbourhood; his longitude not being confirmed, I think, by astronomical observations, and therefore liable to errors, which he could have no method to correct.

As we had now got to the northward of Captain Cartaret's tracks, all hopes of discovering a continent vanished. Islands were all we were to expect to find, until we returned again to the south. I had now, that is on this and my former voyage, crossed this ocean in the latitude of 40° and upwards, without meeting anything that did, in the least, induce me to think I should find what I was in search after. On the contrary, everything conspired to make me believe there is no southern continent, between the meridian of America and New Zealand; at least, this passage did not produce any indubitable signs of any, as will appear by the following remarks. After leaving the coasts of New Zealand, we daily saw, floating in the sea, rock-weed, for the space of 18° of longitude. In my passage to New Zealand in 1769, we also saw

---

[10] "Carteret" is the correct spelling. He named the island after the officer who sighted it. It was here that the *Bounty* mutineers found refuge. The correct position is 25° 3' S., 130° 8' W.

of this weed, for the space of 12° or 14° of longitude, before we made the land. The weed is, undoubtedly, the produce of New Zealand; because, the nearer the coast, the greater quantity you see. At the greatest distance from the coast, we saw it only in small pieces, generally more rotten, and covered with barnacles; an indubitable sign that it had been long at sea. Were it not for this, one might be led to conjecture that some other large land lay in the neighbourhood; for it cannot be a small extent of coast to produce such a quantity of weed, as to cover so large a space or sea. It has been already mentioned, that we were no sooner clear of the Straits, than we met with a large hollow swell from the south-east which continued till we arrived in the longitude of 177° W., and latitude 46°. There we had large billows from the north and north-east for five days successively, and until we got 5° of longitude more to the east, although the wind, great part of the time, blew from different directions. This was a strong indication that there was no land between us and my track to the west in 1769. After this, we had, as is usual in all great oceans, large billows from every direction in which the wind blew a fresh gale, but more especially from the south-west. These billows never ceased with the cause that first put them in motion; a sure indication, that we were not near any large land, and that there is no continent to the south, unless in a very high latitude. But this was too important a point to be left to opinions and conjectures. Facts were to determine it; and these could only be obtained by visiting the southern parts; which was to be the work of the ensuing summer, agreeably to the plan I had laid down.

As the winds continued to blow from the north-west and west, we had no other choice but to stand to the north, inclining more or less every day to the east.[11]

August 15   On the 15th, at five o'clock in the morning, we saw

[11] A few days later Cook writes "The sickly state of the *Adventure's* crew made it necessary for me to make the best of my way to Otaheite." On the way thither they passed many small islands discovered by Bougainville, whose account he criticises thus: "What excuse can M. de Bougainville have for not once mentioning the situation of any one place in his whole run through this sea; this is what he seems carefully to have avoided, for reasons which can only be known to himself."

Osnaburg Island or Maitea, discovered by Captain Wallis, bearing S. by W. ½ W. Soon after I brought to, and waited for the *Adventure* to come up with us, to acquaint Captain Furneaux, that it was my intention to put into Oaiti-piha Bay [Waitepeha], near the south-east end of Otaheite, in order to get what refreshments we could from that part of the island, before we went down to Matavai. This done, we made sail, and at six in the evening saw the island bearing west. We continued to stand on till midnight, when we brought to, till four o'clock in the morning; and then made sail in for the land with a fine breeze at east.

At daybreak we found ourselves not more than half a league from the reef. The breeze now began to fail us, and at last fell to a calm. This made it necessary to hoist out our boats to tow the ships off; but all their efforts were not sufficient to keep them from being carried near the reef. A number of the inhabitants came off in canoes from different parts, bringing with them a little fish, a few coconuts, and other fruits, which they exchanged for nails, beads, etc. The most of them knew me again; and many inquired for Mr. Banks and others who were with me before; but not one asked for Tupia. As the calm continued, our situation became still more dangerous. We were, however, not without hopes of getting round the western point of the reef and into the bay till about two o'clock in the afternoon, when we came before an opening or break in the reef, through which I hoped to get with the ships. But on sending to examine it, I found there was not a sufficient depth of water; though it caused such an indraught of the tide of flood through it, as was very near proving fatal to the the *Resolution*; for as soon as the ships got into this stream, they were carried with great impetuosity towards the reef. The moment I perceived this, I ordered one of the warping machines, which we had in readiness, to be carried out with about four hundred fathoms of rope; but it had not the least effect. The horrors of shipwreck now stared us in the face. We were not more than two cables' length from the breakers; and yet we could find no bottom to anchor, the only probable means we had left to save the ships. We however dropped an anchor; but, before it took hold, and brought us up, the ship was in less than three fathoms of water, and struck at every fall of the sea, which broke close under our stern in a dreadful surf, and threatened us every moment with shipwreck. The *Adventure*, very luckily, brought up close upon our bow without striking.

We presently carried out two kedge anchors, with hawsers to each. These found ground a little without the bower, but in what depth we never knew. By heaving upon them, and cutting away the bower anchor, we got the ship afloat, where we lay some time in the greatest anxiety, expecting every minute that either the kedges would come home, or the hawsers be cut in two by the rocks. At length the tide ceased to act in the same direction. I ordered all the boats to try to tow off the *Resolution*; and when I saw this was practicable, we hove up the two kedges. At that moment, a light air came off from the land, which so much assisted the boats, that we soon got clear of all danger. Then I ordered all the boats to assist the *Adventure*; but before they reached her, she was under sail with the land breeze, and soon after joined us, leaving behind her three anchors, her coasting cable, and two hawsers, which were never recovered. Thus we were once more safe at sea, after narrowly escaping being wrecked on the very island we, but a few days before, so ardently wished to be at. The calm, after bringing us into this dangerous situation, very fortunately continued; for had the sea breeze, as is usual, set in, the *Resolution* must inevitably have been lost, and probably the *Adventure* too.

During the time we were in this critical situation, a number of the natives were on board and about the ships; they seemed to be insensible of our danger, showing not the least surprise, joy, or fear, when we were striking, and left us little before sunset, quite unconcerned.

We spent the night, which proved squally and rainy, making short boards [tacks]; and the next morning, being the 17th, we anchored in Oaiti-piha Bay in twelve fathoms of water, about two cables' length from the shore; both ships being by this time crowded with a great number of the natives, who brought with them coconuts, plantains, bananas, apples, yams, and other roots, which they exchanged for nails and beads. To several who called themselves chiefs, I made presents of shirts, axes, and several other articles; and in return, they promised to bring me hogs and fowls; a promise they never did, nor ever intended to perform.

In the afternoon I landed, in company with Captain Furneaux, in order to view the watering-place, and to sound the disposition of the natives. I also sent a boat to get some water for present use, having scarcely any left on board. We found this article as convenient as could be expected, and the natives to behave with great civility.

Early in the morning I sent the two launches, and the *Resolution's* cutter, under the command of Mr. Gilbert, to endeavour to recover the anchors we had left behind us. They returned about noon with the *Resolution's* bower anchor; but could not recover any of the *Adventure's*. The natives came off again with fruit, as the day before, but in no great quantity. I also had a party on shore, trading under the protection of a guard; nothing, however, was brought to market but fruit and roots, though many hogs were seen (I was told) about the houses of the natives. The cry was that they belonged to Waheatoua [Vehiatua] the *Earee de hi*, or king; and him we had not yet seen, nor, I believe, any other chief of note; many, however, who called themselves *Earees*, came on board, partly with a view of getting presents, and partly to pilfer whatever came in their way.

One of this sort of *Earees* I had, most of the day, in the cabin, and made presents to him and all his friends, which were not a few. At length he was caught taking things which did not belong to him, and handing them out of the quarter-gallery. Many complaints of the like nature were made to me against those on deck; which occasioned my turning them all out of the ship. My cabin guest made good haste to be gone. I was so much exasperated at his behaviour, that after he had got some distance from the ship, I fired two muskets over his head, which made him quit the canoe, and take to the water. I then sent a boat to take up the canoe; but as she came near the shore, the people from thence began to pelt her with stones. Being in some pain for her safety, as she was unarmed, I went myself in another boat to protect her, and ordered a great gun, loaded with ball, to be fired along the coast, which made them all retire from the shore, and I was suffered to bring away two canoes without the least show of opposition. In one of the canoes was a little boy, who was much frightened; but I soon dissipated his fears, by giving him beads, and putting him on shore. A few hours after we were all good friends again; and the canoes were returned to the first person who came for them.

It was not till the evening of this day that anyone inquired after Tupia, and then but two or three. As soon as they learnt the cause of his death, they were quite satisfied; indeed, it did not appear to me, that it would have caused a moment's uneasiness in the breast of anyone, had his death been occasioned by any other means than by sickness. As little inquiry was made after Aotourou, the man who went away with M. de Bougainville; but they were continually asking for Mr. Banks, and several others who were with me in my former voyage.

These people informed us, that Toutaha, the regent of the greater peninsula of Otaheite, had been killed in a battle, which was fought between the two kingdoms about five months before; and that Otoo was the reigning prince. Tubourai Tamaide, and several more of our principal friends about Matavai, fell in this battle, as also a great number of common people; but at present, a peace subsisted between the two kingdoms.[12] . . .

In the evening I was informed that Waheatoua was come into the neighbourhood, and wanted to see me. In consequence of this information, I determined to wait one day longer in order to have an interview with this prince. Accordingly, early the next morning, I set out in company with Captain Furneaux, Mr. Forster, and several of the natives. We met the chief about a mile from the landing-place, towards which he was advancing to meet us; but as soon as he saw us he stopped, with his numerous train in the open air. I found him seated upon a stool, with a circle of people round him, and knew him at first sight and he me; having seen each other several times in 1769. At that time he was but

[12] In consequence of a civil war fought during Cook's absence, there were now two independent kingdoms in the island of Tahiti. Vehiatua ruled over the eastern one, and Otu over the western. For the fate of Aotourou, see above, p. 114, note 2.

a boy, and went by the name of Tearee, but upon the death of his father Waheatoua, he took upon him that name.

After the first salutation was over, having seated me on the same stool with himself, and the other gentlemen on the ground by us, he began to inquire after several by name who were with me on my former voyage. He next inquired how long I would stay; and when I told him no longer than next day, he seemed sorry, asked me to stay some months, and at last came down to five days; promising that, in that time, I should have hogs in plenty. But as I had been here already a week, without so much as getting one, I could not put any faith in this promise. And yet, I believe, if I had stayed, we should have fared much better than at Matavai. The present I made him consisted of a shirt, a sheet, a broad axe, spike nails, knives, looking-glasses, medals, beads, etc. In return, he ordered a pretty good hog to be carried to our boat. We stayed with him all the morning, during which time he never suffered me to go from his side, where he was seated. I was also seated on the same stool, which was carried from place to place by one of his attendants, whom we called stool-bearer. At length we took leave, in order to return on board to dinner; after which we visited him again, and made him more presents; and he in return gave Captain Furneaux and me each of us an hog. Some others were got by exchanges at the trading places: so that we got, in the whole to-day, as much fresh pork as gave the crews of both ships a meal; and this in consequence of our having this interview with the chief.

The 24th, early in the morning, we put to sea with a light land-breeze. Soon after we were out, we got the wind at west, which blew in squalls, attended with heavy showers of rain. Many canoes accompanied us out to sea with coconuts, and other fruits; and did not leave us till they had disposed of their cargoes.

The fruits we got here greatly contributed towards the recovery of the *Adventure's* sick people. Many of them who had been so ill as not to be able to move without assistance, were, in this short time, so far recovered, that they could walk about of themselves. When we put in here, the *Resolution* had but one scorbutic man on board, and a marine, who had long been sick, and who died, the second day after our arrival, of a complication of disorders without the least mixture of the scurvy.

August 26   After having given directions to pitch tents for the reception of the sick, coopers, sail-makers, and the guard, I set out on the 26th for Oparree;[13] accompanied by Captain Furneaux, Mr. Forster, and others, Maritata and his wife. As soon as we landed, we were conducted to Otoo, whom we found seated on the ground, under the shade of a tree, with an immense crowd round him. After the first compliments were over, I presented him with such articles as I guessed were most valuable in his eyes; well knowing that it was my interest to gain the friendship of this man. I also made presents to several of his attendants; and, in return, they offered me cloth, which I refused to accept; telling them that what I had given was for *tiyo* (friendship). The king inquired for Tupia, and all the gentlemen that were with me in my former voyage, by name; although I do not remember that he was personally acquainted with any of us. He promised that I should have some hogs the next day; but I had much ado to obtain a promise from him to visit on board. He said he was *mataou no to poupoue*, that is, afraid of the guns. Indeed, all his actions showed him to be a timorous prince. He was about thirty years of age, six feet high, and a fine, personable, well-made man as one can see. All his subjects appeared uncovered before him, his father not excepted. What is meant by uncovering, is the making bare the head and shoulders, or wearing no sort of clothing above the breast.

When I returned from Oparree, I found the tents, and the astronomer's observatories, set up, on the same spot where we observed the transit of Venus in 1769. In the afternoon I had the sick landed; twenty from the *Adventure*, all ill of the scurvy; and one from the *Resolution*. I also landed some marines for a guard, and left the command to Lieutenant Edgcumbe of the marines.

On the 27th, early in the morning, Otoo, attended by a numerous train, paid me a visit. He first sent into the ship a large

---

[13] The ships were now anchored in Matavai Bay, Tahiti; Maritata was one of the chiefs.

quantity of cloth, fruits, a hog, and two large fish; and, after some persuasion, came aboard himself, with his sister, a younger brother, and several more of his attendants. To all of them I made presents; and, after breakfast, took the king, his sister, and as many more as I had room for, into my boat and carried them home to Oparree. I had no sooner landed than I was met by a venerable old lady, the mother of the late Toutaha. She seized me by both hands, and burst into a flood of tears, saying, *Toutaha Tiyo no Toutee matty Toutaha*—(Toutaha, your friend, or the friend of Cook, is dead). I was so much affected with her behaviour, that it would have been impossible for me to have refrained mingling my tears with hers, had not Otoo come and taken me from her. I, with some difficulty, prevailed on him to let me see her again, when I gave her an axe and some other things. Captain Furneaux, who was with me, presented the king with two fine goats, male and female, which, if taken care of, or rather if no care at all is taken of them, will no doubt multiply. After a short stay we took leave and returned on board.

September 7   Before we quitted this island[14] Captain Furneaux agreed to receive on board his ship a young man named Omai, a native of Ulietea, where he had had some property, of which he had been dispossessed by the people of Bolabola. I at first rather wondered that Captain Furneaux would encumber himself with this man, who, in my opinion, was not a proper sample of the inhabitants of these happy islands, not having any advantage of birth, or acquired rank, nor being eminent in shape, figure, or complexion. For their people of the first rank are much fairer, and usually better behaved, and more intelligent, than the middling class of people, among whom Omai is to be ranked. I have, however, since my arrival in England, been convinced of my error: for, excepting his complexion (which is undoubtedly of a

---

[14] *i.e.* Huaheine, west of Tahiti, reached on September 3rd. Omai returned to England in the *Adventure*. He was introduced to London society by Lieutenant James Burney, brother of Fanny Burney, in whose early diary he makes a frequent appearance. Boswell reports Johnson saying of Omai, " Sir, he had passed his time in England only in the best company; so that all that he had acquired of our manners was genteel."

deeper hue than that of the *earees* or gentry, who, as in other countries, live a more luxurious life, and are less exposed to the heat of the sun), I much doubt whether any other of the natives would have given more general satisfaction by his behaviour among us. Omai has most certainly a very good understanding, quick parts, and honest principles; he has a natural good behaviour, which rendered him acceptable to the best company, and a proper degree of pride, which taught him to avoid the society of persons of inferior rank. He has passions of the same kind as other young men, but has judgment enough not to indulge them in an improper excess. I do not imagine that he has any dislike to liquor; and if he had fallen into company where the person who drank the most met with the most approbation, I have no doubt but that he would have endeavoured to gain the applause of those with whom he associated; but, fortunately for him, he perceived that drinking was very little in use but among inferior people, and as he was very watchful into the manners and conduct of the persons of rank who honoured him with their protection, he was sober and modest; and I never heard that, during the whole time of his stay in England, which was two years, he ever once was disguised with wine, or ever showed an inclination to go beyond the strictest rules of moderation.

Soon after his arrival in London, the Earl of Sandwich, the First Lord of the Admiralty, introduced him to His Majesty at Kew, when he met with a most gracious reception, and imbibed the strongest impression of duty and gratitude to that great and amiable prince, which I am persuaded he will preserve to the latest moment of his life. During his stay among us he was caressed by many of the principal nobility, and did nothing to forfeit the esteem of any one of them; but his principal patrons were the Earl of Sandwich, Mr. Banks, and Dr. Solander: the formtr probably thought it a duty of his office to protect and couneenance an inhabitant of that hospitable country, where the wants and distresses of those in his department had been alleviated and supplied in the most ample manner; the others, as a testimony of their gratitude for the generous reception they had met with during their residence in his country. It is to be observed, that though Omai lived in the midst of amusements during his residence in England, his return to his native country was always in his thoughts, and though he was not impatient to go, he expressed a satisfaction as the time of his return approached. He embarked with me in the *Resolution*, when she was fitted out for another voyage, loaded with presents from his several friends, and full of gratitude for the kind reception and treatment he had experienced among us.

AN ACCOUNT OF THE PRESENT STATE OF THE SOCIETY ISLANDS

I shall now give some further account of these islands; for, although I have been pretty minute in relating the daily transactions, some things, which are rather interesting, have been omitted.

Soon after our arrival at Otaheite, we were informed that a ship, about the size of the *Resolution*, had been in at Owhaiurua harbour near the south-east end of the island, where she remained about three weeks; and had been gone about three months before we arrived. We were told that four of the natives were gone away in her, whose names were Debedebea, Paoodou, Tanadooee, and Opahiah. At this time we conjectured this was a French ship; but on our arrival at the Cape of Good Hope, we learnt she was a Spaniard, which had been sent out from America.[15] The Otaheiteans complained of a disease communicated to them by the people in this ship, which they said affected the head, throat, and stomach, and at length killed them. They seemed to dread it much and were continually inquiring if we had it. This ship they distinguished by the name of *Pahai no Pep-pe* (ship of Peppe), and called the disease *Apa no Pep-pe*, just as they call the venereal disease *Apa no Pretane* (English disease), though they, to a man, say it was brought to the island by M. de Bougainville; but I have

[15] This was the *Aguila*, commanded by Don Domingo Boenechea in 1772. This frigate visited Tahiti on four occasions under the command of different captains, once in 1772 between Cook's first and second voyages, three times in 1774 and 1775, between his second and third. The purpose was to annex Tahiti and Easter Island.

already observed that they thought M. Bougainville came from *Pretane*, as well as every other ship which has touched at the island.

Were it not for this assertion of the natives, and none of Captain Wallis's people being affected with the venereal disease, either while they were at Otaheite, or after they left it, I should have concluded that, long before these islanders were visited by Europeans, this, or some disease which is near akin to it, had existed amongst them; for I have heard them speak of people dying of a disorder which we interpreted to be the pox, before that period; but be this as it will, it is now far less common amongst them than it was in the year 1769, when I first visited these islands. They say they can cure it, and so it fully appears; for, notwithstanding most of my people made pretty free with the women, very few of them were afterwards affected with the disorder; and those who were had it in so slight a manner that it was easily removed; but amongst the natives, whenever it turns to a pox, they tell us it is incurable. Some of our people pretend to have seen some of them who had this last disorder in a high degree; but the surgeon, who made it his business to inquire, could never satisfy himself in this point. These people are, and were before the Europeans visited them, very subject to scrophulous diseases; so that a seaman might easily mistake one disorder for another.

The island of Otaheite which, in the years 1767 and 1768, as it were, swarmed with hogs and fowls, was now so ill supplied with these animals, that hardly anything could induce the owners to part with them. The few they had at this time among them, seemed to be at the disposal of the kings; for while we lay at Oaitipiha Bay, in the kingdom of Tiarrabou, or lesser Peninsula, every hog or fowl we saw, we were told, belonged to Waheatoua; and all we saw in the kingdom of Opoureonu, or the greater Peninsula, belonged to Otoo. During the seventeen days we were at this island, we got but twenty-four hogs; the half of which came from the two kings themselves; and, I believe, the other half was sold us by their permission or order: we were, however, abundantly supplied with all the fruits the island produces, except bread fruit, which was not in season either at this or the other islands. Coconuts and plantains were what we got the most of;

the latter, together with a few yams and other roots, were to us a succedaneum for bread. At Otaheite we got great plenty of apples, and a fruit like a nectarine, called by them *Aheeya*. This fruit was common to all the islands; but apples we got only at Otaheite, and found them of infinite use to the scorbutic people. Of all the seeds that have been brought to these islands by Europeans, none have succeeded but pumpkins, and these they do not like; which is not to be wondered at.

The scarcity of hogs at Otaheite may be owing to two causes; first, the number which have been consumed and carried off by the shipping which have touched here of late years; and, secondly, to the frequent wars between the two kingdoms. We know of two since the year 1767: at present a peace subsists between them, though they do not seem to entertain much friendship for each other. I never could learn the cause of the late war, nor who got the better in the conflict. In the battle, which put an end to the dispute, many were killed on both sides. On the part of Opoureo-nu, fell Toutaha, and several other chiefs, who were mentioned to me by name. Toutaha lies interred in the family *marai* at Oparree; and his mother, and several other women who were of his household, are now taken care of by Otoo the reigning prince; a man who, at first, did not appear to us to much advantage. I know but little of Waheatoua of Tiarrabou. This prince, who is not above twenty years of age, appeared with all the gravity of a man of fifty. His subjects do not uncover before him, or pay him any outward obeisance, as is done to Otoo; nevertheless, they seem to show him full as much respect, and he appeared in rather more state. He was attended by a few middle-aged or elderly men, who seemed to be his counsellors. This is what appeared to me to be the then state of Otaheite. The other islands, that is, Huaheine, Ulietea, and Otaha, were in a more flourishing state than they were when I was there before. Since that time, they had enjoyed the blessing of peace; the people seemed to be as happy as any under heaven; and well they may, for they possess not only the necessaries, but many of the luxuries of life in the greatest profusion; and my young man told me that hogs, fowls, and fruits are in equal plenty at Bola-bola, a thing which Tupia would never allow. To clear up this seeming contradiction, I must observe, that the one was prejudiced against, and the other in favour of, this island.

The produce of the islands, the manners and customs of the natives, etc., having been treated at large in the narrative of my former voyage, it will be unnecessary to take notice of these subjects in this, unless where I can add new matter, or clear up any mistakes which may have been committed.

As I had some reason to believe, that amongst their religious customs, human sacrifices were sometimes considered as necessary, I went one day to a *Marai* in Matavai, in company with Captain Furneaux; having with us, as I had upon all other occasions, one of my men who spoke their language tolerably well, and several of the natives, one of whom appeared to be an intelligent, sensible man. In the *Marai* was a *Tupapow*, on which lay a corpse and some viands; so that everything promised success to my inquiries. I began with asking questions relating to the several objects before me, if the plantains, etc., were for the *Eatua*? If they sacrificed to the *Eatua*, hogs, dogs, fowls, etc., to all of which he answered in the affirmative. I then asked, If they sacrificed men to the *Eatua*? He answered, *Taata eno*; that is, bad men they did, first *Tiparrahy*, or beating them till they were dead. I then asked him, If good men were put to death in this manner? His answer was, No, only *Taata eno*. I asked him, If any *Earees* were? He said, they had hogs to give to the *Eatua*, and again repeated *Taata eno*. I next asked him, If *Towtows*, that is, servants or slaves, who had no hogs, dogs, or fowls, but yet were good men, if they were sacrificed to the *Eatua*? His answer was, No, only bad men. I asked him several more questions, and all his answers seemed to tend to this one point, that men for certain crimes were condemned to be sacrificed to the gods, provided they had not wherewithal to redeem themselves. This, I think, implies that, on some occasions, human sacrifices are considered as necessary; particularly when they take such men as have, by the laws of the country, forfeited their lives, and have nothing to redeem them; and such will generally be found among the lower class of people.

The man of whom I made these inquiries, as well as some others, took some pains to explain the whole of this custom to us; but we were not masters enough of their language to understand them. I have since learnt from Omai, that they offer human sacrifices to the Supreme Being. According to his account, what men shall be so sacrificed, depends on the caprice of the high priest, who, when they are assembled on any solemn occasion, retires alone into the house of God, and stays there some time. When he comes out he informs them, that he has seen and conversed with their great god (the high priest alone having that privilege), and that he has asked for a human sacrifice, and tells them that he has desired such a person, naming a man present, whom most probably the priest has an antipathy against. He is immediately killed, and so falls a victim to the priest's resentment, who, no doubt (if necessary), has address enough to persuade the people that he was a bad man. If I except their funeral ceremonies, all the knowledge that has been obtained of their religion, has been from information; and as their language is but imperfectly understood, even by those who pretend to the greatest knowledge of it, very little on this head is yet known with certainty.

The liquor which they make from the plant called *Ava ava*, is expressed from the root, and not from the leaves, as mentioned in the narrative of my former voyage. The manner of preparing this liquor is as simple as it is disgusting to a European. It is thus: several people take some of the root and chew it till it is soft and pulpy; then they spit it out into a platter or other vessel, everyone into the same; when a sufficient quantity is chewed, more or less water is put to it, according as it is to be strong or weak; the juice thus diluted is strained through some fibrous stuff like fine shavings; after which it is fit for drinking, and this is always done immediately. It has a pepperish taste, drinks flat, and rather insipid. But though it is intoxicating, I saw only one instance where it had that effect; as they generally drink it with great moderation, and but little at a time. Sometimes they chew this root in their mouths, as Europeans do tobacco, and swallow their spittle; and sometimes I have seen them eat it wholly.

At Ulietea they cultivate great quantities of this plant. At Otaheite but very little. I believe there are but few islands in this sea, that do not produce more or less of it; and the natives apply it to the same use, as appears by Le Maire's account of Horn Island, wherein he speaks of the natives making a liquor from a plant in the same manner as above mentioned.

Great injustice has been done to the women of Otaheite, and the Society Isles, by those who have represented them, without exception, as ready to grant the last favour to any man who will come up to their price. But this is by no means the case: the favours of married women, and also the unmarried of the better sort, are as difficult to be obtained here, as in any other country whatever. Neither can the charge be understood indiscriminately of the unmarried of the lower class, for many of these admit of no such familiarities. That there are prostitutes here, as well as in other countries, is very true, perhaps more in proportion, and such were those who came on board the ships to our people, and frequented the post we had on shore. By seeing these mix indiscriminately with those of a different turn, even of the first rank, one is, at first, inclined to think that they are all disposed the same way, and that the only difference is in the price. But the truth is, the woman who becomes a prostitute, does not seem, in their opinion, to have committed a crime of so deep a dye as to exclude her from the esteem and society of the community in general. On the whole, a stranger who visits England might with equal justice, draw the characters of the women there, from those which he might meet with on board the ships in one of the naval ports, or in the purlieus of Covent Garden and Drury Lane. I must, however, allow that they are all completely versed in the art of coquetry, and that very few of them fix any bounds to their conversation. It is, therefore, no wonder that they have obtained the character of libertines.[16]

[16] Kippis, the first biographer of Cook, makes this comment: "Every enlightened mind will rejoice at what conduces to the honour of human nature in general, and of the female sex in particular."

BOOK II

From our Departure from the Society Isles to our Return to them and Leaving them the Second Time

1773-1774

Both men and women are of a common size with Europeans; and their colour is that of a lightish copper, and more uniformly so than amongst the inhabitants of Otaheite and the Society Isles.[1] Some of our gentlemen were of opinion these were a much handsomer race; others maintained a contrary opinion, of which number I was one. Be this as it may, they have a good shape, and regular features, and are active, brisk, and lively. The women, in particular, are the merriest creatures I ever met with, and will keep chattering by one's side, without the least invitation, or considering whether they are understood, provided one does but seem pleased with them. In general they appeared to be modest; although there was no want of those of a different stamp; and as we had yet some venereal complaints on board, I took all possible care to prevent the disorder being communicated to them. Upon

---

[1] Sailing west from Tahiti, the two ships reached the Friendly Isles, where they visited Tongatabu (named Amsterdam by Tasman in 1643) and Eua (Middleburg). On his Third Voyage Cook made a long stay in this group.

most occasions they showed a strong propensity to pilfering; in which they were full as expert as the Otaheiteans.

Their hair in general is black, but more especially that of the women. Different colours were found among the men, sometimes on the same head, caused by something they put upon it, which stains it white, red, and blue. Both sexes wear it short; I saw but two exceptions to this custom, and the most of them combed it upwards. Many of the boys had it cut very close, except a single lock on the top of the head, and a small quantity on each side. The men cut or shave their beards quite close, which operation is performed with two shells. They have fine eyes, and in general good teeth, even to an advanced age. The custom of *tattowing* or puncturing the skin prevails. The men are *tattowed* from the middle of the thigh to above the hips. The women have it only on their arms and fingers; and there but very slightly.

The dress of both sexes consists of a piece of cloth, or matting, wrapped round the waist, and hanging down below the knees. From the waist, upwards, they are generally naked; and it seemed to be a custom to anoint these parts every morning. My friend Attago never failed to do it; but whether out of respect to his friend, or from custom, I will not pretend to say; though I rather think from the latter, as he was not singular in the practice.

Their ornaments are, amulets, necklaces, and bracelets of bones, shells, and beads of mother of pearl, tortoise shell, etc., which are worn by both sexes. The women also wear on their fingers neat rings made of tortoise shell, and pieces in their ears about the size of a small quill; but ear-ornaments are not commonly worn, though all have their ears pierced. They have also a curious apron made of the outside fibres of the coconut shell, and composed of a number of small pieces, sewed together in such a manner as to form stars, half-moons, little squares, etc. It is studded with beads of shells, and covered with red feathers, so as to have a pleasing effect. They make the same kind of cloth, and of the same materials, as at Otaheite; though they have not such a variety, nor do they make any so fine; but as they have a method of glazing it, it is more durable, and will resist rain for some time, which Otaheite cloth will not. Their colours are black, brown, purple, yellow, and red; all made from vegetables. They make various sorts of matting; some of a very fine texture, which is generally used for clothing; and the thick and stronger sort serves to sleep on, and to make sails for their canoes, etc. Among other useful utensils, they have various sorts of baskets; some made of the same materials as their mats; and others of the twisted fibres of coconuts. These are not only durable, but beautiful; being generally composed of different colours, and studded with beads made of shells or bones. They have many little nicknacks amongst them; which shows that they neither want taste to design, nor skill to execute whatever they take in hand.

How these people amuse themselves in their leisure hours, I cannot say, as we are but little acquainted with their diversions. The women frequently entertained us with songs, in a manner which was agreeable enough. They accompany the music by snapping their fingers, so as to keep time to it. Not only their voices but their music was very harmonious; and they have a considerable compass in their notes. I saw but two musical instruments amongst them. One was a large flute made of a piece of bamboo, which they fill with their noses as at Otaheite; but these have four holes or stops, whereas those of Otaheite have only two. The other was composed of ten or eleven small reeds of unequal lengths, bound together side by side, as the Doric pipe of the ancients is said to have been; and the open ends of the reeds into which they blow with their mouths are of equal height, or in a line. They have also a drum, which, without any impropriety, may be compared to a hollow log of wood. The one I saw was five feet six inches long, and thirty inches in girth, and had a slit in it, from the one end to the other, about three inches wide, by means of which it had been hollowed out. They beat on the side of this log with two drum-sticks, and produce a hollow sound, not quite so musical as that of an empty cask.

The common method of saluting one another is by touching or meeting noses, as is done in New Zealand; and their sign of peace to strangers is the displaying a white flag or flags; at least such were displayed to us, when we first drew near the shore. But the people who came first on board brought with them some of the pepper-plant, and sent it before them into the ship; a stronger sign of friendship than which one could not wish for. From their unsuspicious manner of coming on board, and of receiving us at first on shore, I am of opinion, they are seldom disturbed by either foreign or domestic troubles. They are, however, not un-provided with very formidable weapons; such as clubs and spears, made of hard wood, also bows and arrows. The clubs are from three to five feet in length, and of various shapes; their bows and arrows are but indifferent: the former being very slight, and the latter only made of a slender reed pointed with hard wood. Some of their spears have many barbs, and must be very dangerous weapons where they take effect. On the inside of the bow is a groove in which is put the arrow; from which it should seem that they use but one.

They have a singular custom of putting everything you give them to their heads, by way of thanks, as we conjectured. This manner of paying a compliment is taught them from their very infancy; for when we gave things to little children, the mother lifted up the child's hand to its head. They also used this custom in their exchanges with us: whatever we gave them for their goods, was always applied to the head, just as if it had been given them for nothing. Sometimes they would look at our goods, and, if not approved, return them back; but whenever they applied them to the head, the bargain was infallibly struck. When I had made a present to the chief of anything curious, I frequently saw it handed from one to another; and everyone, into whose hands it came, put it to the head. Very often the women would take hold of my hand, kiss it, and lift it to their heads. From all this it should seem, that this custom, which, they call *fagafatie*, has various significations according as it is applied; all however com-plimentary.

It must be observed that the sullen chief or king did not pay me any of these compliments for the presents I made him.

A still more singular custom prevails in these islands: we ob-served that the greater part of the people, both men and women, had lost one or both their little fingers. We endeavoured, but in vain, to find out the reason of this mutilation; for no one would take any pains to inform us. It was neither peculiar to rank, age, or sex; nor is it done at any certain age, as I saw those of all ages on whom the amputation had been just made; and, except some young children, we found few who had both hands perfect. As it was more common among the aged than the young, some of us were of opinion that it was occasioned by the death of their parents, or some other near relation. But Mr. Wales one day met with a man, whose hands were both perfect, of such an advanced age, that it was hardly possible his parents could be living. They also burn or make incisions in their cheeks, near the cheekbone. The reason of this was equally unknown to us. In some, the wounds were quite fresh; in others, they could only be known by the scars, or colour of the skin. I saw neither sick nor lame amongst them: all appeared healthy, strong, and vigorous; a proof of the goodness of the climate in which they live.

October 21   At five o'clock in the morning of the 21st, we made the land of New Zealand extending from N.W. by N. to W.S.W.: at noon, Table Cape bore west, distant eight or ten leagues. I was very desirous of having some intercourse with the natives of this country as far to the north as possible; that is, about Poverty or Tolaga Bays, where I apprehended they were more civilized than at Queen Charlotte's Sound; in order to give them some hogs, fowls, seeds, roots, etc., which I had provided for the purpose. The wind veering to the north-west and north, enabled us to fetch in with the land a little to the north of Portland, and we stood as near the shore as we could with safety. We observed several people upon it, but none attempted to come off to us. Seeing this, we bore away under Portland, where we lay to some time, as well to give time for the natives to come off, as to wait for the *Adventure*. There were several people on Portland, but none seemed inclined to come to us; indeed the wind, at this time, blew rather too fresh for them to make the attempt. Therefore as soon as the *Adventure* was up with us, we made sail for Cape Kidnappers, which we passed at five o'clock in the morning, and continued our course alongshore till nine, when, being about three leagues short of Black Head, we saw some canoes put off from the shore. Upon this I brought to, in order to give them time to come on board; but ordered the *Adventure*, by signal, to stand on, as I was willing to lose as little time as possible.

Those in the first canoe, which came alongside, were fishers, and exchanged some fish for pieces of cloth and nails. In the next, were two men, whom, by their dress and behaviour, I took to be chiefs. These two were easily prevailed on to come on board, when they were presented with nails, and other articles. They were so fond of nails, as to seize on all they could find, and with such eagerness, as plainly showed they were the most valuable things we could give them. To the principal of these two men I gave the pigs, fowls, seeds, and roots. I believe, at first, he did not think I meant to give them to him; for he took but little notice of them, till he was satisfied they were for himself. Nor was he then in such a rapture as when I gave him a spike-nail half the length of his arm. However, at his going away, I took notice, that he very well remembered how many pigs and fowls had been given him, as he took care to have them all collected together, and kept a watchful eye over them, lest any should be taken away. He made me a promise not to kill any; and if he keeps his word, and proper care is taken of them, there were enough to stock the whole island in due time; being two boars, two sows, four hens, two cocks. The seeds were such as are most useful, viz. wheat, French and kidney beans, peas, cabbage, turnips, onions, carrots, parsnips, and yams, etc. With these articles they were dismissed. It was evident these people had not forgot the *Endeavour* being on their coast; for the first words they spoke to us were, *Ma taou no te pow pow* (we are afraid of the guns). As they could be no strangers to the affair which happened off Cape Kidnapper in my former voyage, experience had taught them to have some regard to these instruments of death.

As soon as they were gone, we stretched off to the southward, the wind having now veered to the W.S.W. In the afternoon it increased to a fresh gale, and blew in squalls; in one of which we lost our fore-top-gallant mast, having carried the sail a little too long. The fear of losing the land induced me to carry as much sail as possible. At seven in the morning, we tacked and stretched inshore, Cape Turnagain, at this time, bore about N.W. ½ N., distant six or seven leagues. The *Adventure*, being a good way to leeward, we supposed, did not observe the signal, but stood on; consequently was separated from us.[2]

November 3   The first thing we did, after mooring the ship, was to unbend all the sails, there not being one but what wanted repair. Indeed, both our sails and rigging had sustained much damage in beating off the Strait's mouth.[3]

We had no sooner anchored than we were visited by the natives, several of whom I remembered to have seen when I was here in the *Endeavour*, particularly an old man named Goubiah. In the afternoon I gave orders for all the empty water-casks to be landed, in order to be repaired, cleaned, and filled; tents to be set up for the sail-makers, coopers, and others, whose business made it necessary for them to be on shore. The next day we began to caulk the ship's sides and decks, to overhaul her rigging, repair the sails, cut wood for fuel, and set up the smith's forge to repair the ironwork; all of which were absolutely necessary. We also made some hauls with the seine, but caught no fish, which deficiency the natives in some measure made up, by bringing us a good quantity, and exchanging them for pieces of Otaheitean cloth, etc.

On the 5th, the most part of our bread being in casks, I ordered some to be opened, when, to our mortification, we found a good deal of it damaged. To repair this loss in the best manner we could, all the casks were opened, the bread was picked, and the copper oven set up, to bake such parcels of it as by that means could be recovered. Some time this morning, the natives stole out of one of the tents a bag of clothes belonging to one of the seamen. As soon as I was informed of it, I went to them in an adjoining cove, demanded the clothes again, and, after some time

---

[2] In the succeeding rough weather the two ships parted company, the *Adventure* returning independently to England. No news was received of her until Cook reached the Cape of Good Hope seventeen months later. The place of separation was off the eastern entrance to Cook Strait. Forster was shocked by this event, and by "the dreadful energy of the language" of the sailors which it occasioned.

[3] The *Resolution* anchored once more in Ship Cove, Queen Charlotte's Sound.

spent in friendly application, recovered them. Since we were among thieves, and had come off so well, I was not sorry for what had happened, as it taught our people to keep a better look-out for the future.

With these people I saw the youngest of the two sows Captain Furneaux had put on shore in Cannibal Cove, when we were last here: it was lame of one of its hind legs; otherwise in good case, and very tame. If we understood these people right, the boar and other sow were also taken away and separated, but not killed. We were likewise told that the two goats I had put on shore up the Sound had been killed by that old rascal Goubiah. Thus all our endeavours to stock this country with useful animals were likely to be frustrated by the very people we meant to serve. Our gardens had fared somewhat better. Everything in them, except the potatoes, they had left entirely to nature, who had acted her part so well, that we found most articles in a flourishing state; a proof that the winter must have been mild. The potatoes had most of them been dug up; some, however, still remained, and were growing, though I think it is probable they will never be got out of the ground.

November 22   Having now got the ship in a condition for sea, and to encounter the southern latitudes, I ordered the tents to be struck and everything to be got on board.

The boatswain, with a party of men, being in the woods cutting broom, some of them found a private hut of the natives, in which was deposited most of the treasures they had received from us, as well as some other articles of their own. It is very probable some were set to watch this hut; as, soon after it was discovered, they came and took all away. But missing some things, they told our people they had stolen them, and in the evening came and made their complaint to me, pitching upon one of the party as the person who had committed the theft. Having ordered this man to be punished before them, they went away seemingly satisfied, although they did not recover any of the things they had lost, nor could I by any means find out what had become of them; though nothing was more certain than that something had been stolen by some of the party, if not by the very man the natives had pitched upon. It was ever a maxim with me to punish the least crimes any of my people committed against these uncivilized nations. Their robbing us with impunity, is by no means a sufficient reason why we should treat them in the same manner, a conduct we see they themselves cannot justify. They found themselves injured, and sought for redress in a legal way. The best method, in my opinion, to preserve a good understanding with such people, is, first, by showing them the use of firearms, to convince them of the superiority they give you over them, and then to be always upon your guard. When once they are sensible of these things, a regard for their own safety will deter them from disturbing you, or from being unanimous in forming any plan to attack you, and strict honesty and gentle treatment on your part will make it their interest not to do it.

Calm or light airs from the north all day on the 23rd, hindered us from putting to sea as intended. In the afternoon, some of the officers went on shore to amuse themselves among the natives, where they saw the head and bowels of a youth, who had lately been killed, lying on the beach, and the heart stuck on a forked stick which was fixed to the head of one of the largest canoes. One of the gentlemen bought the head and brought it on board, where a piece of the flesh was broiled and eaten by one of the natives, before all the officers and most of the men. I was on shore at this time, but soon after returning on board, was informed of the above circumstances, and found the quarter-deck crowded with the natives, and the mangled head, or rather part of it (for the under jaw and lip were wanting), lying on the taffrail. The skull had been broken on the left side just above the temples, and the remains of the face had all the appearance of a youth under twenty.

The sight of the head, and the relation of the above circumstances, struck me with horror, and filled my mind with indignation against these cannibals. Curiosity, however, got the better of my indignation, especially when I considered that it would avail but little, and being desirous of becoming an eye-witness of a fact which many doubted, I ordered a piece of the flesh to be broiled and brought to the quarterdeck, where one of these cannibals ate it with surprising avidity. This had such an effect on some of our people as to make them sick. Oedidee (who came on board with me), was so affected with the sight as to become perfectly motionless, and seemed as if metamorphosed into the statue of horror. It is utterly impossible for art to describe that passion with half the force that it appeared in his countenance. When roused from this state by some of us, he burst into tears; continued to weep and scold by turns; told them they were vile men; and that he neither was nor would be any longer their friend. He even would not suffer them to touch him; he used the same language to one of the gentlemen who cut off the flesh, and refused to accept or even touch the knife with which it was done. Such was Oedidee's indignation against the vile custom, and worthy of imitation by every rational being.

I was not able to find out the reason for their undertaking this expedition. All I could understand for certain was, that they went from hence into Admiralty Bay (the next inlet to the west) and there fought with their enemies, many of whom they killed. They counted to me fifty, a number which exceeded probability, as they were not more if so many themselves. I think I understood them clearly, that this youth was killed there; and not brought away prisoner and afterwards killed. Nor could I learn that they had brought away any more than this one; which increased the improbability of their having killed so many. We had also reason to think that they did not come off without loss; for a young woman was seen more than once to cut herself, as is the custom when they lose a friend or relation.

That the New Zealanders are cannibals can now no longer be doubted. The account given of this in my former voyage, being partly founded on circumstances, was, as I afterwards understood, discredited by many persons. Few consider what a savage man is in his natural state, and even after he is in some degree civilized. The New Zealanders are certainly in some state of civilization; their behaviour to us was manly and mild, showing on all occasions a readiness to oblige. They have some arts among them which they execute with great judgment, and unwearied patience; they are far less addicted to thieving than the other islanders of the South Sea; and I believe those in the same tribe, or such as are at peace one with another, are strictly honest among themselves. This custom of eating their enemies slain in battle (for I firmly believe they eat the flesh of no others) has, undoubtedly, been handed down to them from the earliest times; and we know it is not an easy matter to wean a nation from their ancient customs, let them be ever so inhuman and savage; especially if that nation has no manner of connection or commerce with strangers. For it is by this that the greatest part of the human race has been civilized; an advantage which the New Zealanders from their situation never had. An intercourse with foreigners would reform their manners, and polish their savage minds. Or, were they more united under a settled form of government, they would have fewer enemies; consequently, this custom would be less in use, and might in time be in a manner forgotten. At present, they have but little idea of treating others as themselves would *wish* to be treated, but treat them as they *expect* to be treated. If I remember right, one of the arguments they made use of to Tupia, who frequently expostulated with them against this custom, was, that there could be no harm in killing and eating the man who would do the same by them, if it was in his power. For, said they: "Can there be any harm in eating our enemies whom we have killed in battle? Would not those very enemies have done the same to us?" I have often seen them listen to Tupia with great attention, but I never found his arguments have any weight with them, or that, with all his rhetoric, he could persuade any one of them that this custom was wrong; and when Oedidee and several of our people showed their abhorrence of it, they only laughed at them. . . .

Everyone being unanimously of opinion that the *Adventure* could neither be stranded on the coast, nor be in any of the harbours thereof, I gave up looking for her, and all thoughts of seeing her any more during the voyage; as no rendezvous was absolutely fixed upon after leaving New Zealand. Nevertheless, this did not discourage me from fully exploring the southern parts of the Pacific Ocean, in the doing of which I intended to employ the whole of the ensuing season.

On our quitting the coast, and, consequently, all hopes of being joined by our consort, I had the satisfaction to find that not a man was dejected, or thought the dangers we had yet to go through were in the least increased by being alone; but as cheerfully proceeding to the south, or wherever I might think proper to lead them, as if the *Adventure*, or even more ships, had been in our company.[4]

January 29 At four o'clock in the morning of the 29th, the fog began to clear away; and the day becoming clear and serene, we again steered to the south with a gentle gale at N.E. and N.N.E.[5] The variation was found to be 22° 41' E. This was in the latitude of 69° 45' S., longitude 108° 5' W.; and, in the afternoon, being in the same longitude, and in the latitude of 70° 23' S., it was 24° 81' E. Soon after, the sky became clouded, and the air very cold. We continued our course to the south, and passed a piece of weed covered with barnacles, which a brown albatross was picking off. At ten o'clock, we passed a very large ice-island; it was not less than three or four miles in circuit. Several more being seen ahead, and the weather becoming foggy, we hauled the wind to the northward; but in less than two hours, the weather cleared up, and we again stood south.

On the 30th, at four o'clock in the morning, we perceived the clouds, over the horizon to the south, to be of an unusual snow-white brightness, which we knew announced our approach

---

[4] The ship sailed on 25 November. Before leaving, Cook left a message for Furneaux in a bottle buried at the foot of a tree.

[5] In his second attempt to discover the supposed continent in the Southern Pacific, Cook's course lay far to the south of his run to Tahiti six months earlier. He crossed the Antarctic Circle on two occasions, but each time his progress was checked by the presence of pack-ice. The highest latitude he was ever in was 71° 10' S. A few days before the date of this passage he had described how the snow and sleet of a northerly gale "froze to the rigging as it fell, making the ropes like wires, and the sails like boards or plates of metal. The sheaves (wheels) also were frozen so fast in the blocks, that it required our utmost efforts to get a top-sail down and up; the cold so intense as hardly to be endured; the whole sea in a manner covered with ice, a hard gale, and a thick fog." Forster, who suffered from rheumatism, was more bitter: "The whole scene looked like the wrecks of a shattered world, or as the poets describe some regions of hell; an idea which struck us the more forcibly as execrations, oaths, and curses re-echoed about us on all sides." However, the Journal of a gunner's mate (Marra) states that "under all these hardships the men were cheerful over their grog."

to field-ice. Soon after, it was seen from the top-mast head; and at eight o'clock, we were close to its edge. It extended east and west, far beyond the reach of our sight. In the situation we were in, just the southern half of our horizon was illuminated, by the rays of light reflected from the ice, to a considerable height. Ninety-seven ice-hills were distinctly seen within the field, besides those on the outside; many of them very large, and looking like a ridge of mountains, rising one above another till they were lost in the clouds. The outer, or northern edge of this immense field, was composed of loose or broken ice close packed together; so that it was not possible for anything to enter it. This was about a mile broad; within which was solid ice in one continued compact body. It was rather low and flat (except the hills), but seemed to increase in height, as you traced it to the south; in which direction it extended beyond our sight. Such mountains of ice as these, were, I believe, never seen in the Greenland seas; at least, not that I ever heard or read of; so that we cannot draw a comparison between the ice here, and there. It must be allowed that these prodigious ice-mountains must add such additional weight to the ice-fields which enclose them, as cannot but make a great difference between the navigating this icy sea and that of Greenland.

I will not say it was impossible anywhere to get farther to the south; but the attempting it would have been a dangerous and rash enterprise; and what, I believe, no man in my situation would have thought of. It was, indeed, *my* opinion, as well as the opinion of most on board, that this ice extended quite to the pole, or, perhaps, joined to some land, to which it had been fixed from the earliest time; and that it is here, that is to the south of this parallel, where all the ice we find scattered up and down to the north, is first formed, and afterwards broken off by gales of wind, or other causes, and brought to the north by the currents, which we always found to set in that direction in the high latitudes. As we drew near this ice, some penguins were heard, but none seen; and but few other birds, or any other thing, that could induce us to think any land was near. And yet I think there must be some to the south behind this ice; but if there is, it can afford no better retreat for birds, or any other animals, than the ice itself, with which it must be wholly covered. I, who had ambition not only to go farther than anyone had been before, but as far as it was possible for man to go, was not sorry at meeting with this interruption; as it, in some measure, relieved us; at least shortened the dangers and hardships inseparable from the navigation of the southern polar regions. Since, therefore, we could not proceed one inch farther to the south, no other reason need be assigned for my tacking, and standing back to the north; being at this time in the latitude of 71° 10′ S., longitude 106° 54′ W.

February 6   I now came to a resolution to proceed to the north and to spend the ensuing winter within the tropic, if I met with no employment before I came there. I was now well satisfied no continent was to be found in this ocean, but what must lie so far to the south as to be wholly inaccessible on account of ice; and that if one should be found in the southern Atlantic Ocean, it would be necessary to have the whole summer before us to explore it. On the other hand, upon a supposition that there is no land there, we undoubtedly might have reached the Cape of Good Hope by April, and so have put an end to the expedition, so far as it related to the finding a continent; which indeed was the first object of the voyage. But for me at this time to have quitted this Southern Pacific Ocean, with a good ship expressly sent out on discoveries, a healthy crew, and not in want either of stores or of provisions, would have been betraying not only a want of perseverance, but of judgment, in supposing the South Pacific Ocean to have been so well explored, that nothing reremained to be done in it. This, however, was not my opinion; for, although I had proved there was no continent but what must lie far to the south, there remained, nevertheless, room for very large islands in places wholly unexamined: and many of those which were formerly discovered, are but imperfectly explored, and their situations as imperfectly known. I was besides of opinion, that my remaining in this sea some time longer, would be productive of improvements in navigation and geography, as well as other sciences. I had several times communicated my thoughts on this subject to Captain Furneaux; but as it then wholly depended on what we might meet with to the south, I could not give it in orders without running the risk of drawing us from the main object.

Since now nothing had happened to prevent me from carrying these views into execution, my intention was first to go in search of the land, said to have been discovered by Juan Fernandez, above a century ago, in about the latitude of 38°; if I should fail in finding this land, then to go in search of Easter Island or Davis's Land, whose situation was known with so little certainty that the attempts lately made to find it had miscarried.[6] I next intended to get within the tropic, and then proceed to the west, touching at, and settling the situations of such islands as we might meet with till we arrived at Otaheite, where it was necessary I should stop to look for the *Adventure*. I had also thoughts of running as far west as the Tierra Austral del Espiritu Santo, discovered by Quiros, and which M. de Bougainville calls the Great Cyclades. Quiros speaks of this land as being large, or lying in the neighbourhood of large lands; and as this was a point which Bougainville had neither confirmed nor refuted, I thought it was worth clearing up. From this land my design was to steer to the south and so back to the east, between the latitudes of 50° and 60°; intending if possible to be the length of Cape Horn in November next, when we should have the best part of the summer before us to explore the southern part of the Atlantic Ocean. Great as this design appeared to be, I, however, thought it possible to be executed; and when I came to communicate it to the officers, I had the satisfaction to find, that they all heartily concurred in it. I should not do these gentlemen justice if I did not take some opportunity to declare, that they always showed the utmost readiness to carry into execution, in the most effectual manner, every measure I thought proper to take. Under such circumstances, it is hardly necessary to say that the seamen were always obedient and alert; and, on this occasion, they were so far from wishing

---

[6] Juan Fernandez, a soldier in Pizarro's army, is supposed to have discovered the island which bears his name in 1563 and thence sailed west to a hypothetical land in mid-Pacific. Davis Land is equally mythical, the name being transferred to Easter Island, discovered by Roggevein in 1722.

the voyage at an end, that they rejoiced at the prospect of its being prolonged another year, and of soon enjoying the benefits of a milder climate.

February 25   I was now taken ill of the bilious colic, which was so violent as to confine me to my bed; so that the management of the ship was left to Mr. Cooper, the first officer, who conducted her very much to my satisfaction. It was several days before the most dangerous symptoms of my disorder were removed; during which time Mr. Patten, the surgeon, was to me not only a skilful physician, but an affectionate nurse; and I should ill deserve the care he bestowed on me, if I did not make this public acknowledgement. When I began to recover, a favourite dog, belonging to Mr. Forster, fell a sacrifice to my tender stomach. We had no other fresh meat whatever on board; and I could eat of this flesh, as well as broth made of it, when I could taste nothing else. Thus I received nourishment and strength from food which would have made most people in Europe sick; so true it is, that necessity is governed by no law.[7]

March 11   At eight o'clock in the morning on the 11th, land was seen, from the mast-head, bearing west, and at noon from the deck, extending from W. ¾ N. to W. by S., about twelve leagues distant. I made no doubt that this was Davis's Land, or Easter Island, as its appearance from this situation corresponded very well with Wafer's account; and we expected to have seen the low sandy isle that Davis fell in with, which would have been a confirmation; but in this we were disappointed.[8] At seven o'clock in the evening, the island bore from N. 62° W. to N. 87° W., about five leagues distant; in which situation we sounded, without finding ground, with a line of a hundred and forty fathoms. Here we spent the night, having alternately light airs

[7] Forster states that earlier in the month "Captain Cook himself was likewise pale and lean, entirely lost his appetite and laboured under a perpetual costiveness." He recovered early in March.

[8] Lionel Wafer, a companion of Dampier, published an account in 1699 of an island supposed to have been discovered by another buccaneer, Captain Davis. Every circumnavigator searched for this non-existent island.

and calms, till ten o'clock the next morning, when a breeze sprung up at west-south-west. With this we stretched in for the land; and, by the help of our glass, discovered people, and some of those colossian statues or idols mentioned by the authors of *Roggewin's Voyage*. At four o'clock in the afternoon, we were half a league south-south-east, and north-north-west of the north-east point of the island; and, on sounding, found thirty-five fathoms, a dark sandy bottom. I now tacked and endeavoured to get into what appeared to be a bay, on the west side of the point, or south-east side of the island; but before this could be accomplished, night came upon us, and we stood on and off under the land till the next morning, having soundings from seventy-five to a hundred and ten fathoms, the same bottom as before. . . .

Having anchored too near the edge of the bank, a fresh breeze from the land, about three o'clock the next morning, drove us off it; on which the anchor was heaved up, and sail made to re-gain the bank again. While the ship was plying in, I went ashore, accompanied by some of the gentlemen, to see what the island was likely to afford us. We landed at the sandy beach, where some hundreds of the natives were assembled, and who were so im-patient to see us, that many of them swam off to meet the boats. Not one of them had so much as a stick or weapon of any sort in their hands. After distributing a few trinkets amongst them, we made signs for something to eat; on which they brought down a few potatoes, plantains, and sugar-canes, and exchanged them for nails, looking-glasses, and pieces of cloth.

We presently discovered that they were as expert thieves, and as tricking in their exchanges, as any people we had yet met with. It was with some difficulty we could keep the hats on our heads, but hardly possible to keep anything in our pockets, not even what themselves had sold us: for they would watch every oppor-tunity to snatch it from us, so that we sometimes bought the same thing two or three times over, and after all did not get it.

Before I sailed from England, I was informed that a Spanish ship has visited this island in 1769.[9] Some signs of it were seen among the people now about us; one man had a pretty good

[9] See above, p. 152, note 15.

broad-brimmed European hat on, another had a grego jacket, and another a red silk handkerchief. They also seemed to know the use of a musket, and to stand in much awe of it; but this they probably learnt from Roggewin, who, if we are to believe the authors of that voyage, left them sufficient tokens.

Near the place where we landed, were some of those statues before mentioned, which I shall describe in another place. The country appeared barren and without wood; there were, nevertheless, several plantations of potatoes, plantains, and sugar-canes; we also saw some fowls, and found a well of brackish water. As these were articles we were in want of, and as the natives seemed not unwilling to part with them, I resolved to stay a day or two,

A DESCRIPTION OF EASTER ISLAND

I shall now give some further account of this island, which is undoubtedly the same that Admiral Roggewin touched at in April 1722, although the description given of it by the authors of that voyage does by no means agree with it now. It may also be the same that was seen by Captain Davis in 1686; for when seen from the east, it answers very well to Wafer's description, as I have before observed. In short, if this is not the land, his discovery cannot lie far from the coast of America, as this latitude has been well explored from the meridian of 80° to 110°. Captain Carteret carried it much farther, but his track seems to have been a little too far south. Had I found fresh water, I intended spending some days looking for the low sandy island Davis fell in with, which would have determined the point; but as I did not find water, and had a long run to make before I was assured of getting any, and being in want of refreshments, I declined the search, as a small delay might have been attended with bad consequences to the crew, many of them beginning to be more or less affected with the scurvy.

No nation need contend for the honour of the discovery of this island, as there can be few places which afford less convenience for shipping than it does. Here is no safe anchorage, no wood for fuel, nor any fresh water worth taking on board. Nature has been exceedingly sparing of her favours to this spot. As everything must be raised by dint of labour, it cannot be supposed the inhabitants plant much more than is sufficient for themselves; and as they are but few in number, they cannot have much to spare to supply the wants of visitant strangers. The produce is sweet potatoes, yams, taraoreddy-root, plantains, and sugar-canes, all pretty good, the potatoes especially, which are the best of the kind I ever tasted. Gourds they have also; but so very few, that a coconut shell was the most valuable thing we could give them. They have a few tame fowls, such as cocks and hens, small but well tasted. They have also rats, which it seems they eat; for I saw a man with some dead ones in his hand, and he seemed unwilling to part with them, giving me to understand they were for food. Land birds there were hardly any, and sea birds but few; these were, men-of-war, tropic, and egg-birds, nodies, tern, etc. The coast seemed not to abound with fish; at least we could catch none with hook and line, and it was but very little we saw amongst the natives.

Such is the produce of Easter Island, or Davis's Land, which is situated in the latitude of 27° 5′ 30″ S., longitude 109° 46′ 20″ W. It is about ten or twelve leagues in circuit, has a hilly and stony surface, and an iron-bound shore. The hills are of such a height as to be seen fifteen or sixteen leagues. Off the south end, are two rocky islets lying near the shore. The north and east points of the island rise directly from the sea to a considerable height; between them, on the south-east side, the shore forms an open bay, in which I believe the Dutch anchored. We anchored, as has been already mentioned, on the west side of the island, three miles to the north of the south point, with the sandy beach bearing E.S.E. This is a very good road with easterly winds, but a dangerous one with westerly, as the other on the south-east side must be with easterly winds.

For this and other bad accommodations already mentioned, nothing but necessity will induce anyone to touch at this island, unless it can be done without going much out of the way; in which case touching here may be advantageous, as the people willingly and readily part with such refreshments as they have, and at an easy rate. We certainly received great benefit from the little we got; but few ships can come here without being in want of water, and this want cannot be here supplied. The little we took on board, could not be made use of; it being only salt water which had filtrated through a stony beach into a stone well. This the natives had made for the purpose, a little to the southward of the sandy beach so often mentioned, and the water ebbed and flowed into it with the tide.

The inhabitants of this island do not seem to exceed six or seven hundred souls; and above two-thirds of those we saw were males. They either have but few females among them, or else many were restrained from making their appearance during our stay; for though we saw nothing to induce us to believe the men were of a jealous disposition, or the women afraid to appear in public, something of this kind was probably the case.

In colour, features and language, they bear such affinity to the people of the more western islands, that no one will doubt that they have had the same origin. It is extraordinary that the same nation should have spread themselves over all the islands in this vast ocean, from New Zealand to this island, which is almost one-fourth part of the circumference of the globe. Many of them have now no other knowledge of each other than what is preserved by antiquated tradition; and they have by length of time become, as it were, different nations, each having adopted some peculiar custom or habit, etc. Nevertheless, a careful observer will soon see the affinity each has to the other.

In general, the people of this island are a slender race. I did not see a man that would measure six feet; so far are they from being giants, as one of the authors of Roggewin's voyage asserts. They are brisk and active, have good features, and not disagreeable countenances; are friendly and hospitable to strangers, but as much addicted to pilfering as any of their neighbours.

Tatooing, or puncturing the skin, is much used here. The men are marked from head to foot, with figures all nearly alike; only some give them one direction, and some another, as fancy leads. The women are but little punctured; red and white paint is an ornament with *them*, as also with the men; the former is made of tamarick; but what composes the latter I know not. . . .

Of the power or authority of these chiefs, or of the government of these people, I confess myself quite ignorant.

Nor are we better acquainted with their religion. The gigantic statues so often mentioned, are not, in my opinion, looked upon as idols by the present inhabitants, whatever they might have been in the days of the Dutch; at least, I saw nothing that could induce me to think so. On the contrary, I rather suppose that they are burying-places for certain tribes or families. I, as well as some others, saw a human skeleton lying on one of the platforms, just covered with stones. Some of these platforms of masonry, are thirty or forty feet long, twelve or sixteen broad, and from three to twelve in height; which last in some measure depends on the nature of the ground. For they are generally at the brink of the bank facing the sea, so that this face may be ten or twelve feet or more high, and the other may not be above three or four. They are built, or rather faced, with hewn stones of a very large size; and the workmanship is not inferior to the best plain piece of masonry we have in England. They use no sort of cement; yet the joints are exceedingly close, and the stones mortised and tenanted one into another, in a very artful manner. The side walls are not perpendicular, but inclining a little inwards, in the same manner that breastworks, etc., are built in Europe: yet had not all this care, pains, and sagacity been able to preserve these curious structures from the ravages of all-devouring time.

The statues, or at least many of them, are erected on these platforms which serve as foundations. They are, as near as we could judge, about half length, ending in a sort of stump at the bottom, on which they stand. The workmanship is rude, but not bad; nor are the features of the face ill formed, the nose and chin in particular; but the ears are long beyond proportion; and, as to the bodies, there is hardly anything like a human figure about them.

I had an opportunity of examining only two or three of these statues, which are near the landing-place; and they were of a grey stone, seemingly of the same sort as that with which the platforms were built. But some of the gentlemen who travelled over the island, and examined many of them, were of opinion that the stone of which they were made was different from any other they saw on the island, and had much the appearance of being factitious. We could hardly conceive how these islanders, wholly unacquainted with any mechanical power, could raise such stupendous figures, and afterwards place the large cylindrical stones, before mentioned, upon their heads. The only method I can conceive, is by raising the upper end by little and little, supporting it by stones as it is raised, and building about it till they got it erect; thus a sort of mount, or scaffolding, would be made, upon which they might roll the cylinder, and place it upon the head of the statue, and then the stones might be removed from about it. But if the stones are factitious, the statues might have been put together on the place in their present position, and the cylinder put on by building a mount round them as above mentioned. But, let them have been made and set up, by this or any other method, they must have been a work of immense time, and sufficiently show the ingenuity and perseverance of the islanders in the age in which they were built; for the present inhabitants have most certainly had no hand in them, as they do not even repair the foundations of those which are going to decay. They give different names to them, such as Gotomoara, Marapate, Kanaro, Gowaytoo-goo, Matta Matta, etc., etc., to which they sometimes prefix the word Moi, and sometimes annex Areekee. The latter signifies chief, and the former, burying, or sleeping-place, as well as we could understand.[10]

April 21   We made the high land of Otaheite on the 21st, and at noon were about thirteen leagues east of Point Venus, for which we steered, and got pretty well in with it by sunset, when we shortened sail; and, having spent the night, which was squally,

[10] Two of these statues used to stand outside the British Museum. Many attempts have been made to explain the existence of an earlier civilisation on Easter Island, e.g. Macmillan Brown, *The Riddle of the Pacific* and B. G. Corney, *Voyage of Gonzalez* (Hakluyt Soc. 1908).

After leaving the island Cook steered north for the Marquesas group, discovered by Mendana in 1595 and never seen again. Cook's description of the group is brief, but he calls the inhabitants (painted by Gauguin) "without exception the finest race of people in this sea". Thence he made his way back to Tahiti.

with rain, standing on and off, at eight o'clock the next morning anchored in Matavai Bay in seven fathoms of water. This was no sooner known to the natives than many of them made us a visit, and expressed not a little joy at seeing us again.

As my chief reason for putting in at this place was to give Mr. Wales an opportunity to know the error of the watch by the known longitude, and to determine anew her rate of going, the first thing we did was to land his instruments, and to erect tents for the reception of a guard and such other people as it was necessary to have on shore. Sick we had none; the refreshments we got at the Marquesas had removed every complaint of that kind.

On the 23rd, showery weather. Our very good friends the natives supplied us with fruit and fish sufficient for the whole crew.

On the 24th, Otoo the king, and several other chiefs, with a train of attendants, paid us a visit, and brought as presents ten or a dozen large hogs, besides fruits, which made them exceedingly welcome. I was advised of the king's coming, and looked upon it as a good omen. Knowing how much it was my interest to make this man my friend, I met him at the tents, and conducted him and his friends on board, in my boat, where they stayed for dinner; after which they were dismissed with suitable presents, and highly pleased with the reception they had met with.

Next day we had much thunder, lightning, and rain. This did not hinder the king from making me another visit, and a present of a large quantity of refreshments. It has been already mentioned, that when we were at the island of Amsterdam we had collected, amongst other curiosities, some red parrot feathers. When this was known here, all the principal people of both sexes endeavoured to ingratiate themselves into our favour by bringing us hogs, fruit, and every other thing the island afforded, in order to obtain these valuable jewels. Our having these feathers was a fortunate circumstance; for as they were valuable to the natives, they became so to us; but more especially as my stock of trade was, by this time, greatly exhausted; so that, if it had not been for the feathers, I should have found it difficult to have supplied the ship with the necessary refreshments.

When I put in at this island, I intended to stay no longer than till

Mr. Wales had made the necessary observations for the purposes already mentioned; thinking we should meet with no better success than we did the last time we were here. But the reception we had already met with, and the few excursions we had made, which did not exceed the plains of Matavai and Oparree, convinced us of our error. We found at these two places, built and building a great number of large canoes, and houses of every kind; people living in spacious habitations, who had not a place to shelter themselves in eight months before; several large hogs about every house; and every other sign of a rising state.

Judging from these favourable circumstances that we should not mend ourselves by removing to another island, I resolved to make a longer stay, and to begin with the repairs of the ship and stores, etc. Accordingly I ordered the empty casks and sails to be got ashore to be repaired; the ship to be caulked; and the rigging to be overhauled; all of which the high southern latitudes had made indispensably necessary.

In the morning of the 26th, I went down to Oparree, accompanied by some of the officers and gentlemen, to pay Otoo a visit by appointment. As we drew near we observed a number of large canoes in motion; but were surprised, when we arrived, to see upwards of three hundred ranged in order, for some distance, along the shore, all completely equipped and manned, besides a vast number of armed men upon the shore. So unexpected an armament collected together in our neighbourhood, in the space of one night, gave rise to various conjectures. We landed however in the midst of them, and were received by a vast multitude, many of them under arms, and many not. The cry of the latter was *Tiyo no Otoo*, and that of the former *Tiyo no Towha*. This chief, we afterwards learned, was admiral or commander of the fleet and troops present. The moment we landed, I was met by a chief whose name was Tee, uncle to the king, and one of his prime ministers, of whom I inquired for Otoo. Presently after we were met by Towha, who received me with great courtesy. He took me by the one hand, and Tee by the other; and, without my knowing where they intended to carry me, dragged me as it were through the crowd that was divided into two parties, both of which professed themselves my friends by crying out *Tiyo no Tootee*. One party wanted me to go to Otoo, and the other to remain with Towha. Coming to the usual place of audience, a mat was spread for me to sit down upon, and Tee left me to go and bring the king. Towha was unwilling I should sit down, partly insisting on my going with him; but, as I knew nothing of this chief, I refused to comply. Presently Tee returned, and wanted to conduct me to the king, taking hold of my hand for that purpose. This Towha opposed; so that between the one party and the other, I was like to have been torn in pieces; and was obliged to desire Tee to desist, and to leave me to the admiral and his party, who conducted me down to the fleet. As soon as we came before the admiral's vessel, we found two lines of armed men drawn up before her, to keep off the crowd, as I supposed, and to clear the way for me to go in. But, as I was determined not to go, I made the water, which was between me and her, an excuse. This did not answer; for a man immediately squatted himself down at my feet, offering to carry me; and then I declared I would not go. That very moment Towha quitted me, without my seeing which way he went, nor would anyone inform me. Turning myself round I saw Tee, who, I believe, had never lost sight of me. Inquiring of him for the king, he told me he was gone into the country *Mataou*, and advised me to go to my boat; which we accordingly did, as soon as we could get collected together; for Mr. Edgcumbe was the only person that could keep with me; the others being jostled about in the crowd in the same manner we had been.

When we got into our boat, we took our time to view this grand fleet. The vessels of war consisted of a hundred and sixty large double canoes very well equipped, manned, and armed. But I am not sure that they had their full complement of men or rowers; I rather think not. The chiefs, and all those on the fighting stages, were dressed in their war habits; that is, in a vast quantity of cloth, turbans, breast-plates, and helmets. Some of the latter were of such a length as greatly to encumber the wearer. Indeed, their whole dress seemed to be ill calculated for the day of battle, and to be designed more for show than use. Be this as

it may, it certainly added grandeur to the prospect, as they were
so complaisant as to show themselves to the best advantage. The
vessels were decorated with flags, streamers, etc., so that the
whole made a grand and noble appearance, such as we had never
seen before in this sea, and what no one would have expected.
Their instruments of war were clubs, spears, and stones. The
vessels were ranged close alongside of each other, with their
heads ashore, and their stern to the sea; the admiral's vessel being
nearly in the centre. Besides the vessels of war, there were a
hundred and seventy sail of smaller double canoes, all with a little
house upon them, and rigged with mast and sail, which the war
canoes had not. These, we judged, were designed for transports,
victuallers, etc., for in the war canoes was no sort of provisions
whatever. In these three hundred and thirty vessels, I guessed
there were no less than seven thousand seven hundred and sixty
men;[11] a number which appears incredible, especially as we were
told they all belonged to the districts of Attahourou and Ahopatea.
In this computation, I allow to each war canoe forty men, troops
and rowers, and to each of the small canoes eight. Most of the
gentlemen who were with me, thought the number of men belonging to the war canoes exceeded this. It is certain that the most
of them were fitted to row with more paddles than I have allowed
them men; but at this time I think they were not complete. Tupia
informed us, when I was first here, that the whole island raised
only between six and seven thousand men, but we now saw two
districts only raise that number; so that he must have taken his
account from some old establishment, or else he only meant
Tatatous, that is, warriors, or men trained from their infancy to
arms, and did not include the rowers, and those necessary to
navigate the other vessels. I should think he only spoke of this
number as the standing troops or militia of the island, and not
their whole force. This point I shall leave to be discussed in
another place, and return to the subject.

After we had well viewed this fleet, I wanted much to have
seen the admiral, to have gone with him on board the war canoes.

[11] Forster estimated 4,000 oarsmen and 1,500 warriors; he thought the total
population was at least 120,000.

We inquired for him as we rowed past the fleet to no purpose. We put ashore and inquired, but the noise and crowd was so great, that no one attended to what we said. At last Tee came and whispered us in the ear, that Otoo was gone to Matavai, advising us to return thither, and not to land where we were. We accordingly proceeded for the ship, and this intelligence and advice received from Tee gave rise to new conjectures. In short, we concluded that this Towha was some powerful disaffected chief, who was upon the point of making war against his sovereign; for we could not imagine Otoo had any other reason for leaving Oparree in the manner he did.

We had not been long gone from Oparree before the whole fleet was in motion, to the westward from whence it came. When we got to Matavai, our friends there told us, that this fleet was part of the armament intended to go against Eimeo, whose chief had thrown off the yoke of Otaheite, and assumed an independency. We were likewise informed that Otoo neither was nor had been at Matavai; so that we were still at a loss to know why he fled from Oparree. This occasioned another trip thither in the afternoon, where we found him, and now understood that the reason of his not seeing me in the morning was, that some of his people having stolen a quantity of my clothes which were on shore washing, he was afraid I should demand restitution. He repeatedly asked me if I was not angry; and when I assured him that I was not, and that they might keep what they had got, he was satisfied. Towha was alarmed partly on the same account. He thought I was displeased when I refused to go aboard his vessel; and I was jealous of seeing such a force in our neighbourhood without being able to know anything of its design. Thus by mistaking one another, I lost the opportunity of examining more narrowly into part of the naval force of this island, and making myself better acquainted with its manœuvres. Such an opportunity may never occur; as it was commanded by a brave, sensible, and intelligent chief, who would have satisfied us in all the questions we had thought proper to ask; and, as the objects were before us, we could not well have misunderstood each other. It happened unluckily that Oedidee was not with us in the morning; for Tee, who was the only man we could depend on, served only to perplex us. Matters being thus cleared up, and mutual presents having passed between Otoo and me, we took leave and returned on board.

April 29 Early on the morning of the 29th, Otoo, Towha, and several other grandees, came on board, and brought with them as presents, not only provisions, but some of the most valuable curiosities of the island. I made them returns, with which they were well pleased. I likewise took this opportunity to repay the civilities I had received from Towha.

The night before, one of the natives attempting to steal a water-cask from the watering-place, he was caught in the act, sent on board, and put in irons; in which situation Otoo and the other chiefs saw him. Having made known his crime to them, Otoo begged he might be set at liberty. This I refused, telling him, that since I punished my people, when they committed the least offence against his, it was but just this man should be punished also; and, as I knew he would not do it, I was resolved to do it myself. Accordingly, I ordered the man to be carried on shore to the tents, and having followed myself with Otoo, Towha, and others, I ordered the guard out under arms, and the man to be tied up to a post. Otoo, his sister, and some others begged hard for him; Towha said not one word, but was very attentive to everything going forward. I expostulated with Otoo on the conduct of this man, and of his people in general; telling him, that neither I, nor any of my people, took anything from them, without first paying for it; enumerating the articles we gave in exchange for such and such things, and urging that it was wrong in them to steal from us who were their friends. I, moreover, told him, that the punishing this man would be the means of saving the lives of others of his people, by deterring them from committing crimes of this nature, in which some would certainly be shot dead, one time or another. With these and other arguments, which I believe he pretty well understood, he seemed satisfied, and only desired the man might not be *Matterou* (or killed). I then ordered the crowd, which was very great, to be kept at a proper distance, and, in the presence of them all, ordered the fellow two dozen of lashes with a cat-of-nine-tails, which he bore with great firmness, and was then set at liberty. After this, the natives were going away; but Towha stepped forth, called them back, and harangued them for near half an hour. His speech consisted of short sentences, very little of which I understood; but, from what we could gather, he recapitulated part of what I had said to Otoo; named several advantages they had received from us; condemned their present conduct, and recommended a different one for the future. The gracefulness of his action, and the attention with which he was heard, bespoke him a great orator.

Otoo said not one word. As soon as Towha had ended his speech, I ordered the marines to go through their exercise, and to load and fire in volleys with ball; and as they were very quick in their manœuvres, it is easier to conceive than to describe the amazement the natives were under the whole time, especially those who had not seen anything of the kind before.

May 12 On the 12th, old Oberea, the woman, who, when the *Dolphin* was here in 1767, was thought to be queen of the island, and whom I had not seen since 1769, paid us a visit, and brought us a present of hogs and fruit. Soon after came Otoo with a great retinue, and a large quantity of provisions. I was pretty liberal in my returns, thinking it might be the last time I should see these good people, who had so liberally relieved our wants; and, in the evening, entertained them with fireworks.

On the 13th, winds easterly, fair weather. Nevertheless, we were not ready to sail, as Otoo had made me promise to see him again, and I had a present to make him, which I reserved to the last. Oedidee was not yet come back from Attahourou; various reports arose concerning him; some said he had returned to Matavai; others that he would not return; and some would have it that he was at Oparree. In order to know more of the truth, a party of us in the evening went down to Oparree, where we found him, and likewise Towha, who, notwithstanding his illness, had resolved to see me before I sailed, and had gotten thus far on his journey. He was afflicted with a swelling in his feet and legs, which had entirely taken away the use of them. As the day was far spent, we were obliged to shorten our stay; and, after seeing Otoo, we returned with Oedidee on board.

This youth, I found, was desirous of remaining at this island, having before told him, as likewise many others, that we should not return. I now mentioned to him that he was at liberty to remain here, or to quit us at Ulietea, or to go with us to England, frankly owning that if he chose the latter, it was very probable he would never return to his country; in which case I would take care of him, and he must afterwards look upon me as his father. He threw his arms about me, and wept much, saying many people persuaded him to remain at Otaheite. I told him to go ashore and speak to his friends, and then come to me in the morning. He was well beloved in the ship, so that everyone was persuading him to go with us, telling him what great things he would see in England, and the immense riches (according to his idea of riches) he would return with. But I thought proper to undeceive him, as knowing that the only inducement to his going, was the expectation of returning, and I could see no prospect of an opportunity of that kind happening, unless a ship should be expressly sent out for that purpose; which neither I, nor anyone else, had a right to expect. I thought it an act of the highest injustice to take a person from these islands, under any promise which was not in my power to perform. At this time, indeed, it was quite unnecessary, for many youths voluntarily offered themselves to go, and even to remain and die in *Pretanee*; as they call our country. Otoo importuned me much to take one or two, to collect red feathers for him at Amsterdam, willing to risk the chance of their returning. Some of the gentlemen on board were likewise desirous of taking some as servants; but I refused every solicitation of this kind, knowing, from experience, they would be of no use to us in the course of the voyage; and further my views were not extended. What had the greatest weight with me, was the thinking myself bound to see they were afterwards properly taken care of, as they could not be carried from their native spot without consent.

Next morning early, Oedidee came on board with a resolution

to remain at the island; but Mr. Forster prevailed upon him to go with us to Ulietea. Soon after, Towha, Poatatou, Oamo, Happi, Oberea, and several more of our friends, came on board with fruit, etc. Towha was hoisted in and placed on a chair on the quarterdeck; his wife was with him. Amongst the various articles which I gave this chief, was an English pendant, which pleased him more than all the rest, especially after he had been instructed in the use of it.

May 14   Our treatment at this island was such as had induced one of our gunner's mates to form a plan to remain at it.[12] He knew he could not execute it with success while we lay in the bay, therefore took the opportunity, as soon as we were out, the boats in, and sails set, to slip overboard, being a good swimmer. But he was discovered before he got clear of the ship; and we presently hoisted a boat out and took him up. A canoe was observed, about halfway between us and the shore, seemingly coming after us. She was intended to take him up; but as soon as the people in her saw our boat they kept at a distance. This was a preconcerted plan between the man and them, which Otoo was acquainted with, and had encouraged. When I considered this man's situation in life, I did not think him so culpable, nor the resolution he had taken of staying here so extraordinary as it may at first appear. He was an Irishman by birth, and had sailed in the Dutch service. I picked him up at Batavia on my return from my former voyage, and he had been with me ever since. I never learnt that he had either friends or connections to confine him to any particular part of the world. All nations were alike to him. Where then could such a man be more happy than at one of these islands? Where, in one of the finest climates in the world, he could enjoy

---

[12] The ship was about to leave Tahiti for the last time on this voyage. The name of the gunner's mate was James Marra, who published an anonymous account of the voyage in 1775 in which regret is expressed that "he happened to be discovered, as from him a more copious and accurate account of the religion and civil government of these people might have been expected after a few years' stay among them. . . . But this attempt failing, and the man taken up, he was brought back, and laid in irons to bewail his ill-fortune, having flattered himself, as a man of enterprise and courage, with being made king of the country, or at least prime minister."

not only the necessaries, but the luxuries of life, in ease and plenty. I know not if he might not have obtained my consent, if he had applied for it in proper time. As soon as we had got him on board, and the boat in, I steered for Huaheine, in order to pay a visit to our friends there.

June 4   At last, when we were about to weigh, they[13] took a most affectionate leave. Oreo's last request was for me to return; when he saw he could not obtain that promise, he asked the name of my *Marai* (burying-place). As strange a question as this was, I hesitated not a moment to tell him Stepney; the parish in which I live, when in London. I was made to repeat it several times over till they could pronounce it: then, Stepney, *Marai no Toote*, was echoed through a hundred mouths at once. I after-wards found the same question had been put to Mr. Forster by a man on shore; but he gave a different, and, indeed, more proper answer, by saying, no man, who used the sea, could say where he should be buried. It is the custom at these islands for all the great families to have burial-places of their own, where their remains are interred. These go with the estate to the next heir. The *Marai* at Oparree at Otaheite, when Tootaha swayed the sceptre, was called *Marai no Tootaha*; but now it is called *Marai no Otoo*. What greater proof could we have of these people esteeming us as friends, than their wishing to remember us, even beyond the period of our lives? They had been repeatedly told that we should see them no more; they then wanted to know where we were to mingle with our parent dust.

As I could not promise, or even suppose, that more English ships would be sent to those islands, our faithful companion Oedidee chose to remain in his native country. But he left us with a regret fully demonstrative of the esteem he bore to us; nor could anything, but the fear of never returning, have torn him from us. When the chief teased me so much about returning, I sometimes gave such answers as left them hopes. Oedidee would

---

[13] *i.e.* The natives of Ulietea (Raiatea), whither Oedidee had taken a passage from Tahiti. On leaving the Society Isles Cook made his way once more to the Friendly Isles.

instantly catch at this, take me on one side, and ask me over again. In short, I have not words to describe the anguish which appeared in this young man's breast, when he went away. He looked up at the ship, burst into tears, and then sank down into the canoe. The maxim that a prophet has no honour in his own country, was never more fully verified than in this youth. At Otaheite he might have had anything that was in their power to bestow; whereas here he was not in the least noticed. He was a youth of good parts, and, like most of his countrymen, of a docile, gentle, and humane disposition; but, in a manner, wholly ignorant of their religion, government, manners, customs, and traditions; consequently no material knowledge could have been gathered from him, had I brought him away. Indeed, he would have been a better specimen of the nation, in every respect, than Omai. Just as Oedidee was going out of the ship, he asked me to *Tatou* some *Parou* for him, in order to show the commanders of any other ships which might stop here. I complied with his request, gave him a certificate of the time he had been with us, and recommended him to the notice of those who might touch at the island after me.

We did not get clear of our friends till eleven o'clock, when we weighed, and put to sea; but Oedidee did not leave us till we were almost out of the harbour. He stayed in order to fire some guns; for it being His Majesty's birthday, we fired the salute at going away.

When I first came to these islands, I had some thought of visiting Tupia's famous Bolabola. But as I had now got on board a plentiful supply of all manner of refreshments, and the route I had in view allowing me no time to spare, I laid this design aside, and directed my course to the west; taking our final leave of these happy islands, on which benevolent nature has spread her luxuriant sweets with a lavish hand. The natives, copying the bounty of nature, are equally liberal; contributing plentifully and cheerfully to the wants of navigators. During the six weeks we had remained at them, we had fresh pork, and all the fruits which were in season, in the utmost profusion; besides fish at Otaheite, and fowls at the other islands. All these articles we got in exchange for axes, hatchets, nails, chisels, cloth, red feathers, beads, knives, scissors, looking-glasses, etc., articles which will ever be valuable here. I ought not to omit shirts as a very capital article in making presents; especially with those who have any connections with the fair sex. A shirt here is full as necessary as a piece of gold in England. The ladies at Otaheite, after they had pretty well stripped their lovers of shirts, found a method of clothing themselves with their own cloth. It was their custom to go on shore every morning, and to return on board in the evening, generally clad in rags. This furnished a pretence to importune the lover for better clothes; and when he had no more of his own, he was to dress them in new cloth of the country, which they always left ashore; and appearing again in rags, they must again be clothed. So that the same suit might pass through twenty different hands, and be as often sold, bought, and given away.

BOOK III

From the Society Isles to New Zealand

1774

June 28   Early in the morning of the 28th, Lieutenant Clerke,
with the Master and fourteen or fifteen men, went on shore in
the launch for water.[1] I did intend to have followed in another
boat myself, but rather unluckily deferred it till after breakfast.
The launch was no sooner landed than the natives gathered about
her, behaving in so rude a manner, that the officers were in some
doubt if they should land the casks; but, as they expected me on
shore soon, they ventured, and, with difficulty, got them filled,
and into the boat again. In the doing of this, Mr. Clerke's gun
was snatched from him, and carried off; as were also some of the
cooper's tools; and several of the people were stripped of one
thing or another. All this was done, as it were, by stealth; for they
laid hold of nothing by main force. I landed just as the launch was
ready to put off; and the natives, who were pretty numerous on
the beach, as soon as they saw me, fled; so that I suspected something had happened. However, I prevailed on many to stay, and
Mr. Clerke came, and informed me of all the preceding circumstances. I quickly came to a resolution to oblige them to make

---

[1] A visit to another island in the Friendly group—Annamocka (Nomuka, or
Rotterdam as Tasman called it). It was on this occasion that Cook named the
group, as is shown by a pencilled note in his MS.: "This group I have named the
Friendly Archipelago, as a lasting friendship seems to subsist among its inhabitants
and their courtesy to strangers entitles them to that name."

restitution; and, for this purpose, ordered all the marines to be armed, and sent on shore. Mr. Forster and his party being gone into the country, I ordered two or three guns to be fired from the ship, in order to alarm him; not knowing how the natives might act on this occasion. These orders being given, I sent all the boats off but one, with which I stayed, having a good many of the natives about me, who behaved with their usual courtesy. I made them so sensible of my intention, that long before the marines came, Mr. Clerke's musket was brought, but they used many excuses to divert me from insisting on the other. At length Mr. Edgecumbe arriving with the marines, this alarmed them so much, that some of them fled. The first step I took was to seize on two large double sailing-canoes, which were in the cove. One fellow making resistance, I fired some small shot at him, and sent him limping off. The natives being now convinced that I was in earnest, all fled; but on my calling to them, many returned; and, presently after, the other musket was brought, and laid at my feet. That moment I ordered the canoes to be restored, to show them on what account they were detained. The other things we had lost being of less value, I was the more indifferent about them. By this time the launch was ashore for another turn of water, and we were permitted to fill the casks without anyone daring to come near us; except one man, who had befriended us during the whole affair, and seemed to disapprove of the conduct of his countrymen.

On my returning from the pond to the cove, I found a good many people collected together, from whom we understood that the man I had fired at was dead. This story I treated as improbable, and addressed a man, who seemed of some consequence, for the restitution of a cooper's adze we had lost in the morning. He immediately sent away two men, as I thought, for it; but I soon found that we had greatly mistaken each other; for, instead of the adze, they brought the wounded man, stretched out on a board, and laid him down by me, to all appearance dead. I was much moved at the sight; but soon saw my mistake, and that he was only wounded in the hand and thigh. I therefore desired he might be carried out of the sun, and sent for the surgeon to dress his wounds. In the meantime, I addressed several people for the adze; for as I had now nothing else to do, I determined to have it. The one I applied the most to, was an elderly woman, who had always a great deal to say to me, from my first landing; but, on this occasion, she gave her tongue full scope. I understood but little of her eloquence; and all I could gather from her arguments was, that it was mean in me to insist on the return of so trifling a thing. But when she found I was determined, she and three or four more women went away; and soon after the adze was brought me, but I saw her no more. This I was sorry for, as I wanted to make her a present, in return for the part she had taken in all our transactions, private as well as public. For I was no sooner returned from the pond, the first time I landed, than this old lady presented to me a girl, giving me to understand she was at my service. Miss, who probably had received her instructions, wanted, as a preliminary article, a spike-nail, or a shirt, neither of which I had to give her, and soon made them sensible of my poverty. I thought, by that means, to have come off with flying colours; but I was mistaken; for they gave me to understand I might retire with her on credit. On my declining this proposal, the old lady began to argue with me; and then abuse me. Though I comprehended little of what she said, her actions were expressive enough, and showed that her words were to this effect, sneering in my face, saying, what sort of a man are you, thus to refuse the embraces of so fine a young woman? For the girl certainly did not want beauty; which, however, I could better withstand, than the abuses of this worthy matron, and therefore hastened into the boat. They wanted me to take the young lady aboard; but this could not be done, as I had given strict orders, before I went ashore, to suffer no woman, on any pretence whatever, to come into the ship, for reasons which I shall mention in another place.

As soon as the surgeon got ashore, he dressed the man's wounds, and bled him; and was of opinion that he was in no sort of danger, as the shot had done little more than penetrate the skin. In the operation, some poultice being wanting, the surgeon asked for ripe plantains; but they brought sugar-cane, and having chewed it to a pulp, gave it him to apply to the wound. This being of a more balsamic nature than the other, proves that these people have some knowledge of simples. As soon as the man's wounds were dressed, I made him a present, which his master, or at least the man who owned the canoe, took most probably to himself. Matters being thus settled, apparently to the satisfaction of all parties, we repaired on board to dinner, where I found a good supply of fruit and roots, and therefore gave orders to get everthing in readiness to sail.

I now was informed of a circumstance which was observed on board: several canoes being at the ship, when the great guns were fired in the morning, they all retired, but one man, who was bailing the water out of his canoe, which lay alongside, directly under the guns. When the first was fired, he just looked up, and then, quite unconcerned, continued his work; nor had the second gun any other effect upon him; he did not stir till the water was all out of his canoe, when he paddled leisurely off. This man had several times been observed to take fruit and roots out of other canoes, and sell them to us. If the owners did not willingly part with them, he took them by force; by which he obtained the appellation of custom-house officer. One time, after he had been collecting tribute, he happened to be lying alongside of a sailing-canoe which was on board. One of her people seeing him look another way, and his attention otherwise engaged, took the opportunity of stealing somewhat out of his canoe; they then put off, and set their sail; but the man, perceiving the trick they had played him, darted after them, and having soon got on board their canoe, beat him who had taken his things, and not only brought back his own but many other articles which he took from them. This man had likewise been observed making collections on shore at the trading-place. I remembered to have seen him there; and, on account of his gathering tribute, took him to be a man of consequence, and was going to make him a present; but some of their people would not let me; saying he was no *Areeke* (that is, chief). He had his hair always powdered with some kind of white dust.

July 21   We had no sooner anchored than several of the natives came off in canoes.[2] They were very cautious at first; but, at last, trusted themselves alongside, and exchanged, for pieces of cloth, arrows; some of which were pointed with bone, and dipped in some green gummy substance, which we naturally supposed was poisonous. Two men having ventured on board, after a short stay I sent them away with presents. Others probably induced by this, came off by moonlight; but I gave orders to permit none to come alongside; by which means we got clear of them for the night.

Next morning early, a good many came round us, some in canoes, and others swimming. I soon prevailed on one to come on board; which he no sooner did than he was followed by more than I desired; so that not only our deck but rigging was presently filled with them. I took four into the cabin, and gave them various articles, which they showed to those in the canoes, and seemed much pleased with their reception. While I was thus making friends with those in the cabin, an accident happened that threw all into confusion, but in the end, I believe, proved advantageous to us. A fellow in a canoe having been refused admittance into one of our boats that lay alongside, bent his bow to shoot a poisoned arrow at the boatkeeper. Some of his countrymen prevented his doing it that instant, and gave time to acquaint me with it. I ran instantly on deck, and saw another man struggling with him; one of those who had been in the cabin, and had leapt out of the window for this purpose. The other seemed resolved, shook him off, and directed his bow again to the boatkeeper; but on my calling to him, pointed it at me. Having a musket in my hand, loaded with small shot, I gave him the contents. This staggered him for a moment, but did not prevent him from holding his bow still in the attitude of shooting. Another discharge of the same nature made him drop it, and the others, who were in the canoe, to paddle off with all speed. At this time,

[2] At Mallicollo ("Manicolo" according to Quiros, who in 1606 discovered the northern part of the chain of islands which Cook called the New Hebrides; its modern name is Malekula). Two islands named by Bougainville, the Isle of Lepers and Aurora, had already been passed. Cook sailed down the east side of the archipelago and then up the west side to reach the northernmost island, Espiritu Santo. In the space of three weeks he named, charted and fixed the position of the whole of this 350 mile chain of islands.

some began to shoot arrows on the other side. A musket discharged in the air had no effect; but a four-pound shot over their
heads sent them off in the utmost confusion. Many quitted their
canoes and swam on shore: those in the great cabin leaped out
of the windows; and those who were on the deck, and on different
parts of the rigging, all leaped overboard. After this we took no
further notice of them, but suffered them to come off and pick
up their canoes; and some even ventured again alongside the
ship. Immediately after the great gun was fired, we heard the
beating of drums on shore; which was, probably, the signal for
the country to assemble in arms. We now got everything in
readiness to land, to cut some wood, of which we were in want,
and to try to get some refreshments, nothing of this kind having
been seen in any of the canoes.

About nine o'clock, we put off in two boats, and landed in the
face of four or five hundred people, who were assembled on the
shore. Though they were all armed with bows and arrows, clubs
and spears, they made not the least opposition. On the contrary,
seeing me advance alone, with nothing but a green branch in my
hand, one of them, who seemed to be a chief, giving his bow and
arrows to another, met me in the water, bearing also a green
branch, which having exchanged for the one I held, he then took
me by the hand, and led me up to the crowd. I immediately distributed presents to them, and, in the meantime, the marines were
drawn upon the beach. I then made signs (for we understood not
a word of their language) that we wanted wood; and they made
signs to us to cut down the trees. By this time, a small pig being
brought down and presented to me, I gave the bearer a piece of
cloth, with which he seemed well pleased. This made us hope
that we should soon have some more; but we were mistaken. The
pig was not brought to be exchanged for what we had, but on
some other account; probably as a peace-offering. For all we
could say or do did not prevail on them to bring down, after this,
above half a dozen coconuts, and a small quantity of fresh water.
They set no value on nails, or any sort of iron tools; nor indeed
on anything we had. They would, now and then, exchange an
arrow for a piece of cloth; but very seldom would part with a

bow. They were unwilling we should go off the beach, and very desirous we should return on board. At length, about noon, after sending what wood we had cut on board, we embarked ourselves; and they all retired, some one way and some another.

Before we had dined, the afternoon was too far spent to do anything on shore; and all hands were employed, setting up the rigging, and repairing some defects in it. But seeing a man bring along the strand a buoy, which they had taken in the night from the kedge-anchor, I went on shore for it, accompanied by some of the gentlemen. The moment we landed, it was put into the boat by a man who walked off again without speaking one word. It ought to be observed, that this was the only thing they took, or even attempted to take from us, by any means whatever. Being landed near some of their plantations and houses, which were just within the skirts of the woods, I prevailed on one man to conduct me to them; but, though they suffered Mr. Forster to go with me, they were unwilling any more should follow. These houses were something like those of the other isles; rather low, and covered with palm thatch; some were enclosed, or walled round with boards; and the entrance to these was by a square hole at one end, which at this time was shut up, and they were unwilling to open it for us to look in. There were here about six houses, and some small plantations of roots, etc., fenced round with reeds as at the Friendly Isles. There were, likewise, some bread-fruit, coconut, and plantain trees; but very little fruit on any of them. A good many fine yams were piled up upon sticks, or a kind of raised platform; and about twenty pigs, and a few fowls, were running about loose. After making these observations, having embarked, we proceeded to the south-east point of the harbour, where we again landed and walked along the beach till we could see the islands to the south-east already mentioned. The names of these we now obtained, as well as the name of that on which we were. This they called Mallicollo: the island that first appeared over the south end of Ambrym is called Apee; and the other, with the hill on it, Paoom. We found on the beach a fruit like an orange, called by them *Abbi-mora*, but whether it be fit for eating, I cannot say, as this was decayed.

Proceeding next to the other side of the harbour, we there landed, near a few houses, at the invitation of some people who came down to the shore; but we had not been there five minutes before they wanted us to be gone. We complied, and proceeded up the harbour in order to sound it, and to look for fresh water, of which, as yet, we had seen none, but the very little that the natives brought, which we knew not where they got. Nor was our search now attended with success; but this is no proof that there is not any. The day was too far spent to examine the place well enough to determine this point. Night having brought us on board, I was informed that no soul had been off to the ship; so soon was the curiosity of these people satisfied. As we were coming on board, we heard the sound of a drum, and, I think, of some other instruments, and saw people dancing, but as soon as they heard the noise of the oars, or saw us, all was silent.

Being unwilling to lose the benefit of the moonlight nights, which now happened, at 7 a.m. on the 23rd we weighed; and, with a light air of wind, and the assistance of our boats, proceeded out of the harbour; the south end of which, at noon, bore W.S.W. distant about two miles.

When the natives saw us under sail, they came off in canoes, making exchanges with more confidence than before, and giving such extraordinary proofs of their honesty as surprised us. As the ship at first had fresh way through the water, several of them dropped astern after they had received our goods, and before they had time to deliver theirs in return. Instead of taking advantage of this, as our friends at the Society Isles would have done, they used their utmost efforts to get up with us, and to deliver what they had already been paid for. One man, in particular, followed us a considerable time, and did not reach us till it was calm, and the thing was forgotten. As soon as he came alongside, he held up the thing which several were ready to buy; but he refused to part with it, till he saw the person to whom he had before sold it, and to him he gave it. The person not knowing him again, offered him something in return, which he refused, and showed him what he had given him before. Pieces of cloth and marbled paper were in most esteem with them; but edge tools, nails, and beads, they seemed to disregard. The greatest number of canoes we had alongside at once did not exceed eight, and not more than four or five people in each; who would frequently retire to the shore all on a sudden, before they had disposed of half their things, and then others would come off.

At the time we came out of the harbour, it was about low water, and great numbers of people were then on the shoals or reefs which lie along the shore, looking, as we supposed, for shell and other fish. Thus our being on their coast, and in one of their ports, did not hinder them from following the necessary employments. By this time they might be satisfied we meant them no harm; so that, had we made a longer stay, we might soon have been upon good terms with this ape-like nation; for, in general, they are the most ugly, ill-proportioned people I ever saw, and in every respect different from any we had met with in this sea. They are a very dark-coloured and rather diminutive race; with long heads, flat faces, and monkey countenances. Their hair mostly black or brown, is short and curly; but not quite so soft and woolly as that of a negro. Their beards are very strong, crisp, and bushy, and generally black and short. But what most adds to their deformity, is a belt, or cord, which they wear round the waist and tie so tight over the belly that the shape of their bodies is not unlike that of an overgrown pismire [ant]. The men go quite naked, except a piece of cloth or leaf used as a wrapper.

We saw but few women, and they were not less ugly than the men; their heads, faces, and shoulders are painted red; they wear a kind of petticoat; and some of them had something over their shoulders like a bag, in which they carry their children. None of them came off to the ship, and they generally kept at a distance when we were on shore. Their ornaments are ear-rings made of tortoise-shell and bracelets. A curious one of the latter four or five inches broad, wrought with thread or cord, and studded with shells, is worn by them just above the elbow. Round the right wrist they wear hogs' tusks bent circular, and rings made of shells; and round their left, a round piece of wood which we judged was to ward off the bow-string. The bridge of the nose is pierced, in which they wear a piece of white stone about an inch and a half long. As signs of friendship they present a green branch, and sprinkle water with the hand over the head.

Their weapons are clubs, spears, and bows and arrows. The two former are made of hard or iron wood. Their bows are about four feet long, made of a stick split down the middle, and are not circular. The arrows, which are a sort of reed, are sometimes armed with a long and sharp point, made of the hard wood, and sometimes with a very hard point made of bone; and these points are all covered with a substance which we took for poison. Indeed, the people themselves confirmed our suspicions, by making signs to us not to touch the point, and giving us to understand, that if we were pricked by them we should die. They are very careful of them themselves, and keep them always wrapped up in a quiver. Some of these arrows are armed with two or three points, each with small prickles on the edges, to prevent the arrow being drawn out of the wound.

The people of Mallicollo seemed to be a quite different nation from any we had yet met with, and speak a different language.

August 14   Next morning, after breakfast, a party of us set out for the country, to try if we could not get a nearer and better view of the volcano.[3] We went by the way of one of those hot smoking places before mentioned, and dug a hole in the hottest part, into which a thermometer of Fahrenheit's construction was put; and the mercury presently rose to 100°. It remained in the hole two minutes and a half without either rising or falling. The earth about this place was a kind of white clay, had a sulphureous smell, and was soft and wet, the surface only excepted, over which was spread a thin dry crust, that had upon it some sulphur, and a vitriolic substance, tasting like alum. The place affected by the heat was not above eight or ten yards square; and near it were some fig trees, which spread their branches over a part of it, and seemed to like their situation. We thought that this extraordinary heat was caused by the steam of boiling water, strongly impregnated with sulphur. I was told that some of the other places were

[3] A landing on the volcanic island of Tanna, the southernmost of the New Hebrides.

larger than this; though we did not go out of the road to look
at them, but proceeded up the hill through a country so covered
with trees, shrubs, and plants, that the bread-fruit and coconut
trees, which seem to have been planted here by nature, were in
a manner choked up. Here and there we met with a house, some
few people, and plantations. These latter we found in different
states; some of long standing; others lately cleared; and some only
clearing, and before anything had been planted. The clearing a
piece of ground for a plantation seemed to be a work of much
labour, considering the tools they had to work with, which,
though much inferior to those at the Society Isles, are of the same
kind. Their method is, however, judicious, and as expeditious as
it can well be. They lop off the small branches of the large trees,
dig under the roots, and there burn the branches and small
shrubs and plants which they root up. The soil, in some parts, is a
rich black mould; in other parts, it seemed to be composed of
decayed vegetables, and of the ashes the volcano sends forth
throughout all its neighbourhood. Happening to turn out of the
common path, we came into a plantation, where we found a
man at work, who, either out of good nature, or to get us the
sooner out of his territories, undertook to be our guide. We followed him accordingly, but had not gone far before we came to
the junction of two roads, in one of which stood another man
with a sling and a stone, which he thought proper to lay down
when a musket was pointed at him. The attitude in which we
found him, the ferocity appearing in his looks, and his behaviour
after, convinced us that he meant to defend the path he stood in.
He, in some measure, gained his point; for our guide took the
other road, and we followed; but not without suspecting he was
leading us out of the common way. The other man went with us
likewise, counting us several times over, and hallooing, as we
judged, for assistance; for we were presently joined by two or
three more, among whom was a young woman with a club in
her hand. By these people we were conducted to the brow of a
hill, and shown a road leading down to the harbour, which they
wanted us to take. Not choosing to comply, we returned to that
we had left, which we pursued alone, our guide refusing to go

with us. After ascending another ridge, as thickly covered with wood as those we had come over, we saw yet other hills between us and the volcano, which seemed as far off as at our first setting-out. This discouraged us from proceeding farther, especially as we could get no one to be our guide. We therefore came to a resolution to return; and had but just put this in execution, when we met between twenty and thirty people, whom the fellow before mentioned had collected together, with a design, as we judged, to oppose our advancing into the country; but as they saw us returning, they suffered us to pass unmolested. Some of them put us into the right road, accompanied us down the hill, made us stop by the way to entertain us with coconuts, plantains, and sugar-cane; and what we did not eat on the spot, they brought down the hill with us. Thus, we found these people hospitable, civil, and good-natured, when not prompted to a contrary conduct by jealousy; a conduct I cannot tell how to blame them for, especially when I consider the light in which they must view us. It was impossible for them to know our real design; we enter their ports without their daring to oppose; we endeavour to land in their country as friends, and it is well if this succeeds; we land, nevertheless, and maintain the footing we have got, by the superiority of our firearms. Under such circumstances, what opinion are they to form of us? Is it not as reasonable for them to think that we come to invade their country, as to pay them a friendly visit? Time, and some acquaintance with us, can only convince them of the latter. These people are yet in a rude state; and, if we may judge from circumstances and appearances, are frequently at war, not only with their neighbours, but among themselves; consequently must be jealous of every new face. I will allow there are some exceptions to this rule to be found in this sea; but there are few nations who would willingly suffer visitors like us to advance far into their country.

Before this excursion, some of us had been of opinion, that these people were addicted to an unnatural passion, because they had endeavoured to entice some of our men into the woods; and, in particular, I was told, that one who had the care of Mr. Forster's plant bag, had been, once or twice, attempted. As the carrying of bundles, etc., is the office of the women in this country, it had occurred to me, and I was not singular in this, that the natives might mistake him, and some others, for women. My conjecture was fully verified this day: for this man, who was one of the party, and carried the bag as usual, following me down the hill, by the words which I understood of the conversation of the natives, and by their actions, I was well assured that they considered him as a female; till, by some means, they discovered their mistake, on which they cried out, *Erramange! Erramange!* It's a man! It's a man! The thing was so palpable that everyone was obliged to acknowledge, that they had before mistaken his sex; and that, after they were undeceived, they seemed not to have the least notion of what we had suspected. This circumstance will show how liable we are to form wrong conjectures of things, among people whose language we are ignorant of. Had it not been for this discovery, I make no doubt that these people would have been charged with this vile custom.

DESCRIPTION OF TANNA

At first we thought the people of this island, as well as those of Erromango, were a race between the natives of the Friendly Isles and those of Mallicollo; but a little acquaintance with them convinced us that they had little or no affinity to either, except it be in their hair, which is much like what the people of the latter island have.[4] The general colours of it are black and brown, growing to a tolerable length, and very crisp and curly. They separate it into small locks, which they woold or cue round with the rind of a slender plant, down to about an inch of the ends; and, as the hair grows, the woolding is continued. Each of these cues or locks is somewhat thicker than common whipcord; and they look like a parcel of small strings hanging down from the crown of their heads. Their beards, which are strong and bushy, are generally short. The women do not wear their hair so, but cropped;

[4] The inhabitants of Malekula are affected by the Polynesian strain; those of the more southerly islands of Erromango and Tanna are pure Melanesian.

nor do the boys, till they approach manhood. Some few men, women, and children, were seen, who had hair like ours; but it was obvious that these were of another nation; and I think we understood they came from Erronan. It is to this island they ascribe one of the two languages which they speak, and which is nearly, if not exactly, the same as that spoken at the Friendly Isles. It is therefore more than probable that Erronan was peopled from that nation, and that, by long intercourse with Tanna and the other neighbouring islands, each has learnt the other's language, which they use indiscriminately.

The other language which the people of Tanna speak, and, as we understood, those of Erromango and Annattom, is properly their own. It is different from any we had before met with, and bears no affinity to that of Mallicollo; so that, it should seem, the people of these islands are a distinct nation of themselves. Mallicollo, Apee, etc., were names entirely unknown to them; they even knew nothing of Sandwich Island, which is much the nearer. I took no small pains to know how far their geographical knowledge extended; and did not find that it exceeded the limits of their horizon.

These people are of the middle size, rather slender than otherwise; many are little, but few tall or stout; the most of them have good features, and agreeable countenances; are, like all the tropical race, active and nimble; and seem to excel in the use of arms, but not to be fond of labour. They never would put a hand to assist in any work we were carrying on, which the people of the other islands used to delight in. But what I judge most from, is their making the females do the most laborious work, as if they were pack-horses. I have seen a woman carrying a large bundle on her back, or a child on her back and a bundle under her arm, and a fellow strutting before her with nothing but a club or spear, or some such thing. We have frequently observed little troops of women pass, to and fro, along the beach, laden with fruit and roots, escorted by a party of men under arms; though, now and then, we have seen a man carry a burden at the same time, but not often. I know not on what account this was done, nor that an armed troop was necessary. At first, we thought they were moving out of the neighbourhood with their effects; but we afterwards saw them both carry out and bring in every day.

I cannot say the women are beauties; but I think them handsome enough for the men, and too handsome for the use that is made of them. Both sexes are of a very dark colour, but not black; nor have they the least characteristic of the negro about them. They make themselves blacker than they really are, by painting their faces with a pigment of the colour of black lead. They also use another sort which is red, and a third sort brown, or a colour between red and black. All these, but especially the first, they lay on, with a liberal hand, not only on the face, but on the neck, shoulders, and breast. The men wear nothing but a belt, and the wrapping leaf as at Mallicollo. The women have a kind of petticoat made of the filaments of the plantain tree, flags, or some such thing, which reaches below the knee. Both sexes wear ornaments, such as bracelets, earrings, necklaces, and amulets. The bracelets are chiefly worn by the men; some made of sea-shells, and others of those of the coconut. The men also wear amulets; and those of most value being made of a greenish stone, the green stone of New Zealand is valued by them for this purpose. Necklaces are chiefly used by the women, and made mostly of shells. Earrings are common to both sexes, and those valued most are made of tortoise-shell. Some of our people having got some at the Friendly Isles, brought it to a good market here, where it was of more value than anything we had besides; from which I conclude that these people catch but few turtle, though I saw one in the harbour, just as we were getting under sail. I observed that, towards the latter end of our stay, they began to ask for hatchets, and large nails; so that it is likely they had found that iron is more serviceable than stone, bone, or shells, of which all their tools I have seen are made. Their stone hatchets, at least all those I saw, are not in the shape of adzes, as at the other islands, but more like an axe. In the helve, which is pretty thick, is made a hole into which the stone is fixed.

These people, besides the cultivation of ground, have few other arts worth mentioning. They know how to make a coarse kind of matting, and a coarse cloth of the bark of a tree, which is used chiefly for belts. The workmanship of their canoes, I have before observed, is very rude; and their arms, with which they take the most pains in point of neatness, come far short of some others we had seen. Their weapons are clubs, spears, or darts, bows and arrows, and stones. The clubs are of three or four kinds, and from three to five feet long. They seem to place more dependence on the darts, which are pointed, with three bearded edges. In throwing them they make use of a becket, that is, a piece of stiff plaited cord about six inches long, with an eye in one end and a knot at the other. The eye is fixed on the forefinger of the right hand, and the other end is hitched round the dart, where it is nearly on an equipoise. They hold the dart between the thumb and remaining fingers, which serve only to give it direction, the velocity being communicated by the becket and forefinger. The former flies off from the dart the instant its velocity becomes greater than that of the hand, but it remains on the finger ready to be used again. With darts they kill both birds and fish, and are sure of hitting a mark, within the compass of the crown of a hat, at the distance of eight or ten yards; but, at double that distance, it is chance if they hit a mark the size of a man's body, though they will throw the weapon sixty or seventy yards. They always throw with all their might, let the distance be what it will. Darts, bows and arrows, are to them what muskets are to us. The arrows are made of reeds pointed with hard wood: some are bearded and some not, and those for shooting birds have two, three, and sometimes four points. The stones they use are, in general, the branches of coral rocks from eight to fourteen inches long, and from an inch to an inch and a half in diameter. I know not if they employ them as missive weapons; almost every one of them carries a club, and besides that, either darts, or a bow and arrows, but never both: those who had stones kept them generally in their belts.

I cannot conclude this account of their arms without adding an entire passage out of Mr. Wales's journal. As this gentleman was continually on shore amongst them, he had a better opportunity of seeing what they could perform than any of us. The passage is as follows:

"I must confess I have been often led to think the feats which Homer represents his heroes as performing with their spears a little too much of the marvellous to be admitted into an heroic poem; I mean when confined within the straight stays of Aristotle. Nay, even so great an advocate for him as Mr. Pope acknowledges them to be *surprising*. But since I have seen what these people can do with their wooden spears, and them badly pointed, and not of a very hard nature, I have not the least exception to any one passage in that great poet on this account. But, if I see fewer exceptions, I can find infinitely more beauties in him; as he has, I think, scarce an action, circumstance, or description of any kind whatever, relating to a spear, which I have not seen and recognized among these people; as their whirling motion, and whistling noise, as they fly; their quivering motion, as they stick in the ground when they fall; their meditating their aim, when they are going to throw; and their shaking them in their hands as they go along, etc., etc."

August 25   At daybreak, on the 25th, we were on the north side of the island (which is of a moderate height, and three leagues in circuit), and steered west for the bluff-head along the low land under it.[5] At sunrise an elevated coast came in sight beyond the bluff-head, extending to the north as far as N.W. by W. After doubling the head we found the land to trend south, a little easterly, and to form a large, deep bay, bounded on the west by the coast just mentioned.

Everything conspired to make us believe this was the bay of St. Philip and St. Jago, discovered by Quiros in 1606. To determine this point it was necessary to proceed farther up; for at this time we saw no end to it. The wind being at south, we were obliged to ply, and first stretched over for the west shore, from which we were three miles at noon, when our latitude was 14° 55' 30" S., longitude 167° 3' E.; the mouth of the bay extending from N. 64° W. to S. 86° E., which last direction was the bluff-head,

[5] Having sailed up the western side of the New Hebrides, Cook passed through the Bougainville Passage to the eastern coast of Quiros's Espiritu Santo, the most northerly island of the archipelago. Quiros imagined this island to be the north-west point of *Terra Australis*.

distant three leagues. In the afternoon, the wind veering to
E.S.E., we could look up to the head of the bay; but as the breeze
was faint, a north-east swell hurled us over to the west shore; so
that, at half-past four o'clock in the afternoon we were no more
than two miles from it, and tacked in one hundred and twenty
fathoms of water, a soft muddy bottom. The bluff-head, or east
point of the bay, bore N. 53° E.

We had no sooner tacked than it fell calm, and we were left
to the mercy of the swell, which continued to hurtle us towards
the shore, where large troops of people were assembled. Some
ventured off in two canoes; but all the signs of friendship we
could make, did not induce them to come alongside, or near
enough to receive any present from us. At last they took sudden
fright at something, and returned ashore. They were naked,
except having some long grass, like flags, fastened to a belt, and
hanging down before and behind, nearly as low as the knee. Their
colour was very dark, and their hair woolly; or cut short, which
made it seem so. The canoes were small, and had outriggers. The
calm continued till near eight o'clock, in which time we drove
into eighty-five fathoms of water, and so near the shore, that I
expected we should be obliged to anchor. A breeze of wind
sprung up at E.S.E., and first took us on the wrong side; but,
contrary to all our expectations, and when we had hardly room
to veer, the ship came about, and having filled on the starboard
tack, we stood off N.E. Thus we were relieved from the apprehensions of being forced to anchor in a great depth, on a lee shore,
and in a dark and obscure night.

We continued to ply upwards, with variable light breezes between E.S.E. and S., till ten next morning, when it fell calm. We
were, at this time, about seven or eight miles from the head of the
bay, which is terminated by a low beach; and behind that is an
extensive flat covered with wood, and bounded on each side by
a ridge of mountains. At noon we found the latitude to be 15° 5'
S., and were detained here by the calm till one o'clock in the
afternoon, when we got a breeze at N. by W., with which we
steered up to within two miles of the head of the bay; and then I
sent Mr. Cooper and Mr. Gilbert to sound and reconnoitre the

coast, while we stood to and fro with the ship. This gave time to
three sailing-canoes, which had been following us some time, to
come up. There were five or six men in each; and they approached
near enough to receive such things as were thrown to them
fastened to a rope, but would not advance alongside. They were
the same sort of people as those we had seen the preceding evening; indeed we thought they came from the same place. They
seemed to be stouter and better shaped men than those of Mallicollo; and several circumstances concurred to make us think they
were of another nation. They named the numerals as far as five
or six, in the language of Anamocka, and understood us when we
asked the names of the adjacent lands in that language. Some,
indeed, had black short frizzled hair, like the natives of Mallicollo;
but others had it long, tied up on the crown of the head, and ornamented with feathers, like the New Zealanders. Their other ornaments were bracelets and necklaces; one man had something like
a white shell on his forehead; and some were painted with a
blackish pigment. I did not see that they had any other weapon but
darts and gigs [harpoons], intended only for striking of fish. Their
canoes were much like those of Tanna, and navigated in the same
manner, or nearly so. They readily gave us the names of such
parts as we pointed to: but we could not obtain from them the
name of the island. At length, seeing our boats coming, they
paddled in for the shore, notwithstanding all we could say or do
to detain them.

September 5   After dinner I went on shore with two armed
boats, having with us one of the natives who had attached himself to me.[6] We landed on a sandy beach before a vast number of
people, who had got together with no other intent than to see us;
for many of them had not a stick in their hands; consequently we
were received with great courtesy, and with the surprise natural
for people to express at seeing men and things so new to them as
we must be. I made presents to all those my friends pointed out,
who were either old men, or such as seemed to be of some note;

[6] Having set course south-west from Santo, Cook now reached the island of
Balade (Balabea) off the north coast of New Caledonia.

but he took not the least notice of some women who stood behind the crowd, holding my hand when I was going to give them some beads and medals. Here we found the same chief who had been seen in one of the canoes in the morning. His name, we now learnt, was Teabooma; and we had not been on shore above ten minutes, before he called for silence. Being instantly obeyed by every individual present, he made a short speech; and soon after another chief having called for silence, made a speech also. It was pleasing to see with what attention they were heard. Their speeches were composed of short sentences; to each of which two or three old men answered, by nodding their heads, and giving a kind of grunt, significant, as I thought, of approbation. It was impossible for us to know the purport of these speeches; but we had reason to think they were favourable to us, on whose account they doubtless were made. I kept my eyes fixed on the people all the time, and saw nothing to induce me to think otherwise. While we were with them, having inquired, by signs, for fresh water, some pointed to the east, and others to the west. My friend undertook to conduct us to it, and embarked with us for that purpose. We rowed about two miles up the coast to the east, where the shore was mostly covered with mangrove trees; and entering amongst them, by a narrow creek or river, which brought us to a little straggling village above all the mangroves, there we landed, and were shown fresh water. The ground near this village was finely cultivated, being laid out in plantations of sugar-canes, plantains, yams, and other roots; and watered by little rills, conducted by art from the main stream, whose source was in the hills. Here were some coconut trees, which did not seem burdened with fruit. We heard the crowing of cocks, but saw none. Some roots were baking on a fire, in an earthen jar, which would have held six or eight gallons; nor did we doubt its being their own manufacture. As we proceeded up the creek, Mr. Forster having shot a duck flying over our heads, which was the first use these people saw made of our firearms, my friend begged to have it; and when he landed, told his countrymen in what manner it was killed. The day being far spent, and the tide not permitting us to stay longer in the creek, we took leave of the people, and got on board a little after sunset. From this little excursion, I found that we were to expect nothing from these people but the privilege of visiting their country undisturbed. For it was easy to see they had little else than good nature to bestow. In this they exceeded all the nations we had yet met with; and, although it did not satisfy the demands of nature, it at once pleased and left our minds at ease.

September 7   In the afternoon I made a little excursion alongshore to the westward, in company with Mr. Wales. Besides making observations on such things as we met, we got the names of several places, which I then thought were islands; but upon further inquiry, I found they were districts upon this same land. This afternoon, a fish being struck by one of the natives near the watering-place, my clerk purchased it, and sent it to me after my return on board. It was of a new species, something like a sunfish, with a large, long, ugly head. Having no suspicion of its being of a poisonous nature, we ordered it to be dressed for supper; but very luckily, the operation of drawing and describing took up so much time, that it was too late, so that only the liver and row were dressed, of which the two Mr. Forsters and myself did but taste. About three o'clock in the morning, we found ourselves seized with an extraordinary weakness and numbness all over our limbs. I had almost lost the sense of feeling, nor could I distinguish between light and heavy bodies, of such as I had strength to move; a quart pot full of water and a feather being the same in my hand. We each of us took an emetic, and after that a sweat, which gave us much relief. In the morning, one of the pigs which had eaten the entrails was found dead. When the natives came on board and saw the fish hung up, they immediately gave us to understand it was not wholesome food, and expressed the utmost abhorrence of it; though no one was observed to do this when the fish was to be sold, or even after it was purchased.

On the 8th, the guard and a party of men were on shore as usual. In the afternoon I received a message from the officer, acquainting me that Teabooma, the chief, was come with a

present, consisting of a few yams and sugar-canes. In return I sent
him, amongst other articles, a dog and a bitch, both young, but
nearly full grown. The dog was red and white, but the bitch was
all red, or the colour of an English fox. I mention this, because
they may prove the Adam and Eve of their species in that country. When the officer returned on board in the evening, he informed me that the chief came attended by about twenty men,
so that it looked like a visit of ceremony. It was some time before
he would believe the dog and bitch were intended for him; but
as soon as he was convinced, he seemed lost in an excess of joy,
and sent them away immediately.

DESCRIPTION OF NEW CALEDONIA

I shall conclude our transactions at this place with some account
of the country and its inhabitants. They are strong, robust, active,
well-made people, courteous and friendly, and not in the least
addicted to pilfering, which is more than can be said of any other
nation in this sea. They are nearly of the same colour as the natives
of Tanna, but have better features, more agreeable countenances,
and are a much stouter race; a few being seen who measured six
feet four inches. I observed some who had thick lips, flat noses,
and full cheeks, and, in some degree, the features and look of a
negro. Two things contributed to the forming of such an idea;
first, their ruff mop heads; and secondly, their besmearing their
faces with black pigment. Their hair and beards are, in general,
black. The former is very much frizzled; so that, at first sight, it
appears like that of a negro. It is, nevertheless, very different;
though both coarser and stronger than ours. Some, who wear it
long, tie it up on the crown of the head; others suffer only a large
lock to grow on each side, which they tie up in clubs; many
others, as well as all the women, wear it cropped short. These
rough heads, most probably, want frequent scratching, for which
purpose they have a most excellent instrument. This is a kind of
comb made of sticks of hard wood, from seven to nine inches
long, and about the thickness of knitting needles. A number of

these, seldom exceeding twenty, but generally fewer, are fastened together at one end, parallel to, and near one-tenth of an inch from each other. The other ends, which are a little pointed, will spread out or open like the sticks of a fan, by which means they can beat up the quarters of an hundred lice at a time. These combs or scratchers, for I believe they serve both purposes, they always wear in their hair, on one side of their head. The people of Tanna have an instrument of this kind, for the same use; but theirs is forked, I think never exceeding three or four prongs; and sometimes only a small pointed stick. Their beards, which are of the same crisp nature as their hair, are, for the most part, worn short. Swelled and ulcerated legs and feet are common among the men; as also a swelling of the scrotum. I know not whether this is occasioned by disease, or by the mode of applying the wrapper before mentioned, and which they use as at Tanna and Mallicollo. This is their only covering, and is made generally of the bark of a tree, but sometimes of leaves. The small pieces of cloth, paper, etc., which they got from us, were commonly applied to this use. We saw coarse garments amongst them, made of a sort of matting, but they seemed never to wear them, except when out in their canoes and unemployed. Some had a kind of concave, cylindrical, stiff black cap, which appeared to be a great ornament among them, and, we thought, was only worn by men of note, or warriors. A large sheet of strong paper, when they got one from us, was generally applied to this use.

The women's dress is a short petticoat, made of the filaments of the plantain tree, laid over a cord, to which they are fastened, and tied round the waist. The petticoat is made at least six or eight inches thick, but not one inch longer than necessary for the use designed. The outer filaments are dyed black; and, as an additional ornament, the most of them have a few pearl oyster-shells fixed on the right side. The general ornaments of both sexes, are earrings of tortoise-shell, necklaces or amulets, made both of shells and stones, and bracelets, made of large shells, which they wear above the elbow. They have punctures, or marks on the skin, on several parts of the body; but none, I think, are black, as at the eastern islands. I know not if they have any other design than ornament; and the people of Tanna are marked much in the same manner.

Were I to judge of the origin of this nation, I should take them to be a race between the people of Tanna and of the Friendly Isles; or between those of Tanna and the New Zealanders, or all three; their language, in some respects, being a mixture of them all. In their disposition they are like the natives of the Friendly Isles, but in affability and honesty they excel them.

Notwithstanding their pacific inclination, they must sometimes have wars, as they are well provided with offensive weapons; such as clubs, spears, darts, and slings for throwing stones. The clubs are about two feet and a half long, and variously formed; some like a scythe, others like a pick-axe; some have a head like an hawk, and others have round heads; but all are neatly made. Many of their darts and spears are no less neat, and ornamented with carvings. The slings are as simple as possible; but they take some pains to form the stones that they use into a proper shape; which is something like an egg, supposing both ends to be like the small one. They use a becket, in the same manner as at Tanna, in throwing the dart, which, I believe, is much used in striking fish, etc. In this they seem very dexterous; nor, indeed, do I know that they have any other method of catching large fish; for I neither saw hooks nor lines among them.

It is needless to mention their working tools, as they are made of the same materials, and nearly in the same manner, as at the other islands. Their axes, indeed, are a little different; some, at least; which may be owing to fancy as much as custom.

Their houses, or at least most of them, are circular; something like a beehive, and full as close and warm. The entrance is by a small door, or long square hole, just big enough to admit a man bent double. The side walls are about four feet and a half high; but the roof is lofty, and peaked to a point at the top, above which is a post or stick of wood, which is generally ornamented either with carving or shells, or both. The framing is of small spars, reeds, etc., and both sides and roof are thick and close covered with thatch, made of coarse long grass. In the inside of the house are set up posts, to which cross spars are fastened and platforms made for the conveniency of laying anything on. Some houses have two floors, one above the other. The floor is laid with dry grass, and here and there mats are spread for the principal people to sleep or sit on. In most of them we found two fireplaces, and commonly a fire burning, and, as there was no vent for the smoke but by the door, the whole house was both smoky and hot, in so much that we, who are not used to such an atmosphere, could hardly endure it a moment. This may be the reason why we found these people so chilly when in the open air and without exercise. We frequently saw them make little fires anywhere, and hustle round them, with no other view than to warm themselves. Smoke within doors may be a necessary evil, as it prevents the mosquitoes from coming in, which are pretty numerous here. In some respects their habitations are neat; for, besides the ornaments at top, I saw some with carved doorposts. Upon the whole, their houses are better calculated for a cold than a hot climate; and as there are no partitions in them, they can have little privacy. . . . It seems to be a country unable to support many inhabitants. Nature has been less bountiful to it than to any other tropical island we know in this sea. The greatest part of its surface, or at least what we saw of it, consists of barren, rocky mountains, and the grass, etc., growing on them, is useless to people who have no cattle.

The sterility of the country will apologize for the natives not contributing to the wants of the navigator. The sea may, perhaps, in some measure, compensate for the deficiency of the land: for a coast surrounded by reefs and shoals as this is, cannot fail of being stored with fish.

I have before observed, that the country bears great resemblance to New South Wales, or New Holland, and that some of its natural productions are the same. In particular, we found here the tree which is covered with a soft white ragged bark, easily peeled off, and is, as I have been told, the same that in the East Indies is used for caulking of ships. The wood is very hard, the leaves are long and narrow, of a pale dead green, and a fine aromatic; so that it may properly be said to belong to that continent.

Nevertheless, here are several plants, etc., common to the eastern and northern islands, and even a species of the passion flower, which, I am told, has never before been known to grow wild anywhere but in America. Our botanists did not complain for want of employment at this place; every day bringing something new in botany or other branches of natural history. Land-birds, indeed, are not numerous, but several are new. One of these is a kind of crow, at least so we called it, though it is not half so big, and its feathers are tinged with blue. They also have some very beautiful turtle-doves, and other small birds, such as I never saw before.

All our endeavours to get the name of the whole island proved ineffectual. Probably, it is too large for them to know by one name. Whenever we made this inquiry, they always gave us the name of some district or place, which we pointed to; and, as before observed, I got the names of several, with the name of the king or chief of each. Hence, I conclude, that the country is divided into several districts, each governed by a chief; but we know nothing of the extent of his power. Balade was the name of the district we were at, and Teabooma the chief. He lived on the other side of the ridge of hills, so that we had but little of his company, and therefore could not see much of his power. *Tea* seems a title prefixed to the names of all or most of their chiefs or great men. My friend honoured me by calling me *Tea* Cook.

They deposit their dead in the ground. I saw none of their burying-places; but several of the gentlemen did. In one, they were informed, lay the remains of a chief, who was slain in battle; and his grave, which bore some resemblance to a large mole-hill, was decorated with spears, darts, paddles, etc., all stuck upright in the ground round about it. . . .

The women of this country, and likewise those of Tanna, are, so far as I could judge, far more chaste than those of the more eastern islands. I never heard that one of our people obtained the least favour from any one of them. I have been told, that the ladies here would frequently divert themselves, by going a little aside with our gentlemen, as if they meant to be kind to them, and then would run away laughing at them. Whether this was chastity or coquetry, I shall not pretend to determine; nor is it material, since the consequences were the same.[7]

October 10   After leaving Norfolk Isle,[8] I steered for New Zealand, my intention being to touch at Queen Charlotte's Sound, to refresh my crew, and put the ship in a condition to encounter the southern latitudes.

On the 17th, at daybreak, we saw Mount Egmont, which was covered with everlasting snow, bearing S.E. ½ E. Our distance from the shore was about eight leagues, and, on sounding, we found seventy fathoms of water, a muddy bottom. The wind soon fixed in the western board, and blew a fresh gale, with which we steered S.S.E. for Queen Charlotte's Sound, with a view of falling in with Cape Stephens. At noon Cape Egmont bore E.N.E., distant three or four leagues; and though the Mount was hid in the clouds, we judged it to be in the same direction as the Cape; latitude observed 39° 24′. The wind increased in such a manner as to oblige us to close-reef our top-sails, and strike top-gallant-yards. At last we could bear no more sail than the two courses, and two close-reefed top-sails; and under them we stretched for Cape Stephens, which we made at eleven o'clock at night.

At midnight we tacked, and made a trip to the north till three o'clock next morning, when we bore away for the Sound. At nine we hauled round Point Jackson, through a sea which looked terrible, occasioned by a rapid tide and a high wind; but as we knew the coast, it did not alarm us. At eleven o'clock we anchored before Ship Cove; the strong flurries from off the land not permitting us to get in.

In the afternoon, as we could not move the ship, I went into the cove, with the seine, to try to catch some fish. The first thing

[7] Cook did not have time to explore the west coast of New Caledonia. "I was obliged, as it were by necessity, for the first time to leave a coast I had discovered before it was fully explored. I called it New Caledonia; and, if we except New Zealand, it is perhaps the largest island in the South Pacific Ocean. . . . It seems not improbable that a chain of islands, sandbanks, and reefs, may extend to the west as far as the coast of New South Wales." He withdrew this opinion later, see below, p. 240, note 10.

[8] Cook discovered this uninhabited island (between New Caledonia and New Zealand) on October 10.

I did after landing was to look for the bottle I left hid when last here, in which was the memorandum. It was taken away; but by whom it did not appear. Two hauls with the seine producing only four small fish, we, in some measure, made up for this deficiency, by shooting several birds, which the flowers in the garden had drawn thither, as also some old shags, and by robbing the nests of some young ones.

Being little wind next morning, we weighed, and warped the ship into the cove, and there moored with the two bowers. We unbent the sails to repair them, several having been split, and otherwise damaged in the late gale. The main and fore courses, already worn to the very utmost, were condemned as useless. I ordered the top-masts to be struck and unrigged, in order to fix to them movable chocks or knees, for want of which the trestle-trees were continually breaking; the forge to be set up, to make bolts and repair our ironwork; and tents to be erected on shore for the reception of a guard, coopers, sailmakers, etc. I likewise gave orders that vegetables (of which there were plenty) should be boiled every morning with oatmeal and portable broth for breakfast, and with peas and broth every day for dinner for the whole crew, over and above their usual allowance of salt malt.

In the afternoon, as Mr. Wales was setting up his observatory, he discovered that several trees, which were standing when we last sailed from this place, had been cut down with saws and axes; and a few days after, the place where an observatory, clock, etc., had been set up, was also found, in a spot different from that where Mr. Wales had placed his. It was therefore now no longer to be doubted that the *Adventure* had been in this cove after we had left it.

Next day, winds southerly, hazy cloudy weather. Everybody went to work at their respective employments, one of which was to caulk the ship's sides, a thing much wanted. The seams were paid with putty, made with cook's fat and chalk; the gunner happening to have a quantity of the latter on board.

The 21st, wind southerly, with continual rains.

The weather being fair in the afternoon of the 22nd, accompanied by the botanists, I visited our gardens on Motuara, which

we found almost in a state of nature, having been wholly neglected by the inhabitants. Nevertheless, many articles were in a
flourishing condition, and showed how well they liked the soil
in which they were planted. None of the natives having yet
made their appearance, we made a fire on the point of the island;
in hopes, if they saw the smoke, they might be induced to come
to us.

Nothing remarkable happened till the 24th, when, in the morning, two canoes were seen coming down the Sound; but as soon
as they perceived the ship, they retired behind a point on the west
side. After breakfast I went in a boat to look for them; and as we
proceeded along the shore, we shot several birds. The report of
the muskets gave notice of our approach, and the natives discovered themselves in Shag Cove by hallooing to us; but as we
drew near to their habitations, they all fled to the woods, except
two or three men, who stood on a rising ground near the shore,
with their arms in their hands. The moment we landed, they
knew us. Joy then took place of fear, and the rest of the natives
hurried out of the woods, and embraced us over and over again,
leaping and skipping about like madmen; but I observed that
they would not suffer some women, whom we saw at a distance,
to come near us. After we had made them presents of hatchets,
knives, and what else we had with us, they gave us in return a
large quantity of fish, which they had just caught. There were
only a few amongst them whose faces we could recognize; and
on our asking why they were afraid of us, and inquiring for some
of our old acquaintances by name, they talked much about killing, which was so variously understood by us, that we could
gather nothing from it; so that, after a short stay, we took leave,
and went on board.

Next morning early, our friends, according to a promise they
made us the preceding evening, paying us a visit, brought with
them a quantity of fine fish, which they exchanged for Otaheitean cloth, etc., and then returned to their habitations.

On the 26th we got into the after-hold four boatloads of shingle
ballast, and struck down six guns, keeping only six on deck. Our
good friends the natives having brought us a plentiful supply of

fish, afterwards went on shore to the tents, and informed our people there, that a ship like ours had been lately lost in the Strait; that some of the people got on shore; and that the natives stole their clothes, etc., for which several were shot; that afterwards, when they could fire no longer, the natives having got the better, killed them with their *Patapatoos*, and eat them; but that they themselves had no hand in the affair, which, they said, happened at Vanna Aroa, near Teerawhitte, on the other side of the Strait. One man said it was two moons ago; but another contradicted him, and counted on his fingers about twenty or thirty days. They described by actions how the ship was beat to pieces, by going up and down against the rocks, till at last it was all scattered abroad.

The next day some others told the same story, or nearly to the same purport, and pointed over the East Bay, which is on the east side of the Sound, as to the place where it happened. These stories making me very uneasy about the *Adventure*, I desired Mr. Wales, and those on shore, to let me know if any of the natives should mention it again, or to send them to me; for I had not heard anything from them myself. When Mr. Wales came on board to dinner, he found the very people who had told him the story on shore, and pointed them out to me. I inquired about the affair, and endeavoured to come at the truth by every method I could think of. All I could get from them was, *Caurey* (no); and they not only denied every syllable of what they had said on shore, but seemed wholly ignorant of the matter; so that I began to think our people had misunderstood them, and that the story referred to some of their own people and boats.[9]

[9] This mystery was not cleared up until Cook read Furneaux's narrative; see below, p. 233. The Maoris maintained a conspiracy of silence about the event.

BOOK IV

From Leaving New Zealand to our Return to England
1774-1775

November 10   At daybreak on the 10th, with a fine breeze at W.N.W., we weighed and stood out of the Sound; and, after getting round the Two Brothers, steered for Cape Campbell, which is at the south-west entrance of the Strait, all sails set, with a fine breeze at north. At four in the afternoon, we passed the Cape, at the distance of four or five leagues, and then steered S.S.E. ½ E. with the wind at N.W. a gentle gale, and cloudy weather.

Next morning, the wind veered round by the west to south, and forced us more to the east than I intended. At seven o'clock in the evening, the snowy mountains bore W. by S., and Cape Palliser N. ½ W. distant sixteen or seventeen leagues; from which Cape I for the third time took my departure. After a few hours' calm, a breeze springing up at north, we steered S. by E., all sails set, with a view of getting into the latitude of 54° or 55°; my intention being to cross this vast ocean nearly in these parallels, and so as to pass over those parts which were left unexplored the preceding summer.[1]

[1] It was not till he reached longitude 138° W. that Cook "gave up all hope of finding any more land in this ocean and came to a resolution to steer directly for the west entrance of the Straits of Magellan, with a view to coasting the south side of Tierra del Fuego". When that coast was sighted on December 17, after an

December 25   The next morning, the 25th, the natives made us another visit.[2] I found them to be of the same nation I had formerly seen in Success Bay; and the same which M. de Bougainville distinguishes by the name of Pecheras; a word which these had, on every occasion, in their mouths. They are a little, ugly, half-starved, beardless race. I saw not a tall person amongst them. They were almost naked; their clothing was a seal-skin; some had two or three sewed together, so as to make a cloak which reached to the knees; but the most of them had only one skin, hardly large enough to cover their shoulders; and all their lower parts were quite naked. The women, I was told, cover their nakedness with a flap of a seal-skin, but in other respects are clothed like the men. They, as well as the children, remained in the canoes. I saw two young children at the breast entirely naked; thus they are inured from their infancy to cold and hardships. They had with them bows and arrows, and darts, or rather harpoons, made of bone, and fitted to a staff. I suppose they were intended to kill seals and fish; they may also kill whales with them, as the Esquimaux do. I know not if they resemble them in their love of train-oil; but they, and everything they had, smelt most intolerably of it. I ordered them some biscuit, but did not observe them so fond of it as I had been told. They were much better pleased when I gave them some medals, knives, etc.

The women and children, as before observed, remained in the canoes. These were made of bark; and in each was a fire, over which the poor creatures huddled themselves. I cannot suppose that they carry a fire in their canoes for this purpose only; but rather that it may be always ready to remove ashore wherever they land; for let their method of obtaining fire be what it may, they cannot be always sure of finding dry fuel that will kindle from a spark. They likewise carry in their canoes large seal hides, which, I judged, were to shelter them when at sea, and to serve

uneventful crossing in forty-one days, he noted: "I have now done with the Southern Pacific Ocean and flatter myself that no one will think that I have left it unexplored."

[2] The *Resolution* was now at Christmas Sound, a little to the west of Cape Horn. Cook repeats his former opinion of the natives, as being "of all nations I have seen the most wretched".

as covering to their huts on shore; and occasionally to be used for sails.

They all retired before dinner, and did not wait to partake of our Christmas cheer. Indeed I believe no one invited them, and for good reasons; for their dirty persons, and the stench they carried about them, were enough to spoil the appetite of any European; and that would have been a real disappointment, as we had not experienced such fare for some time. Roast and boiled geese, goose pie, etc., was a treat little known to us; and we had yet some Madeira wine left, which was the only article of our provision that was mended by keeping. So that our friends in England, did not, perhaps, celebrate Christmas more cheerfully than we did.

On the 26th, little wind, next to a calm, and fair weather, except in the morning, when we had some showers of rain. In the evening, when it was cold, the natives made us another visit; and it being distressing to see them stand trembling and naked on the deck, I could do no less than to give them some baize and old canvas to cover themselves.

January 1   Next day being January 1st, 1775, finding that nothing was wanting but a good harbour to make this a tolerable place for ships to refresh at, whom chance or design might bring hither, I sent Mr. Gilbert over to Staten Land in the cutter, to look for one. Appearances promised success, in a place opposite the ship.[3] I sent also two other boats for the lions, etc., we had killed the preceding day; and soon after, I went myself and observed the sun's meridian altitude at the north-east end of the island, which gave the latitude 54° 40′ 5″ S. After shooting a few geese, some other birds, and plentifully supplying ourselves with young shags, we returned on board, laden with sea-lions, sea-bears, etc. The old lions and bears were killed chiefly for the sake of their blubber, or fat, to make oil of; for, except their harslets, [entrails] which were tolerable, the flesh was too rank to be eaten with any degree of relish. But the young cubs were very palatable;

[3] Having rounded Cape Horn, the *Resolution* anchored at New Year Harbour on the north coast of Staten Island.

and even the flesh of some of the old lionesses was not much amiss; but that of the old males was abominable. In the afternoon, I sent some people on shore to skin and cut off the fat of those which yet remained dead on shore; for we had already more carcasses on board than necessary; and I went myself, in another boat, to collect birds. About ten o'clock Mr. Gilbert returned from Staten Land, where he found a good port, situated three leagues to the westward of Cape St. John, and in the direction of north, a little easterly, from the north-east end of the eastern island. It may be known by some small islands lying in the entrance. The channel, which is on the east side of these islands, is half a mile broad. The course in is S.W. by S. turning gradually to W. by S. and W. The harbour lies nearly in this last direction; is almost two miles in length; in some places near a mile broad; and hath in it from fifty to ten fathoms of water, a bottom of mud and sand. Its shores are covered with wood fit for fuel; and in it are several streams of fresh water. On the islands were sea-lions, etc., and such an innumerable quantity of gulls as to darken the air when disturbed, and almost to suffocate our people with their dung. This they seemed to void in a way of defence, and it stank worse than asafoetida, or as it is commonly called, devil's dung. Our people also saw several geese, ducks, and racehorses, which is also a kind of duck. The day on which this port was discovered, occasioned my calling it New Year's Harbour. It would be convenient for ships bound to the west, or round Cape Horn, if its situation would permit them, to put to sea with an easterly and northerly wind. This inconvenience, however, is of little consequence, since these winds are never known to be of long duration. The southerly and westerly are the prevailing winds; so that a ship can never be detained long in this port.

January 20   As we advanced to the south-west, land opened off this point, in the direction of N. 60° W., and nine leagues beyond it.[4] It proved an island quite detached from the main, and ob-

---

[4] Since Dalrymple marked in his charts an equally extensive coast in the South Atlantic as in the South Pacific, Cook sailed south-east of Staten Island to see how much actually existed. His first discovery was the "savage and horrible" country

tained the name of Pickersgill Island, after my third officer. Soon after, a point of the main, beyond this island, came in sight, in the direction of N. 55° W.; which exactly united the coast at the very point we had seen, and taken the bearing of, the day we first came in with it, and proved to a demonstration that this land, which we had taken for part of a great continent, was no more than an island of seventy leagues in circuit.

Who would have thought that an island of no greater extent than this, situated between the latitude of 54° and 55°, should, in the very height of summer, be in a manner wholly covered many fathoms deep with frozen snow, but more especially the south-west coast? The very sides and craggy summits of the lofty mountains were cased with snow and ice; but the quantity which lay in the valleys is incredible; and at the bottom of the bays, the coast was terminated by a wall of ice of considerable height. It can hardly be doubted that a great deal of ice is formed here in the winter, which in the spring is broken off and dispersed over the sea; but this island cannot produce the ten-thousandth part of what we saw; so that either there must be more land, or the ice is formed without it. These reflections led me to think that the land we had seen the preceding day might belong to an extensive track; and I still had hopes of discovering a continent. I must confess the disappointment I now met with, did not affect me much, for to judge of the bulk by the sample, it would not be worth the discovery.

I called this land the Isle of Georgia, in honour of His Majesty. It is situated between the latitude of 53° 57′ and 54° 57′ S.; and between 38° 13′ and 35° 34′ W. longitude. It extends S.E. by E., and N.W. by W. and is thirty-one-leagues long in that direction; and its greatest breadth is about ten leagues. It seems to abound with bays and harbours, the north-east coast especially; but the vast quantity of ice must render them inaccessible the greatest part of the year; or, at least, it must be dangerous lying in them, on account of the breaking up of the ice-cliffs.

of South Georgia, where "not a tree was to be seen, nor a shrub even big enough to make a toothpick". Other icebound coasts discovered further east were called Southern Thule and Sandwich Land.

January 27   I now reckoned we were in latitude 60° S., and farther I did not intend to go, unless I observed some certain signs of soon meeting with land; for it would not have been prudent in me to have spent my time in penetrating to the south, when it was at least as probable that a large tract of land might be found near Cape Circumcision. Besides, I was tired of these high southern latitudes, where nothing was to be found but ice and thick fogs. We had now a long hollow swell from the west, a strong indication that there was no land in that direction; so that I think I may venture to assert that the extensive coasts, laid down in Mr. Dalrymple's chart of the ocean between Africa and America, and the Gulf of Saint Sebastian, does not exist. . . .

It is true, however, that the greatest part of this southern continent (supposing there is one) must lie within the polar circle, where the sea is so pestered with ice that the land is thereby inaccessible. The risk one runs in exploring a coast, in these unknown and icy seas, is so very great, that I can be bold enough to say that no man will ever venture farther than I have done; and that the lands which may lie to the south will never be explored. Thick fogs, snowstorms, intense cold, and every other thing that can render navigation dangerous, must be encountered; and these difficulties are greatly heightened, by the inexpressibly horrid aspect of the country; a country doomed by nature never once to feel the warmth of the sun's rays, but to lie buried in everlasting snow and ice. The ports which may be on the coast, are, in a manner, wholly filled up with frozen snow of vast thickness; but if any should be so far open as to invite a ship into it, she would run a risk of being fixed there for ever, or of coming out in an ice-island. The islands and floats on the coast, the great falls from the ice-cliffs in the port, or a heavy snowstorm attended with a sharp frost, would be equally fatal.

After such an explanation as this, the reader must not expect to find me much farther to the south. It was, however, not for want of inclination, but for other reasons. It would have been rashness in me to have risked all that had been done during the voyage, in discovering and exploring a coast, which, when discovered and explored, would have answered no end whatever, or have been of the least use, either to navigation or geography, or indeed to any other science. Bouvet's discovery was yet before us, the existence of which was to be cleared up;[5] and besides all this, we were not now in a condition to undertake great things; nor indeed was there time, had we been ever so well provided.

These reasons induced me to alter the course to E., with a very strong gale at N., attended with an exceedingly heavy fall of snow. The quantity which lodged in our sails was so great, that we were frequently obliged to throw the ship up in the wind to shake it out of them, otherwise neither they nor the ship could have supported the weight. In the evening it ceased to snow; the weather cleared up; the wind backed to the west; we spent the night in making two short boards [tacks], under close-reefed top-sails and fore-sail.

February 26   I had, at this time, some thoughts of revisiting the place where the French discovery is said to lie.[6] But then I considered that, if they had really made this discovery, the end would be as fully answered as if I had done it myself. We know it can only be an island; and if we may judge from the degree of cold we found in that latitude, it cannot be a fertile one. Besides, this would have kept me two months longer at sea, and in a tempestuous latitude, which we were not in a condition to struggle with. Our sails and rigging were so much worn, that something was giving way every hour; and we had nothing left, either to repair or replace them. Our provisions were in a state of decay, and consequently afforded little nourishment, and we had been a long time without refreshments. My people, indeed, were yet healthy, and would have cheerfully gone wherever I had thought proper to lead them; but I dreaded the scurvy laying hold of them, at a time when we had nothing left to remove it. I must say further, that it would have been cruel in me to have continued the fatigues and hardships they were continually exposed to longer than was absolutely necessary. Their behaviour,

[5] Thirteen degrees of longitude were run down in the latitude assigned to Bouvet's Island, but Cook never found it, though it does exist.

[6] *i.e.* Kerguelen's land, much to the east of Bouvet's Island, rediscovered on the Third Voyage.

throughout the voyage, merited every indulgence which it was in my power to give them. Animated by the conduct of the officers, they showed themselves capable of surmounting every difficulty and danger which came in their way, and never once looked either upon the one or the other as being at all heightened by our separation from our consort the *Adventure*.

All these considerations induced me to lay aside looking for the French discoveries, and to steer for the Cape of Good Hope.

March 16   At daylight, on the 16th, we saw two sail in the north-west quarter standing to the westward, and one of them showing Dutch colours. At ten o'clock we tacked and stood to the west also, being at this time in the latitude of 35° 9' S., longitude 22° 38' E.

I now, in pursuance of my instructions, demanded of the officers and petty officers, the log-books and journals they had kept; which were delivered to me accordingly, and sealed up for the inspection of the Admiralty. I also enjoined them, and the whole crew, not to divulge where we had been, till they had their Lordships' permission so to do. In the afternoon the wind veered to the west, and increased to a hard gale, which was of short duration; for, the next day, it fell, and at noon veered to S.E. At this time we were in the latitude of 34° 49' S., longitude 22° E.; and, on sounding, found fifty-six fathoms of water. In the evening we saw the land in the direction of E.N.E., about six leagues distant; and, during the forepart of the night, there was a great fire or light upon it.

At daybreak on the 18th, we saw the land again, bearing N.N.W., six or seven leagues distant, and the depth of water forty-eight fathoms. At nine o'clock, having little or no wind, we hoisted out a boat and sent on board one of the two ships before mentioned, which were about two leagues from us; but we were too impatient after news to regard the distance. Soon after, a breeze sprung up at west, with which we stood to the south; and, presently, three sail more appeared in sight to windward, one of which showed English colours.

At 1 p.m. the boat returned from on board the *Bownkerke*

Polder, Captain Cornelius Bosch, a Dutch Indiaman from Bengal. Captain Bosch, very obligingly offered us sugar, arrack, and whatever he had to spare. Our people were told by some English seamen on board this ship, that the *Adventure* had arrived at the Cape of Good Hope twelve months ago, and that the crew of one of her boats had been murdered and eaten by the people of New Zealand; so that the story which we heard in Queen Charlotte's Sound was now no longer a mystery.

We had light airs, next to a calm, till ten o'clock the next morning, when a breeze sprung up at west, and the English ship, which was to windward, bore down to us. She proved to be the *True Briton*, Captain Broadly, from China. As he did not intend to touch at the Cape, I put a letter on board him for the Secretary of the Admiralty.

The account which we had heard of the *Adventure* was now confirmed to us by this ship. We also got, from on board her, a parcel of old newspapers, which were new to us, and gave us some amusement; but these were the least favours we received from Captain Broadly. With a generosity peculiar to the commanders of the India Company's ships, he sent us fresh provisions, tea, and other articles, which were very acceptable; and deserve from me this public acknowledgement. In the afternoon we parted company. The *True Briton* stood out to sea, and we in for the land; having a fresh gale at west, which split our fore-top-sail in such a manner, that we were obliged to bring another to the yard. At six o'clock we tacked within four or five miles of the shore; and, as we judged, about five or six leagues to the east of Cape Aguilas. We stood off till midnight, when, the wind having veered round to the south, we tacked, and stood alongshore to the west. The wind kept veering more and more in our favour, and at last fixed at E.S.E., and blew, for some hours, a perfect hurricane.

As soon as the storm began to subside we made sail, and hauled in for the land. Next day at noon, the Table Mountain over the Cape Town bore N.E. by E., distant nine or ten leagues. By making use of this bearing and distance to reduce the longitude shown by the watch to the Cape Town, the error was found to be no more than 18′ in longitude, which it was too far to the east

Indeed, the difference we found between it and the lunar observations, since we left New Zealand, had seldom exceeded half a degree, and always the same way.

The next morning, being with us Wednesday, the 22nd, but with the people here Tuesday, the 21st, we anchored in Table Bay, where we found several Dutch ships; some French; and the *Ceres*, Captain Newte, an English East India Company's ship, from China, bound directly to England, by whom I sent a copy of the preceding parts of this journal, some charts, and other drawings, to the Admiralty.

Before we had well got to an anchor, I despatched an officer to acquaint the Governor with our arrival, and to request the necessary stores and refreshments, which were readily granted. As soon as the officer came back, we saluted the garrison with thirteen guns, which compliment was immediately returned with an equal number.

I now learnt that the *Adventure* had called here, on her return; and I found a letter from Captain Furneaux, acquainting me with the loss of his boat, and of ten of his best men, in Queen Charlotte's Sound. The captain, afterwards, on my arrival in England, put into my hands a complete narrative of his proceedings, from the time of our second and final separation, which I now lay before the public in the following section.

CAPTAIN FURNEAUX'S NARRATIVE

After a passage of fourteen days from Amsterdam [Island], we made the coast of New Zealand near the Table Cape, and stood alongshore till we came as far as Cape Turnagain. The wind then began to blow strong at west, with heavy squalls and rain, which split many of our sails, and blew us off the coast for three days; in which time we parted company with the *Resolution*, and never saw her afterwards. . . .

Whilst we lay here,[7] we were employed about the rigging,

[7] Tolaga Bay, on the east coast of the North Island of New Zealand. The *Adventure* reached Queen Charlotte's Sound on November 30, the *Resolution* having sailed thence on November 24, 1773. The two ships must have passed close to each other off the eastern entrance of Cook Strait.

which was much damaged by the constant gales of wind we had met with since we made the coast. We got the booms down on the decks, and having made the ship as snug as possible, sailed again on the 16th. After this we met with several gales of wind off the mouth of the Strait; and continued beating backwards and forwards till the 30th, when we were so fortunate as to get a favourable wind, which we took every advantage of, and at last got safe into our desired port. We saw nothing of the *Resolution*, and began to doubt her safety; but on going ashore, we discerned the place where she had erected her tents; and, on an old stump of a tree in the garden, observed these words cut out: "Look underneath." There we dug, and soon found a bottle corked and waxed down, with a letter in it from Captain Cook, signifying their arrival on the 3rd instant, and departure on the 24th; and that they intended spending a few days in the entrance of the Straits to look for us.

We immediately set about getting the ship ready for sea as fast as possible; erected our tents; sent the cooper on shore to repair the casks; and began to unstow the hold, to get at the bread that was in butts; but on opening them found a great quantity of it entirely spoiled, and most part so damaged that we were obliged to fix our copper oven on shore to bake it over again, which undoubtedly delayed us a considerable time. Whilst we lay here, the inhabitants came on board as before, supplying us with fish, and other things of their own manufacture, which we bought of them for nails, etc., and appeared very friendly; though twice in the middle of the night, they came to the tent, with an intention to steal, but were discovered before they could get anything into their possession.

On the 17th of December, having refitted the ship, completed our water and wood, and got everything ready for sea, we sent our large cutter, with Mr. Rowe, a midshipman, and the boat's crew, to gather wild greens for the ship's company; with orders to return that evening, as I intended to sail the next morning. But, on the boat's not returning the same evening, nor the next morning, being under great uneasiness about her, I hoisted out the launch, and sent her, with the second lieutenant, Mr. Burney,

manned with the boat's crew and ten marines, in search of her.
My orders to Mr. Burney were, first to look well into East Bay,
and then to proceed to Grass Cove, the place to which Mr. Rowe
had been sent; and if he heard nothing of the boat there, to go
farther up the Sound, and come back along the west shore. As
Mr. Rowe had left the ship an hour before the time proposed,
and in a great hurry, I was strongly persuaded that his curiosity
had carried him into East Bay, none in our ship having ever been
there; or else, that some accident had happened to the boat, either
by going adrift through the boat-keeper's negligence, or by being
stove among the rocks. This was almost everybody's opinion;
and on this supposition the carpenter's mate was sent in the
launch, with some sheets of tin. I had not the least suspicion that
our people had received any injury from the natives; our boats
having frequently been higher up, and worse provided. How
much I was mistaken, too soon appeared; for Mr. Burney having
returned about eleven o'clock the same night, made his report or
a horrible scene indeed, which cannot be better described than in
his own words, which now follow.[8]

"On the 18th we left the ship; and having a light breeze in our
favour, we soon got round Long Island, and within Long Point.
I examined every cove, on the larboard hand, as we went along,
looking well all around with a spy-glass, which I took for that
purpose. At half-past one, we stopped at a beach, on the left-
hand side going up East Bay, to boil some victuals, as we brought
nothing but raw meat with us. Whilst we were cooking, I saw an
Indian on the opposite shore, running along a beach to the head
of the bay. Our meat being dressed, we got into the boat and
put off; and, in a short time, arrived at the head of this reach,
where we saw an Indian settlement.

"As we drew near, some of the Indians came down on the
rocks, and waved for us to be gone; but seeing we disregarded
them, they altered their notes. Here we found six large canoes
hauled up on the beach, most of them double ones, and a great
many people; though not so many as one might expect from the
number of houses and size of the canoes. Leaving the boat's crew

[8] This was the mystery referred to above, p. 221.

to guard the boat, I stepped ashore with the marines (the corporal and five men), and searched a good many of their houses; but found nothing to give me any suspicion. Three or four well-beaten paths led farther into the woods, where were many more houses; but the people continuing friendly, I thought it unnecessary to continue our search. Coming down to the beach, one of the Indians had brought a bundle of *Hepatoos* (long spears), but seeing I looked very earnestly at him, he put them on the ground, and walked about with seeming unconcern. Some of the people appearing to be frightened, I gave a looking-glass to one, and a large nail to another. From this place the bay ran, as nearly as I could guess, N.N.W. a good mile, where it ended in a long sandy beach. I looked all round with the glass, but saw no boat, canoe, or sign of inhabitant. I therefore contented myself with firing some guns, which I had done in every cove as I went along.

"I now kept close to the east shore, and came to another settlement, where the Indians invited us ashore. I inquired of them about the boat, but they pretended ignorance. They appeared very friendly here, and sold us some fish. Within an hour after we left this place, in a small beach adjoining to Grass Cove, we saw a very large double canoe just hauled up, with two men and a dog. The men, on seeing us, left their canoe, and ran up into the woods. This gave me reason to suspect I should here get tidings of the cutter. We went ashore, and searched the canoe, where we found one of the rowlock-ports of the cutter, and some shoes, one of which was known to belong to Mr. Woodhouse, one of our midshipmen. One of the people, at the same time, brought me a piece of meat, which he took to be some of the salt meat belonging to the cutter's crew. On examining this, and smelling to it, I found it was fresh. Mr. Fannin (the master) who was with me, supposed it was dog's flesh, and I was of the same opinion; for I still doubted their being cannibals. But we were soon convinced by most horrid and undeniable proof.

"A great many baskets (about twenty) lying on the beach tied up, we cut them open. Some were full of roasted flesh, and some of fern-root, which serves them for bread. On further search, we found more shoes and a hand, which we immediately knew to have belonged to Thomas Hill, one of our forecastle men, it being marked T.H. with an Otaheite tattow-instrument. I went with some of the people a little way up the woods, but saw nothing else. Coming down again, there was a round spot covered with fresh earth about four feet diameter, where something had been buried. Having no spade, we began to dig with a cutlass; and in the meantime I launched the canoe with intent to destroy her; but seeing a great smoke ascending over the nearest hill, I got all the people into the boat, and made what haste I could to be with them before sunset.

"On opening the next bay, which was Grass Cove, we saw four canoes, one single and three double ones, and a great many people on the beach, who, on our approach, retreated to a small hill within a ship's length of the waterside, where they stood talking to us. A large fire was on the top of the high land beyond the woods, from whence, all the way down the hill the place was thronged like a fair. As we came in, I ordered a musquetoon to be fired at one of the canoes, suspecting they might be full of men lying down in the bottom; for they were all afloat, but nobody was seen in them. The savages on the little hill still kept hallooing and making signs for us to land. However, as soon as we got close in, we all fired. The first volley did not seem to affect them much; but on the second, they began to scramble away as fast as they could, some of them howling. We continued firing as long as we could see the glimpse of any of them through the bushes. Amongst the Indians were two very stout men, who never offered to move till they found themselves forsaken by their companions; and then they marched away with great composure and deliberation; their pride not suffering them to run. One of them however, got a fall, and either lay there or crawled off on all fours. The other got clear without any apparent hurt. I then landed with the marines, and Mr. Fannin stayed to guard the boat.

"On the beach were two bundles of celery, which had been gathered for loading the cutter. A broken oar was stuck upright in the ground, to which the natives had tied their canoes; a proof that the attack had been made here. I then searched all along at the back of the beach, to see if the cutter was there. We found no boat, but instead of her, such a shocking scene of carnage and barbarity as can never be mentioned or thought of but with horror; for the heads, hearts, and lungs of several of our people were seen lying on the beach, and, at a little distance, the dogs gnawing their entrails.

"Whilst we remained almost stupefied on the spot, Mr. Fannin called to us that he heard the savages gathering together in the woods; on which I returned to the boat, and hauling alongside the canoes, we demolished three of them. Whilst this was transacting, the fire on the top of the hill disappeared; and we could hear the Indians in the woods at high words, I suppose quarrelling whether or no they should attack us, and try to save their canoes. It now grew dark, I therefore just stepped out, and looked once more behind the beach to see if the cutter had been hauled up in the bushes; but seeing nothing of her, returned and put off. Our whole force would have been barely sufficient to have gone up the hill, and to have ventured with half (for half must have been left to guard the boat) would have been foolhardiness.

"As we opened the upper part of the Sound, we saw a very large fire about three or four miles higher up, which formed a complete oval, reaching from the top of a hill down almost to the waterside, the middle space being enclosed all round by the fire, like a hedge. I consulted with Mr. Fannin, and we were both of opinion that we could expect to reap no other advantage than the poor satisfaction of killing some more of the savages. At leaving Grass Cove, we had fired a general volley towards where we heard the Indians talking; but, by going in and out of the boat, the arms had got wet, and four pieces missed fire. What was still worse, it began to rain; our ammunition was more than half expended, and we left six large canoes behind us in one place. With so many disadvantages, I did not think it worth while to proceed, where nothing could be hoped for but revenge.

"Coming between two round islands, situated to the southward of East Bay, we imagined we heard somebody calling, we lay on our oars and listened, but heard no more of it; we hallooed several times, but to little purpose; the poor souls were far enough out of hearing; and, indeed, I think it some comfort to reflect that, in all probability, every man of them must have been killed on the spot."

Thus far Mr. Burney's report; and, to complete the account of this tragical transaction, it may not be unnecessary to mention that the people in the cutter were Mr. Rowe; Mr. Woodhouse; Francis Murphy, quartermaster; William Facey, Thomas Hill, Michael Bell, and Edward Jones, forecastle-men; John Cavenaugh and Thomas Milton, belonging to the afterguard; and James Sevilley, the captain's man, being ten in all. Most of these were of our very best seamen, the stoutest and most healthy people in the ship. Mr. Burney's party brought on board two hands, one belonging to Mr. Rowe, known by a hurt he had received on it; the other to Thomas Hill, as before mentioned; and the head of the captain's servant. These, with more of the remains, were tied in a hammock and thrown overboard, with ballast and shot sufficient to sink it. None of their arms nor clothes were found, except part of a pair of trousers, a frock, and six shoes, no two of them being fellows.

I am not inclined to think this was any premeditated plan of these savages; for, the morning Mr. Rowe left the ship, he met two canoes, which came down and stayed all the forenoon in Ship Cove. It might probably happen from some quarrel which was decided on the spot; or the fairness of the opportunity might tempt them, our people being so incautious, and thinking themselves too secure. Another thing which encouraged the New Zealanders, was, they were sensible that a gun was not infallible, that they sometimes missed, and that when discharged, they must be loaded before they could be used again, which time they knew how to take advantage of. After their success, I imagine there was a general meeting on the east side of the sound. The Indians of Shag Cove were there; this we knew by a cock which was in one of the canoes, and by a long single canoe, which some of our people had seen four days before in Shag Cove, where they had been with Mr. Rowe in the cutter.

We were detained in the sound by contrary winds four days after this melancholy affair happened, during which time we saw none of the inhabitants. What is very remarkable, I had been several times up in the same cove with Captain Cook, and never saw the least sign of an inhabitant, except some deserted towns, which appeared as if they had not been occupied for several years; and yet, when Mr. Burney entered the cove, he was of opinion there could not be less than fifteen hundred or two thousand people. I doubt not, had they been appraised of his coming, they would have attacked him. From these considerations I thought it imprudent to send a boat up again; as we were convinced there was not the least probability of any of our people being alive.

On the 23rd, we weighed and made sail out of the Sound, and stood to the eastward to get clear of the Straits; which we accomplished the same evening, but were baffled for two or three days with light winds before we could clear the coast.[9]

March 22   I now resume my own journal, which Captain Furneaux's interesting narrative in the preceding section, had obliged me to suspend.

The day after my arrival at the Cape of Good Hope, I went on shore and waited on the Governor, Baron Plettenberg, and other principal officers, who received and treated us with the greatest politeness, contributing all in their power to make it agreeable. And, as there are few people more obliging to strangers than the Dutch in general at this place, and refreshments of all kinds are nowhere to be got in such abundance, we enjoyed some real repose, after the fatigues of a long voyage.

The good treatment which strangers meet with at the Cape of Good Hope, and the necessity of breathing a little fresh air, has introduced a custom not common anywhere else (at least I have nowhere seen it so strictly observed), which is, for all the officers who can be spared out of the ships to reside on shore. We followed this custom. Myself, the two Mr. Forsters, and Mr. Sparrman, took up our abode with Mr. Brandt, a gentleman well

---

[9] After leaving New Zealand the *Adventure* followed roughly the same route to the Cape of Good Hope as the *Resolution's* a year later. The Pacific was crossed in just over a month; Africa was reached on 17 March 1773; the ship anchored at Spithead on 14 July 1774, almost exactly a year before the *Resolution* returned home.

known to the English by his obliging readiness to serve them. My first care after my arrival, was to procure fresh-baked bread, fresh meat, greens, and wine, for those who remained on board; and, being provided every day during our stay with these articles, they were soon restored to their usual strength. We had only three men on board whom it was thought necessary to send on shore for the recovery of their health; and for these I procured quarters, at the rate of thirty stivers, or half a crown, per day, for which they were provided with victuals, drinks, and lodging.

We now went to work to supply all our defects. For this purpose, by permission, we erected a tent on shore, to which we sent our casks and sails to be repaired. We also struck the yards and topmasts, in order to overhaul the rigging, which we found in so bad a condition, that almost everything, except the standing rigging, was obliged to be replaced with new; and that was purchased at a most exorbitant price. In the article of naval stores, the Dutch here, as well as at Batavia, take a shameful advantage of the distress of foreigners.

That our rigging, sails, etc., should be worn out, will not be wondered at, when it is known, that, during this circumnavigation of the globe, that is, from our leaving this place, to our return to it again, we had sailed no less than twenty thousand leagues; an extent of voyage, nearly equal to three times the equatorial circumference of the earth, and which, I apprehend, was never sailed by any ship in the same space of time before. And yet, in all this great run, which had been made in all latitudes between 9° and 71°, we sprung neither low-masts, top-mast, lower nor top-sail yard, nor so much as broke a lower or top-mast shroud; which, with the great care and abilities of my officers, must be owing to the good properties of our ship.

One of the French ships which were at anchor in the bay, was the *Ajax* Indiaman, bound to Pondicherry, commanded by Captain Crozet. He had been second in command with Captain Marion, who sailed from this place with two ships, in March 1772, as has been already mentioned. Instead of going from hence to America, as was said, he stood away for New Zealand; where, in the Bay of Isles, he and some of his people were killed by the inhabitants. Captain Crozet, who succeeded to the command, returned by the way of the Philippine Isles, with the two ships, to the island of Mauritius. He seemed to be a man possessed of the true spirit of discovery, and to have abilities. In a very obliging manner, he communicated to me a chart, wherein were delineated not only his own discoveries, but also that of Captain Kerguelen, which I found laid down in the very situation where we searched for it; so that I can, by no means, conceive how both we and the *Adventure* missed it.[10]

July 29   On the 29th, we made the land near Plymouth.[11] The next morning, we anchored at Spithead; and the same day, I landed at Portsmouth, and set out for London, in company with Messrs. Wales, Forsters, and Hodges.

Having been absent from England three years and eighteen days, in which time, and under all changes of climate, I lost but four men, and only one of them by sickness, it may not be amiss, at the conclusion of this journal, to enumerate the several causes to which, under the care of Providence, I conceive, this uncommon good state of health experienced by my people was owing.

In the Introduction mention has been made of the extraordinary attention paid by the Admiralty, in causing such articles to be put on board as, either from experience or suggestion, it was judged would tend to preserve the health of the seamen. I shall not trespass upon the reader's time in mentioning them all, but confine myself to such as were found the most useful.

We were furnished with a quantity of malt, of which was made *Sweet Wort*. To such of the men as showed the least symptoms of the scurvy; and also to such as were thought to be threatened with that disorder, this was given from one to two or three pints a

---

[10] For Marion, see above, p. 114, note 2. Cook also learned from Crozet of Surville's expedition (see above, p. 43), which made him withdraw his opinion that New Caledonia was connected with New South Wales.

[11] The voyage home was made by way of St. Helena, Ascension and the Azores. The whole voyage lasted three years and eighteen days. In the course of it Cook sailed about 70,000 miles and not a single life was lost from scurvy. At the end of it, as Cook notes in concluding his MS. Journal at this point, "the error of Mr. Kendall's watch in Longitude was only 7′ 45″, which was too far to the west", *i.e.* slow.

day each man; or in such proportion as the surgeon found necessary, which sometimes amounted to three quarts. This is, without doubt, one of the best antiscorbutic sea medicines yet discovered: and, if used in time, will, with proper attention to other things, I am persuaded, prevent the scurvy from making any great progress for a considerable while. But I am not altogether of opinion that it will cure it at sea.

Sauerkraut, of which we had a large quantity, is not only a wholesome vegetable food, but, in my judgment, highly antiscorbutic; and it spoils not by keeping. A pound of this was served to each man when at sea, twice a week or oftener, as was thought necessary.

Portable Broth was another great article, of which we had a large supply. An ounce of this to each man, or such other proportion as circumstances pointed out, was boiled in their pease, three days in the week; and when we were in places where vegetables were to be got, it was boiled with them, and wheat or oatmeal, every morning for breakfast; and also with pease and vegetables for dinner. It enabled us to make several nourishing and wholesome messes, and was the means of making the people eat a greater quantity of vegetables than they would otherwise have done.

Rob of Lemon and *Orange* is an antiscorbutic we were not without. The surgeon made use of it in many cases, with great success.

Amongst the articles of victualling, we were supplied with *Sugar* in the room of *Oil*, and with *Wheat* for a part of our *Oatmeal*; and were certainly gainers by the exchange. Sugar, I apprehend, is a very good antiscorbutic; whereas oil (such as the navy is usually supplied with), I am of opinion, has the contrary effect.

But the introduction of the most salutary articles, either as provisions or medicines, will generally prove unsuccessful, unless supported by certain regulations. On this principle, many years' experience, together with some hints I had from Sir Hugh Palliser, Captains Campbell, Wallis, and other intelligent officers, enabled me to lay a plan whereby all was to be governed.

The crew were at three watches, except upon some extra-ordinary occasions. By this means they were not so much exposed to the weather as if they had been at watch and watch; and had generally dry clothes to shift themselves, when they happened to get wet. Care was also taken to expose them as little to wet weather as possible.

Proper methods were used to keep their persons, hammocks, bedding, clothes, etc., constantly clean and dry. Equal care was taken to keep the ship clean and dry betwixt decks. Once or twice a week she was aired with fires; and when this could not be done, she was smoked with gunpowder mixed with vinegar or water. I had also frequently a fire made in an iron pot at the bottom of the well, which was of great use in purifying the air in the lower parts of the ship. To this and to cleanliness, as well in the ship as amongst the people, too great attention cannot be paid; the least neglect occasions a putrid and disagreeable smell below, which nothing but fires will remove.

Proper attention was paid to the ship's coppers, so that they were kept constantly clean.

The fat which boiled out of the salt beef and pork, I never suffered to be given to the people; being of opinion that it promotes the scurvy.

I was careful to take in water wherever it was to be got, even though we did not want it. Because I look upon fresh water from the shore, to be more wholesome than that which has been kept some time on board a ship. Of this essential article, we were never at an allowance, but had always plenty for every necessary purpose. Navigators in general cannot, indeed, expect, nor would they wish to meet with, such advantages in this respect, as fell to my lot. The nature of our voyage carried us into very high latitudes. But the hardships and dangers inseparable from that situation, were, in some degree, compensated by the singular felicity we enjoyed, of extracting inexhaustible supplies of fresh water from an ocean strewn with ice.

We came to few places, where either the art of man, or the bounty of nature, had not provided some sort of refreshment or other, either in the animal or vegetable way. It was my first care to procure whatever of any kind could be met with, by every means in my power; and to oblige our people to make use thereof, both by my example and authority; but the benefits arising from refreshments of any kind soon became so obvious, that I had little occasion to recommend the one or to exert the other.

It does not become me to say how far the principal objects of our voyage have been obtained. Though it has not abounded with remarkable events, nor been diversified by sudden transitions of fortune; though my relation of it has been more employed in tracing our course by sea, than in recording our operations on shore; this, perhaps, is a circumstance from which the curious reader may infer, that the purposes for which we were sent into the southern hemisphere were diligently and effectually pursued. Had we found out a continent there, we might have been better enabled to gratify curiosity; but we hope our not having found it, after all our persevering searches, will leave less room for future speculation about unknown worlds remaining to be explored.

But, whatever may be the public judgment about other matters, it is with real satisfaction, and without claiming any merit but that of attention to my duty, that I can conclude this account with an observation which facts enable me to make, that our having discovered the possibility of preserving health amongst a numerous ship's company, for such a length of time, in such varieties of climate, and amidst such continued hardships and fatigues, will make this voyage remarkable in the opinion of every benevolent person, when the disputes about a Southern Continent shall have ceased to engage the attention, and to divide the judgment of philosophers.

The Third Voyage
1776-1780

BOOK I

Transactions from the Beginning of the Voyage till our Departure from New Zealand

1776-1777

DEPARTURE FROM PLYMOUTH—ARRIVAL AT TASMANIA—ACCOUNT OF THE NATIVES—QUEEN CHARLOTTE'S SOUND, NEW ZEALAND

Having, on the ninth day of February, 1776, received a commission to command His Majesty's sloop the *Resolution*, I went on board the next day, hoisted the pendant, and began to enter men. At the same time, the *Discovery*, of three hundred tons burden, was purchased into the service, and the command of her given to Captain Clerke, who had been my second Lieutenant on board the *Resolution*, in my second voyage round the world, from which we had lately returned.[1]

These two ships were, at this time, in the dock at Deptford, under the hands of the shipwrights; being ordered to be equipped to make further discoveries in the Pacific Ocean, under my direction.

On the 9th of March, the *Resolution* was hauled out of dock

[1] As the *Adventure* was in service elsewhere, another Whitby-built ship, originally called the *Diligence*, was purchased and renamed *Discovery*. The lieutenants on board Cook's ship, the *Resolution*, were John Gore, James King, and John Williamson; her Master was William Bligh (later of the *Bounty*); Lieutenant Molesworth Phillips was in command of the Marines, and William Anderson was the surgeon. The latter's descriptions of the natural history of places visited were incorporated in the published version of Cook's journal. The description of Cook's death and the subsequent part of the voyage was written by King.

Charles Clerke, in command of the *Discovery*, now set out on his fourth voyage round the world. His First Lieutenant was James Burney (whose sister Susan married Lieut. Phillips); one of the midshipmen was George Vancouver. The complement of both ships totalled 192.

into the river; where we completed her rigging, and took on board the stores and provisions requisite for a voyage of such duration. Both ships, indeed, were supplied with as much of every necessary article as we could conveniently stow, and with

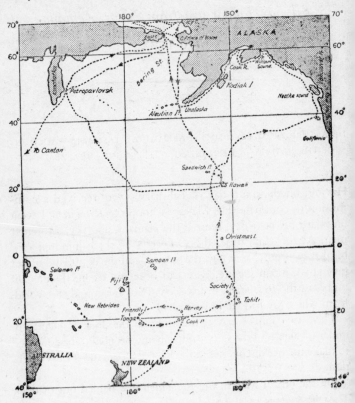

the best of every kind that could be procured. And, besides this, everything that had been found, by the experience acquired during our former extensive voyages, to be of any utility in preserving the health of seamen, was supplied in abundance.

It was our intention to have sailed to Long Reach on the 6th of May, when a pilot came on board to carry us thither; but it was the 29th before the wind would permit us to move; and the

30th before we arrived at that station, where our artillery, powder, shot, and other ordnance stores were received.

While we lay in Long Reach, thus employed, the Earl of
Sandwich, Sir Hugh Palliser, and others of the Board of Admiralty, as the least mark of the very great attention they had all
along shown to this equipment, paid us a visit on the 8th of June,
to examine whether everything had been completed conform-
ably to their intentions and orders, and to the satisfaction of all
who were to embark in the voyage.

They, and several other noblemen and gentlemen, their friends,
honoured me with their company at dinner on that day; and, on
their coming on board, and also on their going ashore, we saluted
them with seventeen guns, and three cheers.

With the benevolent view of conveying some permanent
benefit to the inhabitants of Otaheite, and of the other islands in
the Pacific Ocean, whom we might happen to visit, His Majesty
having commanded some useful animals to be carried out, we
took on board, on the 10th, a bull, two cows with their calves,
and some sheep, with hay and corn for their subsistence; intending to add to these, other useful animals, when I should arrive at
the Cape of Good Hope.

I was also, from the same laudable motives, furnished with a
sufficient quantity of such of our European garden seeds, as could
not fail to be a valuable present to our newly discovered islands,
by adding fresh supplies of food to their own vegetable productions.

Many other articles, calculated to improve the condition of our
friends in the other hemisphere in various ways, were, at the
same time, delivered to us by order of the Board of Admiralty.
And both ships were provided with a proper assortment of iron
tools and trinkets, as the means of enabling us to traffic and to
cultivate a friendly intercourse with the inhabitants of such new
countries as we might be fortunate enough to meet with.

The same humane attention was extended to our own wants.
Some additional clothing, adapted to a cold climate, was ordered
for our crews: and nothing was denied to us, that could be supposed in the least conducive to health, or even to convenience.

Nor did the extraordinary care of those at the head of the naval department stop here. They were equally solicitous to afford us every assistance towards rendering our voyage of public utility. Accordingly, we received on board, next day, several astronomical and nautical instruments, which the Board of Longitude entrusted to me, and to Mr. King, my Second Lieutenant; we having engaged to that Board to make all the necessary observations during the voyage, for the improvement of astronomy and navigation; and, by our joint labours, to supply the place of a professed observator. Such a person had been originally intended to be sent out in my ship.

The Board, likewise, put into our possession the same watch, or timekeeper, which I had carried out in my last voyage, and had performed its part so well. It was a copy of Mr. Harrison's, constructed by Mr. Kendall. This day, at noon, it was found to be too slow for mean time at Greenwich, by 3′, 31″, 890; and by its rate of going, it lost on mean time, 1″, 209 per day.

Another timekeeper, and the same number and sort of instruments for making observations, were put on board the *Discovery*, under the care of Mr. William Bailey; who, having already given satisfactory proofs of his skill and diligence as an observator, while employed in Captain Furneaux's ship, during the late voyage, was engaged a second time, in that capacity, to embark with Captain Clerke.

Mr. Anderson, my surgeon, who, to skill in his immediate profession, added great proficiency in natural history, was as willing as he was qualified to describe everything in that branch of science which should occur worthy of notice. As he had already visited the South Sea Islands in the same ship, and been of singular service, by enabling me to enrich my relation of that voyage with various useful remarks on men and things, I reasonably expected to derive considerable assistance from him in recording our new proceedings.

I had several young men amongst my sea-officers who, under my direction, could be usefully employed in constructing charts, in taking views of the coasts and headlands near which we should pass, and in drawing plans of the bays and harbours in which we should anchor. A constant attention to this I knew to be highly requisite, if we would render our discoveries profitable to future navigators.

And, that we might go out with every help that could serve to make the result of our voyage entertaining to the generality of readers, as well as instructive to the sailor and scholar, Mr. Webber was pitched upon, and engaged to embark with me, for the express purpose of supplying the unavoidable imperfections of written accounts, by enabling us to preserve, and to bring home, such drawings of the most memorable scenes of our transactions, as could only be executed by a professed and skilful artist.

Every preparation being now completed, I received an order to proceed to Plymouth, and to take the *Discovery* under my command. I accordingly gave Captain Clerke two orders; one to put himself under my command, and the other to carry his ship round to Plymouth.

On the 15th, the *Resolution* sailed from Long Reach, with the *Discovery* in company, and the same evening they anchored at the Nore. Next day the *Discovery* proceeded, in obedience to my order; but the *Resolution* was ordered to remain at the Nore till I should join her, being at this time in London.

As we were to touch at Otaheite and the Society Islands, in our way to the intended scene of our fresh operations, it had been determined not to omit this opportunity (the only one ever likely to happen) of carrying Omai back to his native country. Accordingly, everything being ready for our departure, he and I set out together from London on the 24th, at six o'clock in the morning. We reached Chatham between ten and eleven o'clock; and after dining with Commissioner Proby, he very obligingly ordered his yacht to carry us to Sheerness, where my boat was waiting to take us on board.

Omai left London with a mixture of regret and satisfaction. When we talked about England, and about those who, during his stay, had honoured him with their protection or friendship, I could observe that his spirits were sensibly affected, and that it was with difficulty he could refrain from tears. But, the instant the conversation turned to his own islands, his eyes began to sparkle with joy. He was deeply impressed with a sense of the good treatment he had met with in England, and entertained the highest ideas of the country and of the people. But the pleasing prospect he now had before him of returning home, loaded with what he well knew would be esteemed invaluable treasures there, and the flattering hope which the possession of these gave him, of attaining to a distinguished superiority amongst his countrymen, were considerations which operated by degrees to suppress every uneasy sensation; and he seemed to be quite happy when he got on board the ship. . . .

It could not but occur to us as a singular and affecting circumstance, that at the very instant of our departure upon a voyage, the object of which was to benefit Europe by making fresh discoveries in North America, there should be the unhappy necessity of employing others of His Majesty's ships, and of conveying numerous bodies of land forces, to secure the obedience of those parts of that continent which had been discovered and settled by our countrymen in the last century. On the 6th, His Majesty's ships, *Diamond*, *Ambuscade*, and *Unicorn*, with a fleet of transports, consisting of sixty-two sail, bound to America, with the last division of the Hessian troops, and some horse, were forced into the Sound by a strong north-west wind.[2]

January 26   As soon as we had anchored,[3] I ordered the boats to be hoisted out. In one of them I went myself, to look for the most commodious place for furnishing ourselves with the necessary supplies; and Captain Clerke went in his boat upon the same service. Wood and water we found in plenty, and in situations

---

[2] Cook sailed from Plymouth on 12 July 1776. The American Declaration of Independence was issued on July 4. In view of the dangers of war the French Minister of Marine issued orders that "it is the King's pleasure that Captain Cook shall be treated as a commander of a neutral and allied power, and that all Captains of armed vessels who may meet that famous navigator, shall make him acquainted with the King's orders on this behalf". Benjamin Franklin, then in Paris, inserted similar instructions in the Letters of Marque he was empowered to issue to privateers. Those who sailed with Cook first heard of these guarantees three years later.

[3] In Adventure Bay, Tasmania. The ships had left the Cape of Good Hope on 30 November 1776 for a visit to the Marion and Crozet Islands (called by Cook Prince Edward's Islands) and also Kerguelen Land, where Christmas was spent.

convenient enough, especially the first. But grass, of which we stood most in need, was scarce, and also very coarse. Necessity, however, obliged us to take such as we could get.

Next morning early, I sent Lieutenant King to the east side of the bay, with two parties; one to cut wood, and the other to cut grass, under the protection of the marines, whom I judged it prudent to land as a guard. For although, as yet, none of the natives had appeared, there could be no doubt that some were in our neighbourhood, as we had seen columns of smoke, from the time of our approaching the coast; and some now was observed, at no great distance up in the woods. I also sent the launch for water; and afterwards visited all the parties myself. In the evening, we drew the seine at the head of the bay, and, at one haul, caught a great quantity of fish. We should have got many more, had not the net broken in drawing it ashore. Most of them were of that sort known to seamen by the name of elephant fish. After this everyone repaired on board with what wood and grass we had cut, that we might be ready to sail whenever the wind should serve.

This not happening next morning, the people were sent on shore again, on the same duty as the day before. I also employed the carpenter, with part of his crew, to cut some spars for the use of the ship; and despatched Mr. Roberts, one of the mates, in a small boat, to survey the bay.

In the afternoon, we were agreeably surprised, at the place where we were cutting wood, with a visit from some of the natives; eight men and a boy. They approached us from the woods, without betraying any marks of fear, or rather with the greatest confidence imaginable; for none of them had any weapons, except one, who held in his hand a stick about two feet long, and pointed at one end.

They were quite naked, and wore no ornaments; unless we consider as such, and as a proof of their love of finery, some large punctures or ridges raised on different parts of their bodies, some in straight, and others in curved lines.

They were of the common stature, but rather slender. Their skin was black, and also their hair, which was as woolly as that of any native of Guinea; but they were not distinguished by remarkably thick lips or flat noses. On the contrary, their features were far from being disagreeable. They had pretty good eyes; and their teeth were tolerably even, but very dirty. Most of them had their hair and beards smeared with a red ointment; and some had their faces also painted with the same composition.[4]

They received every present we made to them without the least appearance of satisfaction. When some bread was given, as soon as they understood that it was to be eaten, they either returned it, or threw it away, without even tasting it. They also refused some elephant fish, both raw and dressed, which we offered to them. But upon giving some birds to them, they did not return these, and easily made us comprehend that they were fond of such food. I had brought two pigs ashore, with a view to leave them in the woods. The instant these came within their reach, they seized them, as a dog would have done, by the ears, and were for carrying them off immediately; with no other intention, as we could perceive, but to kill them.

Being desirous of knowing the use of the stick which one of our visitors carried in his hand, I made signs to them to show me; and so far succeeded, that one of them set up a piece of wood as a mark, and threw at it, at the distance of about twenty yards. But we had little reason to commend his dexterity; for after repeated trials, he was still very wide from the object. Omai, to show them how much superior our weapons were to theirs, then fired his musket at it; which alarmed them so much, that notwithstanding all we could do or say, they ran instantly into the woods. One of them was so frightened, that he let drop an axe and two knives, that had been given to him. From us, however, they went to the place where some of the *Discovery's* people were employed in taking water into their boat. The officer of that party, not knowing that they had paid us so friendly a visit, nor what their intent might be, fired a musket in the air, which sent them off with the greatest precipitation.

Thus ended our first interview with the natives. Immediately

---

[4] The Tasmanian natives are now extinct. Burney adds that the marines who were landed to protect the watering parties got hold of some brandy "and made themselves so beastly drunk that they were put motionless in the boat and when brought on board were obliged to be hoisted into the ship".

after their final retreat, judging that their fears would prevent their remaining near enough to observe what was passing, I ordered the two pigs, being a boar and sow, to be carried about a mile within the woods, at the head of the bay. I saw them left there, by the side of a freshwater brook. A young bull and a cow, and some sheep and goats, were also, at first, intended to have been left by me, as an additional present to Van Diemen's Land. But I soon laid aside all thoughts of this, from a persuasion that the natives, incapable of entering into my views of improving their country, would destroy them. If ever they should meet with the pigs, I have no doubt this will be their fate. But as that race of animals soon becomes wild, and is fond of the thickest cover of the woods, there is great probability of their being preserved. An open place must have been chosen for the accommodation of the other cattle; and in such a situation, they could not possibly have remained concealed many days.

The morning of the 29th was ushered in with a dead calm, which continued all day, and effectually prevented our sailing. I therefore sent a party over to the east point of the bay to cut grass; having been informed that some of a superior quality grew there. Another party, to cut wood, was ordered to go to the usual place, and I accompanied them myself. We had observed several of the natives, this morning, sauntering along the shore, which assured us, that though their consternation had made them leave us so abruptly the day before, they were convinced that we intended them no mischief, and were desirous of renewing the intercourse. It was natural that I should wish to be present on the occasion.

We had not been long landed, before about twenty of them, men and boys, joined us, without expressing the least sign of fear or distrust. There was one of this company conspicuously deformed; and who was not more distinguishable by the hump upon his back, than by the drollery of his gestures, and the seeming humour of his speeches; which he was very fond of exhibiting, as we supposed, for our entertainment. But, unfortunately, we could not understand him; the language spoken here being wholly unintelligible to us. It appeared to me to be different from that spoken by the inhabitants of the more northern parts of this country, whom I met with in my first voyage; which is not extraordinary, since those we now saw, and those we then visited, differ in many other respects. Nor did they seem to be such miserable wretches as the natives whom Dampier mentions to have seen on its western coast.[5]

Some of our present group wore loose round their necks three or four folds of small cord, made of the fur of some animal; and others of them had a narrow slip of the *kangaroo* skin tied round their ankles. I gave to each of them a string of beads, and a medal; which I thought they received with some satisfaction. They seemed to set no value on iron, or on iron tools. They were even ignorant of the use of fish-hooks, if we might judge from their manner of looking at some of ours which we showed to them.

We cannot, however, suppose it to be possible that a people who inhabit a sea-coast, and who seem to derive no part of their sustenance from the productions of the ground, should not be acquainted with some mode of catching fish, although we did not happen to see any of them thus employed; nor observe any canoe or vessel, in which they could go upon the water. Though they absolutely rejected the sort of fish that we offered to them, it was evident that shell-fish, at least, made a part of their food, from the many heaps of mussel-shells we saw in different parts near the shore, and about some deserted habitations near the head of the bay. These were little sheds or hovels built of sticks, and covered with bark. We could also perceive evident signs of their sometimes taking up their abode in the trunks of large trees, which had been hollowed out by fire, most probably for this very purpose. In or near all these habitations, and wherever there was a heap of shells, there remained the marks of fire; an indubitable proof that they do not eat their food raw.

After staying about an hour with the wooding party and the natives, as I could now be pretty confident that the latter were not likely to give the former any disturbance, I left them, and went over to the grass-cutters on the east point of the bay, and found that they had met with a fine patch. Having seen the boats

[5] See above, p. 66, note 3

loaded, I left that party, and returned on board to dinner; where, some time after, Lieutenant King arrived.

From him I learnt, that I had but just left the shore, when several women and children made their appearance, and were introduced to him by some of the men who attended them. He gave presents to all of them, of such trifles as he had about him. These females wore a *kangaroo* skin (in the same shape as it came from the animal) tied over the shoulders, and round the waist. But its only use seemed to be, to support their children when carried on their backs; for it did not cover those parts which most nations conceal; being, in all other respects, as naked as the men, and as black, and their bodies marked with scars in the same manner. But in this they differed from the men, that though their hair was of the same colour and texture, some of them had their heads completely shorn or shaved; in others this operation had been performed only on one side, while the rest of them had all the upper part of the head shorn close, leaving a circle of hair all round, somewhat like the tonsure of the Romish ecclesiastics. Many of the children had fine features, and were thought pretty; but of the persons of the women, especially those advanced in years, a less favourable report was made. However, some of the gentlemen belonging to the *Discovery*, I was told, paid their addresses, and made liberal offers of presents, which were rejected with great disdain; whether from a sense of virtue, or the fear of displeasing their men, I shall not pretend to determine. That this gallantry was not very agreeable to the latter, is certain: for an elderly man, as soon as he observed it, ordered all the women and children to retire, which they obeyed, though some of them showed a little reluctance.

This conduct of Europeans amongst savages to their women, is highly blameable; as it creates a jealousy in their men, that may be attended with consequences fatal to the success of the common enterprise, and to the whole body of adventurers, without advancing the private purpose of the individual, or enabling him to gain the object of his wishes. I believe it has been generally found amongst uncivilized people, that where the women are easy of access, the men are the first to offer them to strangers; and that, where this is not the case, neither the allurement of presents, nor the opportunity of privacy, will be likely to have the desired effect. This observation, I am sure, will hold good throughout all the parts of the South Sea where I have been. Why then should men act so absurd a part, as to risk their own safety, and that of all their companions, in pursuit of a gratification which they have no probability of obtaining?

February 11   After making the land,[6] I steered for Cape Farewell, which at daybreak, the next morning, bore S. by W., distant about four leagues. At eight o'clock, it bore S.W. by S., about five leagues distant; and, in this situation, we had forty-five fathoms' water over a sandy bottom. In rounding the Cape we had fifty fathoms, and the same sort of bottom.

I now steered for Stephen's Island, which we came up with at nine o'clock at night; and at ten, next morning, anchored in our old station, in Queen Charlotte's Sound. Unwilling to lose any time, our operations commenced that very afternoon, when we landed a number of empty water-casks, and began to clear a place where we might set up the two observatories, and tents for the reception of a guard, and of such of our people whose business might make it necessary for them to remain on shore.

We had not been long at anchor before several canoes, filled with natives, came alongside of the ships; but very few of them would venture on board; which appeared the more extraordinary, as I was well known to them all. There was one man in particular amongst them, whom I had treated with remarkable kindness, during the whole of my stay when I was last here. Yet now, neither professions of friendship, nor presents, could prevail upon him to come into the ship. This shyness was to be accounted for only upon this supposition, that they were apprehensive we had revisited their country, in order to revenge the death of Captain Furneaux's people.[7] Seeing Omai on board my ship now, whom they must have remembered to have seen on board the *Adven-*

[6] *i.e.* New Zealand. Cape Farewell marks the western entrance to Cook Strait.
[7] See above, p. 233f.

ture when the melancholy affair happened, and whose first conversation with them, as they approached, generally turned on that subject, they must be well assured that I was no longer a stranger to it. I thought it necessary, therefore, to use every endeavour to assure them of the continuance of my friendship, and that I should not disturb them on that account. I do not know whether this had any weight with them; but certain it is, that they very soon laid aside all manner of restraint and distrust.

On the 13th we set up two tents, one from each ship; on the same spot where we had pitched them formerly. The observatories were at the same time erected; and Messrs. King and Bayley began their operations immediately, to find the rate of the time-keeper, and to make other observations. The remainder of the empty water-casks were also sent on shore, with the cooper to trim, and a sufficient number of sailors to fill them. Two men were appointed to brew spruce beer; and the carpenter and his crew were ordered to cut wood. A boat, with a party of men, under the direction of one of the mates, was sent to collect grass for our cattle; and the people that remained on board were employed in refitting the ship, and arranging the provisions. In this manner, we were all profitably busied during our stay. For the protection of the party on shore, I appointed a guard of ten marines, and ordered arms for all the workmen; and Mr. King, and two or three petty officers, constantly remained with them. A boat was never sent to any considerable distance from the ships without being armed, and under the direction of such officers as I could depend upon, and who were well acquainted with the natives. During my former visits to this country, I had never taken some of these precautions; nor were they, I firmly believe, more necessary now than they had been formerly. But after the tragical fate of the *Adventure's* boat's crew in this Sound, and of Captain Marion du Fresne, and of some of his people, in the Bay of Islands,[8] it was impossible totally to divest ourselves of all apprehension of experiencing a similar calamity.

If the natives entertained any suspicion of our revenging these acts of barbarity, they very soon laid it aside. For, during the

[8] In 1772; see above, p. 114.

course of this day, a great number of families came from different parts of the coast, and took up their residence close to us; so that there was not a spot in the cove where a hut could be put up, that was not occupied by them, except the place where we had fixed our little encampment. This they left us in quiet possession of; but they came and took away the ruins of some old huts that were there, as materials for their new erections.

It is curious to observe with what facility they build these occasional places of abode. I have seen about twenty of them erected on a spot of ground, that, not an hour before, was covered with shrubs and plants. They generally bring some part of the materials with them; the rest they find upon the premises. I was present when a number of people landed, and built one of these villages. The moment the canoes reached the shore, the men leaped out, and at once took possession of a piece of ground, by tearing up the plants and shrubs, or sticking up some part of the framing of a hut. They then returned to their canoes, and secured their weapons, by setting them up against a tree, or placing them in such a position, that they could be laid hold of in an instant. I took particular notice that no one neglected this precaution. While the men were employed in raising the huts, the women were not idle. Some were stationed to take care of the canoes; others to secure the provisions, and the few utensils in their possession; and the rest went to gather dry sticks, that a fire might be prepared for dressing their victuals. As to the children, I kept them, as also some of the more aged, sufficiently occupied in scrambling for beads, till I had emptied my pockets, and then I left them.

These temporary habitations are abundantly sufficient to afford shelter from the wind and rain, which is the only purpose they are meant to answer. I observed that, generally, if not always, the same tribe or family, though it were ever so large, associated and built together; so that we frequently saw a village, as well as their larger towns, divided into different districts, by low pallisades, or some similar mode of separation.

The advantage we received from the natives coming to live with us, was not inconsiderable. For, every day, when the weather would permit, some of them went out to catch fish; and we generally got, by exchanges, a good share of the produce of their labours. This supply, and what our own nets and lines afforded us, was so ample, that we seldom were in want of fish. Nor was there any deficiency of other refreshments. Celery, scurvy-grass, and portable soup, were boiled with the peas and wheat, for both ships' companies, every day during our whole stay; and they had spruce-beer for their drink. So that, if any of our people had contracted the seeds of the scurvy, such a regimen soon removed them. But the truth is, when we arrived here, there were only two invalids (and these on board the *Resolution*) upon the sick lists in both ships.

Besides the natives who took up their abode close to us, we were occasionally visited by others of them, whose residence was not far off; and by some who lived more remote. Their articles of commerce were, curiosities, fish, and women. The two first always came to a good market; which the latter did not. The seamen had taken a kind of dislike to these people; and were either unwilling, or afraid, to associate with them; which produced this good effect, that I knew no instance of a man's quitting his station, to go to their habitations.

A connection with women I allow, because I cannot prevent it; but never encourage, because I always dread its consequences. I know, indeed, that many men are of opinion, that such an intercourse is one of our greatest securities amongst savages; and perhaps they who, either from necessity or choice, are to remain and settle with them, may find it so. But with travellers and transient visitors, such as we were, it is generally otherwise; and, in our situation, a connection with their women betrays more men than it saves. What else can be reasonably expected, since all their views are selfish, without the least mixture of regard or attachment? My own experience, at least, which has been pretty extensive, has not pointed out to me one instance to the contrary.

BOOK II

From Leaving New Zealand to our Arrival at Tahiti

1777

THE COOK ISLANDS VISITED—OMAI AS INTERPRETER—THEORY OF
CORAL FORMATION—STAY AT THE FRIENDLY ISLANDS—ANNAMOOKA
—DINNER AT HAPAEE—A GRAND NATCHE AT TONGATABU

April 3   Omai was sent upon this expedition;[1] and, perhaps, his
being Mr. Gore's interpreter was not the only service he performed this day. He was asked by the natives a great many questions concerning us, our ships, our country, and the sort of arms
we used; and, according to the account he gave me, his answers
were not a little upon the marvellous. As, for instance, he told
them, that our country had ships as large as their island; on
board which were instruments of war (describing our guns), of
such dimensions, that several people might sit within them; and
that one of them was sufficient to crush the whole island at one
shot. This led them to inquire of him, what sort of guns we actually had in our two ships. He said, that though they were but
small, in comparison with those he had just described, yet, with
such as they were, we could, with the greatest ease, and at the

---

1 After leaving New Zealand on February 25, Cook set course for Tahiti. On
his way thither he sighted the Cook Islands, on one of which (Atiu, or Wateeoo)
a party consisting of Omai, Gore, Burney and Anderson landed. Cook says the
islanders "seemed to know nothing of the existence of any other land-animals,
besides hogs, dogs, and birds", and that they imagined the sheep and goats on
board were species of birds. According to a note made by Bligh, in his copy
now in the Admiralty Library, they did not intend this literally.

distance the ships were from the shore, destroy the island, and kill every soul in it. They persevered in their inquiries, to know by what means this could be done; and Omai explained the matter as well as he could. He happened luckily to have a few cartridges in his pocket. These he produced; the balls, and the gunpowder which was to set them in motion, were submitted to inspection; and to supply the defects of his description, an appeal was made to the senses of the spectators. It has been mentioned above, that one of the chiefs had ordered the multitude to form themselves into a circle. This furnished Omai with a convenient stage for his exhibition. In the centre of this amphitheatre, the inconsiderable quantity of gunpowder, collected from his cartridges, was properly disposed upon the ground, and, by means of a bit of burning wood from the oven, where dinner was dressing, set on fire. The sudden blast, and loud report, the mingled flame and smoke, that instantly succeeded, now filled the whole assembly with astonishment; they no longer doubted the tremendous power of our weapons, and gave full credit to all that Omai had said.

If it had not been for the terrible ideas they conceived of the guns of our ships, from this specimen of their mode of operation, it was thought that they would have detained the gentlemen all night. For Omai assured them, that if he and his companions did not return on board the same day, they might expect that I would fire upon the island. And as we stood in nearer the land in the evening than we had done any time before, of which position of the ships they were observed to take great notice, they, probably, thought we were meditating this formidable attack; and therefore suffered their guests to depart; under the expectation, however, of seeing them again on shore next morning. But I was too sensible of the risk they had already run, to think of a repetition of the experiment.

This day, it seems, was destined to give Omai more occasions than one of being brought forward to bear a principal part in its transactions. The island, though never before visited by Europeans, actually happened to have other strangers residing in it; and it was entirely owing to Omai's being one of Mr. Gore's attendants, that this curious circumstance came to our knowledge.

Scarcely had he been landed upon the beach, when he found amongst the crowd there assembled, three of his own countrymen, natives of the Society Islands. At the distance of about two hundred leagues from those islands, an immense unknown ocean intervening, with such wretched sea-boats as their inhabitants are known to make use of, and fit only for a passage where sight of land is scarcely ever lost, such a meeting, at such a place, so accidentally visited by us, may well be looked upon as one of those unexpected situations, with which the writers of feigned adventures love to surprise their readers, and which, when they really happen in common life, deserve to be recorded for their singularity.

It may easily be guessed with what mutual surprise and satisfaction Omai and his countrymen engaged in conversation. Their story, as related by them, is an affecting one. About twenty persons in number, of both sexes, had embarked on board a canoe at Otaheite, to cross over to the neighbouring island Ulietea. A violent contrary wind arising, they could neither reach the latter, nor get back to the former. Their intended passage being a very short one, their stock of provisions was scanty and soon exhausted; the hardships they suffered, while driven along by the storm, they knew not whither, are not to be conceived; they passed many days without having anything to eat or drink; their numbers gradually diminished, worn out by famine and fatigue; four men only survived, when the canoe overset, and then the perdition of this small remnant seemed inevitable. However, they kept hanging by the side of their vessel during some of the last days, till Providence brought them in sight of the people of this island, who immediately sent out canoes, took them off their wreck, and brought them ashore. Of the four who were thus saved, one was since dead; the other three, who lived to have this opportunity of giving an account of their almost miraculous transplantation, spoke highly of the kind treatment they here met with; and so well satisfied were they with their situation, that they refused the offer made to them by our gentlemen, at

Omai's request, of giving them a passage on board our ships, to restore them to their native islands. The similarity of manners and language had more than naturalized them to this spot; and the fresh connections which they had here formed, and which it would have been painful to have broken off, after such a length of time, sufficiently account for their declining to revisit the places of their birth. They had arrived upon this island at least twelve years ago.

April 6   Being thus disappointed at all the islands we had met with, since our leaving New Zealand,[2] and the unfavourable winds, and other unforeseen circumstances, having unavoidably retarded our progress so much, it was now impossible to think of doing anything this year, in the high latitudes of the northern hemisphere, from which we were still at so great a distance, though the season for our operations there was already begun. In this situation, it was absolutely necessary to pursue such measures as were most likely to preserve the cattle we had on board, in the first place; and, in the next place (which was still a more capital object), to save the stores and provisions of the ships, that we might be better enabled to prosecute our northern discoveries, which could not now commence till a year later than was originally intended.

If I had been so fortunate as to have procured a supply of water, and of grass, at any of the islands we had lately visited, it was my purpose to have stood back to the south, till I had met with a westerly wind. But the certain consequence of doing this without such a supply, would have been the loss of all the cattle, before we could possibly reach Otaheite, without gaining any one advantage with regard to the great object of our voyage.

I therefore determined to bear away for the Friendly Islands, where I was sure of meeting with abundance of everything I wanted, and it being necessary to run in the night as well as in the day, I ordered Captain Clerke to keep about a league ahead of the *Resolution*. I used this precaution, because his ship could

---

[2] *i.e.* of obtaining supplies at a suitable anchorage in the Cook Islands, which lie between Tahiti and the Friendly Islands.

best claw off the land,[3] and it was very possible we might fall in with some, in our passage.

April 17   The nine or ten low islets, comprehended under the name of Palmerston's Island,[4] may be reckoned the heads or summits of the reef of coral rock, that connects them together, covered only with a thin coat of sand, yet clothed, as already observed, with trees and plants; most of which are of the same sorts that are found on the low grounds of the high islands of this ocean.

There are different opinions amongst ingenious theorists, concerning the formation of such low islands as Palmerston's. Some will have it, that, in remote times, these little separate heads or islets were joined, and formed one continued and more elevated tract of land, which the sea, in the revolution of ages, has washed away, leaving only the higher grounds; which, in time, also, will, according to this theory, share the same fate. Another conjecture is, that they have been thrown up by earthquakes, and are the effect of internal convulsions of the globe. A third opinion, and which appears to me as the most probable one, maintains, that they are formed from shoals, or coral banks, and of consequence increasing. Without mentioning the several arguments made use of in support of each of these systems, I shall only describe such parts of Palmerston's Island, as fell under my own observation when I landed upon it.

The foundation is, everywhere, a coral rock; the soil is coral sand, with which the decayed vegetables have, but in a few places, intermixed, so as to form any thing like mould. From this, a very strong presumption may be drawn, that these little spots of land, are not of very ancient date, nor the remains of larger islands now buried in the ocean. For, upon either of these suppositions, more mould must have been formed, or some part of the original soil would have remained. Another circumstance confirmed this doctrine of the increase of these islets. We found upon them, far

[3] *i.e.* beat to windward off a lee shore. The decision to steer west for the Friendly Islands (Tonga) was made on leaving Hervey Island in the Cook group.
[4] This group of atolls, discovered in 1774, lies between the Cook and the Friendly Islands.

beyond the present reach of the sea, even in the most violent storms, elevated coral rocks, which, on examination, appeared to have been perforated, in the same manner that the rocks are, that now compose the outer edge of the reef. This evidently shows, that the sea had formerly reached so far; and some of these perforated rocks were almost in the centre of the land.

But the strongest proof of the increase, and from the cause we have assigned, was the gentle gradation observable in the plants round the skirts of the islands; from within a few inches of high-water mark, to the edge of the wood. In many places, the divisions of the plants, of different growths, were very distinguishable, especially on the lee, or west side. This, I apprehend, to have been the operation of extraordinary high tides, occasioned by violent, accidental gales from the westward; which have heaped up the sand beyond the reach of common tides. The regular and gentle operation of these latter, again, throw up sand enough to form a barrier against the next extraordinary high tide, or storm, so as to prevent its reaching as far as the former had done, and destroying the plants that may have begun to vegetate from coconuts, roots, and seed brought thither by birds, or thrown up by the sea. This, doubtless, happens very frequently; for we found many coconuts, and some other things, just sprouting up, only a few inches beyond where the sea reaches at present, in places where, it was evident, they could not have had their origin from those, farther in, already arrived at their full growth. At the same time, the increase of vegetables will add fast to the height of this new-created land; as the fallen leaves, and broken branches, are, in such a climate, soon converted into a true black mould, or soil.

Perhaps there is another cause, which, if allowed, will accelerate the increase of these islands as much as any other; and will also account for the sea having receded from those elevated rocks before mentioned. This is, the spreading of the coral bank, or reef, into the sea; which, in my opinion, is continually, though imperceptibly, affected. The waves receding, as the reef grows in breadth and height, leave a dry rock behind, ready for the reception of the broken coral and sand, and every other deposit necessary for the formation of land fit for the vegetation of plants.

In this manner, there is little doubt, that, in time, the whole reef will become one island; and, I think, it will extend gradually inward, either from the increase of the islets already formed, or from the formation of new ones, upon the beds of coral, within the enclosed lake, if once they increase so as to rise above the level of the sea.

May 1   At four o'clock next morning, I ordered a boat to be hoisted out, and sent the master to sound the south-west side of Annamooka;[5] where there appeared to be a harbour, formed by the island on the north-east, and by small islets and shoals, to the south-west and south-east. In the meantime the ships were got under sail, and wrought up to the island.

When the master returned, he reported, that he had sounded between Great and Little Annamooka, where he found ten and twelve fathoms' depth of water, the bottom coral sand; that the place was very well sheltered from all winds; but that there was no fresh water to be found, except at some distance inland; and that, even there, little of it was to be got, and that little not good. For this reason only, and it was a very sufficient one, I determined to anchor on the north side of the island, where, during my last voyage, I had found a place fit both for watering and landing.

It was not above a league distant; and yet we did not reach it till five o'clock in the afternoon, being considerably retarded by the great number of canoes that continually crowded round the ships, bringing to us abundant supplies of the produce of their island. Amongst these canoes, there were some double ones, with a large sail, that carried between forty and fifty men each. These sailed round us apparently with the same ease, as if we had been at anchor. There were several women in the canoes, who were, perhaps, incited by curiosity to visit us; though, at the same time, they bartered as eagerly as the men and used the paddle with equal labour and dexterity. I came to an anchor in eighteen fathoms of water, the bottom coarse coral sand; the island extend-

5 Nomuka or Rotterdam in the Friendly group, visited in 1772; see above, p. 158

ing from east to south-west; and the west point of the western-most cove south-east, about three quarters of a mile distant. Thus I resumed the very same station which I had occupied when I visited Annamooka three years before; and, probably, almost in the same place where Tasman, the first discoverer of this, and some of the neighbouring islands, anchored in 1643.

The following day, while preparations were making for watering, I went ashore, in the forenoon, accompanied by Captain Clerke, and some of the officers, to fix on a place where the observatories might be set up, and a guard be stationed; the natives having readily given us leave. They also accommodated us with a boat-house, to serve as a tent, and showed us every other mark of civility. Toobou, the chief of the island, conducted me and Omai to his house. We found it situated on a pleasant spot, in the centre of his plantation. A fine grass plot surrounded it, which he gave us to understand, was for the purpose of cleaning their feet, before they went within doors. I had not before observed such an instance of attention to cleanliness at any of the places I had visited in this ocean; but afterward found, that it was very common at the Friendly Islands. The floor of Toobou's house was covered with mats; and no carpet in the most elegant English drawing-room could be kept neater. While we were on shore, we procured a few hogs, and some fruit, by bartering; and, before we got on board again, the ships were crowded with the natives. Few of them coming empty-handed, every necessary refreshment was now in the greatest plenty.

May 6 On the 6th we were visited by a great chief from Tongataboo, whose name was Feenou, and whom Taipa[6] was pleased to introduce to us as king of all the Friendly Isles. I was now told, that on my arrival, a canoe had been despatched to Tongataboo with the news; in consequence of which, this chief immediately passed over to Annamooka. The officer on shore informed me, that when he first arrived, all the natives were ordered out to meet him, and paid their obeisance by bowing their heads as low as his feet, the soles of which they also touched

---

[6] Taipa, a chief of Nomuka, apparently acted as Prime Minister to Feenou.

with each hand, first with the palm, and then with the back part. There could be little room to suspect that a person, received with so much respect, could be anything less than the king.

In the afternoon, I went to pay this great man a visit, having first received a present of two fish from him, brought on board by one of his servants. As soon as I landed, he came up to me. He appeared to be about thirty years of age, tall but thin, and had more of the European features, than any I had yet seen here. When the first salutation was over, I asked if he was the king; for, notwithstanding what I had been told, finding he was not the man whom I remembered to have seen under that character during my former voyage, I began to entertain doubts. Taipa officiously answered for him, and enumerated no less than one hundred and fifty-three islands, of which he said, Feenou was the sovereign. After a short stay, our new visitor, and five or six of his attendants, accompanied me on board. I gave suitable presents to them all, and entertained them in such a manner, as I thought would be most agreeable.

In the evening, I attended them on shore in my boat, into which the chief ordered three hogs to be put, as a return for the presents he had received from me. I was now informed of an accident which had just happened, the relation of which will convey some idea of the extent of the authority exercised here over the common people. While Feenou was on board my ship, an inferior chief, for what reason our people on shore did not know, ordered all the natives to retire from the post we occupied. Some of them having ventured to return, he took up a large stick and beat them most unmercifully. He struck one man, on the side of the face, with so much violence, that the blood gushed out of his mouth and nostrils; and, after lying some time motionless, he was at last removed from the place in convulsions. The person who had inflicted the blow, being told that he had killed the man, only laughed at it; and, it was evident, that he was not in the least sorry for what had happened. We heard, afterwards, that the poor sufferer recovered.

The *Discovery* having found again her small bower anchor, shifted her berth on the 7th; but not before her best bower cable had shared the fate of the other. This day, I had the company of Feenou at dinner; and also the next day, when he was attended by Taipa, Toobou, and some other chiefs. It was remarkable, that none but Taipa was allowed to sit at table with him, or even to eat in his presence. I own that I considered Feenou as a very convenient guest, on account of this etiquette. For, before his arrival, I had generally a larger company than I could well find room for, and my table overflowed with crowds of both sexes. For it is not the custom at the Friendly Islands, as it is at Otaheite, to deny to their females the privilege of eating in company with the men.

The first day of our arrival at Annamooka, one of the natives had stolen out of the ship a large junk axe. I now applied to Feenou to exert his authority to get it restored to me; and so implicitly was he obeyed, that it was brought on board while we were at dinner. These people gave us very frequent opportunities of remarking what expert thieves they were. Even some of their chiefs did not think this profession beneath them. On the 9th, one of them was detected carrying out of the ship, concealed under his clothes, the bolt belonging to the spun-yarn winch, for which I sentenced him to receive a dozen lashes, and kept him confined till he paid a hog for his liberty. After this we were not troubled with thieves of rank. Their servants, or slaves, however, were still employed in this dirty work; and upon them a flogging seemed to make no greater impression than it would have done upon the mainmast. When any of them happened to be caught in the act, their masters, far from interceding for them, would often advise us to kill them. As this was a punishment we did not choose to inflict, they generally escaped without any punishment at all; for they appeared to us to be equally insensible of the shame and of the pain of corporal chastisement. Captain Clerke at last hit upon a mode of treatment which we thought had some effect. He put them under the hands of the barber, and completely shaved their heads; thus pointing them out as objects of ridicule to their countrymen, and enabling our people to deprive them of future opportunities for a repetition of their rogueries, by keeping them at a distance.

Feenou was so fond of associating with us, that he dined on board every day, though sometimes he did not partake of our fare. On the 10th, some of his servants brought a mess which had been dressed for him on shore. It consisted of fish, soup, and yams. Instead of common water to make the soup, coconut liquor had been made use of, in which the fish had been boiled or stewed, probably in a wooden vessel with hot stones; but it was carried on board in a plantain leaf. I tasted of the mess, and found it so good, that I afterwards had some fish dressed in the same way. Though my cook succeeded tolerably well, he could produce nothing equal to the dish he imitated.

May 18   Next morning early, Feenou and Omai, who scarcely ever quitted the chief, and now slept on shore, came on board. The object of the visit, was to require my presence upon the island.[7] After some time I accompanied them, and upon landing was conducted to the same place where I had been seated the day before, and where I saw a large concourse of people already assembled. I guessed that something more than ordinary was in agitation, but could not tell what, nor could Omai inform me.

I had not been long seated, before near a hundred of the natives appeared in sight, and advanced laden with yams, bread-fruit, plantains, coconuts, and sugar-canes. They deposited their burdens in two heaps or piles, upon our left, being the side they came from. Soon after, arrived a number of others from the right, bearing the same kind of articles; which were collected into two piles upon that side. To these were tied two pigs and six fowls, and to those upon the left six pigs and two turtles. Earoupa seated himself before the several articles upon the left, and another chief before those upon the right; they being as I judged, the two chiefs who had collected them, by order of Feenou, who seemed to be as implicitly obeyed here as he had been at Annamooka;

---

[7] Hapaee (Haabai) north of Nomuka. Zimmermann, a Swiss, who signed on as an ordinary seaman and kept a private diary, says that Feenou was their pilot, from Nomuka to this island: "Finau went ahead in his own boat, and without the assistance of the magnetic needle, and without even having his face toward the island, he not only showed us the way—to the great astonishment of our captain— but he also indicated the depth of the water by extending his arms and we were able to follow him in our large ships, with the greatest confidence."

and, in consequence of his commanding superiority over the chiefs of Hapaee, had laid his tax upon them for the present occasion.

As soon as this munificent collection of provisions was laid down in order, and disposed to the best advantage, the bearers of it joined the multitude, who formed a large circle round the whole. Presently after a number of men entered this circle or area before us, armed with clubs, made of the green branches of the coconut tree. These paraded about for a few minutes, and then retired, the one half to one side, and the other half to the other side; seating themselves before the spectators. Soon after they successively entered the lists, and entertained us with single combats. One champion rising up and stepping forward from one side, challenged those of the other side, by expressive gestures, more than by words, to send one of their body to oppose him. If the challenge was accepted, which was generally the case, the two combatants put themselves in proper attitudes, and then began the engagement, which continued till one or other owned himself conquered, or till their weapons were broken. As soon as each combat was over, the victor squatted himself down facing the chief, then rose up and retired. At the same time some old men, who seemed to sit as judges, gave their plaudit in a few words; and the multitude, especially those on the side to which the victor belonged, celebrated the glory he had acquired in two or three huzzas.

This entertainment was now and then suspended for a few minutes. During these intervals, there were both wrestling and boxing matches. The first were performed in the same manner as at Otaheite, and the second differed very little from the method practised in England. But what struck us with most surprise, was to see a couple of lusty wenches step forth and begin boxing, without the least ceremony, and with as much art as the men. This contest, however, did not last above half a minute before one of them gave it up. The conquering heroine received the same applause from the spectators, which they bestowed upon the successful combatants of the other sex. We expressed some dislike at this part of the entertainment, which, however, did not prevent two other females from entering the lists. They seemed to be girls of spirit, and would certainly have given each other a good drubbing, if two old women had not interposed to part them. All these combats were exhibited in the midst of at least three thousand people; and were conducted with the greatest good humour on all sides, though some of the champions, women as well as men, received blows, which, doubtless, they must have felt for some time after.

As soon as these diversions were ended, the chief told me that the heaps of provisions on our right hand were a present to Omai, and that those on our left hand, being about two-thirds of the whole quantity, were given to me. He added, that I might take them on board whenever it was convenient; but that there would be no occasion to set any of our people as guards over them, as I might be assured that not a single coconut would be taken away by the natives. So it proved, for I left everything behind, and returned to the ship to dinner, carrying the chief with me; and when the provisions were removed on board in the afternoon, not a single article was missing. There was as much as loaded four boats; and I could not but be struck with the munificence of Feenou; for this present far exceeded any I had ever received from any of the sovereigns of the various islands I had visited in the Pacific Ocean. I lost no time in convincing my friend that I was not insensible of his liberality; for before he quitted my ship, I bestowed upon him such of our commodities as I guessed were most valuable in his estimation. And the return I made was so much to his satisfaction, that as soon as he got on shore, he left me still indebted to him, by sending me a fresh present, consisting of two large hogs, a considerable quantity of cloth, and some yams.

Feenou had expressed a desire to see the marines go through their military exercise. As I was desirous to gratify his curiosity, I ordered them all ashore from both ships, in the morning of the 20th. After they had performed various evolutions, and fired several volleys, with which the numerous body of spectators seemed well pleased, the chief entertained us in his turn, with an exhibition, which, as was acknowledged by us all, was performed with a dexterity and exactness far surpassing the specimen we had given of our military manœuvres. It was a kind of dance, so entirely different from anything I had ever seen, that I fear I can give no description that will convey any tolerable idea of it to my readers. It was performed by men, and 105 persons bore their parts in it. Each of them had in his hand an instrument neatly made, shaped somewhat like a paddle, of two feet and a half in length, with a small handle and a thin blade, so that they were very light. With these instruments they made many and various flourishes, each of which was accompanied with a different attitude of the body, or a different movement. At first, the performers ranged themselves in three lines; and by various evolutions, each man changed his station in such a manner, that those who had been in the rear came into the front. Nor did they remain long in the same position, but these changes were made by pretty quick transitions. At one time they extended themselves in one line; they then formed into a semicircle; and, lastly, into two square columns. While this last movement was executing, one of them advanced, and performed an antic dance before me, with which the whole ended.

The musical instruments consisted of two drums, or rather two hollow logs of wood, from which some varied notes were produced, by beating on them with two sticks. It did not, however, appear to me, that the dancers were much assisted or directed by these sounds, but by a chorus of vocal music, in which all the performers joined at the same time. Their song was not destitute of pleasing melody; and all their corresponding motions were executed with so much skill, that the numerous body of dancers seemed to act, as if they were one great machine. It was the opinion of everyone of us, that such a performance would have met with universal applause on a European theatre; and it so far exceeded any attempt we had made to entertain them, that they seemed to pique themselves upon the superiority they had over us. As to our musical instruments, they held none of them in the least esteem, except the drum; and even that they did not think equal to their own. Our French horns in particular, seemed to be held in great contempt; for neither here, nor at any other of the islands, would they pay the smallest attention to them.

In order to give them a more favourable opinion of English amusements, and to leave their minds fully impressed with the deepest sense of our superior attainments, I directed some fire-works to be got ready; and, after it was dark, played them off in the presence of Feenou, the other chiefs, and a vast concourse of their people. Some of the preparations we found damaged; but others of them were in excellent order, and succeeded so per-fectly, as to answer the end I had in view. Our water and sky-rockets, in particular, pleased and astonished them beyond all conception; and the scale was now turned in our favour.

June 20   In this walk we met with about half a dozen women in one place at supper. Two of the company, I observed, being fed by the others, on our asking the reason, they said *taboo mattee*.[8] On further inquiry we found that one of them had, two months before, washed the dead corpse of a chief; and that, on this account, she was not to handle any food for five months. The other had performed the same office to the corpse of another person of inferior rank, and was now under the same restriction, but not for so long a time. At another place hard by, we saw another woman fed; and we learnt that she had assisted in wash-ing the corpse of the above-mentioned chief.

Early the next morning the king came on board to invite me to an entertainment, which he proposed to give the same day. He had already been under the barber's hands: his head being all besmeared with red pigment, in order to redden his hair, which was naturally of a dark brown colour. After breakfast I attended him to the shore; and we found his people very busy in two places, in the front of our area, fixing, in an upright and square position, thus, [$\begin{smallmatrix} \circ & \circ \\ \circ & \circ \end{smallmatrix}$], four very long posts, near two feet from each other. The space between the posts was afterward filled up with yams; and as they went on filling it, they fastened pieces of sticks across, from post to post, at the distance of about every four feet,

---

[8] *Mattee* means killed. It was here in the Friendly group that Cook first met with the word *taboo*, "which word", he says, "has a very comprehensive meaning, but, in general, signifies that a thing is forbidden". The ships were now at Tonga-tabu, the king of which was named Poulaho; Mareewagee, mentioned later, was one of the chiefs.

to prevent the posts from separating by the weight of the enclosed yams, and also to get up by. When the yams had reached
the top of the first posts, they fastened others to them, and so
continued till each pile was the height of thirty feet or upward.
On the top of one they placed two baked hogs; and on the top
of the other a living one; and another they tied by the legs halfway up. It was a matter of curiosity to observe with what facility
and despatch these two piles were raised. Had our seamen been
ordered to execute such a work, they would have sworn that it
could not be performed without carpenters; and the carpenters
would have called to their aid a dozen different sorts of tools, and
have expended, at least, a hundredweight of nails; and, after all,
it would have employed them as many days as it did these people
hours. But seamen, like most other amphibious animals, are always the most helpless on land. After they had completed these
two piles, they made several other heaps of yams and bread-fruit
on each side of the area; to which were added a turtle and a large
quantity of excellent fish. All this, with a piece of cloth, a mat,
and some red feathers, was the king's present to me; and he
seemed to pique himself on exceeding, as he really did, Feenou's
liberality, which I experienced at Hapaee.

About one o'clock they began the *mai*, or dances; the first of
which was almost a copy of the first that was exhibited at Mareewagee's entertainment. The second was conducted by Captain
Furneaux's Toobou, who, as we mentioned, had also danced
there; and in this, four or five women were introduced, who went
through the several parts with as much exactness as the men. Toward the end, the performers divided to leave room for two
champions, who exercised their clubs as described on a former
occasion. And, in the third dance, which was the last now presented, two more men with their clubs displayed their dexterity.
The dances were succeeded by wrestling and boxing; and one man
entered the lists with a sort of club made from the stem of a coco-
leaf, which is firm and heavy, but could find no antagonist to
engage him at so rough a sport. At night we had the *bomai* repeated; in which Poulaho himself danced, dressed in English
manufacture. But neither these nor the dances in the daytime

were so considerable, nor carried on with so much spirit, as Feenou's or Mareewagee's; and, therefore, there is less occasion to be more particular in our description of them.

In order to be present the whole time, I dined ashore. The king sat down with us; but he neither ate nor drank. I found that this was owing to the presence of a female, whom, at his desire, I had admitted to the dining party; and who, as we afterward understood, had superior rank to himself. As soon as this great personage had dined, she stepped up to the king, who put his hands to her feet, and then she retired. He immediately dipped his fingers into a glass of wine, and then received the obeisance of all her followers. This was the single instance we ever observed of his paying this mark of reverence to any person. At the king's desire, I ordered some fireworks to be played off in the evening; but, unfortunately, being damaged, this exhibition did not answer expectation.

July 6   We were now ready to sail, but the wind being easterly, we had not sufficient daylight to turn through the narrows, either with the morning or with the evening flood; the one falling out too early and the other too late. So that without a leading wind, we were under a necessity of waiting two or three days.

I took the opportunity of this delay to be present at a public solemnity, to which the king had invited us when we went last to visit him, and which he had informed us, was to be performed on the 8th. With a view to this, he and all the people of note quitted our neighbourhood on the 7th, and repaired to Mooa, where the solemnity was to be exhibited.[9] A party of us followed them the next morning. We understood, from what Poulaho had said to us, that his son and heir was now to be initiated into certain privileges; amongst which was that of eating with his father; an honour he had not as yet been admitted to.

We arrived at Mooa about eight o'clock, and found the king, with a large circle of attendants sitting before him, within an enclosure so small and dirty as to excite my wonder that any

[9] Mooa is an island near Tongatabu; the ceremony was a *natche* or solemn feast in honour of the coming of age of Poulaho's son.

such could be found in that neighbourhood. They were intent upon their usual morning occupation, in preparing a bowl of *kava*. As this was no liquor for us, we walked out to visit some of our friends, and to observe what preparations might be making for the ceremony, which was soon to begin. About ten o'clock the people began to assemble in a large area, which is before the *malaee*, or great house, to which we had been conducted the first time we visited Mooa. At the end of a road that opens into this area, stood some men with spears and clubs, who kept constantly reciting or chanting short sentences, in a mournful tone, which conveyed some idea of distress, and as if they called for something. This was continued about an hour; and, in the meantime, many people came down the road, each of them bringing a yam tied to the middle of a pole, which they laid down before the persons who continued repeating the sentences. While this was going on, the king and prince arrived, and seated themselves upon the area; and we were desired to sit down by them, but to pull off our hats, and to untie our hair. The bearers of the yams being all come in, each pole was taken up between two men, who carried it over their shoulders. After forming themselves into companies of ten or twelve persons each, they marched across the place with a quick pace, each company, headed by a man bearing a club or spear, and guarded on the right by several others armed with different weapons. A man carrying a living pigeon on a perch, closed the rear of the procession, in which about two hundred and fifty persons walked.

Omai was desired by me to ask the chief to what place the yams were to be thus carried with so much solemnity? but, as he seemed unwilling to give us the information we wanted, two or three of us followed the procession, contrary to his inclination. We found that they stopped before a *morai* or *fiatooka*[10] of one house standing upon a mount, which was hardly a quarter of a mile from the place where they first assembled. Here we observed them depositing the yams, and making them up into bundles; but for what purpose, we could not learn. And, as our presence seemed to give them uneasiness, we left them and re-

[10] *i.e.* burying place.

turned to Poulaho, who told us we might amuse ourselves by walking about, as nothing would be done for some time. The fear of losing any part of the ceremony, prevented our being long absent. When we returned to the king, he desired me to order the boat's crew not to stir from the boat; for, as everything would very soon be *taboo*, if any of our people, or of their own, should be found walking about, they would be knocked down with clubs; nay, *mateed*, that is, killed. He also acquainted us, that we could not be present at the ceremony; but that we should be conducted to a place where we might see everything that passed. Objections were made to our dress. We were told that, to qualify us to be present, it was necessary that we should be naked as low as the breast with our hats off, and our hair untied. Omai offered to conform to these requisites, and began to strip; other objections were then started; so that the exclusion was given to him equally with ourselves.

I did not much like this restriction; and, therefore, stole out to see what might now be going forward. I found very few people stirring except those dressed to attend the ceremony; some of whom had in their hands small poles about four feet long, and to the underpart of these were fastened two or three other sticks not bigger than one's finger, and about six inches in length. These men were going toward the *morai* just mentioned. I took the same road, and was several times stopped by them, all crying out *taboo*. However, I went forward without much regarding them, till I came in sight of the *morai*, and of the people who were sitting before it. I was now urged very strongly to go back; and, not knowing what might be the consequence of a refusal, I complied. I had observed that the people who carried the poles passed this *morai*, or what I may as well call temple; and guessing, from this circumstance, that something was transacting beyond it which might be worth looking at, I had thoughts of advancing by making a round for this purpose; but I was so closely watched by three men that I could not put my design in execution. In order to shake these fellows off, I returned to the *malaee*, where I had left the king, and from thence made an elopement a second time; but I instantly met with the same three men; so that it

seemed as if they had been ordered to watch my motions. I paid
no regard to what they said or did till I came within sight of the
king's principal *fiatooka* or *morai*, before which a great number of
men were sitting, being the same persons whom I had just before
seen pass by the other *morai*, from which this was but a little distant. Observing that I could watch the proceedings of this company from the king's plantation, I repaired thither, very much to
the satisfaction of those who attended me.

As soon as I got in, I acquainted the gentlemen who had come
with me from the ships with what I had seen; and we took a
proper station to watch the result. The number of people at the
fiatooka, continued to increase for some time; and at length we
could see them quit their sitting posture, and march off in procession. They walked in pairs, one after another, every pair carrying between them one of the small poles above mentioned on
their shoulders. We were told that the small pieces of stick fastened to the poles were yams; so that, probably, they were meant
to represent this root emblematically. The hindmost men of each
couple, for the most part, placed one of his hands to the middle
of the pole, as if, without this additional support, it were not
strong enough to carry the weight that hung to it, and under
which they all seemed to bend as they walked. This procession
consisted of one hundred and eight pairs, and all, or most of them,
men of rank. They came close by the fence behind which we
stood; so that we had a full view of them.

Having waited here till they had all passed, we then repaired
to Poulaho's house, and saw him going out. We could not be
allowed to follow him; but were forthwith conducted to the
place allotted to us, which was behind a fence, adjoining to the
area of the *fiatooka* where the yams had been deposited in the forenoon. As we were not the only people who were excluded from
being publicly present at this ceremony, but allowed to peep
from behind the curtain, we had a good deal of company; and I
observed that all the other enclosures round the place were filled
with people. And yet all imaginable care seemed to be taken that
they should see as little as possible; for the fences had not only
been repaired that morning, but, in many places, raised higher

than common; so that the tallest man could not look over them. To remedy this defect in our station, we took the liberty to cut holes in the fence with our knives; and by this means we could see, pretty distinctly, everything that was transacting on the other side.

On our arrival at our station, we found two or three hundred people sitting on the grass near the end of the road that opened into the area of the *morai*, and the number continually increased, by others joining them. At length arrived a few men carrying some small poles, and branches or leaves of the coconut tree; and, upon their appearance, an old man seated himself in the road, and, with his face towards them, pronounced a long oration in a serious tone. He then retired back, and the others advancing to the middle of the area, began to erect a small shed; employing for that purpose the materials above mentioned. When they had finished their work, they all squatted down for a moment before it, then rose up and retired to the rest of the company. Soon after came Poulaho's son, preceded by four or five men, and they seated themselves a little aside from the shed, and rather behind it. After them appeared twelve or fourteen women of the first rank, walking slowly in pairs, each pair carrying between them a narrow piece of white cloth extended about two or three yards in length. These marched up to the prince, squatted down before him; and having wrapped some of the pieces of the cloth they had brought round his body, they rose up and retired in the same order, to some distance on his left, and there seated themselves. Poulaho himself soon made his appearance, preceded by four men, who walked two and two abreast, and sat down on his son's left hand about twenty paces from him. The young prince, then quitting his first position, went and sat down under the shed with his attendants; and a considerable number more placed themselves on the grass before this royal canopy. The prince himself sat facing the people, with his back to the *morai*. This being done, three companies, of ten or a dozen men in each, started up from amongst the large crowd, a little after each other, and running hastily to the opposite side of the area, sat down for a few seconds, after which they returned in the same manner to their former stations. To them succeeded two men, each of whom held a small green branch in his hand, who got up and approached the prince, sitting down for a few seconds three different times, as they advanced; and then, turning their backs, retired in the same manner, inclining their branches to each other as they sat. In a little time two more repeated this ceremony.

The grand procession which I had seen march off from the other *morai*, now began to come in. To judge of the circuit they had made, from the time they had been absent, it must have been pretty large. As they entered the area, they marched up to the right of the shed, and, having prostrated themselves on the grass, deposited their pretended burdens (the poles above mentioned), and faced round to the prince. They then rose up and retired in the same order, closing their hands, which they held before them, with the most serious aspect, and seated themselves along the front of the area. During all the time that this numerous band were coming in, and depositing their poles, three men, who sat under the shed with the prince, continued pronouncing separate sentences in a melancholy tone. After this a profound silence ensued for a little time, and then a man, who sat in the front of the area, began an oration (or prayer), during which, at several different times, he went and broke one of the poles which had been brought in by those who had walked in procession. When he had ended, the people sitting before the sheds separated, to make a lane, through which the prince and his attendants passed, and the assembly broke up.

Some of our party, satisfied with what they had already seen, now returned to the ships; but I, and two or three more of the officers, remained at Mooa, to see the conclusion of the solemnity, which was not to be till the next day; being desirous of omitting no opportunity which might afford any information about the religious or the political institutions of these people. The small sticks or poles which had been brought into the area by those who walked in procession, being left lying on the ground after the crowd had dispersed, I went and examined them. I found, that, to the middle of each, two or three small sticks were tied, as has been related. Yet we had been repeatedly told by the natives who stood near us, that they were young yams; insomuch that some of our gentlemen believed them rather than their own eyes. As I had the demonstration of my senses to satisfy me that they were not real yams, it is clear that we ought to have understood them, that they were only the artificial representations of these roots.

Our supper was got ready about seven o'clock. It consisted of fish and yams. We might have had pork also; but we did not choose to kill a large hog, which the king had given to us for that purpose. He supped with us, and drank pretty freely of brandy and water; so that he went to bed with a sufficient dose. We passed the night in the same house with him and several of his attendants. . . .

We endeavoured in vain to find out the meaning not only of the ceremony in general, which is called *Natche*, but of its different parts. We seldom got any other answer to our inquiries, but *taboo*; a word which I have before observed, is applied to many other things. But as the prince was evidently the principal person concerned in it; and as we had been told by the king, ten days before the celebration of the *Natche*, that the people would bring in yams for him and his son to eat together; and as he even described some part of the ceremony, we concluded, from what he had then said, and from what we now saw, that an oath of allegiance, if I may so express myself, or solemn promise, was on this occasion made to the prince, as the immediate successor to the regal dignity, to stand by him, and to furnish him with the several articles that were here emblematically represented. This seems the more probable, as all the principal people of the island, whom we had ever seen, assisted in the processions. But, be this as it may, the whole was conducted with a great deal of mysterious solemnity; and that there was a mixture of religion in the institution, was evident, not only from the place where it was performed, but from the manner of performing it. Our dress and deportment had never been called in question upon any former occasion whatever. Now, it was expected that we should be uncovered as low as the waist; that our hair should be loose, and flowing over our shoulders, that we should, like themselves, sit cross-legged; and at times in the most humble posture, with down-cast eyes, and hands locked together; all which requisites were most devoutly observed by the whole assembly. And, lastly, everyone was excluded from the solemnity, but the principal people, and those who assisted in the celebration. All these circumstances were to me a sufficient testimony, that, upon this occasion, they considered themselves as acting under the immediate inspection of a supreme being.

ACCOUNT OF THE FRIENDLY ISLANDS

July 17   Thus we took leave of the Friendly Islands and their inhabitants, after a stay of between two and three months; during which time, we lived together in the most cordial friendship. Some accidental differences, it is true, now and then happened, owing to their great propensity to thieving; but, too often encouraged by the negligence of our own people. But these differences were never attended with any fatal consequences; to prevent which, all my measures were directed; and, I believe, few on board our ships left our friends here without some regret. The time employed amongst them was not thrown away. We expended very little of our sea provisions; subsisting in general upon the produce of the islands, while we stayed; and carrying away with us a quantity of refreshments sufficient to last till our arrival at another station, where we could depend upon a fresh supply. I was not sorry, besides, to have had an opportunity of bettering the condition of these good people, by leaving the useful animals before mentioned among them;[11] and, at the same time, those designed for Otaheite, received fresh strength in the pastures of Tongataboo. Upon the whole, therefore, the advantages we received by touching here were very great; and I had the additional satisfaction to reflect, that they were received, without retarding one

[11] Describing a walk on the island, Cook writes: "While I was surveying this delightful prospect I could not help flattering myself with the pleasing idea that some future navigator may, from the same station, behold these meadows stocked with cattle brought to these islands by the ships of England; and that the completion of this single benevolent purpose, independently of all other considerations, would sufficiently mark to posterity that our voyages had not been useless to the general interests of humanity."

moment the prosecution of the great object of our voyage; the season for proceeding to the north being, as has been already observed, lost, before I took the resolution of bearing away for these islands.

But, besides the immediate advantages, which both the natives of the Friendly Islands, and ourselves, received by this visit, future navigators from Europe, if any such should ever tread our steps, will profit by the knowledge I acquired of the geography of this part of the Pacific Ocean; and the more philosophical reader, who loves to view human nature in new situations, and to speculate on singular, but faithful representations of the persons, the customs, the arts, the religion, the government, and the language of uncultivated man, in remote and fresh discovered quarters of the globe, will, perhaps, find matter of amusement, if not of instruction, in the information which I have been enabled to convey to him, concerning the inhabitants of this archipelago. I shall suspend my narrative, of the progress of the voyage, while I faithfully relate what I had opportunities of collecting on these several topics.

We found by our experience, that the best articles for traffic, at these islands, are iron tools in general. Axes and hatchets; nails from the largest spike down to tenpenny ones; rasps, files, and knives, are much sought after. Red cloth, and linen, both white and coloured; looking-glasses, and beads, are also in estimation; but of the latter those that are blue are preferred to all others; and white ones are thought the least valuable. A string of large blue beads would, at any time, purchase a hog. But it must be observed, that such articles as are merely ornaments, may be highly esteemed at one time, and not so at another. When we first arrived at Annamooka, the people there would hardly take them in exchange even for fruit; but when Feenou came, this great man set the fashion, and brought them into vogue, till they rose in their value to what I have just mentioned.

In return for the favourite commodities which I have enumerated, all the refreshments may be procured that the islands produce. These are hogs, fowls, fish, yams, bread-fruit, plantains, coconuts, sugar-cane, and, in general, every such supply as can be met with at Otaheite, or any of the Society Islands. The yams of the Friendly Islands are excellent, and when grown to perfection, keep very well at sea. But their pork, bread-fruit, and plantains, though far from despicable, are, nevertheless, much inferior in quality to the same articles at Otaheite, and in its neighbourhood. . . .

According to the information that we received there, this archipelago is very extensive. Above one hundred and fifty islands were reckoned up to us by the natives, who made use of bits of leaves to ascertain their number; and Mr. Anderson, with his usual diligence, even procured all their names. Fifteen of them are said to be high or hilly, such as Toofoa and Eooa; and thirty-five of them large. Of these only three were seen this voyage; Hapaee (which is considered by the natives as one island), Tonga-taboo and Eooa: of the size of the unexplored thirty-two, nothing more can be mentioned, but that they must all be larger than Annamooka; with those, from whom we had our information, ranked amongst the smaller isles. Some, or indeed several, of this latter denomination, are mere spots, without inhabitants. Sixty-one of these islands have their proper places and names marked upon our chart of the Friendly Islands, and upon the sketch of the harbour of Tongataboo, to both which I refer the reader. But it must be left to future navigators to introduce into the geography of this part of the South Pacific Ocean, the exact situation and size of near a hundred more islands in this neighbourhood, which we had not an opportunity to explore, and whose existence we only learnt from the testimony of our friends, as above mentioned.

The most considerable islands in this neighbourhood that we now heard of (and we heard a great deal about them), are Hamoa, Vavaoo, and Feejee.[12] Each of these was represented to us as larger than Tongataboo. No European, that we know of, has as yet seen any one of them. Tasman, indeed, lays down in his

[12] Hamoa is Samoa (the islanders being unable to pronounce the letter "s"), lying north-east of the Friendly group (not north-west, as stated in the text); Vavaoo is Vavau, the northernmost island of the Friendly group; Feejee is Fiji, lying due west. It is curious that although Cook was so long in the Friendly group he did not go in search of these larger islands.

chart an island nearly in the situation where I suppose Vavaoo to be; that is, about the latitude of 19°. But, then, that island is there marked as a very small one; whereas Vavaoo, according to the united testimony of all our friends at Tongataboo, exceeds the size of their own island, and has high mountains. I should certainly have visited it; and have accompanied Feenou from Hapaee, if he had not then discouraged me, by representing it to be very inconsiderable, and without any harbour. But Poulaho, the king, afterwards assured me, that it was a large island; and that it not only produced everything in common with Tongataboo, but had the peculiar advantage of possessing several streams of fresh water, with as good a harbour as that which we found at his capital island. He offered to attend me if I would visit it; adding, that, if I did not find everything agreeing with his representation, I might kill him. I had not the least doubt of the truth of his intelligence; and was satisfied that Feenou, from some interested view, attempted to deceive me.

Hamoa, which is also under the dominion of Tongataboo, lies two days' sail north-west from Vavaoo. It was described to me as the largest of all their islands, as affording harbours and good water; and as producing, in abundance, every article of refreshment found at the places we visited. Poulaho himself frequently resides there. It should seem that the people of this island are in high estimation at Tongataboo; for we were told that some of the songs and dances with which we were entertained, had been copied from theirs; and we saw some houses said to be built after their fashion. . . .

Feejee, as we were told, lies three days' sail from Tongataboo, in the direction of north-west by west. It was described to us as a high, but very fruitful island; abounding with hogs, dogs, fowls, and all the kinds of fruit and roots that are found in any of the others; and as much larger than Tongataboo; to the dominion of which, as was represented to us, it is not subject as the other islands of this archipelago are. On the contrary, Feejee and Tongataboo frequently make war upon each other. And it appeared, from several circumstances, that the inhabitants of the latter are much afraid of this enemy. They used to express their sense of their own inferiority to the Feejee men, by bending the body forward, and covering the face with their hands. And it is no wonder that they should be under this dread; for those of Feejee are formidable on account of the dexterity with which they use their bows and slings; but much more so, on account of the savage practice to which they are addicted, like those of New Zealand, of eating their enemies whom they kill in battle. We were satisfied that this was not a misrepresentation. For we met with several Feejee people at Tongataboo, and, on inquiring of them, they did not deny the charge.

Now that I am again led to speak of cannibals, let me ask those who maintain that the want of food first brings men to feed on human flesh, what is it that induces the Feejee people to keep it up in the midst of plenty? This practice is detested very much by those of Tongataboo, who cultivate the friendship of their savage neighbours of Feejee, apparently out of fear; though they sometimes venture to skirmish with them on their own ground; and carry off red feathers as their booty, which are in great plenty there, and, as has been frequently mentioned, are in great estimation amongst our Friendly Islanders. When the two islands are at peace, the intercourse between them seems to be pretty frequent; though they have, doubtless, been but lately known to each other; or we may suppose that Tongataboo and its adjoining islands would have been supplied, before this, with a breed of dogs which abound at Feejee, and had not been introduced at Tongataboo so late as 1773, when I first visited it. The natives of Feejee, whom we met with here, were of a colour that was a full shade darker than that of the inhabitants of the Friendly Islands in general. One of them had his left ear slit, and the lobe was so distended, that it almost reached his shoulder; which singularity I had met with at other islands of the South Sea during my second voyage. It appeared to me that the Feejee men, whom we now saw, were much respected here; not only, perhaps, from the power, and cruel manner of their nation's going to war, but also from their ingenuity. For they seem to excel the inhabitants of Tongataboo in that respect, if we might judge from several specimens of their skill in workmanship which we saw; such as

289

clubs and spears, which were carved in a very masterly manner; cloth beautifully chequered; variegated mats; earthen pots, and some other articles; all which had a cast of superiority in the execution. . . .

The natives of the Friendly Islands seldom exceed the common stature (though we have measured some who were above six feet); but are very strong and well made, especially as to their limbs. They are generally broad about the shoulders; and though the muscular disposition of the men, which seems a consequence of much action, rather conveys the appearance of strength than of beauty, there are several to be seen who are really handsome. Their features are very various; insomuch, that it is scarcely possible to fix on any general likeness by which to characterize them, unless it be a fullness at the point of the nose, which is very common. But, on the other hand, we met with hundreds of truly European faces, and many genuine Roman noses amongst them. Their eyes and teeth are good; but the last neither so remarkably white, nor so well set, as is often found amongst Indian nations; though, to balance that, few of them have any uncommon thickness about the lips, a defect as frequent as the other perfection.

The women are not so much distinguished from the men by their features as by their general form, which is, for the most part destitute of that strong fleshy firmness that appears in the latter. Though the features of some are so delicate, as not only to be a true index of their sex, but to lay claim to a considerable share of beauty and expression, the rule is by no means so general as in many other countries. But, at the same time, this is frequently the most exceptionable part; for the bodies and limbs of most of the females are well proportioned; and some absolutely perfect models of a beautiful figure. But the most remarkable distinction in the women, is the uncommon smallness and delicacy of their fingers, which may be put in competition with the finest in Europe.

The general colour is a cast deeper than the copper brown; but several of the men and women have a true olive complexion; and some of the last are even a great deal fairer; which is probably the effect of being less exposed to the sun; as a tendency to corpulence, in a few of the principal people, seems to be the consequence of a more indolent life. It is also amongst the last, that a soft clear skin is most frequently observed. Amongst the bulk of the people, the skin is more commonly of a dull hue, with some degree of roughness, especially the parts that are not covered; which, perhaps, may be occasioned by some cutaneous disease. We saw a man and boy at Hapaee, and a child at Annamooka, perfectly white. Such have been found amongst all black nations; but, I apprehend that their colour is rather a disease than a natural phenomenon.

There are, nevertheless, upon the whole, few natural defects or deformities to be found amongst them; though we saw two or three with their feet bent inward; and some afflicted with a sort of blindness, occasioned by a disease of the *cornea*. Neither are they exempt from some other diseases. The most common of which is the tetter, or ringworm, that seems to affect almost one half of them, and leaves whitish serpentine marks everywhere behind it. But this is of less consequence than another disease, which is very frequent, and appears on every part of the body, in large broad ulcers, with thick white edges, discharging a thin clear matter; some of which had a very virulent appearance, particularly those on the face, which were shocking to look at; and yet we met with some who seemed to be cured of it, and others in a fair way of being cured; but this was not affected without the loss of the nose, or of the best part of it. As we know for a certainty (and the fact is acknowledged by themselves), that the people of these islands were subject to this loathsome disease before the English first visited them, notwithstanding the similarity of symptoms, it cannot be the effect of the venereal contagion; unless we adopt a supposition, which I could wish had sufficient foundation in truth, that the venereal disorder was not introduced here from Europe, by our ships in 1773. It assuredly was now found to exist amongst them; for we had not been long there before some of our people received the infection; and I had the mortification to learn from thence, that all the care I took, when I first visited these islands, to prevent this dreadful disease from being communicated to their inhabitants, had proved ineffectual. What is extraordinary, they do not seem to regard it much; and as we saw few signs of its destroying effects, probably the climate, and the way of living of these people, greatly abate its virulence. There are two other diseases frequent amongst them; one of which is an indolent firm swelling, which affects the legs and arms, and increases them to an extraordinary size in their whole length. The other is a tumour of the same sort in the testicles, which sometimes exceed the size of the two fists. But, in other respects, they may be considered as uncommonly healthy; not a single person having been seen, during our stay, confined to the house by sickness of any kind. On the contrary, their strength and activity are every way answerable to their muscular appearance; and they exert both, in their usual employment, and in their diversions, in such a manner, that there can be no doubt of their being as yet little debilitated by the numerous diseases that are the consequence of indolence, and an unnatural method of life.

The graceful air and firm step with which these people walk, are not the least obvious proof of their personal accomplishments. They consider this as a thing so natural or so necessary to be acquired, that nothing used to excite their laughter sooner than to see us frequently stumbling upon the roots of trees, or other inequalities of the ground.

Their countenances very remarkably express the abundant mildness or good nature which they possess; and are entirely free from that savage keenness which marks nations in a barbarous state. One would indeed be apt to fancy, that they had been bred up under the severest restrictions, to acquire an aspect so settled, and such a command of their passions as well as steadiness in conduct. But they are at the same time, frank, cheerful, and good-humoured; though sometimes, in the presence of their chiefs, they put on a degree of gravity, and such a serious air as becomes stiff and awkward, and has an appearance of reserve.

Their peaceable disposition is sufficiently evinced, from the friendly reception all strangers have met with who have visited them. Instead of offering to attack them openly or clandestinely, as has been the case with most of the inhabitants of these seas, they have never appeared in the smallest degree hostile; but, on the contrary, like the most civilized people, have courted an inter-course with their visitors by bartering, which is the only medium that unites all nations in a sort of friendship. They understand barter (which they call *fukkatou*) so perfectly, that at first we imagined they might have acquired this knowledge of it by commercial intercourse with the neighbouring islands; but we were afterwards assured that they had little or no traffic, except with Feejee, from which they get the red feathers, and the few other articles mentioned before. Perhaps, no nation in the world traffic with more honesty and less distrust. We could always safely permit them to examine our goods, and to hand them about, one to another; and they put the same confidence in us. If either party repented of the bargain, the goods were re-exchanged with mutual consent and good-humour. Upon the whole, they seem possessed of many of the most excellent qualities that adorn the human mind; such as industry, ingenuity, perseverance, affability, and, perhaps other virtues which our short stay with them might prevent our observing.

The only defect sullying their character, that we knew of, is a propensity to thieving; to which we found those of all ages and both sexes addicted, and to an uncommon degree. It should, however, be considered, that this exceptionable part of their con-duct seemed to exist merely with respect to us; for, in their general intercourse with one another, I had reason to be of opinion, that thefts do not happen more frequently (perhaps less so) than in other countries, the dishonest practices of whose worthless indi-viduals are not supposed to authorize any indiscriminate censure on the whole body of the people. Great allowances should be made for the foibles of these poor natives of the Pacific Ocean, whose minds we overpowered with the glare of objects equally new to them as they were captivating. Stealing amongst the civil-ized and enlightened nations of the world, may well be considered as denoting a character deeply stained with moral turpitude, with avarice unrestrained by the known rules of right, and with pro-fligacy producing extreme indigence, and neglecting the means of relieving it. But at the Friendly and other islands which we visited, the thefts so frequently committed by the natives, of what we had brought along with us, may be fairly traced to less culpable motives. They seemed to arise, solely from an intense curiosity or desire to possess something which they had not been accustomed to before, and belonging to a sort of people so different from themselves. . . .

Their long and general mourning, proves that they consider death as a very great evil. And this is confirmed by a very odd custom which they practise to avert it. When I first visited these islands, during my last voyage, I observed that many of the inhabitants had one or both of their little fingers cut off; and we could not then receive any satisfactory account of the reason of this mutilation. But we now learned that this operation is performed when they labour under some grievous disease, and think themselves in danger of dying. They suppose that the deity will accept of the little finger, as a sort of sacrifice efficacious enough to procure the recovery of their health. They cut it off with one of their stone hatchets. There was scarcely one in ten of them whom we did not find thus mutilated in one or both hands; which has a disagreeable effect, especially as they sometimes cut so close, that they encroach upon the bone of the hand which joins to the amputated finger.

From the rigid severity with which some of these mourning and religious ceremonies are executed, one would expect to find that they meant thereby to secure to themselves felicity beyond the grave; but their principal object relates to things merely temporal. For they seem to have little conception of future punishment for faults committed in this life. They believe, however, that they are justly punished upon earth; and, consequently, use every method to render their divinities propitious. The Supreme Author of most things they call *Kallafootonga*; who, they say, is a female residing in the sky, and directing the thunder, wind, rain; and, in general, all the changes of weather. They believe, that when she is angry with them, the productions of the earth are blasted; that many things are destroyed by lightning; and that they themselves are afflicted with sickness and death, as well as their hogs and other animals. When this anger abates, they suppose that everything is restored to its natural order; and it should seem, that they have a great reliance on the efficacy of their endeavours to appease their offended divinity. They also admit a plurality of deities, though all inferior to *Kallafootonga*. . . .

They have, however, very proper sentiments about the immateriality and the immortality of the soul. They call it life, the living principle, or, what is more agreeable to their notions of it, an *Otooa*; that is, a divinity or invisible being. They say, that, immediately upon death, the souls of their chiefs separate from their bodies, and go to a place called *Boolootoo*; the chief, or god of which is *Gooleho*. This *Gooleho* seemed to be a personification of death; for they used to say to us: "You, and the men of Feejee (by this junction, meaning to pay a compliment, expressive of their confession of our superiority over themselves) are also subject to the power and dominion of *Gooleho*." His country, the general receptacle of the dead, according to their mythology, was never seen by any person; and yet, it seems, they know that it lies to the westward of Feejee; and that they who are once transported thither, live for ever; or, to use their own expression, are not subject to death again; but feast upon all the favourite products of their own country, with which this everlasting abode is supposed to abound. As to the souls of the lower sort of people, they undergo a sort of transmigration; or, as they say, are eaten up by a bird called *loata*, which walks upon their graves for that purpose.

I think I may venture to assert, that they do not worship anything that is the work of their own hands, or any visible part of the creation. They do not make offerings of hogs, dogs, and fruit, as at Otaheite, unless it be emblematically; for their *morais* were perfectly free from everything of the kind. But that they offer real human sacrifices, is with me beyond a doubt. Their *morais* or *fiatookas* (for they are called by both names, but mostly by the latter), are, as at Otaheite and many other parts of the world, burying-grounds, and places of worship; though some of them seemed to be only appropriated to the first purpose; but these were small, and in every other respect inferior to the others. . . .

Taboo, as I have before observed, is a word of an extensive signification. Human sacrifices are called *tangata taboo*; and when anything is forbidden to be eaten, or made use of, they say that it is *taboo*. They tell us, that if the king should happen to go into a house belonging to a subject, that house would be *taboo*, and could never more be inhabited by the owner; so that wherever he travels, there are particular houses for his reception. Old Toobou, at this time, presided over the *taboo*; that is, if Omai comprehended the matter rightly, he and his deputies inspected all the produce of the island; taking care that every man should cultivate and plant his quota; and ordering what should be eaten, and what not. By this wise regulation they effectually guard against a famine; a sufficient quantity of ground is employed in raising provisions; and every article thus raised, is secured from unnecessary waste.

BOOK III

Transactions at the Society Islands and Prosecution of the Voyage to the Coast of North America

1777-1778

LAST VISIT TO TAHITI—FAREWELL TO OMAI—VOYAGE NORTH AND DISCOVERY OF THE SANDWICH ISLANDS—DESCRIPTION OF THE ISLANDS—COAST OF NORTH AMERICA—NOOTKA SOUND, VANCOUVER ISLAND

August 13   I found Omai holding forth to a large company;[1] and it was with some difficulty that he could be got away, to accompany me on board; where I had an important affair to settle.

As I knew that Otaheite and the neighbouring islands could furnish us with a plentiful supply of coconuts, the liquor of which is an excellent *succedaneum* for any artificial beverage, I was desirous of prevailing upon my people to consent to be abridged, during our stay here, of their stated allowance of spirits to mix with water. But as this stoppage of a favourite article, without assigning some reason, might have occasioned a general murmur, I thought it most prudent to assemble the ship's company, and

---

[1] On his return to Tahiti Cook learned that the Spaniards had twice visited the island since he had been there last. The ex-Queen O Berea was dead, but his friend Otoo was there to welcome him. Singularly little interest was shown in Omai's return. He was prodigal in giving away presents bestowed on him in England, and "suffered himself to be duped by every designing knave".

to make known to them the intent of the voyage, and the extent of our future operations. To induce them to undertake which with cheerfulness and perseverance, I took notice of the rewards offered by Parliament to such of His Majesty's subjects, as shall first discover a communication between the Atlantic and Pacific Oceans, in any direction whatever, in the northern hemisphere: and also to such as shall first penetrate beyond the 89th degree of northern latitude. I made no doubt, I told them, that I should find them willing to co-operate with me in attempting, as far as might be possible, to become entitled to one or both these rewards; but that, to give us the best chance of succeeding, it would be necessary to observe the utmost economy in the expenditure of our stores and provisions, particularly the latter, as there was no probability of getting a supply anywhere after leaving these islands. I strengthened my argument, by reminding them, that our voyage must last at least a year longer than had been originally supposed, by our having already lost the opportunity of getting to the north this summer. I begged them to consider the various obstructions and difficulties we might still meet with, and the aggravated hardships they would labour under, if it should be found necessary to put them to short allowance of any species of provisions in a cold climate. For these very substantial reasons, I submitted to them, whether it would not be better to be prudent in time, and rather than to run the risk of having no spirits left, when such a cordial would be most wanted, to consent to be without their grog now, when we had so excellent a liquor as that of coconuts to substitute in its place; but that, after all, I left the determination entirely to their own choice.

I had the satisfaction to find, that this proposal did not remain a single moment under consideration; being unanimously approved of, immediately, without any objection. I ordered Captain Clerke to make the same proposal to his people; which they also agreed to. Accordingly, we stopped serving grog, except on Saturday nights, when the companies of both ships had full allowance of it, that they might drink the healths of their female friends in England; lest these, amongst the pretty girls of Otaheite, should be wholly forgotten.

September 2   The unhappy victim offered to the object of their worship upon this occasion,[2] seemed to be a middle-aged man, and, as we were told, was a *towtow*, that is, one of the lowest class of the people. But, after all my inquiries, I could not learn that he had been pitched upon on account of any particular crime committed by him meriting death. It is certain, however, that they generally make choice of such guilty persons for their sacrifice, or else of common low fellows, who stroll about from place to place and from island to island, without having any fixed abode, or any visible way of getting an honest livelihood, of which description of men enough are to be met with at these islands. Having had an opportunity of examining the appearance of the body of the poor sufferer now offered up, I could observe that it was bloody about the head and face, and a good deal bruised upon the right temple; which marked the manner of his being killed. And we were told, that he had been privately knocked on the head with a stone.

Those who are devoted to suffer, in order to perform this bloody act of worship, are never appraised of their fate till the blow is given that puts an end to their existence. Whenever any one of the great chiefs thinks a human sacrifice necessary on any particular emergency, he pitches upon the victim. Some of his trusty servants are then sent, who fall upon him suddenly, and put him to death with a club or by stoning him. The king is next acquainted with it, whose presence at the solemn rites that follow is, as I was told, absolutely necessary; and, indeed, on the present occasion, we could observe that Otoo bore a principal part. The solemnity itself is called *Poore Eree*, or chief's prayer; and the victim who is offered up *Taata-taboo*, or consecrated man. This is the only instance where we have heard the word *taboo* used at this island, where it seems to have the same mysterious signification as at Tonga, though it is there applied to all cases where things are not to be touched. But at Otaheite, the word *raa* serves the same purpose, and is full as extensive in its meaning.

[2] War between the island of Tahiti and Moorea (Cook calls it "Eimeo") was imminent, so the chiefs prepared a sacrifice to the god Eatooa to obtain his assistance. Before this Cook never believed Bougainville's report that the victim was a human being.

The *morai* (which, undoubtedly, is a place of worship, sacrifice, and burial, at the same time) where the sacrifice was now offered, is that where the supreme chief of the whole island is always buried, and is appropriated to his family and some of the principal people. It differs little from the common ones, except in extent. Its principal part is a large oblong pile of stones, lying loosely upon each other, about twelve or fourteen feet high, contracted towards the top, with a square area on each side loosely paved with pebble stones, under which the bones of the chiefs are buried. At a little distance from the end nearest the sea, is the place where the sacrifices are offered; which, for a considerable extent, is also loosely paved. There is here a very large scaffold or *whatta*, on which the offerings of fruits and other vegetables are laid. But the animals are deposited on a smaller one already mentioned, and the human sacrifices are buried under different parts of the pavement. There are several other relics which ignorant superstition had scattered about this place, such as small stones raised in different parts of the pavement, some with bits of cloth tied round them, others covered with it; and, upon the side of the large pile which fronts the area, are placed a great many pieces of carved wood, which are supposed to be sometimes the residence of their divinities, and, consequently, held sacred. But one place, more particular than the rest, is a heap of stones at one end of the large *whatta*, before which the sacrifice was offered, with a kind of platform at one side. On this are laid the skulls of all the human sacrifices, which are taken up after they have been several months underground. Just above them are placed a great number of the pieces of wood; and it was also here where the *maro*, and the other bundle supposed to contain the god *Ooro* (and which I call the ark), were laid during the ceremony; a circumstance which denotes its agreement with the altar of other nations.

It is much to be regretted, that a practice so horrid in its own nature and so destructive of that inviolable right of self-preservation, which everyone is born with, should be found still existing; and (such is the power of superstition to counteract the first principles of humanity!) existing amongst a people in many other respects emerged from the brutal manners of savage life. What is still worse, it is probable that these bloody rites of worship are prevalent throughout all the wide extended islands of the Pacific Ocean. The similarity of customs and language, which our late voyages have enabled us to trace between the most distant of these islands, makes it not unlikely that some of the most important articles of their religious institutions should agree. And, indeed, we have the most authentic information that human sacrifices continue to be offered at the Friendly Islands. When I described the *Natche* at *Tonga-taboo*, I mentioned that, on the approaching sequel of that festival, we had been told that ten men were to be sacrificed. This may give us an idea of the extent of this religious massacre in that island. And though we should suppose that never more than one person is sacrificed, on any single occasion at Otaheite, it is more than probable that these occasions happen so frequently, as to make a shocking waste of the human race; for I counted no less than forty-nine skulls of former victims lying before the *morai*, where we saw one more added to the number. And as none of those skulls has as yet suffered any considerable change from the weather, it may hence be inferred, that no great length of time had elapsed, since, at least, this considerable number of unhappy wretches had been offered upon this altar of blood.

The custom, though no consideration can make it cease to be abominable, might be thought less detrimental, in some respects, if it served to impress any awe for the divinity or reverence for religion, upon the minds of the multitude. But this is so far from being the case, that though a great number of people had assembled at the *morai* on this occasion, they did not seem to show any proper reverence for what was doing or saying during the celebration of the rites. And Omai happening to arrive after they had begun, many of the spectators flocked round him, and were engaged the remainder of the time in making him relate some of his adventures, which they listened to with great attention, regardless of the solemn offices performing by their priests. Indeed, the priests themselves, except the one who chiefly repeated the prayers, either from their being familiarized to such objects, or from want of confidence in the efficacy of their institutions, observed very little of that solemnity, which is necessary to give to religious performances their due weight. Their dress was only an ordinary one; they conversed together without scruple; and the only attempt made by them to preserve any appearance of decency, was by exerting their authority to prevent the people from coming upon the very spot where the ceremonies were performed, and to suffer us, as strangers, to advance a little forward. They were, however, very candid in their answers to any questions that were put to them concerning the institution. And particularly, on being asked what the intention of it was? they said that it was an old custom, and was agreeable to their god, who delighted in, or, in other words, came and fed upon the sacrifices; in consequence of which, he complied with their petitions. Upon its being objected that he could not feed on these, as he was neither seen to do it, nor were the bodies of the animals quickly consumed; and that, as to the human victim, they prevented his feeding on him, by burying him. But to all this they answered, that he came in the night, but invisibly, and fed only on the soul or immaterial part, which, according to their doctrine, remains about the place of sacrifice, until the body of the victim be entirely wasted by putrefaction.

It were much to be wished that this deluded people may learn to entertain the same horror of murdering their fellow-creatures, in order to furnish such an invisible banquet to their god, as they now have of feeding, corporeally, on human flesh themselves. And, yet, we have great reason to believe, that there was a time when they were cannibals. We were told (and, indeed, partly saw it), that it is a necessary ceremony, when a poor wretch is sacrificed, for the priest to take out the left eye. This he presents to the king, holding it to his mouth, which he desires him to open; but, instead of putting it in, immediately withdraws it. This they call "eating the man", or, "food for the chief"; and, perhaps, we may observe here some traces of former times, when the dead body was really feasted upon.

October 13   The carpenters of both ships were set to work, to build a small house for Omai, in which he might secure the European commodities that were his property.[3] At the same time, some hands were employed in making a garden for his use, planting shaddocks, vines, pineapples, melons, and the seeds of several other vegetable articles; all of which I had the satisfaction of observing to be in a flourishing state before I left the island.

Omai now began seriously to attend to his own affairs, and repented heartily of his ill-judged prodigality while at Otaheite. He found at Huaheine, a brother, a sister, and a brother-in-law; the sister being married. But these did not plunder him, as he had lately been by his other relations. I was sorry, however, to discover, that, though they were too honest to do him any injury, they were of too little consequence in the island to do him any positive good. They had neither authority nor influence to protect his person or his property; and, in that helpless situation, I had reason to apprehend, that he ran great risk of being stripped of everything he had got from us, as soon as he should cease to have us within his reach, to enforce the good behaviour of his countrymen, by an immediate appeal to our irresistible power.

A man who is richer than his neighbours is sure to be envied by numbers who wish to see him brought down to their own level. But in countries where civilization, law, and religion, impose their restraints, the rich have a reasonable ground of security. And, besides, there being, in all such communities, a diffusion of property, no single individual need fear, that the efforts of all the poorer sort can ever be united to injure him, exclusively of others who are equally the objects of envy. It was very different with Omai. He was to live amongst those who are strangers, in a great measure, to any other principle of action besides the immediate impulse of their natural feelings. But what was his principal danger, he was to be placed in the very singular situation, of being the only rich man in the community to which he was to

---

[3] Before proceeding northward on his voyage, Cook established Omai at Huaheine, an island near Tahiti. According to Zimmermann, Omai was dissatisfied with the size of his house, declaring that the King had promised him a two-storied building "and that this was only a one-storied house such as was used in England to house swine. But Cook only laughed and told him he deserved nothing better." Fifty years later the missionary Ellis wrote, "He appears to have passed his life in inglorious indolence or wanton crime." (*Polynesian Researches*, 1834, II, 369).

belong; and having, by a fortunate connection with us, got into his possession an accumulated quantity of a species of treasure which none of his countrymen could create by any art or industry of their own: while all coveted a share of this envied wealth, it was natural to apprehend, that all would be ready to join in attempting to strip its sole proprietor.

To prevent this, if possible, I desired him to make a proper distribution of some of his movables to two or three of the principal chiefs; who, being thus gratified themselves, might be induced to take him under their patronage, and protect him from the injuries of others. He promised to follow my advice; and I heard, with satisfaction, before I sailed, that this very prudent step had been taken. Not trusting, however, entirely to the operation of gratitude, I had recourse to the more forcible motive of intimidation. With this view, I took every opportunity of notifying to the inhabitants, that it was my intention to return to their island again, after being absent the usual time; and that if I did not find Omai in the same state of security in which I was now to leave him, all those whom I should then discover to have been his enemies, might expect to feel the weight of my resentment. This threatening declaration will probably have no inconsiderable effect; for our successive visits of late years have taught these people to believe, that our ships are to return at certain periods; and while they continue to be impressed with such a notion, which I thought it a fair stratagem to confirm, Omai has some prospect of being permitted to thrive upon his new plantation.

November 2 On the 2nd of November, at four in the afternoon, I took the advantage of a breeze, which then sprung up at east, and sailed out of the harbour. Most of our friends remained on board till the ships were under sail; when, to gratify their curiosity, I ordered five guns to be fired. They then all took their leave, except Omai, who remained till we were at sea. We had come to sail by a hawser fastened to the shore. In casting the ship, it parted, being cut by the rocks, and the outer end was left behind; as those who cast it off did not perceive that it was broken; so that it became necessary to send a boat to bring it on board. In this boat, Omai went ashore, after taking a very affectionate farewell of all the officers. He sustained himself with a manly resolution, till he came to me. Then his utmost efforts to conceal his tears failed; and Mr. King, who went in the boat, told me, that he wept all the time in going ashore.

It was no small satisfaction to reflect, that we had brought him safe back to the very spot from which he was taken. And yet, such is the strange nature of human affairs, that it is probable we left him in a less desirable situation, than he was in before his connection with us. I do not by this mean, that, because he has tasted the sweets of civilized life, he must become more miserable from being obliged to abandon all thoughts of continuing them. I confine myself to this single disagreeable circumstance, that the advantages he received from us, have placed him in a more hazardous situation, with respect to his personal safety. Omai, from being much caressed in England, lost sight of his original condition; and never considered in what manner his acquisitions, either of knowledge or of riches, would be estimated by his countrymen at his return; which were the only things he could have to recommend him to them now, more than before, and on which he could build either his future greatness or happiness. He seemed even to have mistaken their genius in this respect; and, in some measure, to have forgotten their customs; otherwise he must have known the extreme difficulty there would be in getting himself admitted as a person of rank, where there is, perhaps, no instance of a man's being raised from an inferior station by the greatest merit. Rank seems to be the very foundation of all distinction here, and, of its attendant, power; and so pertinaciously, or rather blindly adhered to, that, unless a person has some degree of it, he will certainly be despised and hated, if he assumes the appearance of exercising any authority. This was really the case, in some measure, with Omai; though his countrymen were pretty cautious of expressing their sentiments while we remained among them. Had he made a proper use of the presents he brought with him from England, this, with the knowledge he had acquired by travelling so far, might have enabled him to form the most useful connections; but we have given too many instances, in the course of our narrative, of his childish inattention to this obvious means of advancing his interest. His schemes seemed to be of a higher, though ridiculous nature; indeed, I might say, meaner; for revenge, rather than a desire of becoming great, appeared to actuate him from the beginning. This, however, may be excused, if we consider that it is common to his countrymen. His father was, doubtless, a man of considerable property in Ulietea, when that island was conquered by those of Bolabola, and, with many others, sought refuge in Huaheine, where he died, and left Omai with some other children, who by that means became totally dependent. In this situation he was taken up by Captain Furneaux, and carried to England. Whether he really expected, from his treatment there, that any assistance would be given him against the enemies of his father and his country, or whether he imagined that his own personal courage and superiority of knowledge would be sufficient to dispossess the conquerors of Ulietea, is uncertain; but, from the beginning of the voyage, this was his constant theme. He would not listen to our remonstrances on so wild a determination, but flew into a passion, if more moderate and reasonable counsels were proposed for his advantage. Nay, so infatuated and attached to his favourite scheme was he, that he affected to believe these people would certainly quit the conquered island, as soon as they should hear of his arrival at Otaheite. As we advanced, however, on our voyage, he became more sensible of his error; and, by the time we reached the Friendly Islands, had even such apprehensions of his reception at home, that, as I have mentioned in my journal, he would fain have stayed behind at Tongataboo, under Feenou's protection. At these islands he squandered away much of his European treasure very unnecessarily; and he was equally imprudent, as I also took notice of above, at Tiaraboo, where he could have no view of making friends, as he had not any intention of remaining there. At Matavai, he continued the same inconsiderate behaviour, till I absolutely put a stop to his profusion; and he formed such improper connections there, that Otoo, who was at first much disposed to countenance him, afterward openly expressed his dislike of him, on account of his conduct. It was not, however, too late to recover his favour; and he might have settled to great advantage in Otaheite, as he had formerly lived several years there, and was now a good deal noticed by Towha, whose valuable present of a very large double canoe we have seen above. The objection to admitting him to some rank would have also been much lessened, if he had fixed at Otaheite; as a native will always find it more difficult to accomplish such a change of state amongst his countrymen, than a stranger, who naturally claims respect. But Omai remained undetermined to the last, and would not, I believe, have adopted my plan of settlement in Huaheine, if I had not so explicitly refused to employ force in restoring him to his father's possessions. Whether the remains of his European wealth, which after all his improvident waste, was still considerable, will be more prudently administered by him, or whether the steps I took, as already explained, to ensure him protection in Huaheine, shall have proved effectual, must be left to the decision of future navigators of this ocean, with whom it cannot but be a principal object of curiosity to trace the future fortunes of our traveller. At present, I can only conjecture, that his greatest danger will arise from the very impolitic declarations of his antipathy to the inhabitants of Bolabola; for these people, from a principle of jealousy, will, no doubt, endeavour to render him obnoxious to those of Huaheine; as they are at peace with that island at present, and may easily effect their designs, many of them living there. This is a circumstance which, of all others, he might the most easily have avoided; for they were not only free from any aversion to him, but the person mentioned before, whom we found at Tiaraboo as an ambassador, priest, or god, absolutely offered to reinstate him in the property that was formerly his father's. But he refused this peremptorily; and, to the very last, continued determined to take the first opportunity that offered of satisfying his revenge in battle. To this, I guess, he is not a little spurred by the coat of mail he brought from England; clothed in which, and in possession of some firearms, he fancies that he shall be invincible.

Whatever faults belonged to Omai's character, they were more than overbalanced by his great good nature and docile

disposition. During the whole time he was with me, I very seldom had reason to be seriously displeased with his general conduct. His grateful heart always retained the highest sense of the
favours he had received in England; nor will he ever forget those
who honoured him with their protection and friendship, during
his stay there. He had a tolerable share of understanding, but
wanted application and perseverance to exert it; so that his knowledge of things was very general, and, in many instances, im-
perfect. He was not a man of much observation. There were
many useful arts, as well as elegant amusements, amongst the
people of the Friendly Islands, which he might have conveyed to
his own, where they probably would have been readily adopted,
as being so much in their own way. But I never found that he
used the least endeavour to make himself master of any one.
This kind of indifference is, indeed, the characteristic foible of his
nation. Europeans have visited them, at times, for these ten years
past; yet we could not discover the slightest trace of any attempt
to profit by this intercourse; nor have they hitherto copied after us
in any one thing. We are not, therefore, to expect that Omai will
be able to introduce many of our arts and customs among them, or
much improve those to which they have been long habituated. I
am confident, however, that he will endeavour to bring to perfection the various fruits and vegetables we planted, which will be
no small acquisition. But the greatest benefit these islands are likely
to receive from Omai's travels, will be in the animals that have
been left upon them, which, probably, they never would have got,
had he not come to England. When these multiply, of which I
think there is little doubt, Otaheite and the Society Islands will
equal, if not exceed, any place in the known world for provisions.

January 20   The next morning we stood in for the land,[4] and
were met with several canoes filled with people; some of whom
took courage and ventured on board.

---

[4] *i.e.* Atooi (Kauai), the first of the Hawaiian group (named by Cook the
"Sandwich Islands"), which they sighted on 18 January 1778. On their way hither
the small desert island named Christmas Island was discovered. That Cook was
the first to discover the Hawaiian group is now generally admitted, though there is
a legend that the Spaniard Gaetano visited it in 1555.

In the course of my several voyages, I never before met with the natives of any place so much astonished, as these people were, upon entering a ship. Their eyes were continually flying from object to object; the wildness of their looks and gestures fully expressing their entire ignorance about everything they saw, and strongly marking to us, that, till now, they had never been visited by Europeans, nor been acquainted with any of our commodities except iron; which, however, it was plain, they had only heard of, or had known it in some small quantity brought to them at some distant period. They seemed only to understand, that it was a substance much better adapted to the purposes of cutting, or of boring of holes, than anything their own country produced. They asked for it by the name of *hamaite*, probably referring to some instrument, in the making of which iron could be usefully employed; for they applied that name to the blade of a knife, though we could be certain that they had no idea of that particular instrument; nor could they at all handle it properly. For the same reason, they frequently called iron by the name of *toe*, which in their language signifies a hatchet, or rather a kind of adze. On asking them what iron was, they immediately answered: "We do not know; you know what it is, and we only understand it as *toe*, or *hamaite*."[5] When we showed them some beads, they asked first: "What they were; and then, whether they should eat them?" But on their being told, that they were to be hung in their ears, they returned them as useless. They were equally indifferent as to a looking-glass, which was offered them, and returned it, for the same reason; but sufficiently expressed their desire for *hamaite* and *toe*, which they wished might be very large. Plates of earthenware, china cups, and other such things, were so new to them, that they asked if they were made of wood; but wished to have some, that they might carry them to be looked at on shore. They were in some respects naturally well bred, or, at least, fearful of giving offence, asking, where they should sit down, whether they might spit upon the deck, and the like. Some of them repeated a long prayer before they came on board; and others, afterward, sang and made motions with their hands, such as we had been

[5] *Hamaite* means "little scraper" and *toe* means "sharp".

accustomed to see in the dances of the islands we had lately visited. There was another circumstance in which they also perfectly resembled those other islanders. At first, on their entering the ship, they endeavoured to steal everything they came near; or rather to take it openly, as what we either should not resent, or not hinder. We soon convinced them of their mistake; and if they, after some time, became less active in appropriating to themselves whatever they took a fancy to, it was because they found that we kept a watchful eye over them.

At nine o'clock, being pretty near the shore, I sent three armed boats, under the command of Lieutenant Williamson, to look for a landing-place, and for fresh water. I ordered him, that if he should find it necessary to land in search of the latter, not to suffer more than one man to go with him out of the boats. Just as they were putting off from the ship, one of the natives having stolen the butcher's cleaver, leaped overboard, got into his canoe, and hastened to the shore, the boats pursuing him in vain.

The order not to permit the crews of the boats to go on shore was issued, that I might do everything in my power to prevent the importation of a fatal disease into this island, which I knew some of our men laboured under, and which, unfortunately, had been already communicated by us to other islands in these seas. With the same view, I ordered all female visitors to be excluded from the ships. Many of them had come off in the canoes. Their size, colour, and features did not differ much from those of the men; and though their countenances were remarkably open and agreeable, there were few traces of delicacy to be seen, either in their faces, or other proportions. The only difference in their dress, was their having a piece of cloth about the body, reaching from near the middle to halfway down the thighs, instead of the *maro* worn by the other sex. They would as readily have favoured us with their company on board as the men; but I wished to prevent all connection, which might, too probably, convey an irreparable injury to themselves, and through their means, to the whole nation. Another necessary precaution was taken, by strictly enjoining, that no person, known to be capable of propagating the infection, should be sent upon duty out of the ships.[6]

Whether these regulations, dictated by humanity, had the desired effect, or no, time only can discover. I had been equally attentive to the same object, when I first visited the Friendly Islands; yet I afterward found, with real concern, that I had not succeeded. And I am much afraid, that this will always be the case, in such voyages as ours, whenever it is necessary to have a number of people on shore. The opportunities and inducements to an intercourse between the sexes are then too numerous to be guarded against; and however confident we may be of the health of our men, we are often undeceived too late. It is even a matter of doubt with me, if it be always in the power of the most skilful of the faculty to pronounce, with any certainty, whether a person who has been under their care, in certain stages of this malady, is so effectually cured, as to leave no possibility of his being still capable of communicating the taint. I think I could mention some instances which justify my presuming to hazard this opinion. It is likewise well known, that, amongst a number of men, there are generally to be found some so bashful as to endeavour to conceal their labouring under any symptoms of this disorder. And there are others, again, so profligate, as not to care to whom they communicate it. Of this last, we had an instance at Tonga-taboo, in the gunner of the *Discovery*, who had been stationed on shore to manage the trade for that ship. After he knew that he had contracted this disease, he continued to have connections with different women, who were supposed not to have already contracted it. His companions expostulated with him without effect, till Captain Clerke, hearing of this dangerous irregularity of conduct, ordered him on board.

DESCRIPTION OF THE SANDWICH ISLANDS

It is worthy of observation, that the islands in the Pacific Ocean, which our late voyages have added to the geography of the globe,

[6] Zimmermann states that the whole crew underwent a medical examination.

have been generally found lying in groups or clusters; the single intermediate islands, as yet discovered, being few in proportion to the others; though, probably, there are many more of them still unknown, which serve as steps between the several clusters. Of what number this newly discovered Archipelago consists, must be left for future investigation. We saw five of them, whose names, as given to us by the natives, are Woahoo, Atooi, Oneeheow, Oreehoua, and Tahoora.[7] The last is a small elevated island, lying four or five leagues from the south-east point of Oneeheow, in the direction of S. 69° W. We were told, that it abounds with birds, which are its only inhabitants. We also got some information of the existence of a low, uninhabited island, in the neighbourhood, whose name is Tammata pappa. Besides these six, which we can distinguish by their names, it appeared, that the inhabitants of those with whom we had intercourse, were acquainted with some other islands both to the eastward and westward. I named the whole group the Sandwich Islands, in honour of the Earl of Sandwich. Those that I saw, are situated between the latitude of 21° 30', and 22° 15' N., and between the longitude of 199° 20', and 201° 30' E. . . .

The inhabitants are of a middling stature, firmly made, with some exceptions, neither remarkable for a beautiful shape, nor for striking features, which rather express an openness and good nature, than a keen, intelligent disposition. Their visage, especially amongst the women, is sometimes round; but others have it long; nor can we say that they are distinguished, as a nation, by any general cast of countenance. Their colour is nearly of a nut-brown, and it may be difficult to make a nearer comparison, if we take in all the different hues of that colour; but some individuals are darker. The women have been already mentioned, as being little more delicate than the men in their formation; and I may say that, with a very few exceptions, they have little claim to those peculiarities that distinguish the sex in other countries. There is, indeed, a more remarkable equality in the size, colour,

---

[7] On his first visit Cook did not see the largest and most easterly island, Hawaii. The most important of those named above are Woahoo (Oahu), on which Honolulu and Pearl Harbour are situated, Atooi (Kauai) and Oneeheow (Niihau), the most westerly of the group. These islands were left on 2 February.

and figure of both sexes, than in most places I have visited. However, upon the whole, they are far from being ugly, and appear to have few natural deformities of any kind. Their skin is not very soft, nor shining; perhaps for want of oiling, which is practised at the southern islands; but their eyes and teeth are, in general, very tolerable. The hair, for the greatest part, is straight, though, in some, frizzling; and though its natural colour be commonly black, it is stained, as at the Friendly and other islands. We saw but few instances of corpulence; and these oftener among the women than the men; but it was chiefly amongst the latter that personal defects were observed, though, if any of them can claim a share of beauty, it was most conspicuous amongst the young men.

They are vigorous, active, and most expert swimmers; leaving their canoes upon the most trifling occasion; diving under them, and swimming to others though at a great distance. It was very common to see women, with infants at the breast, when the surf was so high that they could not land in the canoes, leap overboard, and without endangering their little ones, swim to the shore, through a sea that looked dreadful.

They seem to be blessed with a frank, cheerful disposition; and were I to draw any comparisons, I should say, that they are equally free from the fickle levity which distinguishes the natives of Otaheite, and the sedate cast observable amongst many of those of Tongataboo. They seem to live very sociably in their intercourse with one another; and, except the propensity to thieving, which seems innate in most of the people we have visited in this ocean, they were exceedingly friendly to us. And it does their sensibility no little credit, without flattering ourselves, that when they saw the various articles of our European manufacture, they could not help expressing their surprise, by a mixture of joy and concern, that seemed to apply the case, as a lesson of humility, to themselves; and, on all occasions, they appeared deeply impressed with a consciousness of their own inferiority; a behaviour which equally exempts their national character from the preposterous pride of the more polished Japanese, and of the ruder Greenlander. It was a pleasure to observe with how much affection the women managed their infants, and how readily the men lent their assistance to such a tender office; thus sufficiently distinguishing themselves from those savages who esteem a wife and child as things rather necessary than desirable, or worthy of their notice.

From the numbers which we saw collected at every village, as we sailed past, it may be supposed that the inhabitants of this island are pretty numerous. Any computation that we make can be only conjectural. But that some notion may be formed, which shall not greatly err on either side, I should suppose that, including the straggling houses, there might be, upon the whole island, sixty such villages, as that before which we anchored; and that, allowing five persons to each house, there would be, in every village, five hundred; or thirty thousand upon the island. This number is, certainly, not exaggerated; for we had sometimes three thousand persons, at least, upon the beach; when it could not be supposed that above a tenth part of the inhabitants were present.

The common dress, both of the women and of the men, has been already described. The first have often much larger pieces of cloth wrapped round them, reaching from just below the breasts to the hams, or lower; and several were seen with pieces thrown loosely about the shoulders, which covered the greatest part of the body; but the children, when very young, are quite naked. They wear nothing upon the head; but the hair, in both sexes, is cut in different forms; and the general fashion, especially among the women, is to have it long before and short behind. The men often had it cut, or shaved, on each side, in such a manner that the remaining part, in some measure, resembles the crest of their caps or helmets, formerly described. Both sexes, however, seem very careless about their hair, and have nothing like combs to dress it with. Instances of wearing it, in a singular manner, were sometimes met with among the men, who twist it into a number of separate parcels, like the tails of a wig, each about the thickness of a finger; though the greatest part of these, which are so long that they reach far down the back, we observed, were artificially fixed upon the head, over their own hair. . . .

Their amusements seem pretty various; for, during our stay, several were discovered. The dances, at which they use the feathered cloaks and caps, were not seen; but from the motions which they made with their hands, on other occasions, when they sang, we could form some judgment that they are, in some degree at least, similar to those we had met with at the southern islands, though not executed so skilfully. Neither had they amongst them either flutes or reeds; and the only two musical instruments which we observed, were of an exceeding rude kind. One of them does not produce a melody exceeding that of a child's rattle.[8] It consists of what may be called a conic cap inverted, but scarcely hollowed at the base above a foot high, made of a coarse sedge-like plant; the upper part of which, and the edges, are ornamented with beautiful red feathers; and to the point, or lower part, is fixed a gourd-shell, larger than the fist. Into this is put something to rattle; which is done by holding the instrument by the small part, and shaking, or rather moving it, from place to place briskly, either to different sides, or backward and forward, just before the face, striking the breast with the other hand at the same time. The other musical instrument (if either of them deserve that name) was a hollow vessel of wood, like a platter, combined with the use of two sticks, on which one of our gentlemen saw a man performing. He held one of the sticks, about two feet long, as we do a fiddle, with one hand, and struck it with the other, which was smaller, and resembled a drum-stick, in a quicker or slower measure; at the same time beating with his foot upon the hollow vessel, that lay inverted upon the ground, and thus producing a tune that was by no means disagreeable. This music was accompanied by the vocal performance of some women, whose song had a pleasing and tender effect. . . .

But whatever resemblance we might discover, in the general manners of the people of Atooi to those of Otaheite, these of course were less striking than the coincidence of language. Indeed, the languages of both places may be said to be almost word for word the same. It is true, that we sometimes remarked particular words to be pronounced exactly as we had found at New

[8] This instrument, however, plays an important part in modern dance bands.

Zealand and the Friendly Islands; but though all the four dialects are indisputably the same, these people in general have neither the strong guttural pronunciation of the former, nor a less degree of it, which also distinguishes the latter; and they have not only adopted the soft mode of the Otaheiteans in avoiding harsh sounds, but the whole idiom of their language, using not only the same affixes and suffixes to their words, but the same measure and cadence in their songs, though in a manner somewhat less agreeable. There seems, indeed, at first hearing, some disagreement to the ear of a stranger, but it ought to be considered, that the people of Otaheite, from their frequent connections with the English, had learnt, in some measure, to adapt themselves to our scanty knowledge of their language by using not only the most common, but even corrupted, expressions in conversation with us; whereas, when they conversed among themselves and used the several parts necessary to propriety of speech, they were scarcely at all understood by those amongst us, who had made the greatest proficiency in their vocabulary. A catalogue of words was collected at Atooi by Mr. Anderson, who lost no opportunity of making our voyage useful to those who amuse themselves in tracing the migrations of the various tribes or families that have peopled the globe, by the most convincing of all arguments, that drawn from affinity of language.

How shall we account for this nation's having spread itself in so many detached islands, so widely disjoined from each other, in every quarter of the Pacific Ocean! We find it from New Zealand in the south, as far as the Sandwich Islands to the north! And in another direction, from Easter Island to the Hebrides! That is, over an extent of sixty degrees of latitude or twelve hundred leagues north and south! And eighty-three degrees of longitude, or sixteen hundred and sixty leagues east and west! How much farther in either direction its colonies reach is not known; but what we know already, in consequence of this and our former voyage, warrants our pronouncing it to be, though perhaps not the most numerous, certainly, by far, the most extensive nation upon earth.

Had the Sandwich Islands been discovered at an early period

by the Spaniards, there is little doubt that they would have taken advantage of so excellent a situation, and have made use of Atooi or some other of the islands as a refreshing place, in the ships that sail annually from Acapulco for Manilla. They lie almost midway between the first place and Guam, one of the Ladrones,[9] which is at present their only port in traversing this vast ocean; and it would not have been a week's sail out of their common route, to have touched at them, which could have been done without running the least hazard of losing the passage, as they are sufficiently within the verge of the easterly Trade wind. An acquaintance with the Sandwich Islands would have been equally favourable to our Buccaneers, who used sometimes to pass from the coast of America to the Ladrones, with a stock of food and water scarcely sufficient to preserve life. Here they might always have found plenty, and have been within a month's sure sail of the very part of California, which the Manilla ship is obliged to make, or else have returned to the coast of America, thoroughly refitted, after an absence of two months. How happy would Lord Anson have been, and what hardships would he have avoided, if he had known that there was a group of islands, halfway between America and Tinian, where all his wants could have been effectually supplied, and in describing which, the elegant historian of that voyage would have presented his reader with a more agreeable picture than I have been able to draw in this chapter?

March 6   On the 6th, at noon, being in the latitude of 44° 10′ N. and the longitude of 234½° E., we saw two sails and several whales; and at daybreak, the next morning, the long-looked-for coast of New Albion[10] was seen, extending from north-east to south-east, distant ten or twelve leagues. At noon our latitude was 44° 33′ N., and our longitude 235° 20′ E.; and the land extended from north-east half north, to south-east by south, about eight leagues distant. In this situation we had seventy-three fathoms of water, over a

[9] Or Marianas, which include Anson's Tinian.

[10] The spot where Drake landed in 1579 is uncertain, but he named the coast New Albion. Cook's landfall was on the coast of Oregon. Burney says that to celebrate the event "the gentlemen in the gunroom dined on a fricassee of rats".

muddy bottom, and about a league farther off found ninety fathoms. The land appeared to be of a moderate height, diversified with hills and valleys, and, almost everywhere, covered with wood. There was, however, no very striking object on any part of it, except one hill, whose elevated summit was flat. This bore east from us, at noon. At the northern extreme the land formed a point, which I called *Cape Foulweather*, from the very bad weather that we soon after met with. I judge it to lie in the latitude of 44° 55' N., and in the longitude of 235° 54' E. . . .

Our difficulties now began to increase. In the evening the wind came to the north-west, blowing in squalls with hail and sleet; and the weather being thick and hazy, I stood out to sea till near noon the next day, when I tacked and stood in again for the land, which made its appearance at two in the afternoon, bearing E.N.E. The wind and weather continued the same; but, in the evening, the former veered more to the west, and the latter grew worse, which made it necessary to tack and stand off till four the next morning, when I ventured to stand in again.

At four in the afternoon we saw the land, which, at six, extended from north-east half east, to south-east by south, about eight leagues distant. In this situation we tacked and sounded; but a line of a hundred and sixty fathoms did not reach the ground. I stood off till midnight, then stood in again; and at half-past six, we were within three leagues of the land, which extended from north by east, half east, to south, half east; each extreme about seven leagues distant. Seeing no signs of a harbour, and the weather being still unsettled, I tacked and stretched off south-west, having then fifty-five fathoms water over a muddy bottom.

That part of the land, which we were so near when we tacked, is of a moderate height, though, in some places, it rises higher within. It was diversified with a great many rising grounds and small hills; many of which were entirely covered with tall straight trees; and others, which were lower, and grew in spots like coppices; but the interspaces and sides of many of the rising grounds, were clear. The whole, though it might make an agreeable summer prospect, had now an uncomfortable appearance, as the bare grounds toward the coast were all covered with snow, which seemed to be of a considerable depth between the little hills and rising grounds; and, in several places toward the sea, might easily have been mistaken, at a distance, for white cliffs. The snow on the rising grounds was thinner spread; and farther inland, there was no appearance of any; from whence we might, perhaps, conclude that what we saw toward the sea had fallen during the night, which was colder than any we had experienced since our arrival on the coast; and we had sometimes a kind of sleet. The coast seemed everywhere almost straight, without any opening or inlet; and it appeared to terminate in a kind of white sandy beach; though some on board thought that appearance was owing to the snow.

March 22   I continued to stand to the north with a fine breeze at west, and west north-west, till near seven o'clock in the evening, when I tacked to wait for daylight. At this time we were in forty-eight fathoms of water, and about four leagues from the land, which extended from north to south east half east, and a small round hill, which had the appearance of being an island, bore north three-quarters east, distant six or seven leagues, as I guessed; it appears to be of a tolerable height, and was but just to be seen from the deck. Between this island or rock, and the northern extreme of the land, there appeared to be a small opening, which flattered us with the hopes of finding an harbour. These hopes lessened as we drew nearer; and, at last, we had some reason to think, that the opening was closed by low land. On this account I called the point of land to the north of it *Cape Flattery*. It lies in the latitude of 48° 15′ N., and in the longitude of 235° 3′ E. There is a round hill of a moderate height over it; and all the land upon this part of the coast is of a moderate and pretty equal height, well covered with wood, and had a very pleasant and fertile appearance. It is in this very latitude where we now were, that geographers have placed the pretended strait of Juan de Fuca. We saw nothing like it; nor is there the least probability that ever any such thing existed.[11]

---

[11] Nevertheless the straits of Juan de Fuca do lie between Vancouver Island and the coast of the State of Washington; Cape Flattery marks the entrance, but bad

March 29   We no sooner drew near the inlet,[12] than we found the coast to be inhabited; and at the place where we were first becalmed, three canoes came off to the ship. In one of these were two men, in another six, and in the third ten. Having come pretty near us, a person in one of the two last stood up, and made a long harangue, inviting us to land, as we guessed by his gestures. At the same time, he kept strewing handfuls of feathers towards us; and some of his companions threw handfuls of red dust or powder in the same manner. The person who played the orator, wore the skin of some animal, and held in each hand something which rattled as he kept shaking it. After tiring himself with his repeated exhortations, of which we did not understand a word, he was quiet; and then others took it, by turns, to say something, though they acted their part neither so long nor with so much vehemence as the other. We observed that two or three had their hair quite strewed over with small white feathers, and others had large ones stuck into different parts of the head. After the tumultuous noise had ceased, they lay at a little distance from the ship, and conversed with each other in a very easy manner; nor did they seem to show the least surprise or distrust. Some of them, now and then got up, and said something after the manner of their first harangues; and one sang a very agreeable air, with a degree of softness and melody which we could not have expected; the word *haela*, being often repeated as the burden of the song. The breeze which soon after sprang up, bringing us nearer to the shore, the canoes began to come off in greater numbers; and we had, at one time, thirty-two of them near the ship, carrying from three to seven or eight persons in each, both men and women. Several of these stood up in their canoes haranguing, and making gestures after the manner of our first visitors. One canoe was remarkable for a singular head, which had a bird's eye and bill, of an enormous size,

---

weather seems to have prevented Cook from noticing the strait. The apocryphal voyage of de Fuca is printed in Purchas; another legendary voyage is that of de Fonte, in 1640, who claimed to have sailed through the North West Passage. Vancouver, who was to explore this coast more thoroughly in 1792–94, was now a midshipman in the *Discovery*.

12 Nootka Sound, on the north-west coast of Vancouver Island. Eleven years later the Spaniards asserted their claim to this area by driving out a settlement of British fur traders, but withdrew under threat of war.

painted on it; and a person who was in it, who seemed to be a chief, was no less remarkable for his uncommon appearance; having many feathers hanging from his head, and being painted in an extraordinary manner. He held in his hand a carved bird of wood, as large as a pigeon, with which he rattled as the person first mentioned had done; and was no less vociferous in his harangue, which was attended with some expressive gestures.

Though our visitors behaved very peaceably, and could not be suspected of any hostile intention, we could not prevail upon any of them to come on board. They showed great readiness, however, to part with anything they had, and took from us whatever we offered them in exchange; but were more desirous of iron, than of any other of our articles of commerce; appearing to be perfectly acquainted with the use of that metal. Many of the canoes followed us to our anchoring-place; and a group of about ten or a dozen of them remained alongside the *Resolution* most part of the night.

These circumstances gave us a reasonable ground of hope, that we should find this a comfortable station to supply all our wants and to make us forget the hardships and delays experienced during a constant succession of adverse winds, and boisterous weather, almost ever since our arrival upon the coast of America.

BOOK IV

Transactions among the Natives of North America and the Voyage Northward to our Return to the Sandwich Islands

1778

March 30 A great many canoes, filled with the natives, were about the ships all day; and a trade commenced betwixt us and them, which was carried on with the strictest honesty on both sides. The articles which they offered to sale were skins of various animals, such as bears, wolves, foxes, deer, racoons, polecats, martins; and, in particular, of the sea otters, which are found at the islands east of Kamtschatka.[1] Besides the skins in their native shape, they also brought garments made of them, and another sort of clothing made of the bark of a tree, or some plant like hemp; weapons, such as bows, arrows, and spears; fish-hooks, and instruments of various kinds; wooden visors of many different monstrous figures; a sort of woollen stuff, or blanketing, bags filled with red ochre; pieces of carved work; beads; and several other little ornaments of thin brass and iron, shaped like a horseshoe, which they hang at their noses; and several chisels,

---

[1] *i.e.* the Aleutians. Zimmermann describes the North American Indians as "the rudest and most uncivilised of all the native peoples we met on our voyage".

or pieces of iron, fixed to handles. From their possessing which metals, we could infer that they had either been visited before by some civilized nation, or had connections with tribes on their continent, who had communication with them. But the most extraordinary of all the articles which they brought to the ships for sale were human skulls, and hands not yet quite stripped of the flesh, which they made our people plainly understand they had eaten; and, indeed, some of them had evident marks that they had been upon the fire. We had but too much reason to suspect, from this circumstance, that the horrid practice of feeding on their enemies is as prevalent here as we had found it to be at New Zealand and other South Sea islands. For the various articles which they brought, they took in exchange knives, chisels, pieces of iron and tin, nails, looking-glasses, buttons, or any kind of metal. Glass beads they were not fond of; and cloth of every sort they rejected.

April 19   After a fortnight's bad weather, the 19th proving a fair day, we availed ourselves of it, to get up the top-masts and yards, and to fix up the rigging.[2] And, having now finished most of our heavy work, I set out the next morning to take a view of the Sound. I first went to the west point, where I found a large village, and before it a very snug harbour, in which was from nine to four fathoms' water, over a bottom of fine sand. The people of this village, who were numerous, and to most of whom I was well known, received me very courteously, everyone pressing me to go into his house, or rather his apartment; for several families live under the same roof. I did not decline the invitations; and my hospitable friends, whom I visited, spread a mat for me to sit upon, and showed me every other mark of civility. In most of the houses were women at work, making dresses of the plant or bark before mentioned, which they executed exactly in the same manner that the New Zealanders manufacture their cloth. Others were occupied in opening sardines. I had seen a large quantity of them brought on shore from canoes, and divided by

---

[2] At Nootka Sound it was also found necessary to step new mizen and fore masts.

measure amongst several people, who carried them up to their houses, where the operation of curing them by smoke-drying is performed. They hang them on small rods; at first, about a foot from the fire; afterward they remove them higher and higher, to make room for others, till the rods, on which the fish hang, reach the top of the house. When they are completely dried, they are taken down and packed close in bales, which they cover with mats. Thus they are kept till wanted; and they are not a disagreeable article of food. Cod, and other large fish, are also cured in the same manner by them; though they sometimes dry these in the open air, without fire.

From this village I proceeded up the west side of the Sound. For about three miles I found the shore covered with small islands, which are so situated as to form several convenient harbours, having various depths of water, from thirty to seven fathoms, with a good bottom. Two leagues within the Sound, on this west side, there runs in an arm in the direction of north north-west; and two miles farther is another nearly in the same direction, with a pretty large island before it. I had no time to examine either of these arms; but have reason to believe that they do not extend far inland, as the water was no more than brackish at their entrances. A mile above the second arm, I found the remains of a village. The logs or framings of the houses were standing; but the boards that had composed their sides and roofs did not exist. Before this village were some large fishing weirs; but I saw nobody attending them. These weirs were composed of pieces of wicker-work made of small rods, some closer than others, according to the size of the fish intended to be caught in them. These pieces of wicker-work (some of whose *superfices* are, at least, twenty feet by twelve), are fixed up edgewise in shallow water, by strong poles or pickets, that stand firm in the ground. Behind this ruined village is a plain of a few hours' extent, covered with the largest pine trees that I ever saw. This was the more remarkable, as the elevated ground, most other parts of this west side of the Sound, was rather naked.

From this place I crossed over to the other, or east side of the Sound, passing an arm of it that runs in north north-east, to appearance not far. I now found what I had before conjectured, that the land, under which the ships lay, was an island; and that there were many smaller ones lying scattered in the Sound on the west side of it.

DESCRIPTION OF NOOTKA SOUND

The persons of the natives are in general under the common stature, but not slender in proportion, being commonly pretty full or plump, though not muscular. Neither doth the soft fleshiness seem ever to swell into corpulence, and many of the older people are rather spare or lean. The visage of most of them is round and full, and sometimes, also, broad, with large prominent cheeks; and above these, the face is frequently much depressed, or seems fallen in quite across between the temples, the nose also flattening at its base, with pretty wide nostrils, and a rounded point. The forehead rather low, the eyes small, black, and rather languishing than sparkling, the mouth round with large round thickish lips, the teeth tolerably equal and well set, but not remarkably white. They have either no beards at all, which was most commonly the case, or a small thin one upon the point of the chin, which does not arise from any natural defect of hair on that part, but from plucking it out more or less; for some of them, and particularly the old men, have not only considerable beards all over the chin, but whiskers or mustachios, both on the upper lip, and running from thence toward the lower jaw obliquely downward. Their eyebrows are also scanty and always narrow, but the hair of the head is in great abundance, very coarse and strong, and without a single exception, black, straight, and lank, or hanging down over the shoulders; the neck is short; the arms and body have no particular mark of beauty or elegance in their formation, but are rather clumsy; and the limbs in all are very small in proportion to the other parts, and crooked or ill made, with large feet badly shaped and projecting ankles. This last defect seems, in a great measure, to arise from their sitting so much on their hams or knees, both in their canoes and houses.

Their colour we could never positively determine, as their bodies were encrusted with paint and dirt; though, in particular cases, when these were well rubbed off, the whiteness of the skin appeared almost to equal that of Europeans, though rather of that pale effete cast which distinguishes those of our southern nations. Their children, whose skins had never been stained with paint, also equalled ours in whiteness. During their youth, some of them have no disagreeable look, if compared to the generality of the people; but this seems to be entirely owing to the particular animation attending that period of life, for after attaining a certain age, there is hardly any distinction. Upon the whole, a very remarkable sameness seems to characterize the countenances of the whole nation, a dull phlegmatic want of expression, with very little variation, being strongly marked in all of them.

The women are nearly of the same size, colour, and form, with the men, from whom it is not easy to distinguish them, as they possess no natural delicacies sufficient to render their persons agreeable; and hardly anyone was seen, even amongst those who are in the prime of life, who had the least pretensions to be called handsome. . . .

Though their bodies are always covered with red paint, their faces are often stained with a black, a bright red, or a white colour by way of ornament. The last of these gives them a ghastly, disgusting aspect. They also strew the brown martial *mica* upon the paint, which makes it glitter, the ears of many of them are perforated in the lobe, where they make a pretty large hole; and two others higher up on the outer edge. In these holes they hang bits of bone; quills fixed upon a leathern thong; small shells; bunches of woollen tassels; or pieces of thin copper, which our beads could never supplant. The *septum* of the nose, in many, is also perforated, through which they draw a piece of soft cord; and others wear, at the same place, small thin pieces of iron, brass, or copper, shaped almost like a horseshoe, the narrow opening of which receives the *septum*, so as that the two points may gently pinch it; and the ornament thus hangs over the upper lip. The rings of our brass buttons, which they eagerly purchased, were appropriated to this use. About their wrists they wear bracelets or bunches of

326

white bugle beads, made of a conic shelly substance; bunches of thongs, with tassels; or a broad black shining horny substance, of one piece. And about their ankles they also frequently wear many folds of leathern thongs, or the sinews of animals twisted to a considerable thickness.

Thus far of their ordinary dress and ornaments; but they have some that seem to be used only on extraordinary occasions; either when they exhibit themselves as strangers, in visits of ceremony, or when they go to war. Amongst the first may be considered the skins of animals, such as wolves or bears, tied on in the usual manner, but ornamented at the edges with broad borders of fur, or of the woollen stuff manufactured by them, ingeniously wrought with various figures. These are worn either separately, or over their other common garments. On such occasions, the most common headdress is a quantity of withe, or half-beaten bark, wrapped about the head; which, at the same time, has various large feathers, particularly those of eagles, stuck in it, or is entirely covered, or, we may say, powdered with small white feathers. The face, at the same time, is variously painted, having its upper and lower parts of different colours, the strokes appearing like fresh gashes; or it is besmeared with a kind of tallow, mixed with paint, which is afterward formed into a great variety of regular figures, and appears like carved work. Sometimes, again, the hair is separated into small parcels, which are tied at intervals of about two inches, to the end, with thread; and others tie it together, behind, after our manner, and stick branches of the *cupressus thyoides* in it. Thus dressed, they have a truly savage and incongruous appearance; but this is much heightened, when they assume what may be called their monstrous decorations. These consist of an endless variety of carved wooden masks or visors, applied on the face, or to the upper part of the head or forehead. Some of these resemble human faces, furnished with hair, beards, and eyebrows; others, the heads of birds, particularly of eagles and quebrantahuessos; and many, the heads of land and sea animals, such as wolves, deer, and porpoises, and others. But, in general, these representations much exceed the natural size; and they are painted, and often strewed with pieces of the foliaceous *mica*, which makes them glitter, and serves to augment their enormous deformity. They even exceed this sometimes, and fix on the same part of the head large pieces of carved work, resembling the prow of a canoe, painted in the same manner, and projecting to a considerable distance. So fond are they of these disguises, that I have seen one of them put his head into a tin kettle he had got from us, for want of another sort of mask. Whether they use these extravagant masquerade ornaments on any particular religious occasion, or diversion, or whether they be put on to intimidate their enemies when they go to battle, by their monstrous appearance; or as decoys when they go to hunt animals, is uncertain. But it may be concluded, that, if travellers or voyagers, in an ignorant and credulous age, when many unnatural or marvellous things were supposed to exist, had seen a number of people decorated in this manner, without being able to approach so near as to be undeceived, they would readily have believed, and in their relations would have attempted to make others believe, that there existed a race of beings, partaking of the nature of man and beast; more especially, when, besides the heads of animals on the human shoulders, they might have seen the whole bodies of their men-monsters covered with quadrupeds' skins.

The only dress amongst the people of Nootka, observed by us, that seems peculiarly adapted to war, is a thick leathern mantle doubled, which, from its size, appears to be the skin of an elk, or buffalo tanned. This they fasten on in the common manner, and it is so contrived, that it may reach up, and cover the breast quite to the throat, falling, at the same time, almost to the heels. It is sometimes ingeniously painted in different compartments; and is not only sufficiently strong to resist arrows, but as they informed us by signs, even spears cannot pierce it; so that it may be considered as their coat of mail, or most complete defensive armour. Upon the same occasion, they sometimes wear a kind of leathern cloak, covered with rows of dried hoofs of deer, disposed horizontally, appended by leathern thongs, covered with quills; which, when they move, make a loud rattling noise, almost equal to that of many small bells. It seems doubtful, however, whether this part of their garb be intended to strike terror in war, or only is to be considered as belonging to their eccentric ornaments on ceremonious occasions; for we saw one of their musical entertainments, conducted by a man dressed in this sort of cloak, with his mask on, and shaking his rattle.

Though these people cannot be viewed without a kind of horror, when equipped in such extravagant dresses, yet when divested of them, and beheld in their common habit and actions, they have not the least appearance of ferocity in their countenances; and seem, on the contrary, as observed already, to be of a quiet, phlegmatic, and inactive disposition; destitute, in some measure, of that degree of animation and vivacity that would render them agreeable as social beings. If they are not reserved, they are far from being loquacious; but their gravity is, perhaps, rather a consequence of the disposition just mentioned, than of any conviction of its propriety, or the effect of any particular mode of education. For, even in the greatest paroxysms of their rage, they seem unable to express it sufficiently, either with warmth of language, or significance of gestures.

Their orations, which are made either when engaged in any altercation or dispute, or to explain their sentiments publicly on other occasions, seem little more than short sentences, or rather single words, forcibly repeated, and constantly in one tone and degree of strength, accompanied only with a single gesture, which they use at every sentence, jerking their whole body a little forward, by bending the knees, their arms hanging down by their sides at the same time. . . .

The nastiness and stench of their houses are, however, at least equal to the confusion; for, as they dry their fish within doors, they also gut them there, which, with their bones and fragments thrown down at meals, and the addition of other sorts of filth, lie everywhere in heaps, and are, I believe, never carried away till it becomes troublesome, from their size, to walk over them. In a word, their houses are as filthy as hog-sties, everything in and about them stinking of fish, train-oil, and smoke.

But, amidst all the filth and confusion that are found in the houses, many of them are decorated with images. These are

z

nothing more than the trunks of very large trees four or five feet high, set up singly or by pairs at the upper end of the apartment, with the front carved into a human face, the arms and hands cut out upon the sides and variously painted; so that the whole is a truly monstrous figure. The general name of these images is *Klumma*,[3] and the names of two particular ones which stood abreast of each other, three or four feet asunder in one of the houses, were *Natchkoa* and *Matseeta*. Mr. Webber's view of the inside of a Nootka house in which these images are represented, will convey a more perfect idea of them than any description. A mat, by way of curtain, for the most part hung before them, which the natives were not willing at all times to remove; and when they did unveil them, they seemed to speak of them in a very mysterious manner. It should seem that they are at times accustomed to make offerings to them, if we can draw this inference from their desiring us, as we interpreted their signs, to give something to these images when they drew aside the mats that covered them. It was natural, from these circumstances, for us to think that they were representatives of their gods, or symbols of some religious or superstitious object; and yet we had proofs of the little real estimation they were in, for with a small quantity of iron or brass, I could have purchased all the gods (if their images were such) in the place. I did not see one that was not offered to me; and I actually got two or three of the very smallest sort.

The chief employment of the men seems to be that of fishing and killing land or sea animals for the sustenance of their families, for we saw few of them doing anything in the houses; whereas the women were occupied in manufacturing their flaxen or woollen garments, and in preparing the sardines for drying, which they also carry up from the beach in twig baskets, after the men have brought them in their canoes. The women are also sent in the small canoes to gather mussels and other shellfish, and perhaps on some other occasions, for they manage these with as much dexterity as the men, who, when in the canoes with them, seem to pay little attention to their sex, by offering to relieve them

Totems.

from the labour of the paddle; nor, indeed, do they treat them with any particular respect or tenderness in other situations. The young men appeared to be the most indolent or idle set in this community, for they were either sitting about in scattered companies, to bask themselves in the sun, or lay wallowing in the sand upon the beach like a number of hogs, for the same purpose, without any covering. But this disregard for decency was confined to the men. The women were always properly clothed, and behaved with the utmost propriety, justly deserving all commendation for a bashfulness and modesty becoming their sex, but more meritorious in them, as the men seem to have no sense of shame. It is impossible, however, that we should have been able to observe the exact mode of their domestic life and employments, from a single visit (as the first was quite transitory) of a few hours.

May 12   From Comptroller's Bay to this point, which I name *Cape Hinchingbroke*, the direction of the coast is nearly east and west. Beyond this, it seemed to incline to the southward; a direction so contrary to the modern charts founded upon the late Russian discoveries,[4] that we had reason to expect that, by the inlet before us, we should find a passage to the north; and that the land to the west and south-west was nothing but a group of islands. Add to this, that the wind was now at south-east, and we were threatened with a fog and a storm; and I wanted to get into some place to stop the leak, before we encountered another gale. These reasons induced me to steer for the inlet, which we had no sooner reached, than the weather became so foggy, that we could not see a mile before us, and it became necessary to secure the ships in some place, to wait for a clearer sky. With this view, I hauled close under Cape Hinchingbroke, and anchored before a small cove, a little within the cape, in eight fathoms' water, a clayey bottom, and about a quarter of a mile from the shore.

The boats were then hoisted out, some to sound, and others to

[4] *i.e.* Vitus Bering (in 1728 and 1741) and his successors. By this date there were a number of Russian trappers on the Alaskan coast. Having worked up the coast of Canada in a vain search for a passage, Cook found that the coast of Alaska trended west. Cape Hinchingbroke is at the entrance of Prince William's Sound.

fish. The seine was drawn in the cove; but without success, for it was torn. At some short intervals, the fog cleared away, and gave us a sight of the lands around us. The cape bore south by west half west, one league distant; the west point of the inlet south-west by west, distant five leagues; and the land on that side extended as far as west by north. Between this point and north-west by west, we could see no land; and what was in the last direction seemed to be at a great distance. The westernmost point we had in sight on the north shore, bore north north-west half west, two leagues distant. Between this point and the shore under which we were at anchor is a bay about three leagues deep; on the south-east side of which there are two or three coves, such as that before which we had anchored; and in the middle some rocky islands.

To these islands Mr. Gore was sent in a boat, in hopes of shooting some eatable birds. But he had hardly got to them, before about twenty natives made their appearance in two large canoes; on which he thought proper to return to the ships, and they followed him. They would not venture alongside, but kept at some distance, halloing aloud, and alternately clasping and extending their arms; and, in a short time, began a kind of song exactly after the manner of those at Nootka. Their heads were also powdered with feathers. One man held out a white garment, which we interpreted as a sign of friendship; and another stood up in the canoe, quite naked, for almost a quarter of an hour, with his arms stretched out like a cross, and motionless. The canoes were not constructed of wood, as at King George's or Nootka Sound. The frame only, being slender laths, was of that substance; the outside consisting of the skins of seals, or of suchlike animals. Though we returned all their signs of friendship, and, by every expressive gesture, tried to encourage them to come alongside, we could not prevail. Some of our people repeated several of the common words of the Nootka language, such as *seekemaile*, and *mahook*; but they did not seem to understand them. After receiving some presents, which were thrown to them, they retired toward that part of the shore from whence they came; giving us to understand by signs, that they would visit us again the next morning.

Two of them, however, each in a small canoe, waited upon us in the night; probably with a design to pilfer something, thinking we should be all asleep; for they retired as soon as they found themselves discovered.

May 20   To the inlet, which we had now left, I gave the name of *Prince William's Sound*. To judge of this Sound, from what we saw of it, it occupies, at least, a degree and a half of latitude, and two of longitude, exclusive of the arms or branches, the extent of which is not known. The direction which they seemed to take, as also the situation and magnitude of the several islands in and about it, will be best seen in the sketch, which is delineated with as much accuracy as the short time and other circumstances would allow.

The natives, who came to make us several visits while we were in the sound, were generally not above the common height; though many of them were under it. They were square, or strong-chested; and the most disproportioned part of their body seemed to be their heads, which were very large, with thick, short necks, and large, broad, or spreading faces; which, upon the whole, were flat. Their eyes, though not small, scarcely bore a proportion to the size of their faces; and their noses had full, round points, hooked, or turned up at the tip. Their teeth were broad, white, equal in size, and evenly set. Their hair was black, thick, straight and strong; and their beards, in general, thin or wanting; but the hairs about the lips of those who have them, were stiff or bristly, and frequently of a brown colour. And several of the elderly men had even large and thick, but straight beards.

Though, in general, they agree in the make of their persons, and largeness of their heads, there is a considerable variety in their features; but very few can be said to be of the handsome sort, though their countenance commonly indicates a considerable share of vivacity, good nature, and frankness. And yet some of them had an air of sullenness and reserve. Some of the women have agreeable faces; and many are easily distinguishable from the men by their features, which are more delicate; but this should be understood chiefly of the younger sort, or middle-aged. The complexion of some of the women, and of the children, is white; but without any mixture of red. And some of the men who were seen naked, had rather a brownish or swarthy cast, which could scarcely be the effect of any stain; for they do not paint their bodies.

Their common dress (for men, women, and children are clothed alike) is a kind of close frock, or rather robe, reaching generally to the ankles, though sometimes only to the knees. At the upper part is a hole just sufficient to admit the head, with sleeves that reach to the wrist. These frocks are made of the skins of different animals; the most common of which are those of the sea-otter, grey fox, racoon, and pine martin; with many of seal skins; and, in general, they are worn with the hairy side outward. Some also have these frocks made of the skins of fowls, with only the down remaining on them, which they glue on other substances. And we saw one or two woollen garments like those of Nootka. At the seams, where the different skins are sewed together, they are commonly ornamented with tassels or fringes of narrow thongs, cut out of the same skins. A few have a kind of cape, or collar, and some a hood; but the other is the most common form, and seems to be their whole dress in good weather. When it rains, they put over this another frock, ingeniously made from the intestines of whales, or some other large animal, prepared so skilfully as almost to resemble our gold-beaters' leaf. It is made to draw tight round the neck; its sleeves reach as low as the wrist, round which they are tied with a string; and its skirts, when they are in their canoes, are drawn over the rim of the hole in which they sit, so that no water can enter. At the same time, it keeps the men entirely dry upward. For no water can penetrate through it, any more than through a bladder. It must be kept continually moist or wet; otherwise it is apt to crack or break. This, as well as the common frock made of the skins, bears a great resemblance to the dress of the Greenlanders, as described by Crantz.[5]

In general, they do not cover their legs or feet; but a few have a kind of skin stockings, which reach halfway up the thigh; and

[5] Author of a History of Greenland.

scarcely any of them are without mittens for the hands, made of the skins of bears' paws. Those who wear anything on their heads, resembled in this respect our friends at Nootka; having high truncated conic caps, made of straw, and sometimes of wood, resembling a seal's head well painted.

The men commonly wear their hair cropped round the neck and forehead; but the women allow it to grow long, and most of them tie a small lock of it on the crown, or a few club it behind, after our manner. Both sexes have the ears perforated with several holes about the outer and lower part of the edge, in which they hang little bunches of beads, made of the same tubulose shelly substance used for this purpose by those of Nootka. The *septum* of the nose is also perforated, through which they frequently thrust the quill-feathers of small birds, or little bending ornaments made of the above shelly substance, strung on a stiff string or cord three or four inches long, which give them a truly grotesque appearance. But the most uncommon and unsightly ornamental fashion adopted by some of both sexes, is their having the under lip slit, or cut quite through, in the direction of the mouth, a little below the swelling part. This incision, which is made even in the sucking children, is often above two inches long; and either by its natural retraction when the wound is fresh, or by the repetition of some artificial management, assumes the true shape of lips, and become so large as to admit the tongue through. This happened to be the case, when the first person having this incision was seen by one of the seamen, who called out that the man had two mouths, and, indeed, it does not look unlike it. In this artificial mouth they stick a flat narrow ornament, made chiefly out of a solid shell or bone, cut into little narrow pieces like small teeth, almost down to the base or thickest part, which has a small projecting bit at each end that supports it when put into the divided lip, the cut part then appearing outward. Others have the lower lip only perforated into separate holes, and then the ornament consists of as many distinct shelly studs, whose points are pushed through these holes, and their heads appear within the lip, as another row of teeth immediately under their own.

June 1   If the discovery of this great river,[6] which promises to vie with the most considerable ones already known to be capable of extensive inland navigation, should prove of use either to the present or to any future age, the time we spent in it ought to be the less regretted. But to us, who had a much greater object in view, the delay thus occasioned was an essential loss. The season was advancing apace. We knew not how far we might have to proceed to the south; and we were now convinced that the continent of North America extended farther to the west than, from the modern most reputable charts, we had reason to expect. This made the existence of a passage into Baffin's or Hudson's Bays less probable, or, at least, showed it to be of greater extent. It was a satisfaction to me, however, to reflect that, if I had not examined this very considerable inlet, it would have been assumed, by speculative fabricators of geography, as a fact that it communicated with the sea to the north, or with Baffin's or Hudson's Bays to the east; and been marked, perhaps, on future maps of the world, with greater precision, and more certain signs of reality, than the invisible, because imaginary, Straits of de Fuca, and de Fonte.

In the afternoon I sent Mr. King again, with two armed boats, with orders to land on the northern point of the low land, on the south-east side of the river; there to display the flag, and to take possession of the country and river in His Majesty's name; and to bury in the ground a bottle, containing some pieces of English coin, of the year 1772, and a paper, on which were inscribed the names of our ships, and the date of our discovery. In the meantime, the ships were got under sail, in order to proceed down the river. The wind still blew fresh, easterly; but a calm ensued not long after we were under way; and the flood tide meeting us off the point where Mr. King landed (and which thence got the name of *Point Possession*), we were obliged to drop anchor in six fathoms of water, with the point bearing south, two miles distant.

June 19   Some time after we had got through this channel,[7] in

[6] As Cook gave no name to this inlet (it is not a river), lying west of Prince William's Sound, the Earl of Sandwich named it Cook's River.

[7] Between Kodiak island and the Alaska peninsula.

which we found forty fathoms water, the *Discovery*, now two miles astern, fired three guns, and brought to, and made the signal to speak with us. This alarmed me not a little; and as no apparent danger had been remarked in the passage through the channel, it was apprehended that some accident, such as springing a leak, must have happened. A boat was immediately sent to her; and in a short time returned with Captain Clerke. I now learned from him that some natives, in three or four canoes, who had been following the ship for some time, at length got under his stern. One of them then made many signs, taking off his cap, and bowing, after the manner of Europeans. A rope being handed down from the ship, to this he fastened a small thin wooden case or box; and having delivered this safe, and spoken something, and made some signs, the canoes dropped astern, and left the *Discovery*. No one on board her had any suspicion that the box contained anything till after the departure of the canoes, when it was accidentally opened, and a piece of paper was found, folded up carefully, upon which something was written in the Russian language, as was supposed. The date 1778 was prefixed to it; and, in the body of the written note, there was a reference to the year 1776. Not learned enough to decipher the alphabet of the writer, his numerals marked sufficiently that others had preceded us in visiting this dreary part of the globe, who were united to us by other ties besides those of our common nature; and the hopes of soon meeting with some of the Russian traders, could not but give a sensible satisfaction to those who had, for such a length of time, been conversant with the savages of the Pacific Ocean, and of the continent of North America.

Captain Clerke was at first of opinion, that some Russians had been shipwrecked here; and that these unfortunate persons, seeing our ships pass, had taken this method to inform us of their situation. Impressed with humane sentiments, on such an occasion, he was desirous of our stopping till they might have time to join us.[8] But no such idea occurred to me. It seemed obvious that

[8] This seems to have been the general attitude. When, shortly afterwards, the *Resolution* nearly ran aground, Zimmermann writes "seeing how near we had been to shipwreck, the crews of both ships gave expression to their indignation at the lack of feeling shown by Captain Cook in refusing to go to the assistance of

if this had been the case, it would have been the first step taken by such shipwrecked persons, in order to secure to themselves, and to their companions, the relief they could not but be solicitous about, to send some of their body off to the ships in the canoes. For this reason, I rather thought that the paper contained a note of information, left by some Russian trader, who had lately been amongst these islands, to be delivered to the next of their country-men who should arrive; and that the natives, seeing our ships pass, and supposing us to be Russians, had resolved to bring off the note, thinking it might induce us to stop. Fully convinced of this, I did not stay to inquire any further into the matter; but made sail, and stood away to the westward, along the coast; per-haps I should say along the islands; for we could not pronounce, with certainty, whether the nearest land within us was continent or islands. If not the latter, the coast here forms some tolerably large and deep bays.

August 3   Mr. Anderson, my surgeon, who had been lingering under a consumption for more than twelve months, expired between three and four this afternoon. He was a sensible young man, an agreeable companion, well skilled in his own profes-sion; and had acquired considerable knowledge of other branches of science. The reader of this Journal will have observed how useful an assistant I had found him in the course of the voyage; and had it pleased God to have spared his life, the public, I make no doubt, might have received from him such communications, on various parts of the natural history of the several places we visited, as would have abundantly shown that he was not un-worthy of this commendation. Soon after he had breathed his last, land was seen to the westward, twelve leagues distant. It was supposed to be an island; and, to perpetuate the memory of the deceased, for whom I had a very great regard, I named it *Ander-son's Island*. The next day, I removed Mr. Law, the surgeon of the *Discovery*, into the *Resolution*, and appointed Mr. Samwell,[9] the

those individuals who had quite evidently sent a request for help through the two men who brought the box."

[9] David Samwell, whose account of Cook's death is printed below. The previous month the ships had passed through the chain of the Aleutian islands near Dutch Harbour on Unalaska, and were now entering the Bering Strait.

surgeon's first mate of the *Resolution*, to be surgeon of the *Discovery*.

August 9   Being now satisfied that the whole was a continued coast, I tacked, and stood away for its north-west part, and came to an anchor under it in seventeen fathoms' water.[10] The weather, at this time, was very thick with rain; but, at four next morning, it cleared up, so that we could see the land about us. A high steep rock or island bore west by south; another island to the north of it, and much larger, bore west by north; the peaked hill above mentioned, south-east by east; and the point under it, S. 32° E. Under this hill lies some low land, stretching out toward the north-west, the extreme point of which, bore north-east by east, about three miles distant. Over, and beyond it, some high land was seen, supposed to be a continuation of the continent.

This point of land, which I named *Cape Prince of Wales*, is the more remarkable, by being the western extremity of all America hitherto known. It is situated in the latitude of 65° 46', and in the longitude of 191° 45'. The observations by which both were determined, though made in sight of it, were liable to some small error, on account of the haziness of the weather. We thought we saw some people upon the coast; and probably we were not mistaken, as some elevations, like stages, and others, like huts, were seen at the same place. We saw the same things on the continent within Sledge Island, and on some other parts of the coast.

It was calm till eight o'clock in the morning, when a faint breeze at north springing up, we weighed; but we had scarcely got our sails set, when it began to blow and rain very hard, with misty weather. The wind and current, being in contrary directions, raised such a sea, that it frequently broke into the ship. We had a few minutes' sunshine at noon; and from the observation then obtained, we fixed the above-mentioned latitude.

August 10   As we were standing into this bay, we perceived on

---

[10] In the Bering Strait, through which the ships were now passing, it is possible in clear weather to see both the shores of Asia and America. Of the Asiatic coastline Cook writes: "In justice to Behring's memory, I must say he delineated this coast very well."

the north shore a village, and some people, whom the sight of the ships seemed to have thrown into confusion, or fear. We could plainly see persons running up the country with burdens upon their backs. At these habitations, I proposed to land; and accordingly went with three armed boats, accompanied by some of the officers. About thirty or forty men, each armed with a spontoon,[11] a bow and arrows, stood drawn up on a rising ground close by the village. As we drew near, three of them came down toward the shore, and were so polite as to take off their caps, and to make us low bows. We returned the civility; but this did not inspire them with sufficient confidence to wait for our landing; for the moment we put the boats ashore, they retired. I followed them alone, without anything in my hand; and by signs and gestures prevailed on them to stop, and receive some trifling presents. In return for these, they gave me two fox skins, and a couple of sea-horse teeth. I cannot say whether they or I made the first present; for it appeared to me, that they had brought down with them these things for this very purpose, and that they would have given them to me, even though I had made no return.

They seemed very fearful and cautious; expressing their desire by signs, that no more of our people should be permitted to come up. On my laying my hand on the shoulder of one of them, he started back several paces. In proportion as I advanced, they retreated backward; always in the attitude of being ready to make use of their spears; while those on the rising ground stood ready to support them with their arrows. Insensibly, myself, and two or three of my companions, got in amongst them. A few beads distributed to those about us, soon created a kind of confidence; so that they were not alarmed when a few more of our people joined us; and, by degrees, a sort of traffic between us commenced. In exchange for knives, beads, tobacco, and other articles, they gave us some of their clothing, and a few arrows. But nothing that we had to offer could induce them to part with a spear or a bow. These they held in constant readiness, never once quitting them, except at one time, when four or five persons laid

[11] *i.e.* a pike. Cook landed on the north east point of the Asiatic coast opposite Cape Prince of Wales. The inhabitants are called the Tschutski.

theirs down, while they gave us a song and a dance. And even then, they placed them in such a manner, that they could lay hold of them in an instant; and for their security, they desired us to sit down.

The arrows were pointed either with bone or stone, but very few of them had barbs; and some had a round blunt point. What use these may be applied to I cannot say; unless it be to kill small animals, without damaging the skin. The bows were such as we had seen on the American coast, and like those used by the Esquimaux. The spears, or spontoons, were of iron or steel, and of European or Asiatic workmanship; in which no little pains had been taken to ornament them with carving, and inlayings of brass and of a white metal. Those who stood ready with bows and arrows in their hands, had a spear slung over their shoulder by a leather strap. A leathern quiver, slung over their left shoulder, contained arrows; and some of these quivers were extremely beautiful; being made of red leather, on which was very neat embroidery, and other ornaments.

Several other things, and in particular their clothing, showed that they were possessed of a degree of ingenuity, far surpassing what one could expect to find amongst so northern a people. All the Americans we had seen since our arrival on that coast, were rather low of stature, with round chubby faces, and high cheekbones. The people we now were amongst, far from resembling them, had long visages, and were stout and well made. In short, they appeared to be a quite different nation. We saw neither women nor children of either sex; nor any aged, except one man, who was bald-headed; and he was the only one who carried no arms. The others seemed to be picked men, and rather under than above the middle age. The old man had a black mark across his face, which I did not see in any others. All of them had their ears bored; and some had glass beads hanging to them. These were the only fixed ornaments we saw about them; for they wear none to their lips. This is another thing in which they differ from the Americans we had lately seen.

Their clothing consisted of a cap, a frock, a pair of breeches, a pair of boots, and a pair of gloves, all made of leather, or of the skins of deer, dogs, seals, etc., and extremely well dressed; some with the hair or fur on; but others without it. The caps were made to fit the head very close; and besides these caps, which most of them wore, we got from them some hoods, made of the skins of dogs, that were large enough to cover both head and shoulders. Their hair seemed to be black; but their heads were either shaved, or the hair cut close off; and none of them wore any beard. Of the few articles which they got from us, knives and tobacco were what they valued most.

We found the village composed both of their summer and their winter habitations. The latter are exactly like a vault, the floor of which is sunk a little below the surface of the earth. One of them which I examined, was of an oval form, about twenty feet long, and twelve or more high. The framing was composed of wood, and the ribs of whales, disposed in a judicious manner, and bound together with smaller materials of the same sort. Over this framing is laid a covering of strong coarse grass; and that again is covered with earth; so that, on the outside, the house looks like a little hillock, supported by a wall of stone, three or four feet high, which is built round the two sides, and one end. At the other end the earth is raised sloping, to walk up to the entrance, which is by a hole in the top of the roof over that end. The floor was boarded, and under it a kind of cellar, in which I saw nothing but water. And at the end of each house was a vaulted room, which I took to be a storeroom. These storerooms communicated with the house by a dark passage; and with the open air, by a hole in the roof, which was even with the ground one walked upon; but they cannot be said to be wholly underground; for one end reached to the edge of the hill, along which they were made, and which was built up with stone. Over it stood a kind of sentry-box, or tower, composed of the large bones of large fish.

The summer huts were pretty large and circular, being brought to a point at the top. The framing was of slight poles and bones, covered with the skins of sea-animals. I examined the inside of one. There was a fireplace just within the door, where lay a few wooden vessels, all very dirty. Their bed-places were close to the side, and took up about half the circuit. Some privacy seemed to

be observed; for there were several partitions made with skins.
The bed and bedding were of deer-skins; and most of them were
dry and clean.

About the habitations were erected several stages, ten or twelve
feet high; such as we had observed on some parts of the American
coast. They were wholly composed of bones; and seemed intended for drying their fish and skins, which were thus placed
beyond the reach of their dogs, of which they had a great many.
These dogs are of the fox kind, rather large, and of different
colours, with long soft hair like wool. They are, probably, used
in drawing their sledges in winter. For sledges they have, as I
saw a good many laid up in one of the winter huts. It is also not
improbable that dogs may constitute a part of their food. Several
lay dead that had been killed that morning.

The canoes of these people are of the same sort with those of
the northern Americans; some, both of the large and of the small
ones, being seen lying in a creek under the village.

By the large fish-bones, and of their sea-animals, it appeared
that the sea supplied them with the greatest part of their subsistence. The country appeared to be exceedingly barren; yielding
neither tree nor shrub, that we could see. At some distance
westward, we observed a ridge of mountains covered with snow
that had lately fallen.

At first we supposed this land to be a part of the island of
Alaschka, laid down in Mr. Stæhlin's map. But from the figure
of the coast, the situation of the opposite shore of America, and
from the longitude, we soon began to think that it was, more
probably, the country of the Tschutski, or the eastern extremity
of Asia, explored by Behring in 1728. But to have admitted
this, without further examination, I must have pronounced Mr.
Stæhlin's map, and his account of the new Northern Archipelago,
to be either exceeding erroneous, even in latitude, or else to be
a mere fiction; a judgment which I had no right to pass upon a
publication so respectably vouched, without producing the
clearest proofs.

August 16   I now steered N.E. by E., thinking by this course to deepen our water.[12] But, in the space of six leagues, it shoaled to eleven fathoms; which made me think it proper to haul close to the wind, that now blew at west. Toward noon, both sun and moon were seen clearly at intervals, and we got some flying observations for the longitude; which, reduced to noon, when the latitude was 70° 33', gave 197° 41'. The timekeeper, for the same time, gave 198°; and the variation was 35° 1' 22" E. We had afterward reason to believe that the observed longitude was within a very few miles of the truth.

Some time before noon we perceived a brightness in the northern horizon, like that reflected from ice, commonly called the blink. It was little noticed, from a supposition that it was improbable we should meet with ice so soon. And yet the sharpness of the air, and gloominess of the weather, for two or three days past, seemed to indicate some sudden change. About an hour after, the sight of a large field of ice left us no longer in doubt about the cause of the brightness of the horizon. At half-past two, we tacked, close to the edge of the ice, in twenty-two fathoms water, being then in the latitude of 70° 41'; not being able to stand on any farther. For the ice was quite impenetrable, and extended from west by south to east by north, as far as the eye could reach. Here were abundance of sea-horses; some in the water, but far more upon the ice. I had the thoughts of hoisting out the boats to kill some; but the wind freshening, I gave up the design, and continued to ply to the southward, or rather to the westward; for the wind came from that quarter.

We gained nothing; for on the 18th at noon our latitude was 70° 44'; and we were near five leagues farther to the eastward. We were, at this time, close to the edge of the ice, which was as compact as a wall, and seemed to be ten or twelve feet high at least. But farther north, it appeared much higher. Its surface was extremely rugged, and here and there we saw upon it pools of water.

We now stood to the southward, and, after running six leagues, shoaled the water to seven fathoms; but it soon deepened to nine fathoms. At this time the weather, which had been hazy, clearing

12 North of the north-west point of Alaska.

up a little, we saw land extending from south to south-east by east, about three or four miles distant. The eastern extreme forms a point, which was much encumbered with ice; for which reason it obtained the name of *Icy Cape*. Its latitude is 70° 29',[13] and its longitude 198° 20'. The other extreme of the land was lost in the horizon; so that there can be no doubt of its being a continuation of the American continent. The *Discovery* being about a mile astern, and to leeward, found less water than we did, and tacking on that account, I was obliged to tack also, to prevent separation.

Our situation was now more and more critical. We were in shoal water, upon a lee shore; and the main body of the ice to windward, driving down upon us. It was evident that if we remained much longer between it and the land, it would force us ashore, unless it should happen to take the ground before us. It seemed nearly to join the land to leeward; and the only direction that was open was to the south-west. After making a short board[14] to the northward, I made the signal for the *Discovery* to tack, and tacked myself at the same time. The wind proved rather favourable, so that we lay up south-west, and south-west by west.

At eight in the morning of the 19th, the wind veering back to west, I tacked to the northward; and at noon the latitude was 70° 6', and the longitude 196° 42'. In this situation we had a good deal of drift-ice about us; and the main ice was about two leagues to the north. At half-past one we got in with the edge of it. It was not so compact as that which we had seen to the northward; but it was too close, and in too large pieces, to attempt forcing the ships through it. On the ice lay a prodigious number of sea-horses; and as we were in want of fresh provisions, the boats from each ship were sent to get some.

By seven o'clock in the evening, we had received on board the *Resolution* nine of these animals, which, till now, we had supposed to be sea-cows, so that we were not a little disappointed, especially some of the seamen, who, for the novelty of the thing,

---

[13] In the original text this position is given as 79° 29', clearly a misprint if compared with the previous figure (his farthest north) of 70° 44'.
[14] *i.e.* a short tack.

had been feasting their eyes for some days past. Nor would they have been disappointed now, nor have known the difference, if we had not happened to have one or two on board, who had been in Greenland, and declared what animals these were, and that no one ever ate of them. But notwithstanding this, we lived upon them as long as they lasted; and there were few on board who did not prefer them to our salt meat.

The fat at first is as sweet as marrow; but in a few days it grows rancid, unless it be salted, in which state it will keep much longer. The lean flesh is coarse, black, and has rather a strong taste, and the heart is nearly as well tasted as that of a bullock. The fat when melted yields a good deal of oil, which burns very well in lamps, and their hides, which are very thick, were very useful about our rigging. The teeth, or tusks, of most of them were at this time very small, even some of the largest and oldest of these animals had them not exceeding six inches in length. From this we concluded that they had lately shed their old teeth.

They lie in herds of many hundreds upon the ice, huddling one over the other like swine, and roar or bray very loud; so that in the night, or in foggy weather, they gave us notice of the vicinity of the ice, before we could see it. We never found the whole herd asleep, some being always upon the watch. These, on the approach of the boat, would wake those next to them, and the alarm being thus gradually communicated, the whole herd would be awake presently. But they were seldom in a hurry to get away, till after they had been once fired at. Then they would tumble one over the other into the sea, in the utmost confusion. And if we did not, at the first discharge, kill those we fired at, we generally lost them, though mortally wounded. They did not appear to us to be that dangerous animal some authors have described, not even when attacked. They are rather more so to appearance than in reality. Vast numbers of them would follow, and come close up to the boats; but the flash of a musket in the pan, or even the bare pointing of one at them, would send them down in an instant. The female will defend the young one to the very last, and at the expense of her own life, whether in the water or upon the ice. Nor will the young one quit the dam, though she be dead, so that, if you kill

346

one, you are sure of the other. The dam, when in the water
olds the young one between her fore-fins.

Mr. Pennant has given a very good description of this animal,
under the name of *Arctic Walrus*; but I have nowhere seen a good
drawing of one. Why they should be called sea-horses, is hard to
say, unless the word be a corruption of the Russian name, *Morse*;
for they have not the least resemblance of a horse. This is, without
doubt, the same animal that is found in the Gulf of St. Lawrence,
and there called sea-cow. It is certainly more like a cow than a
horse, but this likeness consists in nothing but the snout. In short,
it is an animal like a seal, but incomparably larger.

August 29   The season was now so far advanced, and the time
when the frost is expected to set in so near at hand, that I did not
think it consistent with prudence, to make any further attempts
to find a passage into the Atlantic this year, in any direction; so
little was the prospect of succeeding. My attention was now
directed towards finding out some place where we might supply
ourselves with wood and water; and the object uppermost in my
thoughts was, how I should spend the winter, so as to make some
improvements in geography and navigation, and, at the same
time, be in a condition to return to the north, in further search
of a passage, the ensuing summer.[15]

December 6   On the 6th in the evening, being about five leagues
farther up the coast,[16] and near the shore, we had some traffic
with the natives. But, as it had furnished only a trifling supply, I
stood in again the next morning, when we had a considerable
number of visitors; and we lay to, trading with them till two in
the forenoon. By that time, we had procured pork, fruit, and
roots, sufficient for four or five days. We then made sail, and
continued to ply to windward.

Having procured a quantity of sugar-cane; and having, upon

[15] After trying for eleven days to work through to the east, Cook gave up the
search for a passage in lat. 69° 17′, long. 183°, off Cape North. On running down
the coast of Alaska, Norton Sound was discovered and Unalaska in the Aleutians
was visited, where contact was made with Russian traders. On 26 October course
was set for the Sandwich Islands. By now the *Resolution* was leaking badly.

[16] Of Hawaii (Owhyhee), the most easterly of the Sandwich group.

a trial, made but a few days before, found that a strong decoction of it produced a very palatable beer, I ordered some more to be brewed, for our general use. But when the cask was now broached, not one of my crew would even so much as taste it.[17] As I had no motive in preparing this beverage, but to save our spirit for a colder climate, I gave myself no trouble, either by exerting authority, or by having recourse to persuasion, to prevail upon them to drink it; knowing that there was no danger of the scurvy, so long as we could get a plentiful supply of other vegetables. But, that I might not be disappointed in my views, I gave orders that no grog should be served in either ship. I myself, and the officers, continued to make use of this sugar-cane beer, whenever we could get materials for brewing it. A few hops, of which we had some on board, improved it much. It has the taste of new malt beer; and I believe no one will doubt of its being very wholesome. And yet my inconsiderate crew alleged that it was injurious to their health.

They had no better reason to support a resolution, which they took on our first arrival in King George's Sound, not to drink the spruce-beer made there. But, whether from a consideration that it was not the first time of their being required to use that liquor, or from some other reason, they did not attempt to carry their purpose into actual execution; and I had never heard of it till now, when they renewed their ignorant opposition to my best endeavours to serve them. Every innovation whatever, on board a ship, though ever so much to the advantage of seamen, is sure to meet with their highest disapprobation. Both portable soup and sauerkraut were, at first, condemned as stuff unfit for human beings. Few commanders have introduced into their ships more novelties, as useful varieties of food and drink, than I have done. Indeed few commanders have had the same opportunities of trying such experiments, or been driven to the same necessity of trying them. It has, however, been in a great measure owing to

[17] This passage is one of the very few in which Cook speaks harshly of his men. His words have been toned down in the published version, the adjectives "mutinous" and "turbulent" in the MS. being omitted. The last paragraph is erased in the MS., according to King by Captain Gore (cp. Brit. Mus. Egerton MSS., 2177, A & B).

various little deviations from established practice, that I have been able to preserve my people, generally speaking, from that dreadful distemper, the scurvy, which has perhaps destroyed more of our sailors, in their peaceful voyages, than have fallen by the enemy in military expeditions.

January 16   At daybreak on the 16th, seeing the appearance of a bay,[18] I sent Mr. Bligh, with a boat from each ship, to examine it, being at this time three leagues off. Canoes now began to arrive from all parts; so that before ten o'clock there were not fewer than a thousand about the two ships, most of them crowded with people, and well laden with hogs and other productions of the island. We had the most satisfying proof of their friendly intentions; for we did not see a single person who had with him a weapon of any sort. Trade and curiosity alone had brought them off. Among such numbers as we had, at times, on board, it is no wonder that some should betray a thievish disposition. One of our visitors took out of the ship a boat's rudder. He was discovered; but too late to recover it. I thought this a good opportunity to show these people the use of firearms; and two or three muskets, and as many four-pounders, were fired over the canoe, which carried off the rudder. As it was not intended that any of the shot should take effect, the surrounding multitude of natives seemed rather more surprised than frightened.

In the evening Mr. Bligh returned, and reported that he had found a bay in which was good anchorage, and fresh water, in a situation tolerably easy to be come at. Into this bay I resolved to carry the ships, there to refit, and supply ourselves with every refreshment that the place could afford. As night approached, the greater part of our visitors retired to the shore; but numbers of them requested our permission to sleep on board. Curiosity was not the only motive, at least with some; for the next morning several things were missing, which determined me not to entertain so many another night.

[18] Karakakooa (Kealakekua) Bay on the west coast of Hawaii. The last entry in the fair copy of Cook's MS. Journal is dated 6 January, but there is also in the British Museum his rough Journal (Egerton MS. 2177, B) in which the last entry is dated 17 January, and refers to anchoring in the bay. The last two sentences of this extract are therefore written by the editor, Canon Douglas.

At eleven o'clock in the forenoon we anchored in the bay (which is called by the natives *Karakakooa*), in thirteen fathoms' water, over a sandy bottom, and about a quarter of a mile from the north-east shore. In this situation, the south point of the bay bore south by west, and the north point west half north. We moored with the stream-anchor and cable to the northward, unbent the sails, and struck the yards and top-masts. The ships continued to be much crowded with natives, and were surrounded by a multitude of canoes. I had nowhere, in the course of my voyages, seen so numerous a body of people assembled at one place. For besides those who had come off to us in canoes, all the shore of the bay was covered with spectators, and many hundreds were swimming round the ships like shoals of fish. We could not but be struck with the singularity of this scene; and perhaps there were few on board who now lamented our having failed in our endeavours to find a northern passage homeward, last summer. To this disappointment we owed our having it in our power to revisit the *Sandwich Islands*, and to enrich our voyage with a discovery which, though the last, seemed, in many respects, to be the most important that had hitherto been made by Europeans throughout the extent of the Pacific Ocean.

[*Here Captain Cook's* Journal *ends. The remaining transactions of the voyage are related by Captain King.*]

BOOK V

The Death of Captain Cook

1779

January 17   As soon as the inhabitants perceived our intention of anchoring in the bay, they came off from the shore in astonishing numbers, and expressed their joy by singing and shouting, and exhibiting a variety of wild and extravagant gestures. The sides, the decks, and rigging of both ships were soon completely covered with them; and a multitude of women and boys who had not been able to get canoes, came swimming round us in shoals; many of whom, not finding room on board, remained the whole day playing in the water.

Among the chiefs who came on board the *Resolution*, was a young man, called Pareea, whom we soon perceived to be a person of great authority. On presenting himself to Captain Cook, he told him, that he was *Jakanee* to the king of the island, who was at that time engaged on a military expedition at Mowee, and was expected to return within three or four days. A few presents from Captain Cook attached him entirely to our interests, and he became exceedingly useful to us in the management of his countrymen, as we had soon occasion to experience. For we had not been long at anchor, when it was observed that the *Discovery* had such a number of people hanging on one side, as occasioned her to heel considerably: and that the men were unable to keep

351

off the crowds which continued pressing into her. Captain Cook, being apprehensive that she might suffer some injury, pointed out the danger to Pareea, who immediately went to their assistance, cleared the ship of its encumbrances, and drove away the canoes that surrounded her.

The authority of the chiefs over the inferior people appeared, from this incident, to be of the most despotic kind. A similar instance of it happened the same day on board the *Resolution*; where the crowd being so great, as to impede the necessary business of the ship, we were obliged to have recourse to the assistance of Kaneena, another of their chiefs, who had likewise attached himself to Captain Cook. The inconvenience we laboured under being made known, he immediately ordered his countrymen to quit the vessel; and we were not a little surprised to see them jump overboard, without a moment's hesitation; all except one man, who loitering behind, and showing some unwillingness to obey, Kaneena took him up in his arms and threw him into the sea.

Both these chiefs were men of strong and well-proportioned bodies, and of countenances remarkably pleasing. Kaneena especially, whose portrait Mr. Webber has drawn, was one of the finest men I ever saw. He was about six feet high, had regular and expressive features, with lively dark eyes; his carriage was easy, firm, and graceful.

It has been already mentioned, that during our long cruise off this island, the inhabitants had always behaved with great fairness and honesty in their dealings, and had not shown the slightest propensity to theft; which appeared to us the more extraordinary because those with whom we had hitherto held any intercourse, were of the lowest rank, either servants or fishermen. We now found the case exceedingly altered. The immense crowd of islanders, which blocked up every part of the ships, not only afforded frequent opportunity of pilfering without risk of discovery, but our inferiority in number held forth a prospect of escaping with impunity in case of detection. Another circumstance, to which we attributed this alteration in their behaviour, was the presence and encouragement of their chiefs; for generally

tracing the booty into the possession of some men of consequence, we had the strongest reason to suspect that these depreda-
tions were committed at their instigation.

Soon after the *Resolution* had got into her station, our two
friends, Pareea and Kaneena, brought on board a third chief,
named Koah, who, we were told, was a priest, and had been, in
his youth, a distinguished warrior. He was a little old man, of an
emaciated figure; his eyes exceedingly sore and red, and his body
covered with a white leprous scurf, the effects of an immoderate
use of the *ava*. Being led into the cabin, he approached Captain
Cook with great veneration, and threw over his shoulders a piece
of red cloth, which he had brought along with him. Then stepping a few paces back, he made an offering of a small pig, which he
held in his hand, whilst he pronounced a discourse that lasted for
a considerable time. This ceremony was frequently repeated during our stay at Owhyhee, and appeared to us, from many circumstances, to be a sort of religious adoration. Their idols we
found always arrayed with red cloth, in the same manner as was
done to Captain Cook; and a small pig was their usual offering
to the *Eatooas*. Their speeches, or prayers, were uttered too with
a readiness and volubility that indicated them to be according to
some formulary.

When this ceremony was over, Koah dined with Captain
Cook, eating plentifully of what was set before him; but, like the
rest of the inhabitants of the islands in these seas, could scarcely
be prevailed on to taste a second time our wine or spirits. In the
evening, Captain Cook, attended by Mr. Bayley and myself,
accompanied him on shore. We landed at the beach, and were
received by four men, who carried wands tipped with dogs' hair,
and marched before us, pronouncing with a loud voice a short
sentence, in which we could only distinguish the word *Orono*.[1]

---

[1] As far as King could understand, this referred both to a deity and to a great
personage "resembling pretty much the Dalai Lama of the Tartars, and the eccle-
siastical emperor of Japan". The attitude of the natives was first explained by the
missionary Ellis in his *Polynesian Researches* (1834, IV. 134). Cook was mistaken
for the legendary king Rono or Lono, who had been deified as the god of peace
and prosperity. "When, in the attack made upon him, they saw his blood running,
and heard his groans, they said, 'This is not Rono.' Some, however, after his
death, still supposed him to be Rono, and expected he would appear again."

The crowd, which had been collected on the shore, retired at our approach; and not a person was to be seen, except a few lying prostrate on the ground, near the huts of the adjoining village.

January 24   Things continued in this state till the 24th, when we were a good deal surprised to find that no canoes were suffered to put off from the shore, and that the natives kept close to their houses. After several hours' suspense, we learned that the bay was *tabooed*, and all intercourse with us interdicted, on account of the arrival of Terreeoboo.[2] As we had not foreseen an accident of this sort, the crews of both ships were obliged to pass the day without their usual supply of vegetables. The next morning, therefore, they endeavoured, both by threats and promises, to induce the natives to come alongside; and as some of them were at last venturing to put off, a chief was observed attempting to drive them away. A musket was immediately fired over his head, to make him desist, which had the desired effect, and refreshments were soon after purchased as usual. In the afternoon, Terreeoboo arrived, and visited the ships in a private manner, attended only by one canoe, in which were his wife and children, he stayed on board till near ten o'clock, when he returned to the village of Kowrowa.

The next day, about noon, the king, in a large canoe, attended by two others, set out from the village, and paddled toward the ships in great state. Their appearance was grand and magnificent. In the first canoe was Terreeoboo and his chiefs, dressed in their rich feathered cloaks and helmets, and armed with long spears and daggers; in the second came the venerable Kaoo, the chief of the priests, and his brethren, with their idols displayed on red cloth. These idols were busts of a gigantic size, made of wicker-work, and curiously covered with small feathers of various colours, wrought in the same manner with their cloaks. Their eyes were made of large pearl oysters, with a black nut fixed in the centre; their mouths were set with a double row of the fangs of dogs, and, together with the rest of their features, were strangely distorted. The third canoe was filled with hogs and

2 The principal chief of the Hawaiian group.

various sorts of vegetables. As they went along, the priests in the centre canoe sung their hymns with great solemnity; and after paddling round the ships, instead of going on board, as was expected, they made towards the shore at the beach where we were stationed.

As soon as I saw them approaching, I ordered out our little guard to receive the king; and Captain Cook, perceiving that he was going on shore, followed him, and arrived nearly at the same time. We conducted them into the tent, where they had scarcely been seated, when the king rose up, and in a very graceful manner threw over the Captain's shoulders the cloak he himself wore, put a feathered helmet on his head, and a curious fan into his hand. He also spread at his feet five or six other cloaks, all exceedingly beautiful, and of the greatest value. His attendants then brought four very large hogs, with sugar-canes, coconuts, and bread-fruit; and this part of the ceremony was concluded by the king's exchanging names with Captain Cook, which amongst all the islanders of the Pacific Ocean, is esteemed the strongest pledge of friendship. A procession of priests, with a venerable old personage at their head, now appeared, followed by a long train of men leading large hogs, and others carrying plantains, sweet potatoes, etc. By the looks and gestures of Kaireekeea, I immediately knew the old man to be the chief of the priests before mentioned, on whose bounty we had so long subsisted. He had a piece of red cloth in his hands, which he wrapped round Captain Cook's shoulders, and afterwards presented him with a small pig in the usual form. A seat was then made for him, next to the king, after which, Kaireekeea and his followers began their ceremonies, Kaoo and the chiefs joining in the responses.

January 26 The quiet and inoffensive behaviour of the natives having taken away every apprehension of danger, we did not hesitate to trust ourselves amongst them at all times, and in all situations. The officers of both ships went daily up the country in small parties, or even singly, and frequently remained out the whole night. It would be endless to recount all the instances of kindness and civility which we received upon those occasions.

Wherever we went, the people flocked about us, eager to offer every assistance in their power, and highly gratified if their services were accepted. Various little arts were practised to attract our notice, or to delay our departure. The boys and girls ran before, as we walked through their villages, and stopped us at every opening, where there was room to form a group for dancing. At one time, we were invited to accept a draught of coconut milk, or some other refreshment, under the shade of their huts; at another, we were seated within a circle of young women, who exerted all their skill and agility to amuse us with songs and dances.

The satisfaction we derived from their gentleness and hospitality was, however, frequently interrupted by that propensity to stealing, which they have in common with all the other islanders of these seas. This circumstance was the more distressing, as it sometimes obliged us to have recourse to acts of severity, which we should willingly have avoided, if the necessity of the case had not absolutely called for them. Some of their most expert swimmers were one day discovered under the ships, drawing out the filling nails of the sheathing, which they performed very dexterously by means of a short stick, with a flint stone fixed in the end of it. To put a stop to this practice, which endangered the very existence of the vessels, we at first fired small shot at the offenders; but they easily got out of our reach by diving under the ship's bottom. It was therefore found necessary to make an example, by flogging one of them on board the *Discovery*.

February 11   We were employed the whole of the 11th and part of the 12th, in getting out the foremast, and sending it with the carpenters, on shore.[3] Besides the damage which the head of

---

[3] On 4 February the ships sailed to complete the survey of the island, but on the 7th a sprung foremast compelled them to return to the bay. A few days previously an ex-Greenwich pensioner named Watman had died and been buried on the island. According to Zimmermann this fact (together with the removal of some wood from a burial place) "destroyed their previous belief in our immortality, and, this belief being lost, their reverence for us was gone". Furthermore, the ships demanded more supplies; even on their last visit King had noted how the natives were often "stroking the sides and patting the bellies of the sailors and telling them, partly by signs and partly by words, that it was time for them to go".

the mast had sustained, we found the heel exceedingly rotten, having a large hole up the middle of it, capable of holding four or five coconuts. It was not, however, thought necessary to shorten it; and fortunately, the logs of red toa-wood, which had been cut at Eimeo, for anchor-stocks, were found fit to replace the sprung parts of the fishes. As these repairs were likely to take up several days, Mr. Bayley and myself got the astronomical apparatus on shore, and pitched our tents on the *Morai*; having with us a guard of a corporal and six marines. We renewed our friendly correspondence with the priests, who, for the greater security of the workmen, and their tools, *tabooed* the place where the mast lay, sticking their wands round it, as before. The sail-makers were also sent on shore, to repair the damages which had taken place in their department during the late gales. They were lodged in a house adjoining to the *Morai*, that was lent us by the priests. Such were our arrangements on shore. I shall now proceed to the account of those other transactions with the natives, which led, by degrees, to the fatal catastrophe of the 14th.

Upon coming to anchor, we were surprised to find our reception very different from what it had been on our first arrival; no shouts, no bustle, no confusion; but a solitary bay, with only here and there a canoe stealing close along the shore. The impulse of curiosity, which had before operated to so great a degree, might now indeed be supposed to have ceased; but the hospitable treatment we had invariably met with, and the friendly footing on which we parted, gave us some reason to expect that they would again have flocked about us with great joy, on our return.

We were forming various conjectures upon the occasion of this extraordinary appearance, when our anxiety was at length relieved by the return of a boat, which had been sent on shore, and brought us word, that Terreeoboo was absent, and had left the bay under the *taboo*. Though this account appeared very satisfactory to most of us; yet others were of opinion, or rather, perhaps, have been led, by subsequent events, to imagine, that there was something at this time very suspicious in the behaviour of the natives; and that the interdiction of all intercourse with us, on pretence of the king's absence, was only to give him time to consult with his chiefs in what manner it might be proper to treat us. Whether these suspicions were well founded, or the account given by the natives was the truth, we were never able to ascertain. For though it is not improbable that our sudden return, for which they could see no apparent cause, and the necessity of which we afterward found it very difficult to make them comprehend, might occasion some alarm; yet the unsuspicious conduct of Terreeoboo, who, on his supposed arrival, the next morning, came immediately to visit Captain Cook, and the consequent return of the natives to their former friendly intercourse with us, are strong proofs that they neither meant nor apprehended any change of conduct.

In support of this opinion, I may add the account of another accident, precisely of the same kind, which happened to us on our first visit, the day before the arrival of the king. A native had sold a hog on board the *Resolution*, and taken the price agreed on, when Pareea passing by, advised the man not to part with the hog without an advanced price. For this he was sharply spoken to, and pushed away; and the *taboo* being soon after laid on the bay, we had at first no doubt, but that it was in consequence of the offence given to the chief. Both these accidents serve to show how very difficult it is to draw any certain conclusion from the actions of people, with whose customs, as well as language, we are so imperfectly acquainted; at the same time, some idea may be formed from them of the difficulties, at the first view, perhaps, not very apparent, which those have to encounter, who, in all their transactions with these strangers, have to steer their course amidst so much uncertainty, where a trifling error may be attended with even the most fatal consequences. However true or false our conjectures may be, things went on in their usual quiet course, till the afternoon of the 13th.

Toward the evening of that day, the officer who commanded the watering-party of the *Discovery* came to inform me, that several chiefs had assembled at the well near the beach, driving away the natives whom he had hired to assist the sailors in rolling down the casks to the shore. He told me, at the same time, that he thought their behaviour extremely suspicious, and that they meant to give him some further disturbance. At his request, therefore, I sent a marine along with him, but suffered him to take only his side-arms. In a short time the officer returned, and, on his acquainting me that the islanders had armed themselves with stones and were growing very tumultuous, I went myself to the spot, attended by a marine, with his musket. Seeing us approach, they threw away their stones, and, on my speaking to some of the chiefs, the mob were driven away, and those who chose it, were suffered to assist in filling the casks. Having left things quiet here, I went to meet Captain Cook, whom I saw coming on shore, in the pinnace. I related to him what had just passed; and he ordered me, in case of their beginning to throw stones, or behave insolently, immediately to fire a ball at the offenders. I accordingly gave orders to the corporal, to have the pieces of the sentinels loaded with ball, instead of small shot.

Soon after our return to the tents, we were alarmed by a continued fire of muskets from the *Discovery*, which we observed to be directed at a canoe, that we saw paddling toward the shore in great haste, pursued by one of our small boats. We immediately concluded, that the firing was in consequence of some theft, and Captain Cook ordered me to follow him with a marine armed, and to endeavour to seize the people as they came on shore. Accordingly we ran toward the place where we supposed the canoe would land, but were too late; the people having quitted it, and made their escape into the country before our arrival.

We were at this time ignorant, that the goods had been already restored; and as we thought it probable, from the circumstances we had at first observed, that they might be of importance, were unwilling to relinquish our hopes of recovering them. Having therefore inquired of the natives, which way the people had fled, we followed them till it was near dark, when judging ourselves to be about three miles from the tents, and suspecting that the natives, who frequently encouraged us in the pursuit, were amusing us with false information, we thought it in vain to continue our search any longer, and returned to the beach.

During our absence, a difference of a more serious and unpleasant nature had happened. The officer,[4] who had been sent

---

[4] Edgar, Master of the *Discovery*; Vancouver was with him.

in the small boat, and was returning on board with the goods which had been restored, observing Captain Cook and me engaged in the pursuit of the offenders, thought it his duty to seize the canoe, which was left drawn up on the shore. Unfortunately, this canoe belonged to Pareea, who arriving, at the same moment, from on board the *Discovery*, claimed his property, with many protestations of his innocence. The officer refusing to give it up, and being joined by the crew of the pinnace, which was waiting for Captain Cook, a scuffle ensued, in which Pareea was knocked down by a violent blow on the head with an oar. The natives, who were collected about the spot, and had hitherto been peaceable spectators, immediately attacked our people with such a shower of stones as forced them to retreat with great precipitation, and swim off to a rock, at some distance from the shore. The pinnace was immediately ransacked by the islanders; and, but for the timely interposition of Pareea, who seemed to have recovered from the blow, and forgot it at the same instant, would soon have been entirely demolished. Having driven away the crowd, he made signs to our people, that they might come and take possession of the pinnace, and that he would endeavour to get back the things which had been taken out of it. After their departure, he followed them in his canoe, with a midshipman's cap, and some other trifling articles of the plunder, and, with much apparent concern at what had happened, asked, if the *Orono* would kill him, and whether he would permit him to come on board the next day? On being assured that he should be well received, he joined noses (as their custom is) with the officers, in token of friendship, and paddled over to the village of Kowrowa.

When Captain Cook was informed of what had passed, he expressed much uneasiness at it, and as we were returning on board, "I am afraid", said he, "that these people will oblige me to use some violent measures; for", he added, "they must not be left to imagine that they have gained an advantage over us." However, as it was too late to take any steps this evening, he contented himself with giving orders, that every man and woman on board should be immediately turned out of the ship. As soon as this order was executed I returned on shore; and our former confidence in the natives being now much abated, by the events of the day, I posted a double guard on the *Morai*, with orders to call me, if they saw any men lurking about the beach. At about eleven o'clock, five islanders were observed creeping round the bottom of the *Morai*; they seemed very cautious in approaching us, and, at last, finding themselves discovered, retired out of sight. About midnight, one of them venturing up close to the observatory, the sentinel fired over him; on which the men fled, and we passed the remainder of the night without further disturbance.

Next morning [February 14] at daylight, I went on board the *Resolution* for the timekeeper, and, on my way, was hailed by the *Discovery*, and informed that their cutter had been stolen during the night from the buoy where it was moored.

When I arrived on board, I found the marines arming, and Captain Cook loading his double-barrelled gun. Whilst I was relating to him what had happened to us in the night, he interrupted me with some eagerness, and acquainted me with the loss of the *Discovery's* cutter, and with the preparations he was making for its recovery. It had been his usual practice, whenever anything of consequence was lost at any of the islands in this ocean, to get the king, or some of the principal *Erees*, on board, and to keep them as hostages till it was restored. This method, which had been always attended with success, he meant to pursue on the present occasion; and, at the same time, had given orders to stop all the canoes that should attempt to leave the bay, with an intention of seizing and destroying them, if he could not recover the cutter by peaceable means.

Accordingly the boats of both ships, well manned and armed, were stationed across the bay; and, before I left the ship, some great guns had been fired at two large canoes, that were attempting to make their escape.

It was between seven and eight o'clock when we quitted the ship together; Captain Cook in the pinnace, having Mr. Phillips and nine marines with him; and myself in the small boat. The last orders I received from him were, to quiet the minds of the natives, on our side of the bay, by assuring them they should not be hurt; to keep my people together; and to be on my guard. We then parted: the captain went toward Kowrowa, where the king resided; and I proceeded to the beach. My first care, on going ashore, was to give strict orders to the marines to remain within their tent, to load their pieces with ball, and not to quit their arms. Afterward I took a walk to the huts of old Kaoo, and the priests, and explained to them, as well as I could, the object of the hostile preparations, which had exceedingly alarmed them. I found, that they had already heard of the cutter's being stolen, and I assured them, that though Captain Cook was resolved to recover it, and to punish the authors of the theft, yet that they, and the people of the village on our side, need not be under the smallest apprehension of suffering any evil from us. I desired the priests to explain this to the people, and to tell them not to be alarmed, but to continue peaceable and quiet. Kaoo asked me, with great earnestness, if Terreeoboo was to be hurt? I assured him, he was not; and both he and the rest of his brethren seemed much satisfied with this assurance.

In the meantime, Captain Cook having called off the launch, which was stationed at the north point of the bay, and taken it along with him, proceeded to Kowrowa, and landed with the lieutenant and nine marines.[5] He immediately marched into the village, where he was received with the usual marks of respect; the people prostrating themselves before him, and bringing their accustomed offerings of small hogs. Finding that there was no suspicion of his design, his next step was to inquire for Terreeoboo and the two boys, his sons, who had been his constant guests on board the *Resolution*. In a short time, the boys returned along with the natives, who had been sent in search of them, and immediately led Captain Cook to the house where the king had slept. They found the old man just awoke from sleep; and after a short conversation about the loss of the cutter, from which Captain Cook was convinced that he was in no wise privy to it, he invited him to return in the boat, and spend the day on board

[5] Two boats now lay off the beach: the pinnace in charge of Roberts, a Mate, and the launch under Lieut. Williamson. Lieut. Phillips was in command of the marines who landed with Cook.

the *Resolution*. To this proposal the king readily consented, and immediately got up to accompany him.

Things were in this prosperous train, the two boys being already in the pinnace, and the rest of the party having advanced near the waterside, when an elderly woman called Kaneekabareea, the mother of the boys, and one of the king's favourite wives, came after him, and with many tears and entreaties, besought him not to go on board. At the same time, two chiefs who came along with her, laid hold of him, and insisting that he should go no farther, forced him to sit down. The natives, who were collecting in prodigious numbers along the shore, and had probably been alarmed by the firing of the great guns, and the appearances of hostility in the bay, began to throng round Captain Cook and their king. In this situation, the lieutenant of marines observing that his men were huddled close together in the crowd, and thus incapable of using their arms, if any occasion should require it, proposed to the captain to draw them up along the rocks, close to the water's edge; and the crowd readily making way for them to pass, they were drawn up in a line, at the distance of about thirty yards from the place where the king was sitting.

All this time the old king remained on the ground, with the strongest marks of terror and dejection in his countenance. Captain Cook, not willing to abandon the object for which he had come on shore, continuing to urge him, in the most pressing manner, to proceed; whilst, on the other hand, whenever the king appeared inclined to follow him, the chiefs, who stood round him, interposed at first with prayers and entreaties, but afterward, having recourse to force and violence, insisted on his staying where he was. Captain Cook, therefore, finding that the alarm had spread too generally, and that it was in vain to think any longer of getting him off without bloodshed, at last gave up the point; observing to Mr. Phillips, that it would be impossible to compel him to go on board, without the risk of killing a great number of the inhabitants.

Though the enterprise which had carried Captain Cook on shore had now failed, and was abandoned, yet his person did not appear to have been in the least danger, till an accident happened, which gave a fatal turn to the affair. The boats which had been stationed across the bay, having fired at some canoes that were attempting to get out, unfortunately had killed a chief of the first rank. The news of his death arrived at the village where Captain Cook was, just as he had left the king, and was walking slowly toward the shore. The ferment it occasioned was very conspicuous; the women and children were immediately sent off; and the men put on their war-mats, and armed themselves with spears and stones. One of the natives, having in his hands a stone, and a long iron spike (which they call a *pahooa*), came up to the Captain, flourishing his weapon, by way of defiance, and threatening to throw the stone. The Captain desired him to desist; but the man persisting in his insolence, he was at length provoked to fire a load of small shot. The man having his mat on, which the shot were not able to penetrate, this had no other effect than to irritate and encourage them. Several stones were thrown at the marines; and one of the *Erees* attempted to stab Mr. Phillips with his *pahooa*, but failed in the attempt, and received from him a blow with the butt end of his musket. Captain Cook now fired his second barrel, loaded with ball, and killed one of the foremost of the natives. A general attack with stones immediately followed, which was answered by a discharge of musketry from the marines and the people in the boats. The islanders, contrary to the expectations of everyone, stood the fire with great firmness; and before the marines had time to re-load, they broke in upon them with dreadful shouts and yells. What followed was a scene of the utmost horror and confusion.

Four of the marines were cut off amongst the rocks in their retreat, and fell a sacrifice to the fury of the enemy; three more were dangerously wounded; and the Lieutenant, who had received a stab between the shoulders with a *pahooa*, having fortunately reserved his fire, shot the man who had wounded him just as he was going to repeat his blow. Our unfortunate Commander, the last time he was seen distinctly, was standing at the water's edge, and calling out to the boats to cease firing, and to pull in. If it be true, as some of those who were present have imagined, that the marines and boatmen had fired without his orders, and that he was desirous of preventing any further blood-shed, it is not improbable that his humanity, on this occasion, proved fatal to him. For it was remarked, that whilst he faced the natives, none of them had offered him any violence, but that having turned about, to give his orders to the boats, he was stabbed in the back, and fell with his face into the water. On see-ing him fall, the islanders set up a great shout, and his body was immediately dragged on shore, and surrounded by the enemy, who snatching the daggers out of each other's hands, showed a savage eagerness to have a share in his destruction.

Thus fell our great and excellent Commander! After a life of so much distinguished and successful enterprise, his death, as far as regards himself, cannot be reckoned premature; since he lived to finish the great work for which he seems to have been designed; and was rather removed from the enjoyment, than cut off from the acquisition of glory. How sincerely his loss was felt and lamented by those who had so long found their general security in his skill and conduct, and every consolation, under their hard-ships, in his tenderness and humanity, it is neither necessary nor possible for me to describe; much less shall I attempt to paint the horror with which we were struck, and the universal dejection and dismay which followed so dreadful and unexpected a calamity. . . .[6]

---

[6] There are a number of accounts of Cook's death (see R. T. Gould in *Mariner's Mirror*, Vol. XIV), but most were written by men who saw the fatality from afar off. King was on the other side of the bay; Phillips and Burney left full reports; but the most vivid is that by Samwell the surgeon. He adds the following details after Cook's order to the boats to cease firing and come closer in; "Mr. Roberts immediately brought the pinnace as close to the shore as he could, without ground-ing, notwithstanding the showers of stones that fell among the people: but Mr. John Williamson, the lieutenant, who commanded the launch, instead of pulling in to the assistance of Captain Cook, withdrew his boat farther off, at the moment that everything seems to have depended upon the timely exertion of those in the boats. By his own account he mistook the signal; but be that as it may, this circumstance appears to me to have decided the fatal turn of the affair, and to have removed every chance which remained with Captain Cook, of escaping with his life. The business of saving the marines out of the water, in consequence of that, fell altogether upon the pinnace; which thereby became so much crowded, that the crew were, in a great measure, prevented from using their firearms, or giving what assistance they otherwise might have done, to Captain Cook; so that he seems, at the most critical point of time, to have wanted the assistance of both boats, owing to the removal of the launch." In his opinion, Cook was first clubbed on the head and then stabbed; when he fell into the water the boat was

It has been already related that four of the marines who attended Captain Cook were killed by the islanders on the spot. The rest, with Mr. Phillips, their lieutenant, threw themselves into the water, and escaped, under cover of a smart fire from the boats. On this occasion, a remarkable instance of gallant behaviour and of affection for his men, was shown by that officer. For he had scarcely got into the boat, when, seeing one of the marines, who was a bad swimmer, struggling in the water, and in danger of being taken by the enemy, he immediately jumped into the sea to his assistance, though much wounded himself; and after receiving a blow on the head from a stone, which had nearly sent him to the bottom, he caught the man by the hair, and brought him safe off.[7]

Our people continued for some time to keep up a constant fire from the boats (which, during the whole transaction, were not more than twenty yards from the land), in order to afford their unfortunate companions, if any of them should still remain alive, an opportunity of escaping. These efforts, seconded by a few guns, that were fired at the same time, from the *Resolution*, having forced the natives at last to retire, a small boat, manned by five of our young midshipmen, pulled towards the shore, where they saw the bodies, without any signs of life, lying on the ground;

only a few yards off. (Kippis, *Life of Cook*, 1788, and *Trans. of Soc. of Cymmrodorion*, 1928).

Burney says that "being no swimmer, and stunned with the blow, he turned towards the shore again, and a number of Indians surrounded and dragged him on the rocks, where they beat and stabbed him in several places".

The general opinion on board was that Williamson "looked on during these events without attempting to give any assistance" (Zimmermann). It is significant that he had previously differed from Cook on the way to treat natives, and that he was cashiered for cowardice after the battle of Camperdown. Samwell adds "To have come away at such a time as this and forsaken the body of Captain Cook cannot be thought on without feeling the keenest anguish and indignation. The men it must be said were most sincerely affected and had they been left to themselves, would ~~most certainly~~ have ~~brought him off~~. When they came alongside they cried out with tears in their eyes that they had lost their father!"

[7] All other witnesses add their tributes to Phillips, except Bligh, who, in a note in the Admiralty Library copy, writes: "This person, who never was of any real service the whole Voyage, or did anything but eat and Sleep, was a great Croney of C. King's, and he has taken care not to forget, altho' it is very laughable to those who knew the characters. The Man was close to the Boat, and swam nearly as well as the Lieut. The whole affair from the Opening to the End did [not] last 10 Minutes, or [was] their a spark of courage or Conduct shown in [the] whole busyness." Phillips later challenged Williamson to a duel.

but judging it dangerous to attempt to bring them off, with so small a force, and their ammunition being nearly expended, they returned to the ships, leaving them in possession of the islanders, together with ten stands of arms.

As soon as the general consternation, which the news of this calamity occasioned throughout both crews, had a little subsided, their attention was called to our party at the *Morai*, where the mast and sails were on shore, with a guard of only six marines. It is impossible for me to describe the emotions of my own mind, during the time these transactions had been carrying on at the other side of the bay. Being at the distance only of a short mile from the village of Kowrowa, we could see distinctly an immense crowd collected on the spot where Captain Cook had just before landed. We heard the firing of the musketry, and could perceive some extraordinary bustle and agitation in the multitude. We afterward saw the natives flying, the boats retire from the shore, and passing and repassing, in great stillness, between the ships. I must confess that my heart soon misgave me. Where a life so dear and valuable was concerned, it was impossible not to be alarmed, by appearances both new and threatening. But, besides this, I knew that a long and uninterrupted course of success, in his transactions with the natives of these seas, had given the Captain a degree of confidence, that I was always fearful might, at some unlucky moment, put him too much off his guard; and I now saw all the dangers to which that confidence might lead, without receiving much consolation from considering the experience that had given rise to it.

My first care, on hearing the muskets fired, was, to assure the people, who were assembled in considerable numbers round the wall of our consecrated field, and seemed equally at a loss with ourselves how to account for what they had seen and heard, that they should not be molested; and that, at all events, I was desirous of continuing on peaceable terms with them. We remained in this posture, till the boats had returned on board, when Captain Clerke, observing, through his telescope, that we were surrounded by the natives, and apprehending they meant to attack us, ordered two four-pounders to be fired at them. Fortunately these guns, though well aimed, did no mischief, and yet gave the natives a convincing proof of their power. One of the balls broke a coco-nut tree in the middle, under which a party of them were sitting; and the other shivered a rock, that stood in an exact line with them. As I had, just before, given them the strongest assurances of their safety, I was exceedingly mortified at this act of hostility; and, to prevent a repetition of it, immediately dispatched a boat to acquaint Captain Clerke, that, at present, I was on the most friendly terms with the natives; and that, if occasion should here-after arise for altering my conduct toward them, I would hoist a jack, as a signal for him to afford us all the assistance in his power.

We expected the return of the boat with the utmost impatience; and after remaining a quarter of an hour under the most tortur-ing anxiety and suspense, our fears were at length confirmed, by the arrival of Mr. Bligh, with orders to strike the tents as quickly as possible, and to send the sails, that were repairing, on board. Just at the same moment, our friend Kaireekeea having also re-ceived intelligence of the death of Captain Cook from a native, who had arrived from the other side of the bay, came to me with great sorrow and dejection in his countenance, to inquire if it was true?

Our situation was, at this time, extremely critical and impor-tant. Not only our own lives, but the event of the expedition, and the return of at least one of the ships, being involved in the same common danger. We had the mast of the *Resolution*, and the greatest part of our sails, on shore, under the protection of only six marines: their loss would have been irreparable; and though the natives had not as yet shown the smallest disposition to molest us, yet it was impossible to answer for the alteration which the news of the transaction at Kowrowa might produce. I therefore thought it prudent to dissemble my belief of the death of Captain Cook, and to desire Kaireekeea to discourage the report; lest either the fear of our resentment, or the successful example of their countrymen, might lead them to seize the favourable opportunity, which at this time offered itself of giving us a second blow. At the same time I advised him to bring old

Kaoo, and the rest of the priests, into a large house that was close to the *Morai*; partly out of regard to their safety, in case it should have been found necessary to proceed to extremities; and partly to have him near us, in order to make use of his authority with the people, if it could be instrumental in preserving peace.

Having placed the marines on the top of the *Morai*, which formed a strong and advantageous post, and left the command with Mr. Bligh, giving him the most positive directions to act entirely on the defensive, I went on board the *Discovery*, in order to represent to Captain Clerke the dangerous situation of our affairs. As soon as I quitted the spot, the natives began to annoy our people with stones; and I had scarcely reached the ship, before I heard the firing of the marines. I therefore returned instantly on shore, where I found things growing every moment more alarming. The natives were arming, and putting on their mats; and their numbers increased very fast. I could also perceive several large bodies marching toward us, along the cliff which separates the village of Kakooa from the north side of the bay, where the village of Kowrowa is situated.

They began, at first, to attack us with stones from behind the walls of their enclosures, and finding no resistance on our part, they soon grew more daring. A few resolute fellows, having crept along the beach, under cover of the rocks, suddenly made their appearance at the foot of the *Morai*, with a design, as it seemed, of storming it on the side next the sea, which was its only accessible part; and were not dislodged, till after they had stood a considerable number of shot, and seen one of their party fall.

The bravery of one of these assailants well deserves to be particularly mentioned; for having returned to carry off his companion, amidst the fire of our whole party, a wound which he received made him quit the body and retire; but, in a few minutes, he again appeared, and being again wounded, he was obliged a second time to retreat. At this moment I arrived at the *Morai*, and saw him return the third time, bleeding and faint; and being informed of what had happened, I forbade the soldiers to fire, and he was suffered to carry off his friend; which he was just able to perform, and then fell down himself and expired.

About this time, a strong reinforcement from both ships having landed, the natives retreated behind their walls; which giving me access to our friendly priests, I sent one of them to endeavour to bring their countrymen to some terms, and to propose to them, that if they would desist from throwing stones, I would not permit our men to fire. This truce was agreed to, and we were suffered to launch the mast, and carry off the sails, and our astronomical apparatus, unmolested. . . .

I left the ships about four o'clock in the afternoon; and, as we approached the shore, I perceived every indication of a hostile reception. The whole crowd of natives was in motion; the women and children retiring; the men putting on their war mats, and arming themselves with long spears and daggers. We also observed, that, since the morning, they had thrown up stone breastworks along the beach, where Captain Cook had landed, probably in expectation of an attack at that place; and, as soon as we were within reach, they began to throw stones at us with slings, but without doing any mischief. Concluding, therefore, that all attempts to bring them to a parley would be in vain, unless I first gave them some ground for mutual confidence; I ordered the armed boats to stop, and went on, in the small boat, alone, with a white flag in my hand, which, by a general cry of joy from the natives, I had the satisfaction to find was instantly understood. The women immediately returned from the side of the hill, whither they had retired; the men threw off their mats; and all sat down together by the waterside, extending their arms, and inviting me to come on shore.

Though this behaviour was very expressive of a friendly disposition, yet I could not help entertaining some suspicions of its sincerity. But when I saw Koah, with a boldness and assurance altogether unaccountable, swimming off toward the boat, with a white flag in his hand, I thought it necessary to return this mark of confidence, and therefore received him into the boat, though armed; a circumstance which did not tend to lessen my suspicions. I must confess, I had long harboured an unfavourable opinion of this man. The priests had always told us, that he was of a malicious disposition, and no friend of ours; and the repeated detections of his fraud and treachery, had convinced us of the truth of their representations. Add to all this, the shocking transaction of the morning, in which he was seen acting a principal part, made me feel the utmost horror at finding myself so near him; and as he came up to me with feigned tears, and embraced me, I was so distrustful of his intentions, that I could not help taking hold of the point of the *pahooa*, which he held in his hand, and turning it from me. I told him, that I had come to demand the body of Captain Cook; and to declare war against them, unless it was instantly restored. He assured me this should be done as soon as possible; and that he would go himself for that purpose; and, after begging of me a piece of iron, with much assurance, as if nothing extraordinary had happened, he leaped into the sea, and swam ashore, calling out to his countrymen, that we were all friends again.

We waited near an hour, with great anxiety for his return; during which time the rest of the boats had approached so near the shore, as to enter into conversation with a party of the natives, at some distance from us; by whom they were plainly given to understand, that the body had been cut to pieces and carried up the country; but of this circumstance I was not informed till our return to the ships.

I began now to express some impatience at Koah's delay; upon which the chiefs pressed me exceedingly to come on shore; assuring me, that if I would go myself to Terreeoboo, the body would certainly be restored to me. When they found they could not prevail on me to land, they attempted, under a pretence of wishing to converse with more ease, to decoy our boat among some rocks, where they would have had it in their power to cut us off from the rest. It was no difficult matter to see through these artifices; and I was, therefore, strongly inclined to break off all further communication with them, when a chief came to us, who was the particular friend of Captain Clerke, and of the officers of the *Discovery*, on board which ship he had sailed, when we last left the bay, intending to take his passage to *Mowee*. He told us, he came from Terreeoboo to acquaint us, that the body was carried up the country; but that it should be brought to us the next morning. There appeared a great deal of sincerity in his manner; and being asked, if he told a falsehood, he hooked his two forefingers together, which is understood amongst these islanders as the sign of truth; in the use of which they are very scrupulous.

As I was now at a loss in what manner to proceed, I sent Mr. Vancouver to acquaint Captain Clerke with all that had passed; that my opinion was, they meant not to keep their word with us, and were so far from being sorry at what had happened, that, on the contrary, they were full of spirits and confidence on account of their late success, and sought only to gain time, till they could contrive some scheme for getting us into their power. Mr. Vancouver came back with orders for me to return on board; having first given the natives to understand that if the body was not brought the next morning, the town should be destroyed.

When they saw that we were going off, they endeavoured to provoke us by the most insulting and contemptuous gestures. Some of our people said, they could distinguish several of the natives parading about in the clothes of our unfortunate comrades; and, among them, a chief brandishing Captain Cook's hanger, and a woman holding the scabbard. Indeed, there can be no doubt, but that our behaviour had given them a mean opinion of our courage; for they could have but little notion of the motives of humanity that directed it.

In consequence of the report I made to Captain Clerke, of what I conceived to be the present temper and disposition of the islanders, the most effectual measures were taken to guard against any attack they might make in the night. The boats were moored with top-chains; additional sentinels were posted on both ships; and guard-boats were stationed to row round them, in order to prevent the natives from cutting the cables. During the night we observed a prodigious number of lights on the hills, which made some of us imagine they were removing their effects back into the country, in consequence of our threats. But I rather believed them to have been the sacrifices that were performing on account of the war, in which they imagined themselves about to be engaged; and most probably the bodies of our slain countrymen were at that time burning. We afterward saw fires of the same kind, as we passed the island of Morotoi; and which, we were told by some natives then on board, were made on account of the war they had declared against a neighbouring island. And this agrees with what we learned amongst the Friendly and Society Isles, that, previous to any expedition against an enemy, the chiefs always endeavoured to animate and inflame the courage of the people by feasts and rejoicings in the night.

We remained the whole night undisturbed, except by the howlings and lamentations which were heard on shore: and early the next morning, Koah came alongside the *Resolution* with a present of cloth, and a small pig, which he desired leave to present to me. I have mentioned before, that I was supposed by the natives to be the son of Captain Cook; and as he, in his lifetime, had always suffered them to believe it, I was probably considered as the chief, after his death. As soon as I came on deck, I questioned him about the body; and, on his returning me nothing but evasive answers, I refused to accept his presents; and was going to dismiss him, with some expressions of anger and resentment, had not Captain Clerke, judging it best, at all events, to keep up the appearance of friendship, thought it more proper that he should be treated with the usual respect.

This treacherous fellow came frequently to us during the course of the forenoon, with some trifling present or other; and as I always observed him eyeing every part of the ship with great attention, I took care he should see we were well prepared for our defence.

February 15   The greatest part of the day was taken up in getting the foremast into a proper situation on deck, for the carpenters to work upon it; and in making the necessary alterations in the commissions of the officers. The command of the expedition having devolved on Captain Clerke, he removed on board the *Resolution*, appointed Lieutenant Gore to be Captain of the *Discovery*, and promoted Mr. Harvey, a midshipman, who had been with Captain Cook on his two last voyages, to the vacant lieutenancy. During the whole day, we met with no interruption from the natives; and, at night, the launch was again moored with a top-chain; and guard-boats stationed round both ships as before.

About eight o'clock, it being very dark, a canoe was heard paddling toward the ship; and as soon as it was seen, both the sentinels on deck fired into it. There were two persons in the canoe, and they immediately roared out "*Tinnee*" (which was the way in which they pronounced my name), and said they were friends, and had something for me belonging to Captain Cook. When they came on board, they threw themselves at our feet, and appeared exceedingly frightened. Luckily neither of them was hurt, notwithstanding the balls of both pieces had gone through the canoe. One of them was the person, whom I have before mentioned under the name of *Taboo* man, who constantly attended Captain Cook with the circumstances of ceremony I have already described; and who, though a man of rank in the island, could scarcely be hindered from performing for him the lowest offices of a menial servant. After lamenting, with abundance of tears, the loss of the *Orono*, he told us that he had brought us a part of his body. He then presented to us a small bundle, wrapped up in cloth, which he brought under his arm; and it is impossible to describe the horror which seized us, on finding in it a piece of human flesh, about nine or ten pounds' weight. This, he said, was all that remained of the body; that the rest was cut to pieces, and burnt; but that the head and all the bones, except what belonged to the trunk, were in the possession of Terreeoboo, and the other *Erees*: that what we saw had been allotted to Kaoo, the chief of the priests, to be made use of in some religious ceremony; and that he had sent it as a proof of his innocence and attachment to us.

This afforded an opportunity of informing ourselves, whether they were cannibals; and we did not neglect it. We first tried, by many indirect questions, put to each of them apart, to learn in what manner the rest of the bodies had been disposed of; and finding them very constant in one story, that, after the flesh had been cut off, it was all burnt; we at last put the direct question,

Whether they had not ate some of it? They immediately showed as much horror at the idea, as any European would have done; and asked, very naturally, if that was the custom amongst us? They afterward asked us, with great earnestness and apparent apprehension: "When the *Orono* would come again? and what he would do to them on his return?" The same inquiry was frequently made afterward by others; and this idea agrees with the general tenor of their conduct toward him, which showed that they considered him as a being of a superior nature.

February 20   Early in the morning of the 20th, we had the satisfaction of getting the foremast stepped. It was an operation attended with great difficulty, and some danger; our ropes being so exceedingly rotten, that the purchase gave way several times.

Between ten and eleven o'clock, we saw a great number of people descending the hill, which is over the beach, in a kind of procession, each man carrying a sugar-cane or two on his shoulders, and bread-fruit, *taro*, and plantains in his hand. They were preceded by two drummers who, when they came to the water-side, sat down by a white flag, and began to beat their drums, while those who had followed them, advanced one by one, and, having deposited the presents they had brought, retired in the same order. Soon after, Eappo came in sight, in his long feathered cloak, bearing something with great solemnity in his hands; and having placed himself on a rock, he made signs for a boat to be sent him.

Captain Clerke, conjecturing that he had brought the bones of Captain Cook, which proved to be the fact, went himself in the pinnace, to receive them; and ordered me to attend him in the cutter. When we arrived at the beach, Eappo came into the pinnace, and delivered to the captain the bones wrapped up in a large quantity of fine new cloth, and covered with a spotted cloak of black and white feathers. He afterward attended us to the *Resolution*, but could not be prevailed upon to go on board; probably not choosing, from a sense of decency, to be present at the opening of the bundle. We found in it both the hands of

Captain Cook entire, which were well known from a remarkable scar on one of them, that divided the thumb from the forefinger, the whole length of the metacarpal bone; the skull, but with the scalp separated from it, and the bones that form the face wanting; the scalp, with the hair upon it cut short, and the ears adhering to it; the bones of both arms, with the skin of the forearms hanging to them; the thigh and leg-bones joined together, but without the feet. The ligaments of the joints were entire; and the whole bore evident marks of having been in the fire, except the hands, which had the flesh left upon them, and were cut in several places, and crammed with salt, apparently with an intention of preserving them. The scalp had a cut in the back part of it, but the skull was free from any fracture. The lower jaw and feet, which were wanting, Eappo told us, had been seized by different chiefs, and that Terreeoboo was using every means to recover them.

The next morning Eappo, and the king's son, came on board, and brought with them the remaining bones of Captain Cook; the barrels of his gun, his shoes, and some other trifles that belonged to him. Eappo took great pains to convince us, that Terreeoboo, Maiha-maiha, and himself were most heartily desirous of peace; that they had given us the most convincing proof of it in their power; and that they had been prevented from giving it sooner by the other chiefs, many of whom were still our enemies. He lamented, with the greatest sorrow, the death of six chiefs we had killed, some of whom, he said, were amongst our best friends. The cutter, he told us, was taken away by Pareea's people; very probably in revenge for the blow that had been given him; and that it had broken up the next day. The arms of the marines, which we had also demanded, he assured us, had been carried off by the common people, and were irrecoverable; the bones of the chief alone having been preserved, as belonging to Terreeoboo and the *Erees*.

Nothing now remained but to perform the last offices to our great and unfortunate commander. Eappo was dismissed with orders to *taboo* all the bay; and, in the afternoon, the bones having been put into a coffin, and the service read over them, they were committed to the deep with the usual military honours.[8] What our feelings were on this occasion, I leave the world to conceive; those who were present know, that it is not in my power to express them.

Epilogue

by the Editor

Under the command of Captain Clerke, the two ships sailed from their anchorage at Hawaii on 22 February, 1779. A few days later course was set for the Russian harbour of St. Peter and St. Paul (Petropavlosk) on the coast of Kamchatka. Here they were hospitably entertained and the opportunity was taken to send home the news of Cook's death by the Governor, who was returning to St. Petersburg. Clerke then continued north, following the Asiatic shore of the Bering Strait, and turned eastward when he reached polar seas. The ships were, however, forced to turn back on account of pack ice on 19 July at almost the same spot as on the former occasion. "We were all heartily sick of a navigation full of danger", writes King, "and in which the utmost perseverance had not been repaid with the smallest probability of success. We therefore turned our faces towards home, after an absence of three years, with a delight and satisfaction which, notwithstanding the tedious voyage we had still to make, and the immense distance we had to run, were as freely entertained as if we had been already in sight of Land's End."

According to the opinion entertained on board, "it would be madness to attempt to run from the Icy Cape to the known parts of Baffin's Bay", and since "upon the Asiatic side there appears still less probability of success", it was decided to follow their instructions and return home by way of China. On 22 August, before returning to Petropavlosk, Clerke died of consumption. The command now devolved upon Lieut. Gore in the Resolution. *King remained in the* Discovery, *which was now*

---

[8] Ellis states that for many years other remains of Cook were preserved by the natives in a wicker basket covered with precious red feathers; this was carried round the island on an annual procession. About 1820, when the island was converted to Christianity, these relics were hidden and no one has since discovered the place.

leaking badly. The ships ran down the coast of Japan, but made no contact with the inhabitants, because it was known that their "aversion to any intercourse with strangers has led them to commit the most atrocious barbarities".

On reaching Macao and Canton in December they first heard that Britain was at war with France and Spain, as well as with the United States. All logs were impounded (though Zimmermann managed to conceal his Diary). Although they heard that their immunity had been guaranteed, Burney made a copy of his Journal "on China paper in so small a compass as to be easily concealable that if bereft of our other journals there might be one saved for the Admiralty". This calligraphic masterpiece, which can only be deciphered with the aid of a magnifying glass, is preserved in the British Museum (Add. MSS. 8955).

On 12 January 1780, the ships sailed for home. A short visit was made to Cochin China, Batavia being avoided because of the memory of the disease previously contracted there. Passing through the Straits of Sunda, the Cape of Good Hope was visited in April, and both ships reached the Nore on 4 October.

"In the course of our voyage", writes King, "the Resolution lost but five men through sickness, three of whom were in a precarious state of health at our departure from England; the Discovery did not lose a man. An unremitting attention to the regulations established by Captain Cook may be justly considered as the principal cause, under the blessing of Divine Providence, of this singular success." He seizes the opportunity to recommend that Peruvian Bark (the equivalent of quinine) should be carried in future by such ships "as may be exposed to the influence of unwholesome climates", but it does not appear that his advice was generally adopted. The voyage had lasted four years and two months, and only on brief occasions had the ships lost sight of each other—"a stronger proof", concludes King, "cannot be given of the skill and vigilance of our subaltern officers, to whom this share of merit almost entirely belongs."

INDEX

Cook's sketch of the track of The Endea[vour]